It looks like the series is going to end before I get a chance to organize all this research material that I've collected.

From this volume on, the story is entering its final stretch (in a manner of speaking). Looking back, I really feel like we've come a long way.

—*Hiromu Arakawa, 2009*

Born in Hokkaido (northern Japan), Hiromu Arakawa first attracted national attention in 1999 with her award-winning manga *Stray Dog*. Her series *Fullmetal Alchemist* debuted in 2001 in Square Enix's monthly manga anthology *Shonen Gangan*.

FULLMETAL ALCHEMIST VOL. 21

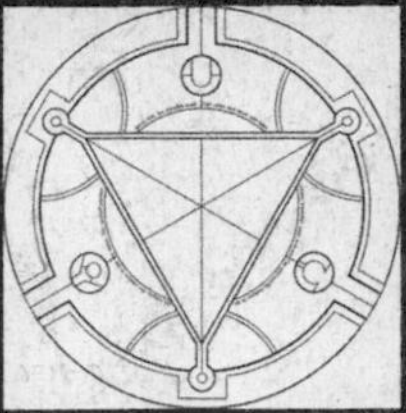

VIZ Media Edition

Story and Art by Hiromu Arakawa

Translation/Akira Watanabe
English Adaptation/Jake Forbes
Touch-up Art & Lettering/Wayne Truman
Design/Julie Behn
Editor/Alexis Kirsch

VP, Production/Alvin Lu
VP, Publishing Licensing/Rika Inouye
VP, Sales & Product Marketing/Gonzalo Ferreyra
VP, Creative/Linda Espinosa
Publisher/Hyoe Narita

Printed in the U.S.A.

Published by VIZ Media, LLC
P.O. Box 77010
San Francisco, CA 94107

10 9 8 7 6 5 4 3 2 1
First printing, November 2009

www.viz.com

RATED T FOR TEEN

PARENTAL ADVISORY
FULLMETAL ALCHEMIST is rated T for Teen and is recommended for ages 13 and up. Contains mildly strong language, tobacco/alcohol use and fantasy violence.

ratings.viz.com

鋼の錬金術師

FULLMETAL ALCHEMIST

21

荒川弘

HIROMU ARAKAWA

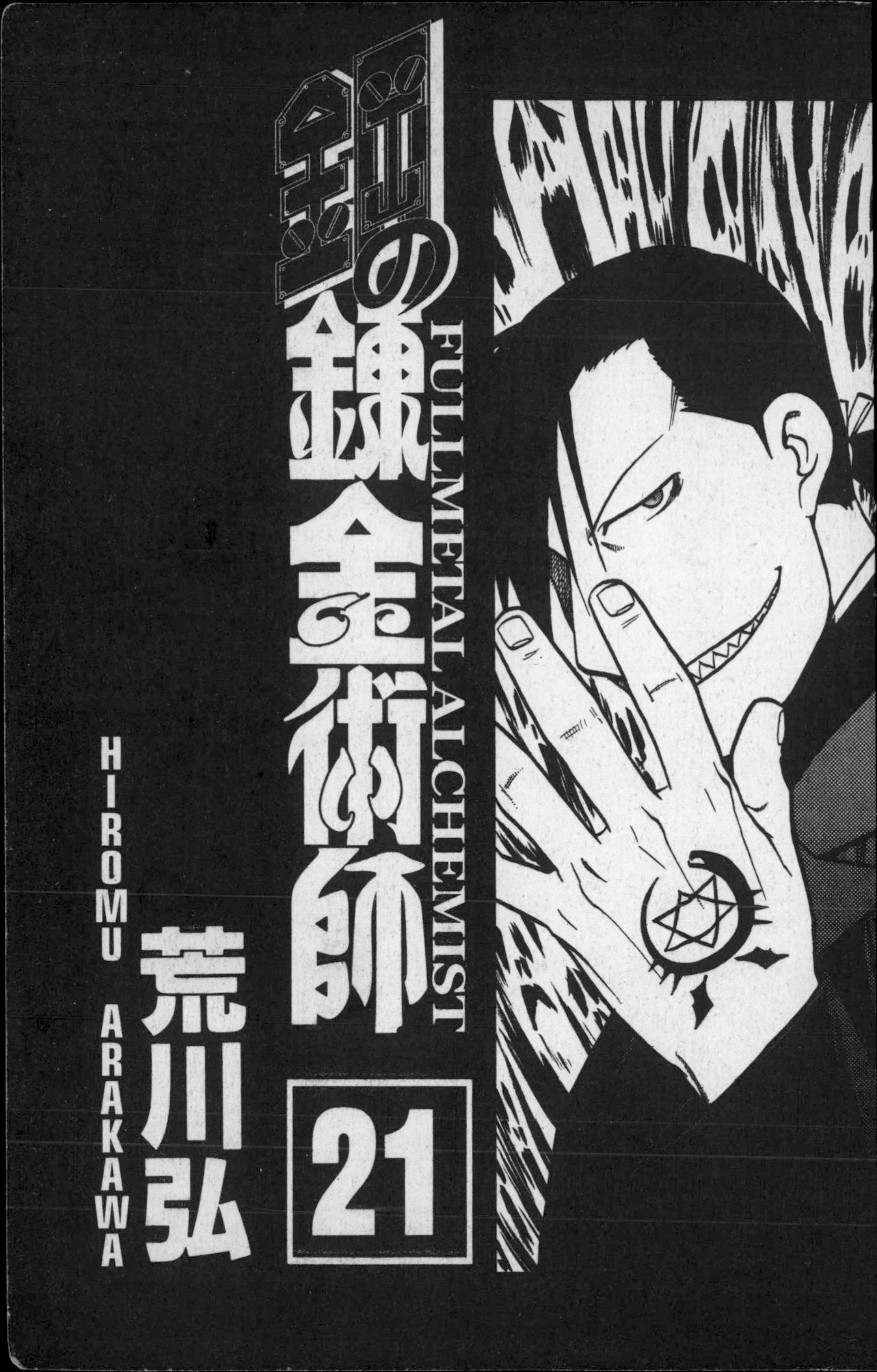

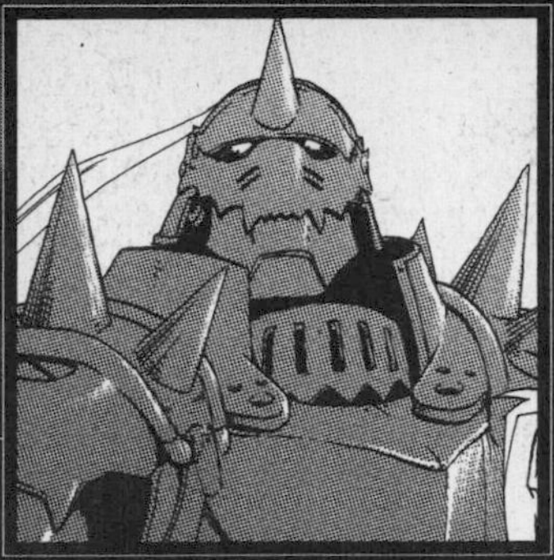

アルフォンス・エルリック

Alphonse Elric

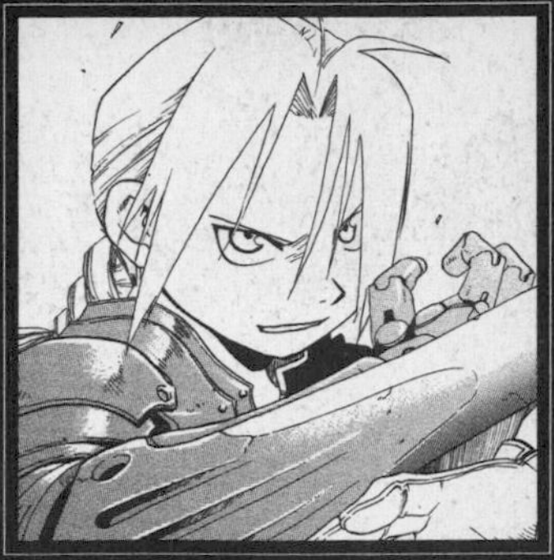

エドワード・エルリック

Edward Elric

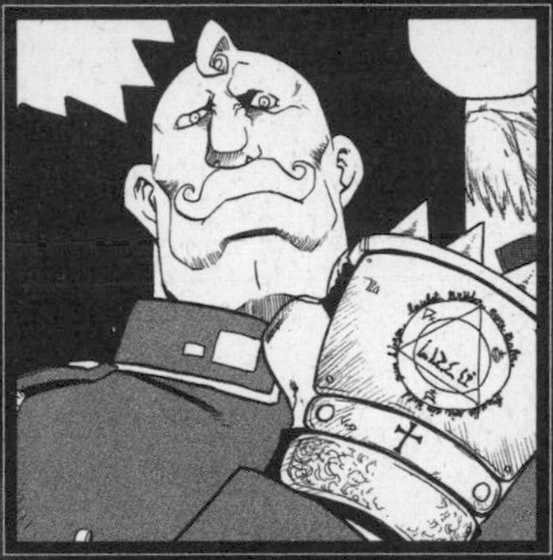

アレックス・ルイ・アームストロング

Alex Louis Armstrong

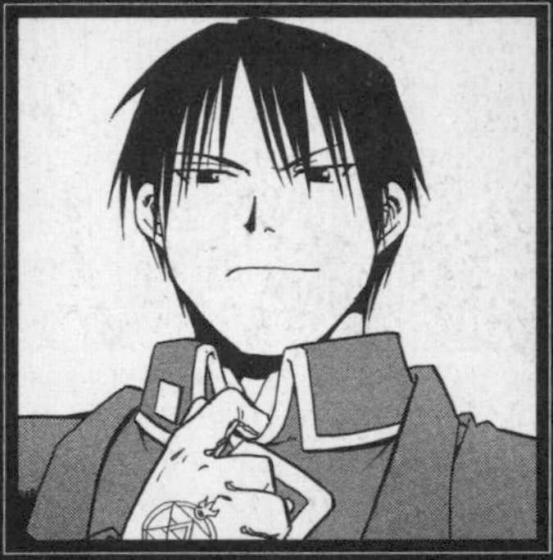

ロイ・マスタング

Roy Mustang

OUTLINE

FULLMETAL ALCHEMIST

Using a forbidden alchemical ritual, the Elric brothers attempted to bring their dead mother back to life. But the ritual went wrong, consuming Edward Elric's leg and Alphonse Elric's entire body. At the cost of his arm, Edward was able to graft his brother's soul into a suit of armor. Equipped with mechanical "auto-mail" to replace his missing limbs, Edward becomes a state alchemist in hopes of finding a way to restore their bodies. Their search embroils them in a deadly conspiracy that threatens to take the innocence, if not the lives, of everyone involved.

As the "Day of Reckoning" approaches, an intricate chess game has emerged in Amestris. On one side stand the Elrics, Mustang's crew, Olivier Armstrong and a ragtag bunch of chimeras; on the other, Military Command, Kimblee, the Homunculi and their mysterious "Father." At stake–the lives and souls of every last person in the country! But there is one "piece" who refuses to take sides–Prince Lin of Xing, now fused with the Homunculus Greed. With time running out, Ed swears fealty to Greed in the hopes of tipping the balance. Will the gambit pay off…?

鋼の錬金術師
FULLMETAL ALCHEMIST

CHARACTERS
FULLMETAL ALCHEMIST

■ ウィンリィ・ロックベル

Winry Rockbell

■ スカー

Scar

■ オリヴィエ・ミラ・アームストロング

Olivier Mira Armstrong

■ キング・ブラッドレイ

King Bradley

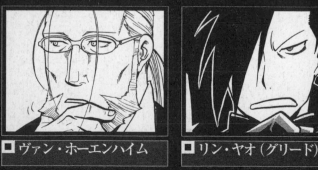

■ ヴァン・ホーエンハイム

Van Hohenheim

■ リン・ヤオ（グリード）

Lin Yao (Greed)

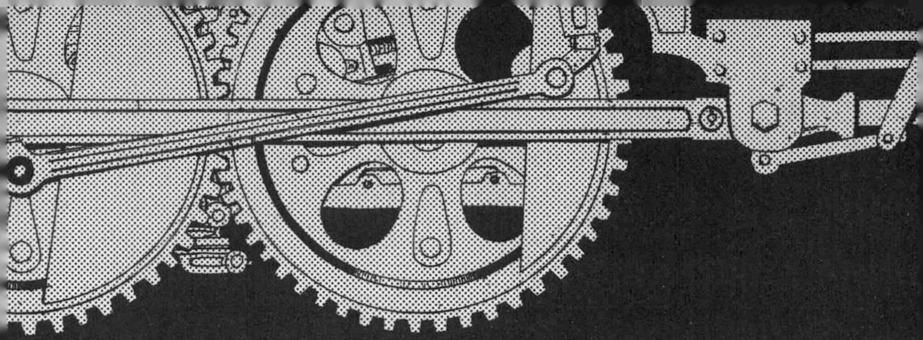

CONTENTS

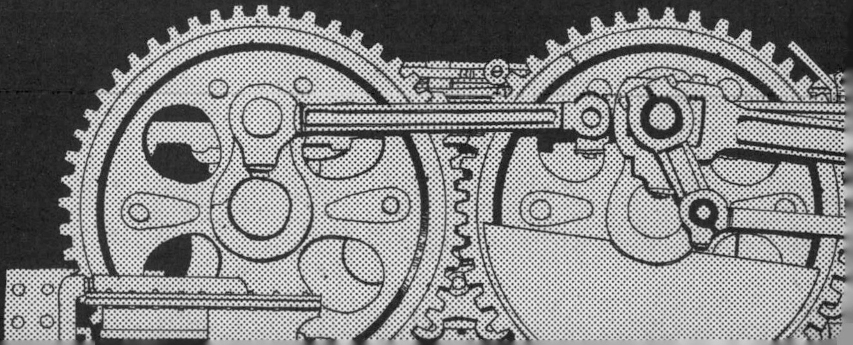

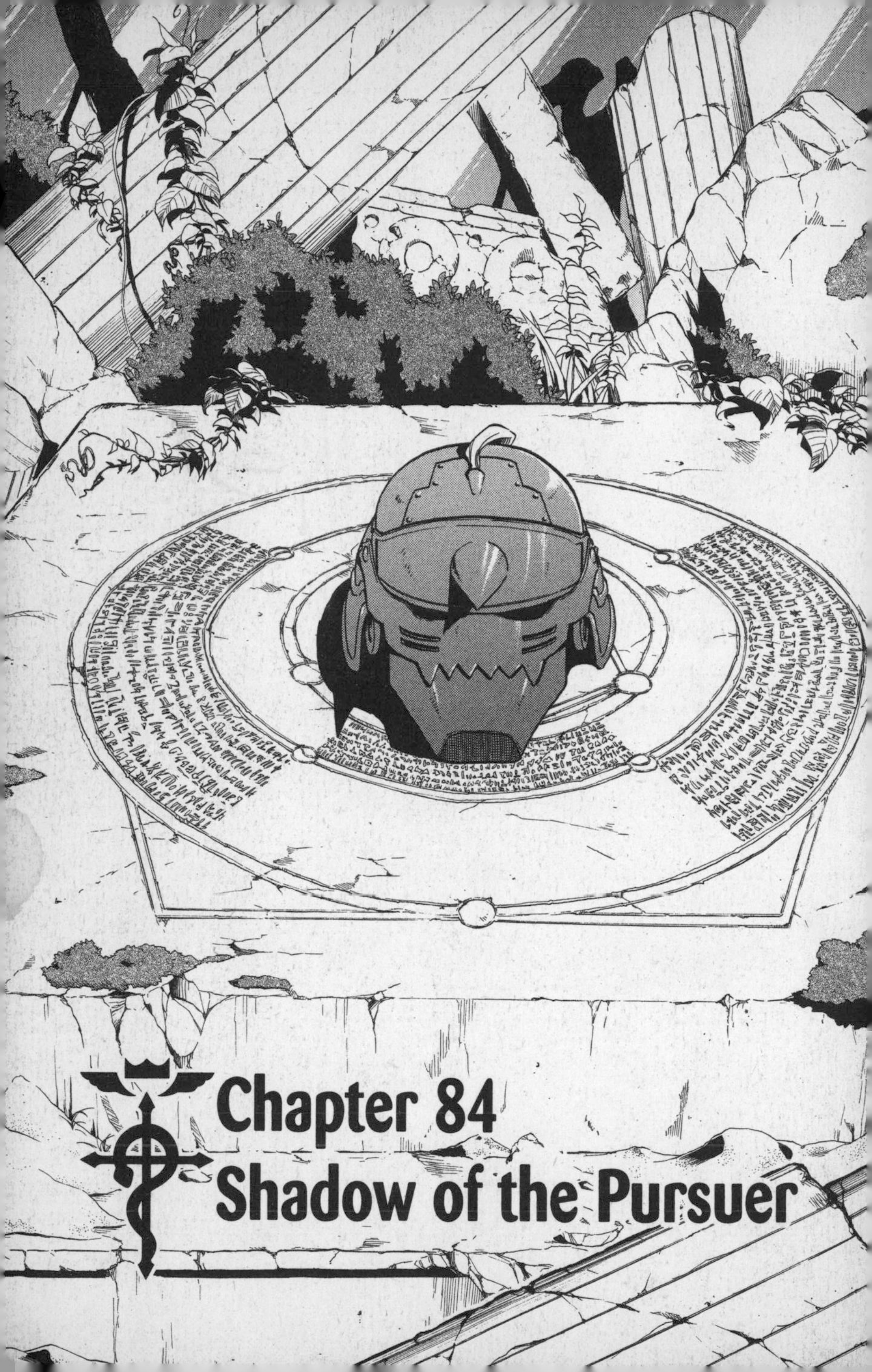
Chapter 84
Shadow of the Pursuer

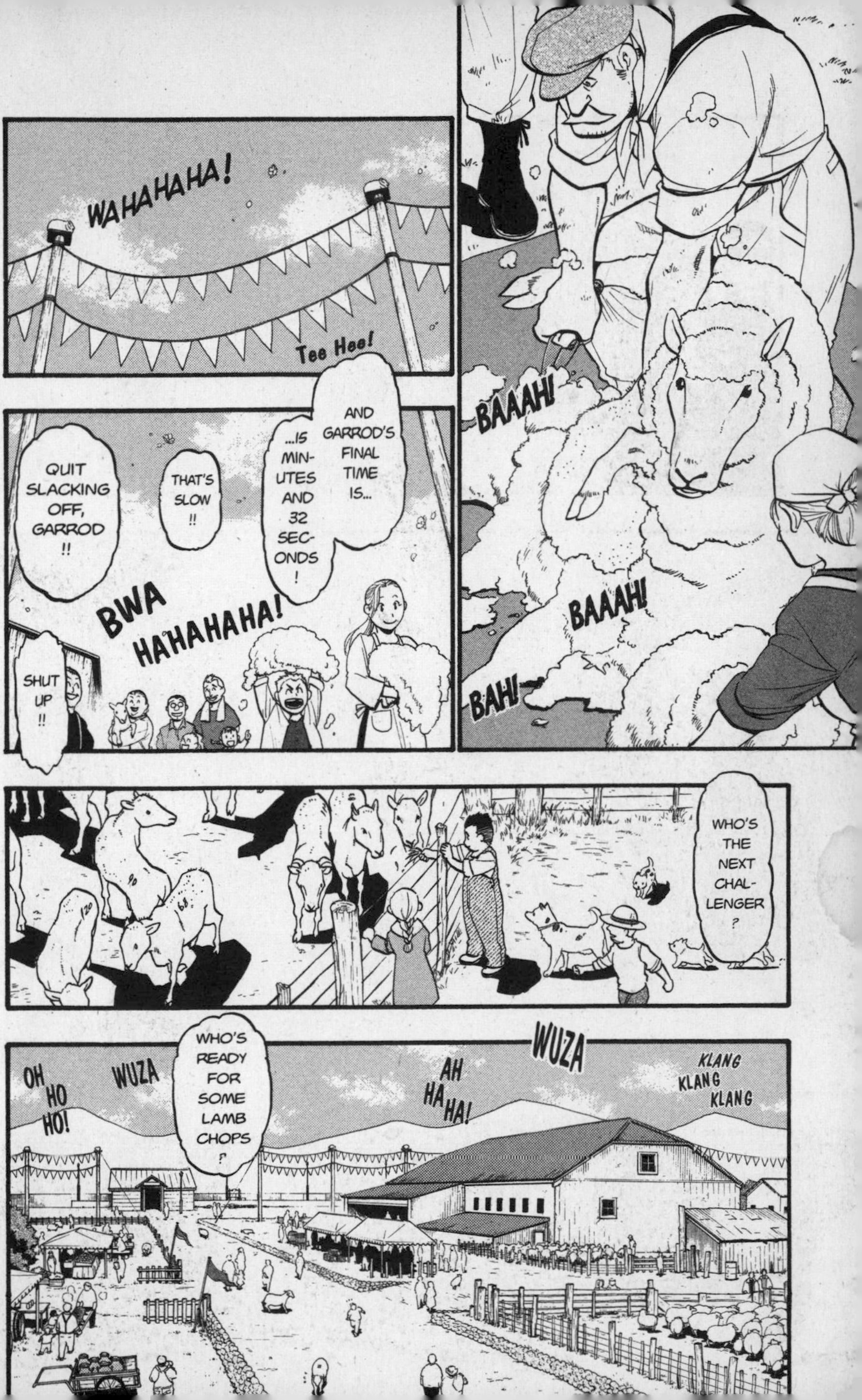
BAAAH!
BAAAH!
BAH!
WAHAHAHA!
Tee Hee!
AND GARROD'S FINAL TIME IS...
...15 MINUTES AND 32 SECONDS!
THAT'S SLOW!!
QUIT SLACKING OFF, GARROD!!
BWA HAHAHAHA!
SHUT UP!!
WHO'S THE NEXT CHALLENGER?
KLANG KLANG KLANG
WUZA
AH HA HA!
WHO'S READY FOR SOME LAMB CHOPS?
WUZA
OH HO HO!

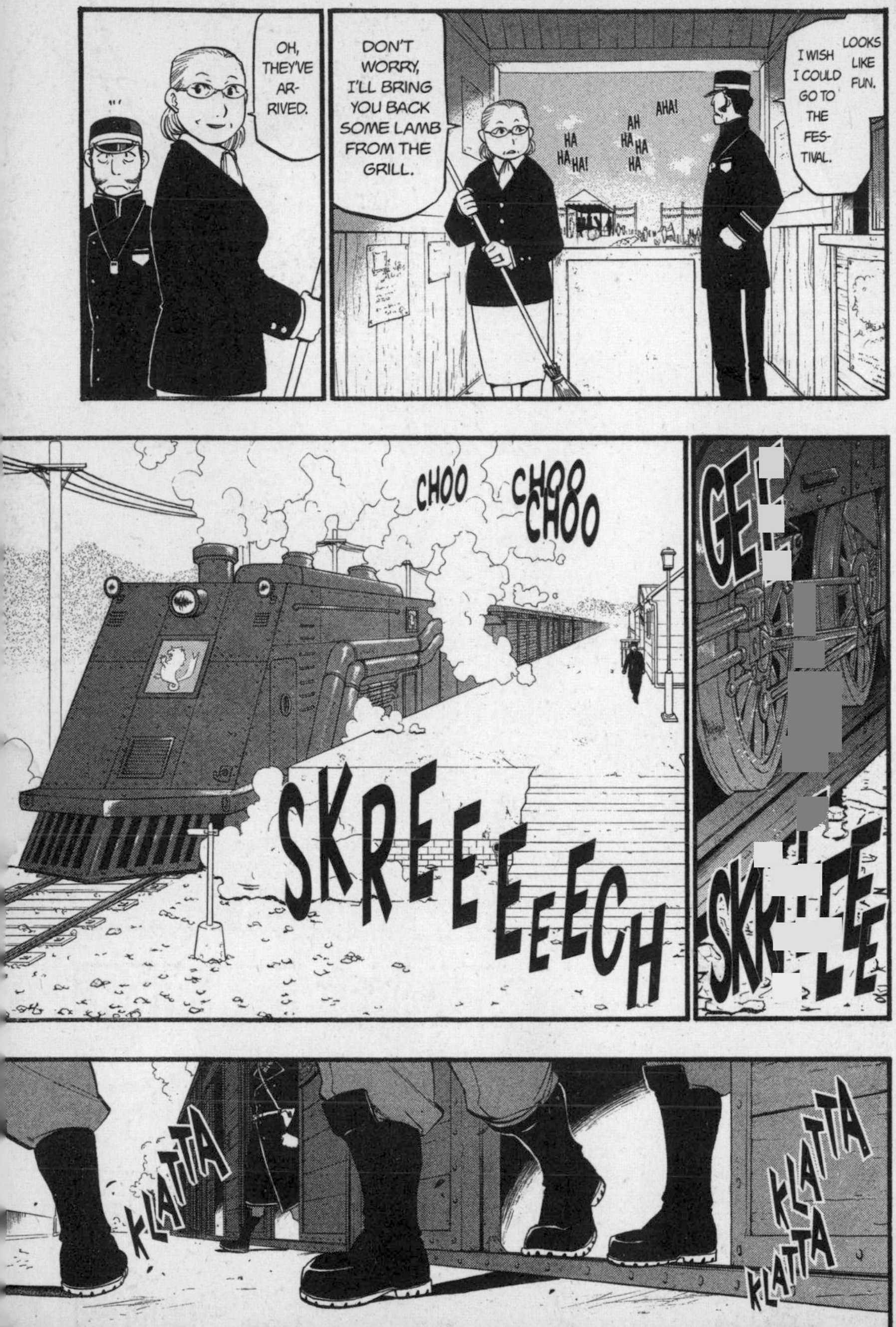
LOOKS LIKE FUN.
I WISH I COULD GO TO THE FES-TIVAL.
AHA!
AH HA HA HA HA
HA HA HA!
DON'T WORRY, I'LL BRING YOU BACK SOME LAMB FROM THE GRILL.
OH, THEY'VE AR-RIVED.
CHOO CHOO CHOO
SKREEEEECH
KLATTA KLATTA
KLATTA

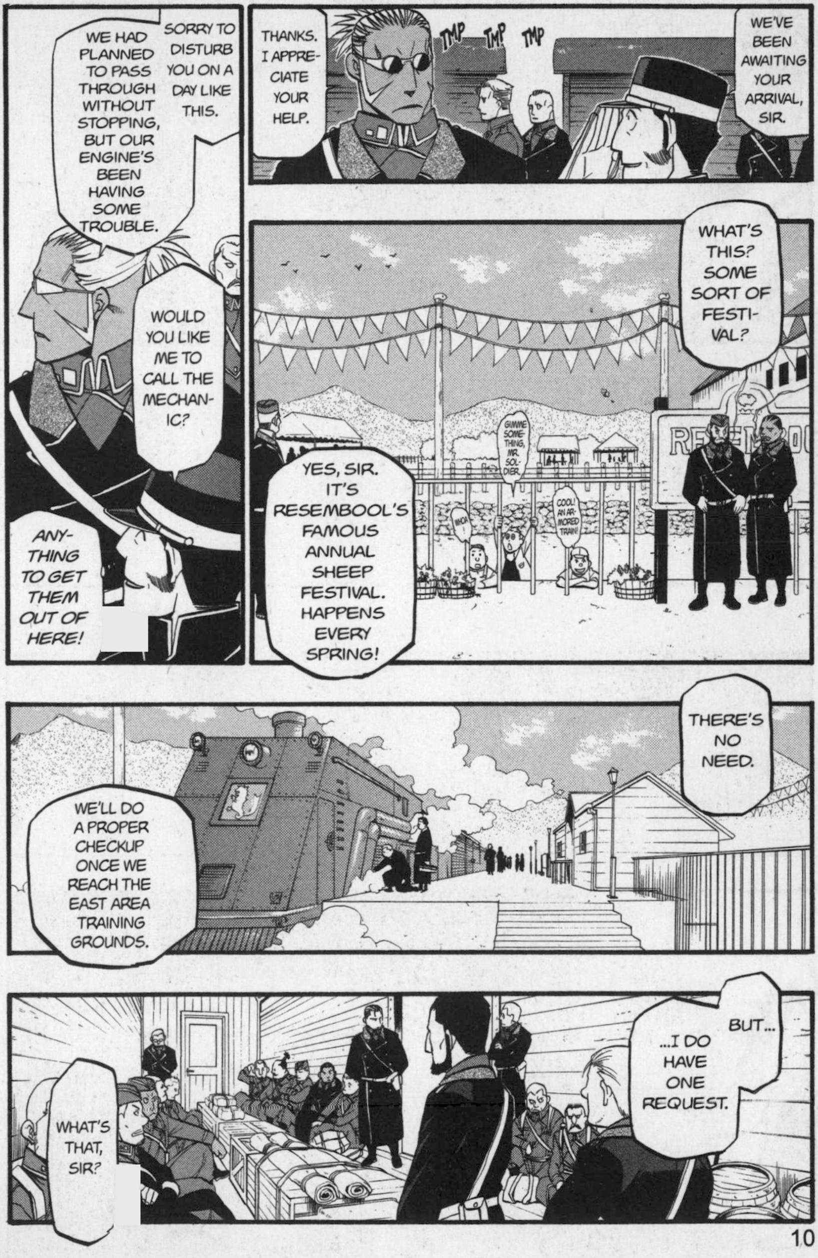
WE'VE BEEN AWAITING YOUR ARRIVAL, SIR.
TMP TMP TMP
THANKS. I APPRECIATE YOUR HELP.
WHAT'S THIS? SOME SORT OF FESTIVAL?
GIMME SOMETHING, MR. SOLDIER.
COOL! AN ARMORED TRAIN!
WHOA!
YES, SIR. IT'S RESEMBOOL'S FAMOUS ANNUAL SHEEP FESTIVAL. HAPPENS EVERY SPRING!
SORRY TO DISTURB YOU ON A DAY LIKE THIS.
WE HAD PLANNED TO PASS THROUGH WITHOUT STOPPING, BUT OUR ENGINE'S BEEN HAVING SOME TROUBLE.
WOULD YOU LIKE ME TO CALL THE MECHANIC?
ANYTHING TO GET THEM OUT OF HERE!
THERE'S NO NEED.
WE'LL DO A PROPER CHECKUP ONCE WE REACH THE EAST AREA TRAINING GROUNDS.
BUT...
...I DO HAVE ONE REQUEST.
WHAT'S THAT, SIR?

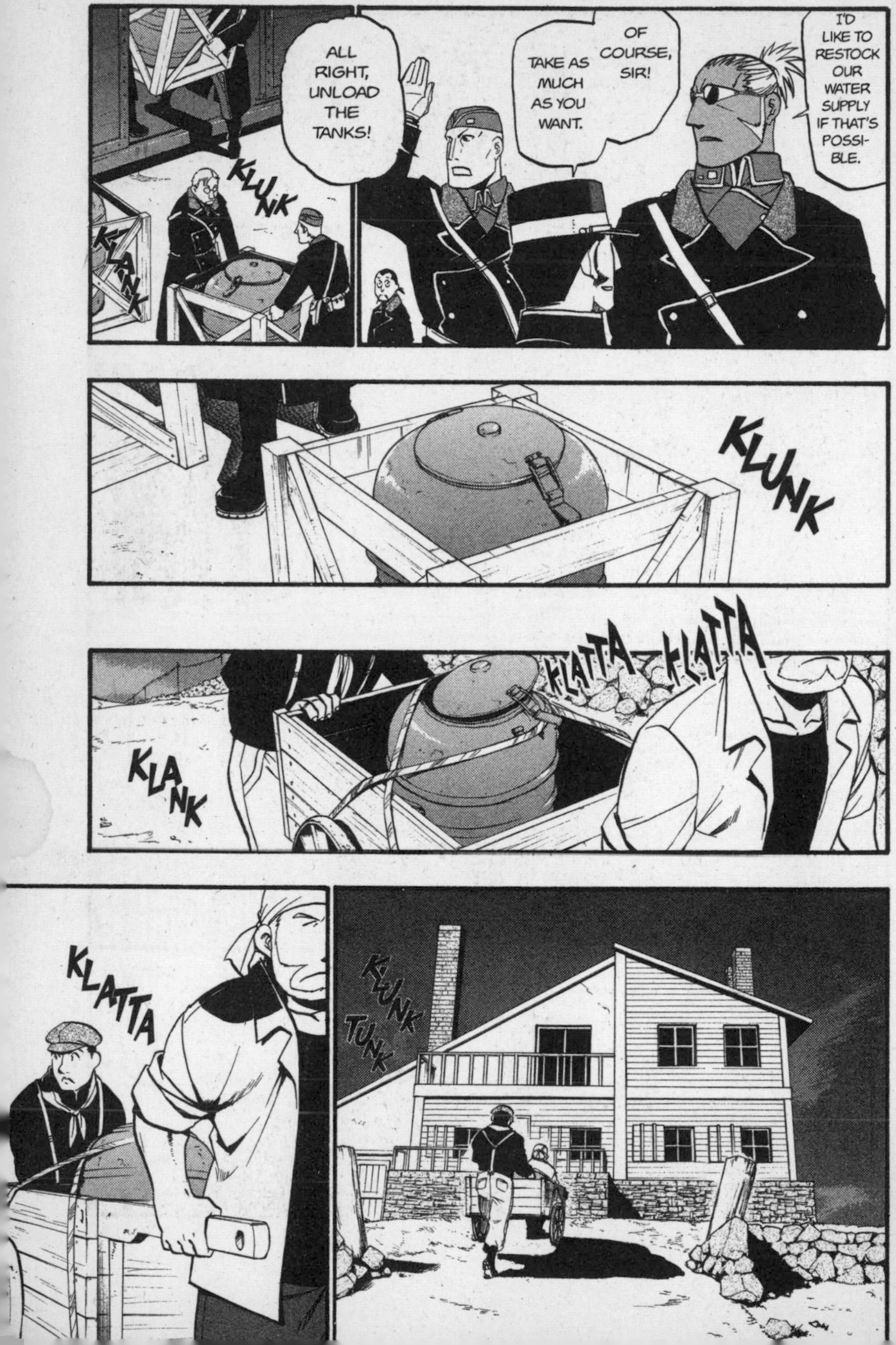
I'D LIKE TO RESTOCK OUR WATER SUPPLY IF THAT'S POSSIBLE.
OF COURSE, SIR!
TAKE AS MUCH AS YOU WANT.
ALL RIGHT, UNLOAD THE TANKS!
KLUNK
KLANK
KLUNK
KLATTA KLATTA
KLANK
KLUNK TUNK
KLATTA

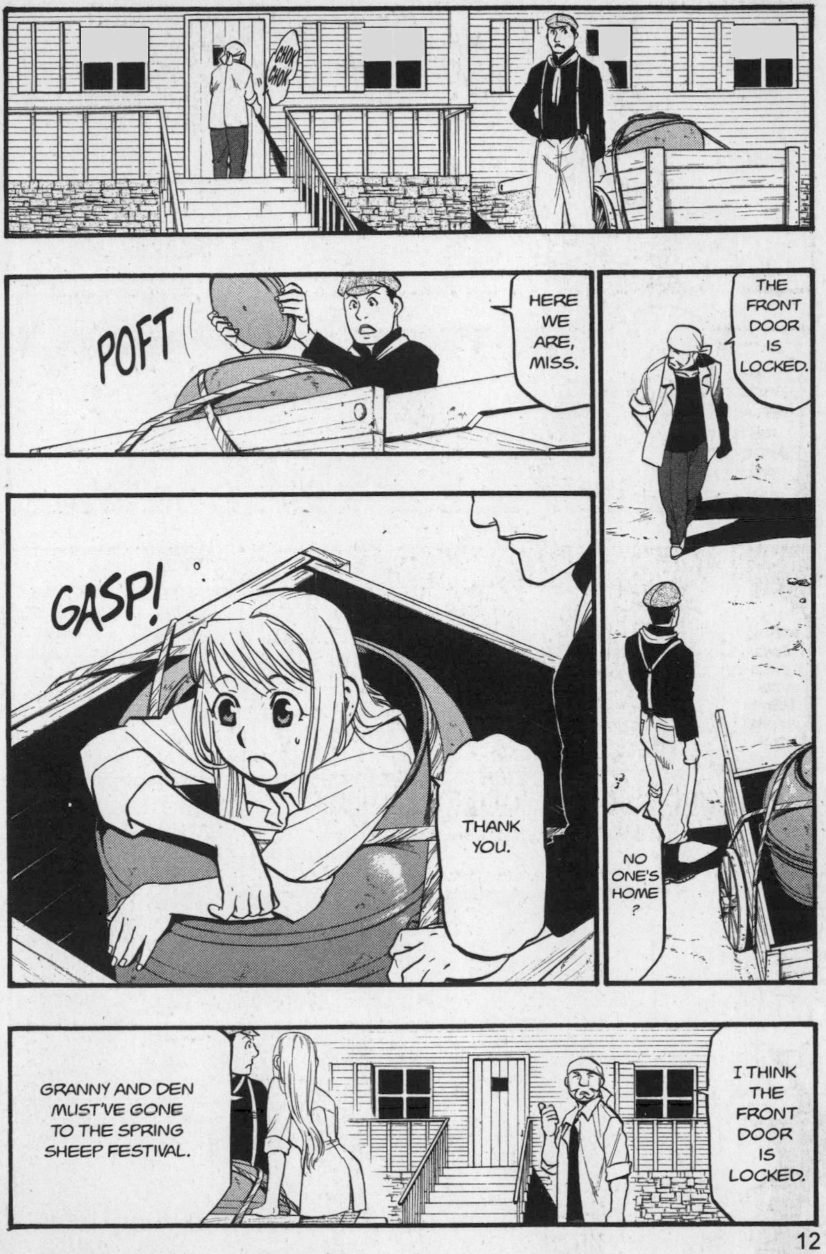
CHOK CHOK
THE FRONT DOOR IS LOCKED.
NO ONE'S HOME?
POFT
HERE WE ARE, MISS.
GASP!
THANK YOU.
I THINK THE FRONT DOOR IS LOCKED.
GRANNY AND DEN MUST'VE GONE TO THE SPRING SHEEP FESTIVAL.

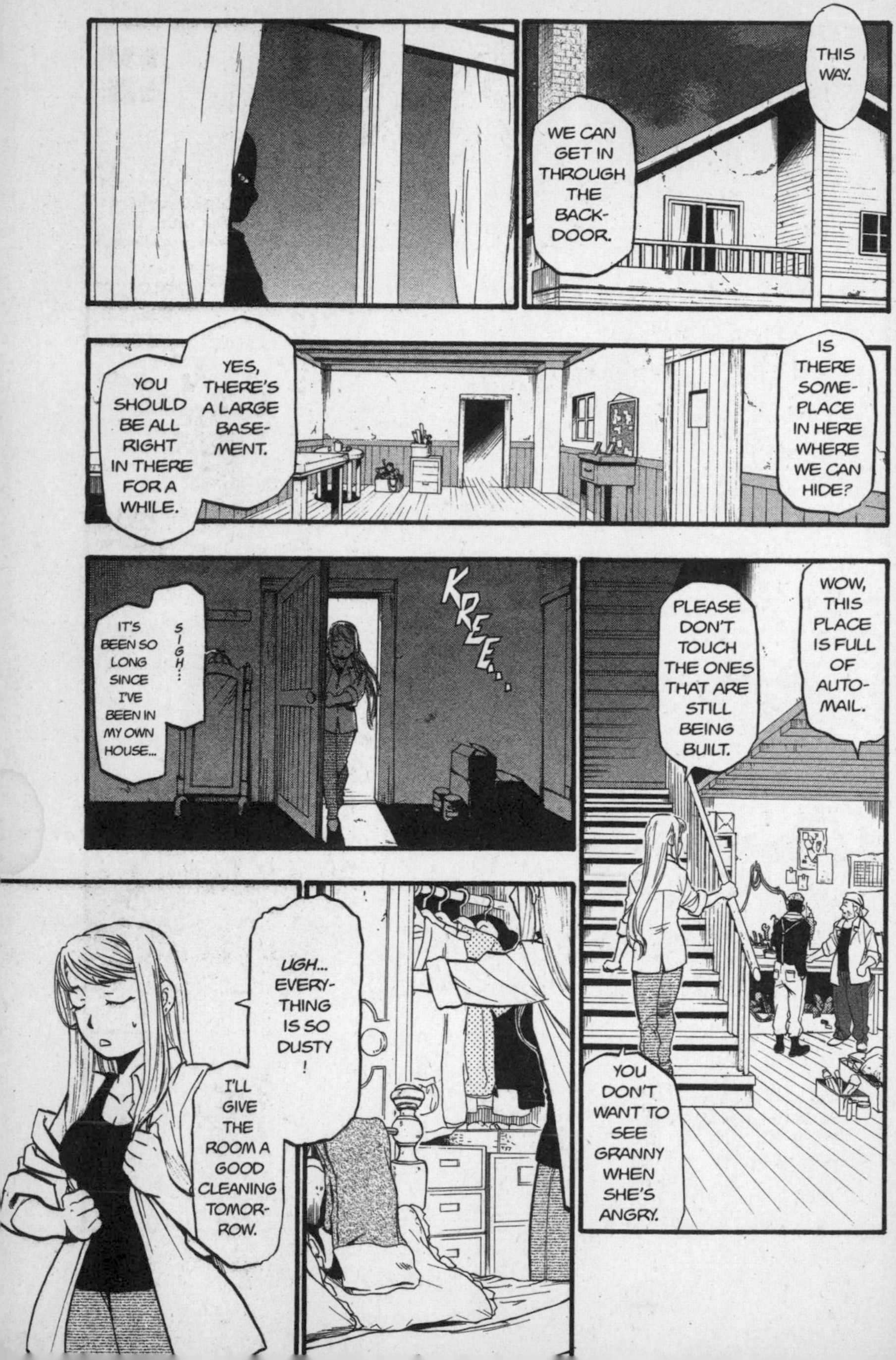
THIS WAY.
WE CAN GET IN THROUGH THE BACK-DOOR.
IS THERE SOME-PLACE IN HERE WHERE WE CAN HIDE?
YES, THERE'S A LARGE BASE-MENT.
YOU SHOULD BE ALL RIGHT IN THERE FOR A WHILE.
WOW, THIS PLACE IS FULL OF AUTO-MAIL.
PLEASE DON'T TOUCH THE ONES THAT ARE STILL BEING BUILT.
YOU DON'T WANT TO SEE GRANNY WHEN SHE'S ANGRY.
KREE...
SIGH...
IT'S BEEN SO LONG SINCE I'VE BEEN IN MY OWN HOUSE...
UGH... EVERY-THING IS SO DUSTY!
I'LL GIVE THE ROOM A GOOD CLEANING TOMOR-ROW.

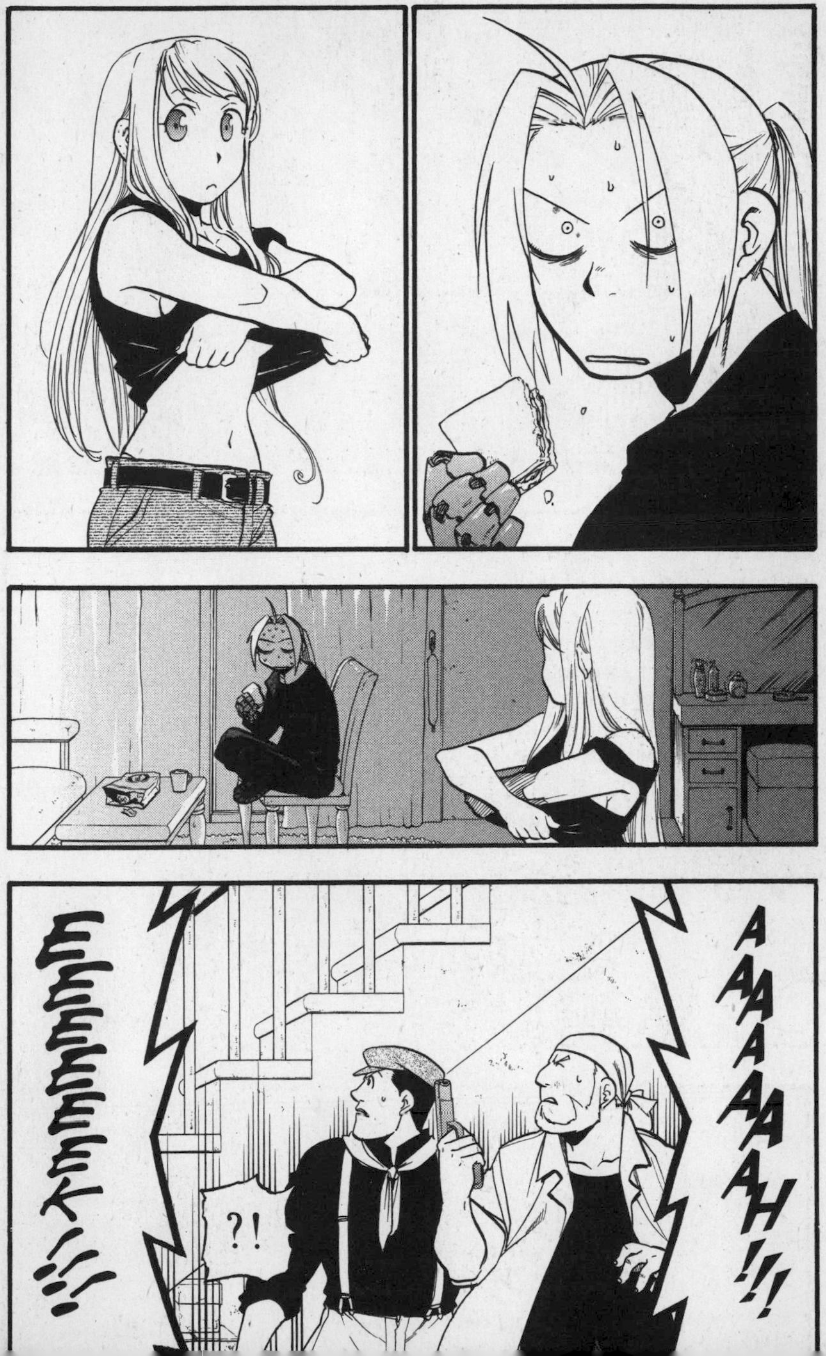
AAAAAAAAAH!!!
?!
EEEEEEEEEK!!!

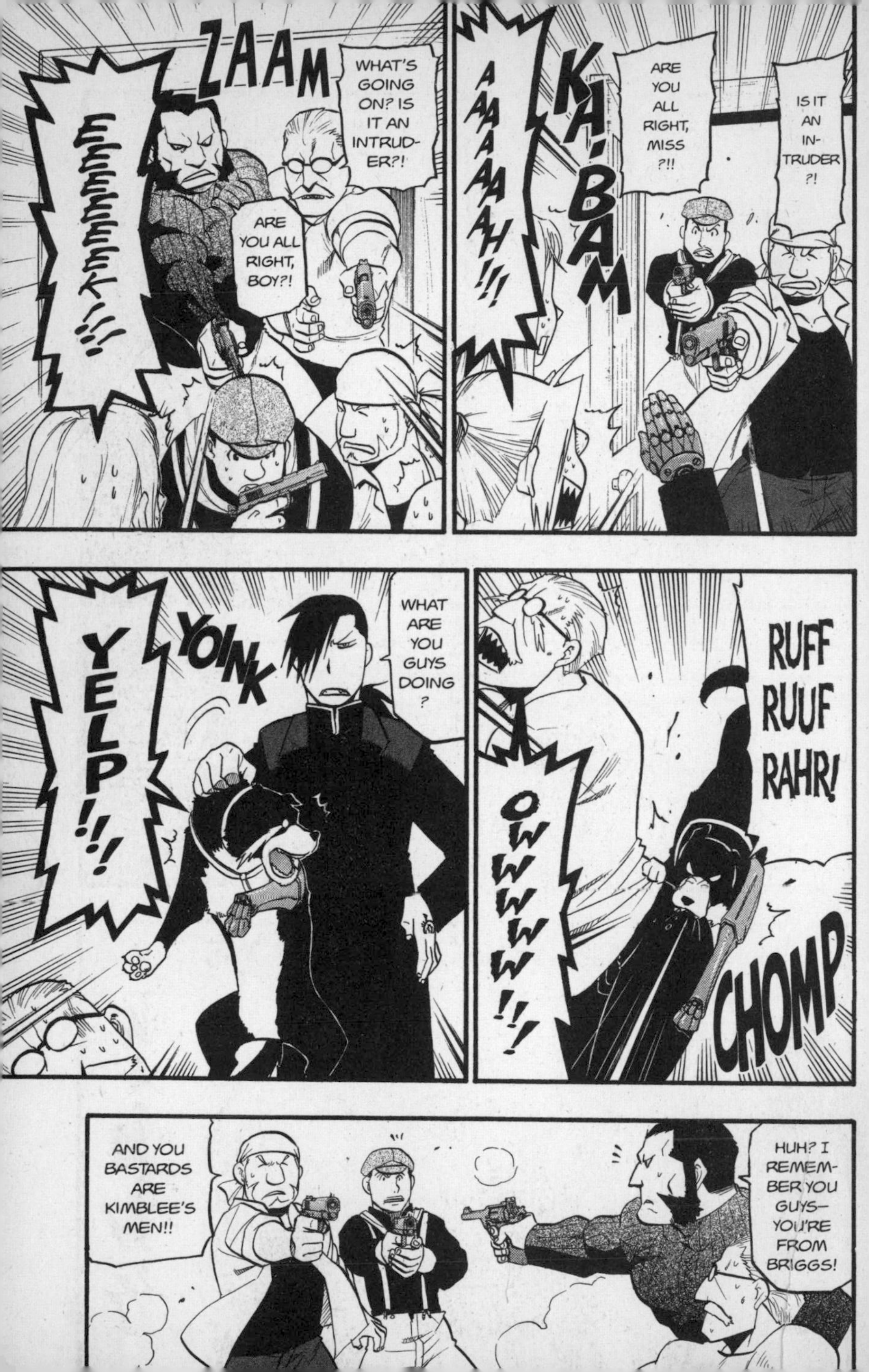
IS IT AN IN-TRUDER?!
ARE YOU ALL RIGHT, MISS?!!
KA-BAM
AAAAAAAH!!!
WHAT'S GOING ON? IS IT AN INTRUD-ER?!
ZAAM
ARE YOU ALL RIGHT, BOY?!
EEEEEEEEK!!!
RUFF RUUF RAHR!
OWWWWWW!!!
CHOMP
WHAT ARE YOU GUYS DOING?
YOINK
YELP!!!
HUH? I REMEM-BER YOU GUYS—YOU'RE FROM BRIGGS!
AND YOU BASTARDS ARE KIMBLEE'S MEN!!

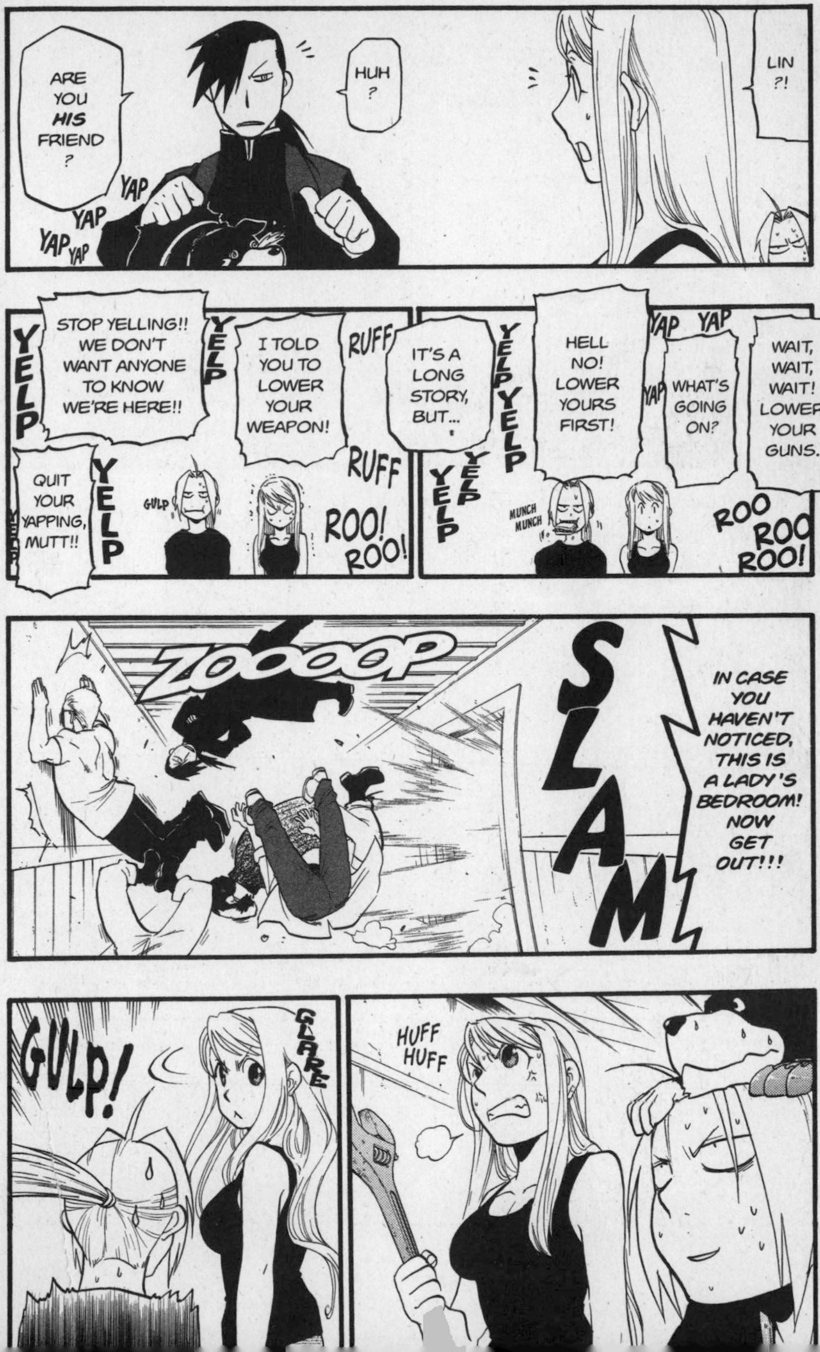
LIN ?!
HUH ?
ARE YOU HIS FRIEND ?
YAP YAP YAP YAP
WAIT, WAIT, WAIT! LOWER YOUR GUNS.
YAP YAP
WHAT'S GOING ON?
YAP
HELL NO! LOWER YOURS FIRST!
YELP YELP
IT'S A LONG STORY, BUT...
YELP YELP
MUNCH MUNCH
ROO ROO ROO!
RUFF
I TOLD YOU TO LOWER YOUR WEAPON!
YELP
STOP YELLING!! WE DON'T WANT ANYONE TO KNOW WE'RE HERE!!
YELP
QUIT YOUR YAPPING, MUTT!!
YELP
GULP
RUFF
ROO! ROO!
IN CASE YOU HAVEN'T NOTICED, THIS IS A LADY'S BEDROOM! NOW GET OUT!!!
SLAM
ZOOOOP
HUFF HUFF
GLARE
GULP!

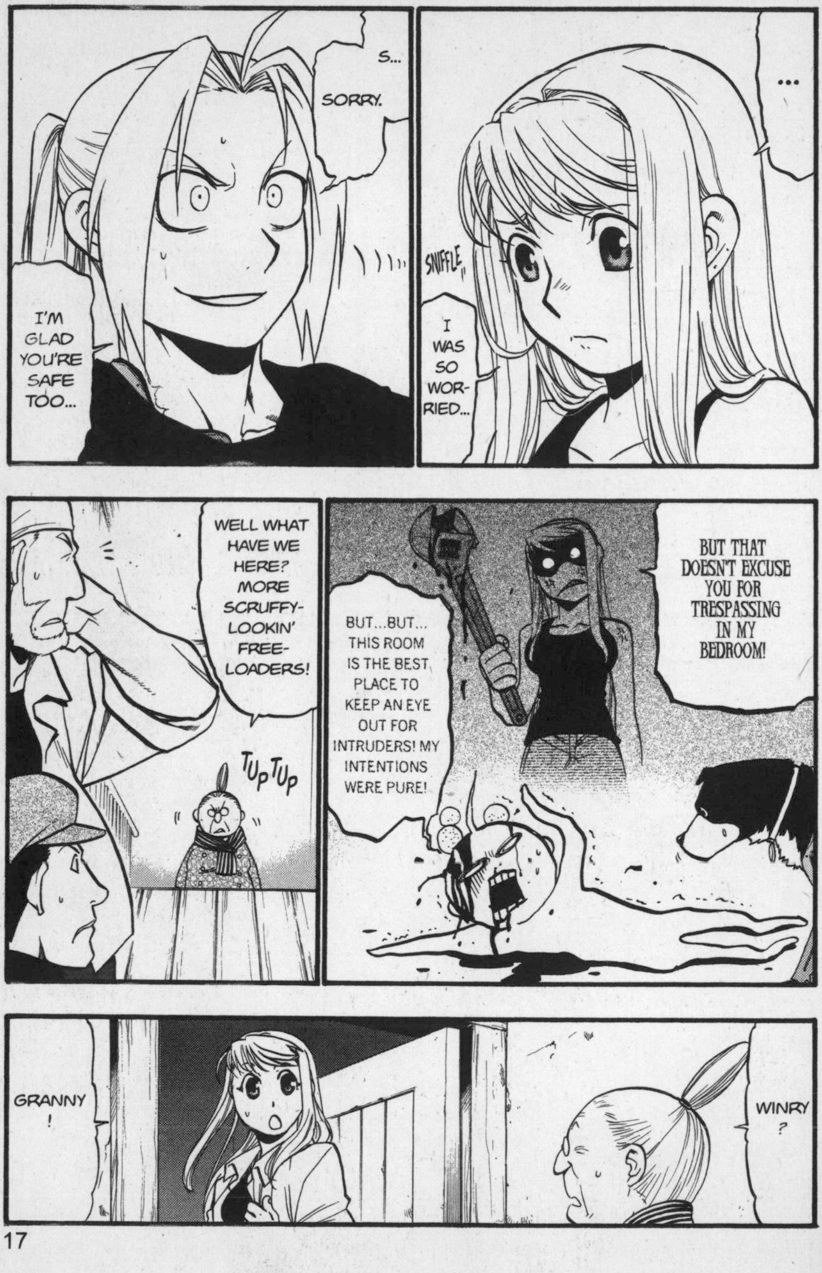
...
SNIFFLE
I WAS SO WOR-RIED...
S... SORRY.
I'M GLAD YOU'RE SAFE TOO...
BUT THAT DOESN'T EXCUSE YOU FOR TRESPASSING IN MY BEDROOM!
BUT...BUT... THIS ROOM IS THE BEST PLACE TO KEEP AN EYE OUT FOR INTRUDERS! MY INTENTIONS WERE PURE!
WELL WHAT HAVE WE HERE? MORE SCRUFFY-LOOKIN' FREE-LOADERS!
TUP TUP
WINRY?
GRANNY!

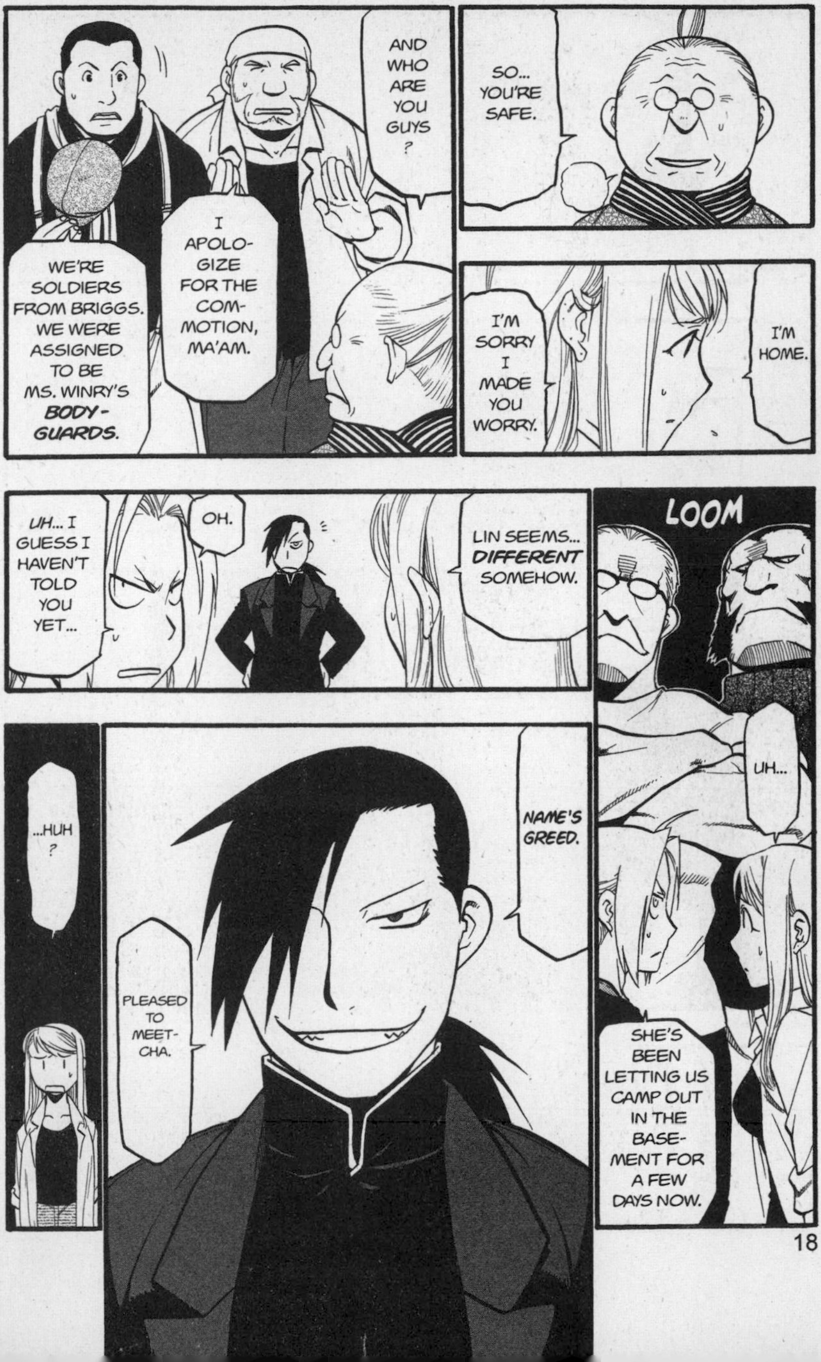
SO... YOU'RE SAFE.
I'M HOME.
I'M SORRY I MADE YOU WORRY.
AND WHO ARE YOU GUYS?
I APOLOGIZE FOR THE COMMOTION, MA'AM.
WE'RE SOLDIERS FROM BRIGGS. WE WERE ASSIGNED TO BE MS. WINRY'S **BODYGUARDS.**
LOOM
UH...
SHE'S BEEN LETTING US CAMP OUT IN THE BASEMENT FOR A FEW DAYS NOW.
LIN SEEMS... **DIFFERENT** SOMEHOW.
OH.
UH... I GUESS I HAVEN'T TOLD YOU YET...
NAME'S GREED.
PLEASED TO MEET-CHA.
...HUH?

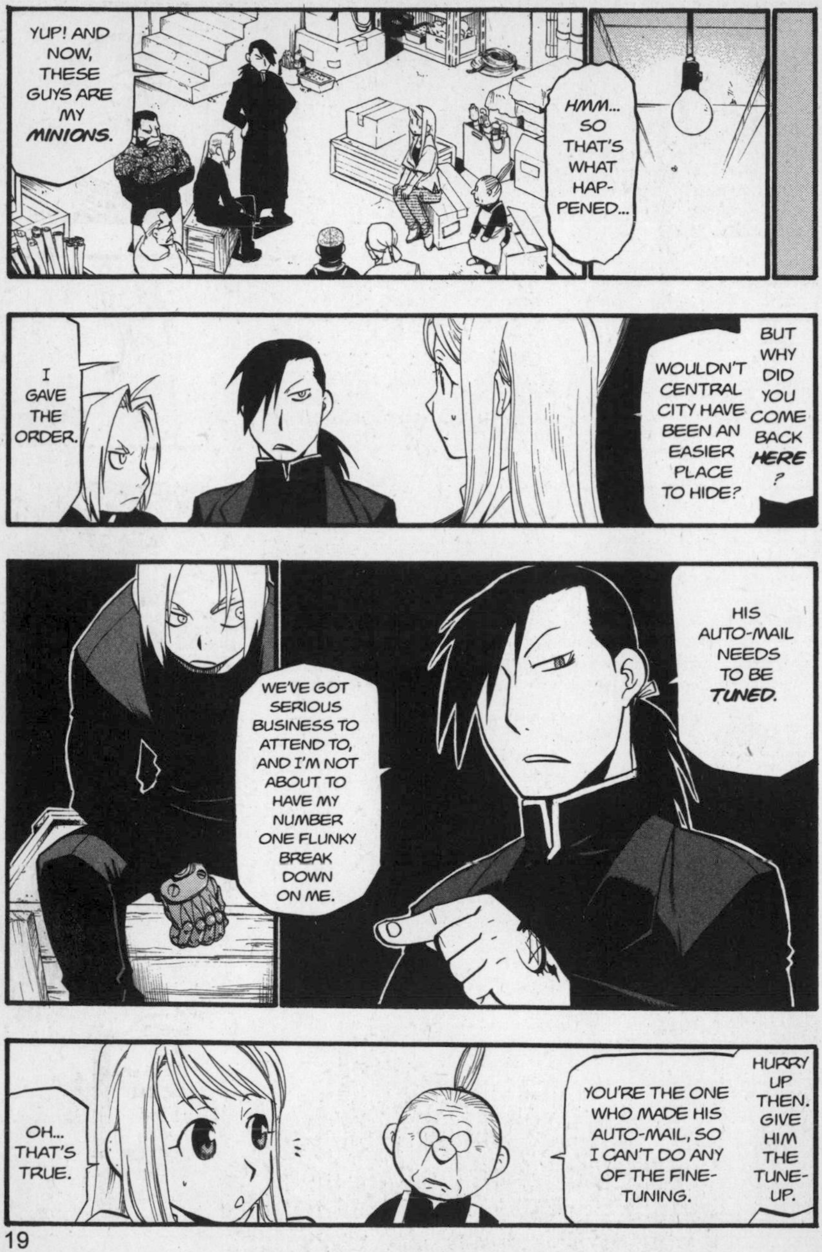
HMM... SO THAT'S WHAT HAP-PENED...
YUP! AND NOW, THESE GUYS ARE MY **MINIONS**.
BUT WHY DID YOU COME BACK **HERE**?
WOULDN'T CENTRAL CITY HAVE BEEN AN EASIER PLACE TO HIDE?
I GAVE THE ORDER.
HIS AUTO-MAIL NEEDS TO BE **TUNED**.
WE'VE GOT SERIOUS BUSINESS TO ATTEND TO, AND I'M NOT ABOUT TO HAVE MY NUMBER ONE FLUNKY BREAK DOWN ON ME.
HURRY UP THEN. GIVE HIM THE TUNE-UP.
YOU'RE THE ONE WHO MADE HIS AUTO-MAIL, SO I CAN'T DO ANY OF THE FINE-TUNING.
OH... THAT'S TRUE.

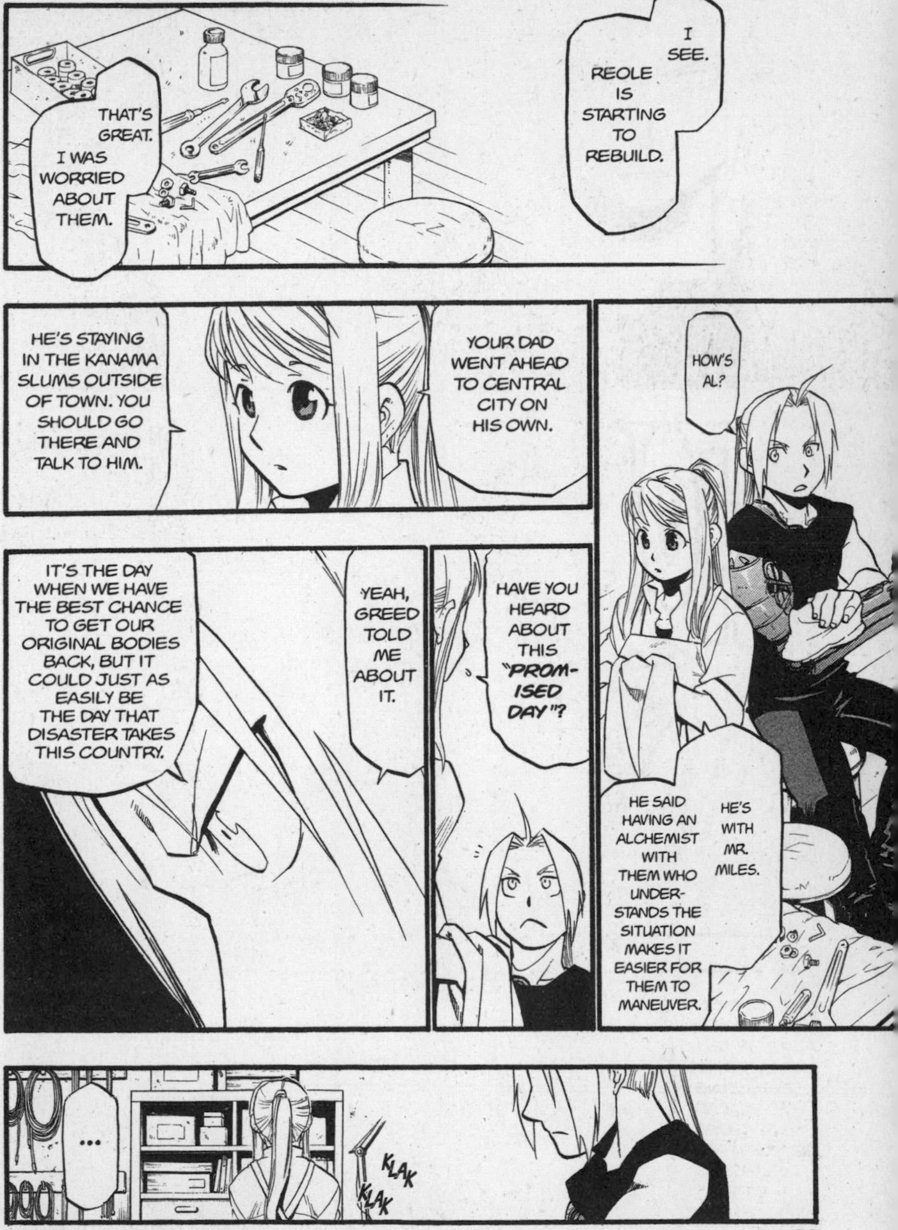
I SEE. REOLE IS STARTING TO REBUILD.
THAT'S GREAT. I WAS WORRIED ABOUT THEM.
HOW'S AL?
HE'S WITH MR. MILES.
HE SAID HAVING AN ALCHEMIST WITH THEM WHO UNDER-STANDS THE SITUATION MAKES IT EASIER FOR THEM TO MANEUVER.
YOUR DAD WENT AHEAD TO CENTRAL CITY ON HIS OWN.
HE'S STAYING IN THE KANAMA SLUMS OUTSIDE OF TOWN. YOU SHOULD GO THERE AND TALK TO HIM.
HAVE YOU HEARD ABOUT THIS "PROM-ISED DAY"?
YEAH, GREED TOLD ME ABOUT IT.
IT'S THE DAY WHEN WE HAVE THE BEST CHANCE TO GET OUR ORIGINAL BODIES BACK, BUT IT COULD JUST AS EASILY BE THE DAY THAT DISASTER TAKES THIS COUNTRY.
KLAK
KLAK
...

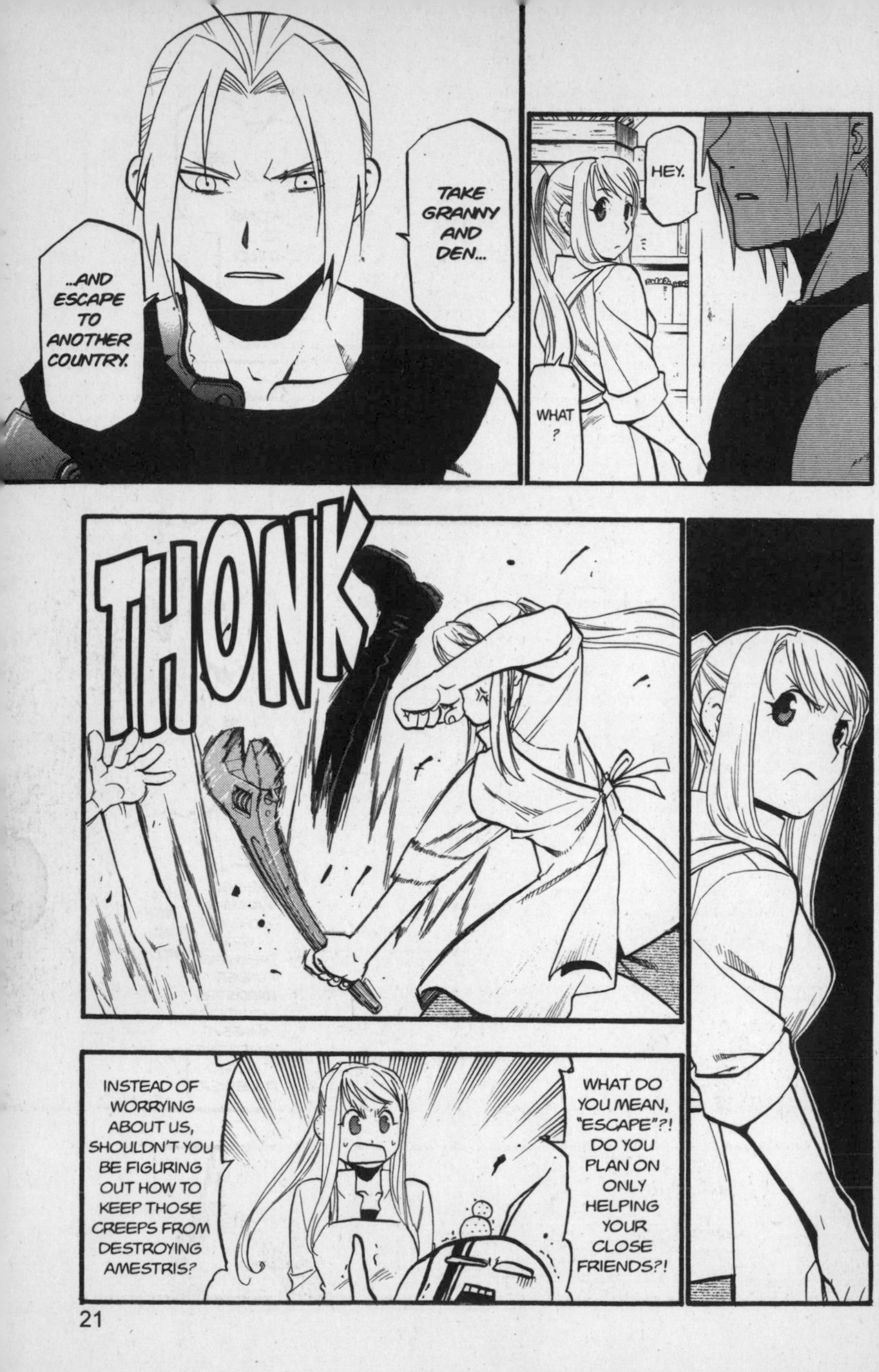
HEY.
WHAT?
TAKE GRANNY AND DEN...
...AND ESCAPE TO ANOTHER COUNTRY.
THONK
WHAT DO YOU MEAN, "ESCAPE"?! DO YOU PLAN ON ONLY HELPING YOUR CLOSE FRIENDS?!
INSTEAD OF WORRYING ABOUT US, SHOULDN'T YOU BE FIGURING OUT HOW TO KEEP THOSE CREEPS FROM DESTROYING AMESTRIS?

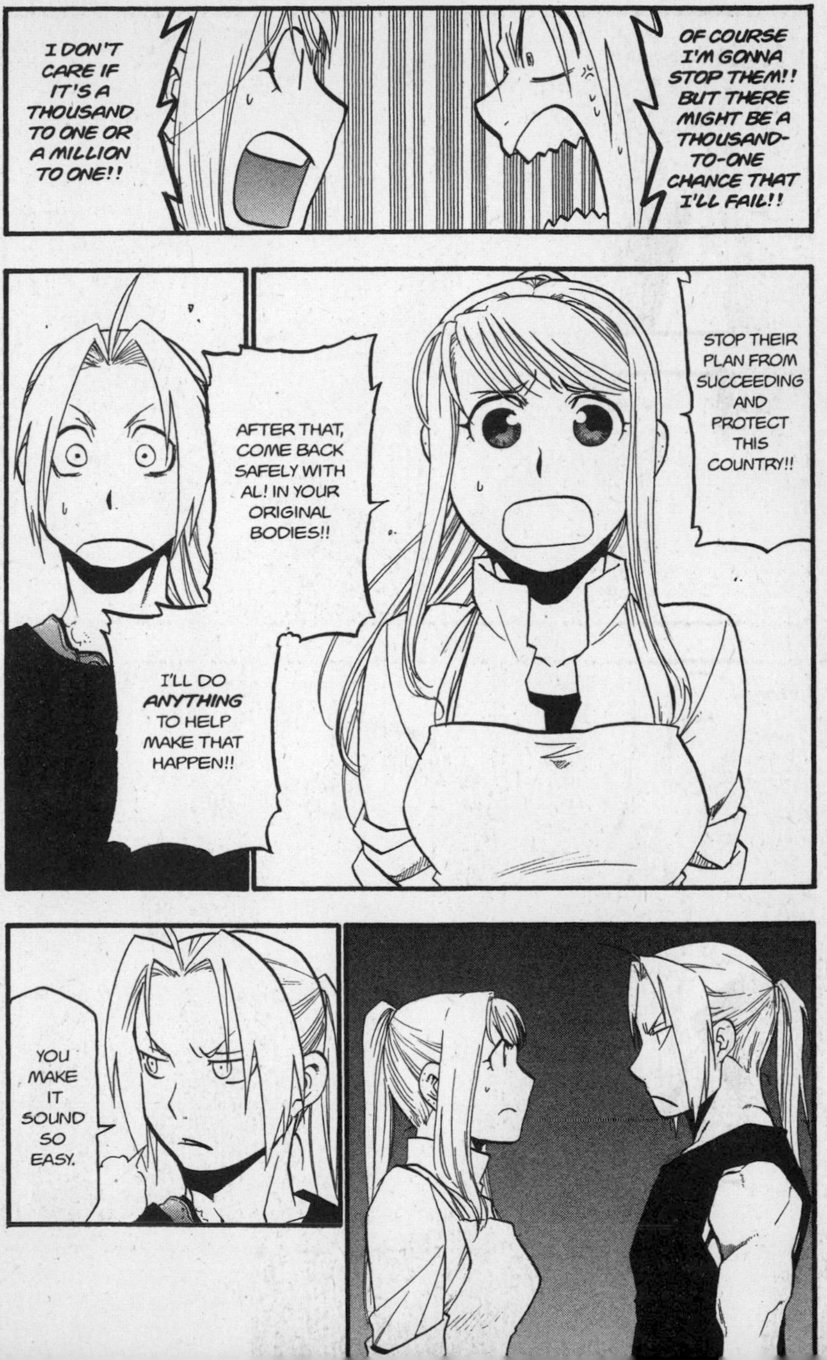
OF COURSE I'M GONNA STOP THEM!! BUT THERE MIGHT BE A THOUSAND-TO-ONE CHANCE THAT I'LL FAIL!!
I DON'T CARE IF IT'S A THOUSAND TO ONE OR A MILLION TO ONE!!
STOP THEIR PLAN FROM SUCCEEDING AND PROTECT THIS COUNTRY!!
AFTER THAT, COME BACK SAFELY WITH AL! IN YOUR ORIGINAL BODIES!!
I'LL DO ***ANYTHING*** TO HELP MAKE THAT HAPPEN!!
YOU MAKE IT SOUND SO EASY.

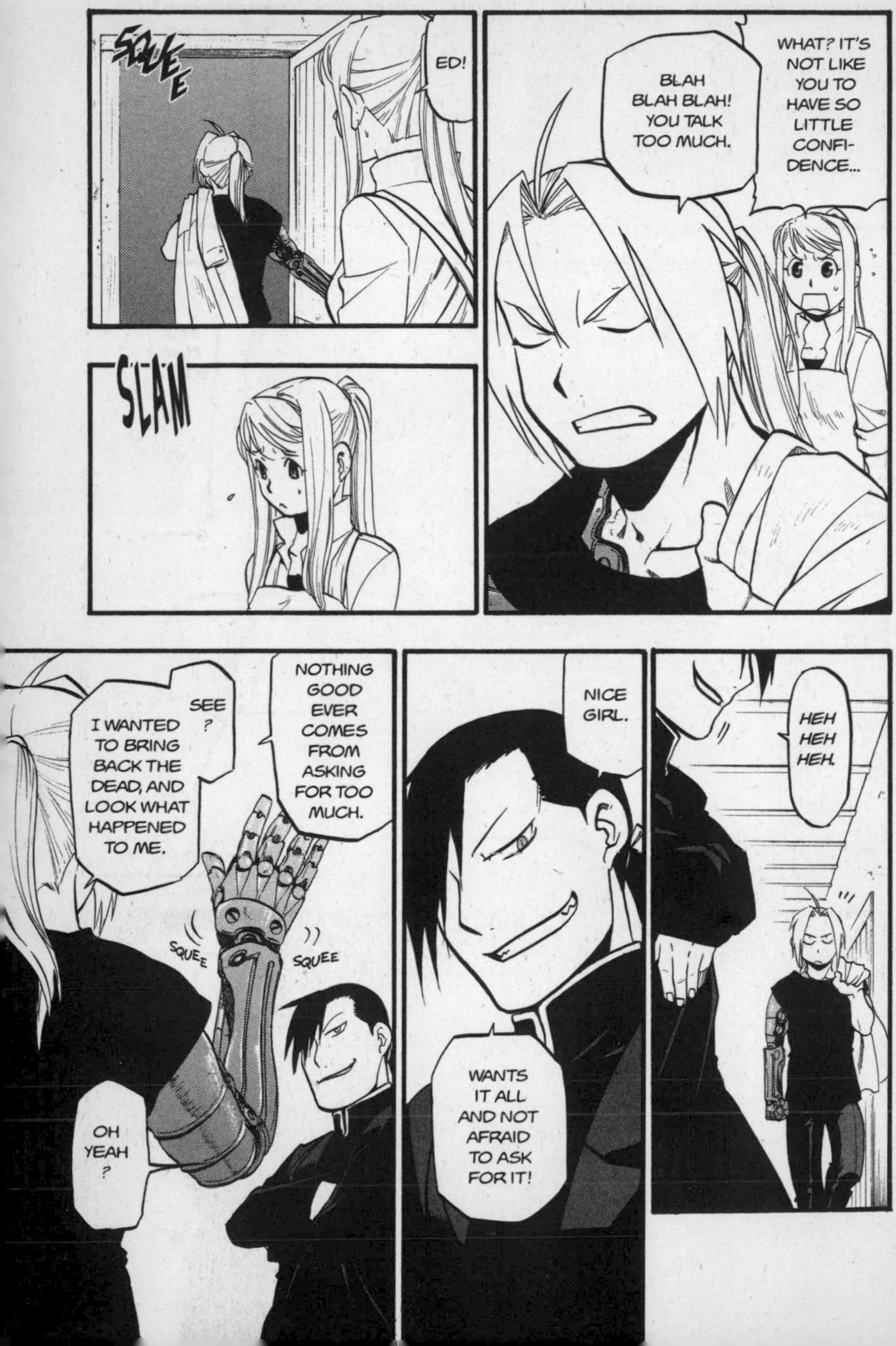
WHAT? IT'S NOT LIKE YOU TO HAVE SO LITTLE CONFIDENCE...
BLAH BLAH BLAH! YOU TALK TOO MUCH.
SQUEE
ED!
SLAM
HEH HEH HEH.
NICE GIRL.
WANTS IT ALL AND NOT AFRAID TO ASK FOR IT!
NOTHING GOOD EVER COMES FROM ASKING FOR TOO MUCH.
SEE? I WANTED TO BRING BACK THE DEAD, AND LOOK WHAT HAPPENED TO ME.
SQUEE
SQUEE
OH YEAH?

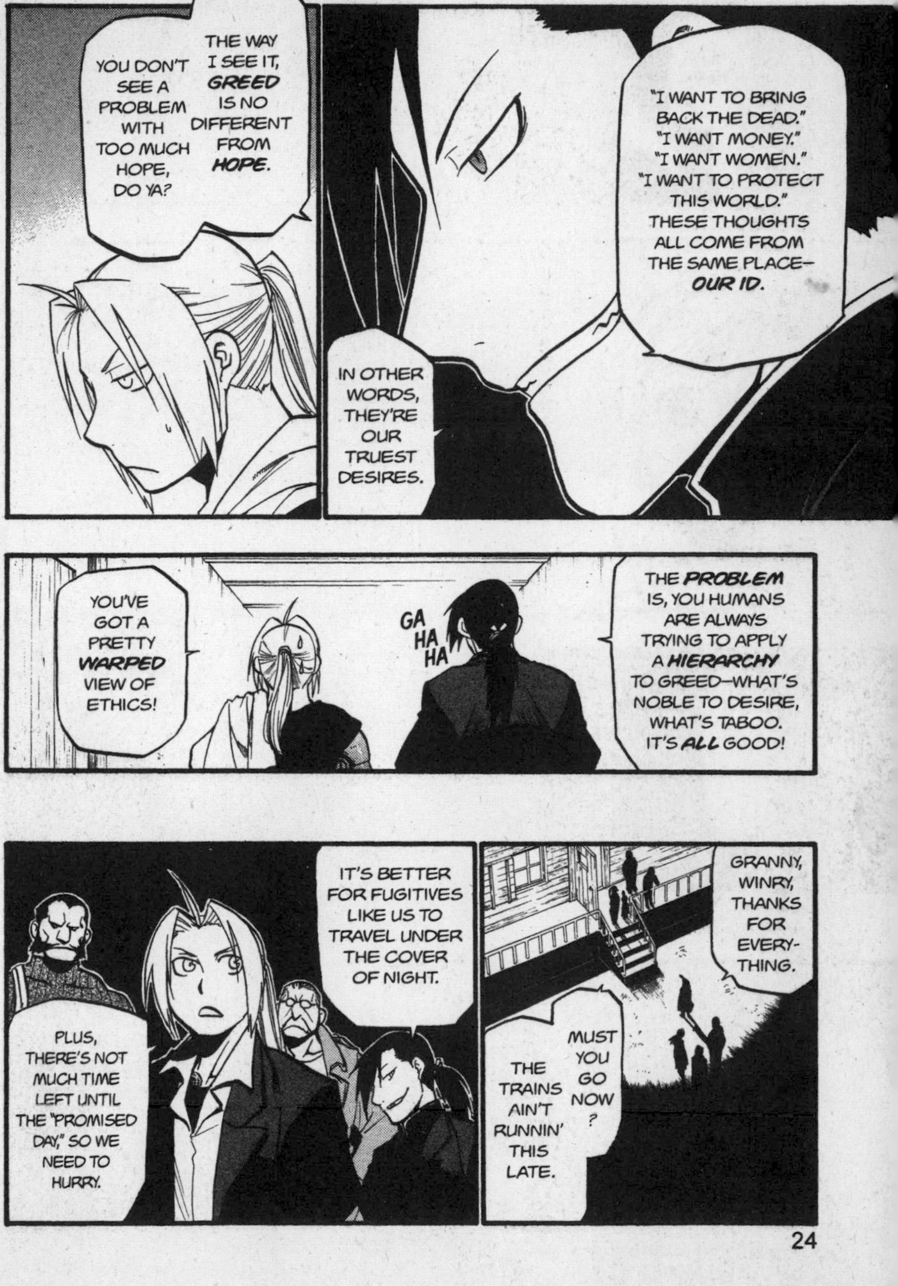
"I WANT TO BRING BACK THE DEAD." "I WANT MONEY." "I WANT WOMEN." "I WANT TO PROTECT THIS WORLD." THESE THOUGHTS ALL COME FROM THE SAME PLACE—OUR ID.
IN OTHER WORDS, THEY'RE OUR TRUEST DESIRES.
THE WAY I SEE IT, GREED IS NO DIFFERENT FROM HOPE.
YOU DON'T SEE A PROBLEM WITH TOO MUCH HOPE, DO YA?
THE PROBLEM IS, YOU HUMANS ARE ALWAYS TRYING TO APPLY A HIERARCHY TO GREED—WHAT'S NOBLE TO DESIRE, WHAT'S TABOO. IT'S ALL GOOD!
GA HA HA
YOU'VE GOT A PRETTY WARPED VIEW OF ETHICS!
GRANNY, WINRY, THANKS FOR EVERY-THING.
MUST YOU GO NOW?
THE TRAINS AIN'T RUNNIN' THIS LATE.
IT'S BETTER FOR FUGITIVES LIKE US TO TRAVEL UNDER THE COVER OF NIGHT.
PLUS, THERE'S NOT MUCH TIME LEFT UNTIL THE "PROMISED DAY," SO WE NEED TO HURRY.

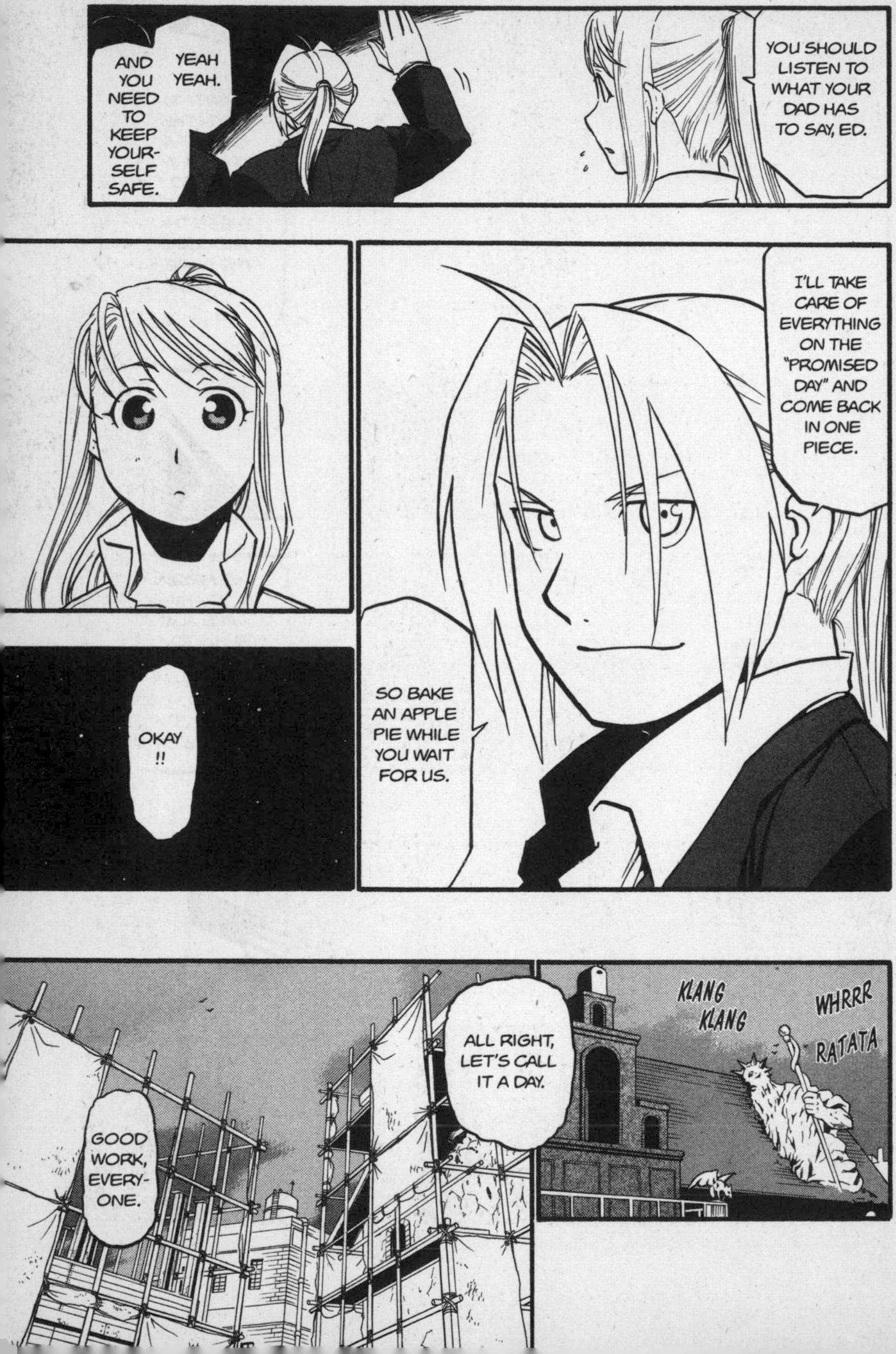
YOU SHOULD LISTEN TO WHAT YOUR DAD HAS TO SAY, ED.
YEAH YEAH.
AND YOU NEED TO KEEP YOUR-SELF SAFE.
I'LL TAKE CARE OF EVERYTHING ON THE "PROMISED DAY" AND COME BACK IN ONE PIECE.
SO BAKE AN APPLE PIE WHILE YOU WAIT FOR US.
OKAY !!
KLANG KLANG
WHRRR RATATA
ALL RIGHT, LET'S CALL IT A DAY.
GOOD WORK, EVERY-ONE.

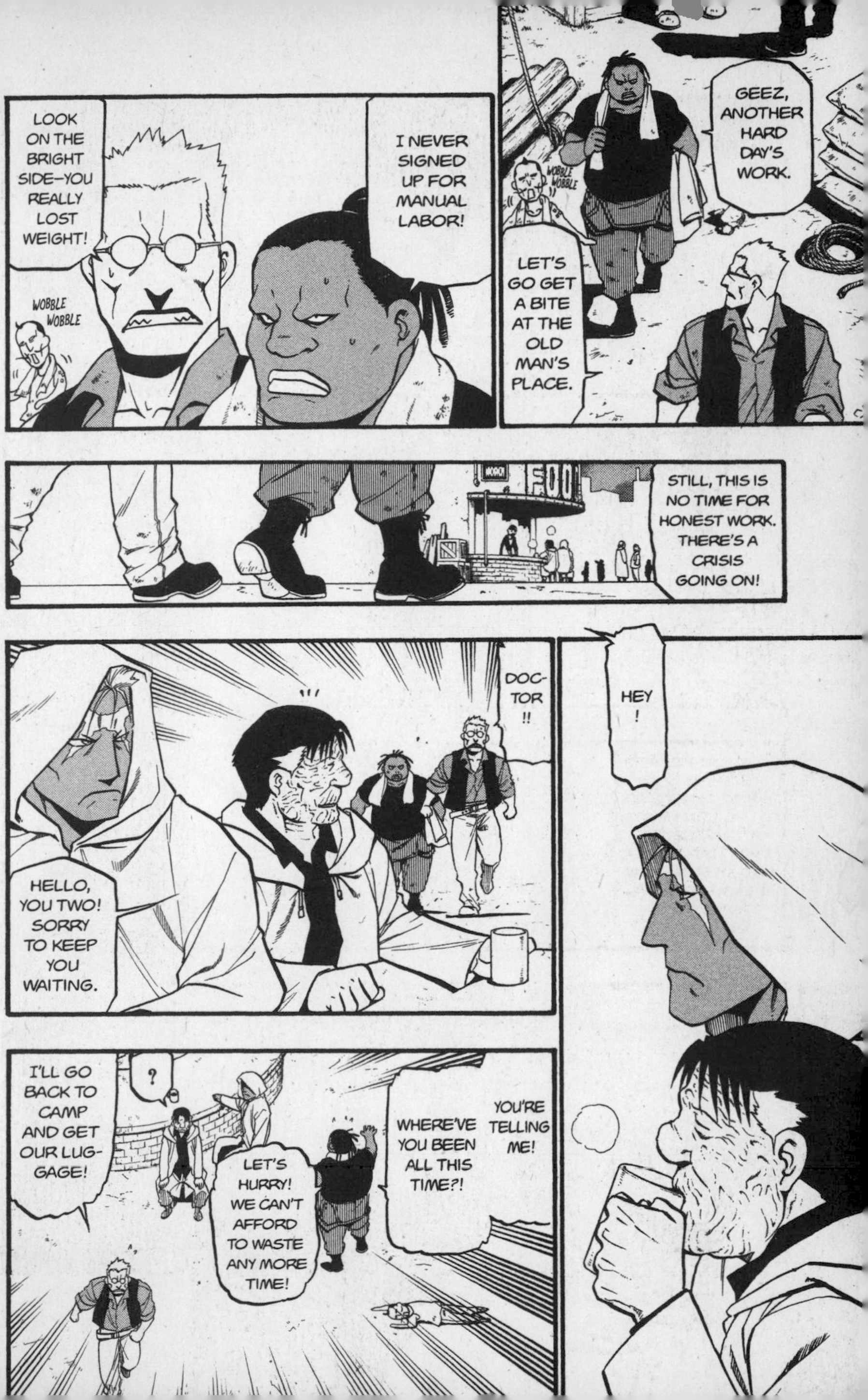
GEEZ, ANOTHER HARD DAY'S WORK.
WOBBLE WOBBLE
LET'S GO GET A BITE AT THE OLD MAN'S PLACE.
I NEVER SIGNED UP FOR MANUAL LABOR!
LOOK ON THE BRIGHT SIDE—YOU REALLY LOST WEIGHT!
WOBBLE WOBBLE
STILL, THIS IS NO TIME FOR HONEST WORK. THERE'S A CRISIS GOING ON!
HEY!
DOCTOR!!
HELLO, YOU TWO! SORRY TO KEEP YOU WAITING.
YOU'RE TELLING ME!
WHERE'VE YOU BEEN ALL THIS TIME?!
?
LET'S HURRY! WE CAN'T AFFORD TO WASTE ANY MORE TIME!
I'LL GO BACK TO CAMP AND GET OUR LUGGAGE!

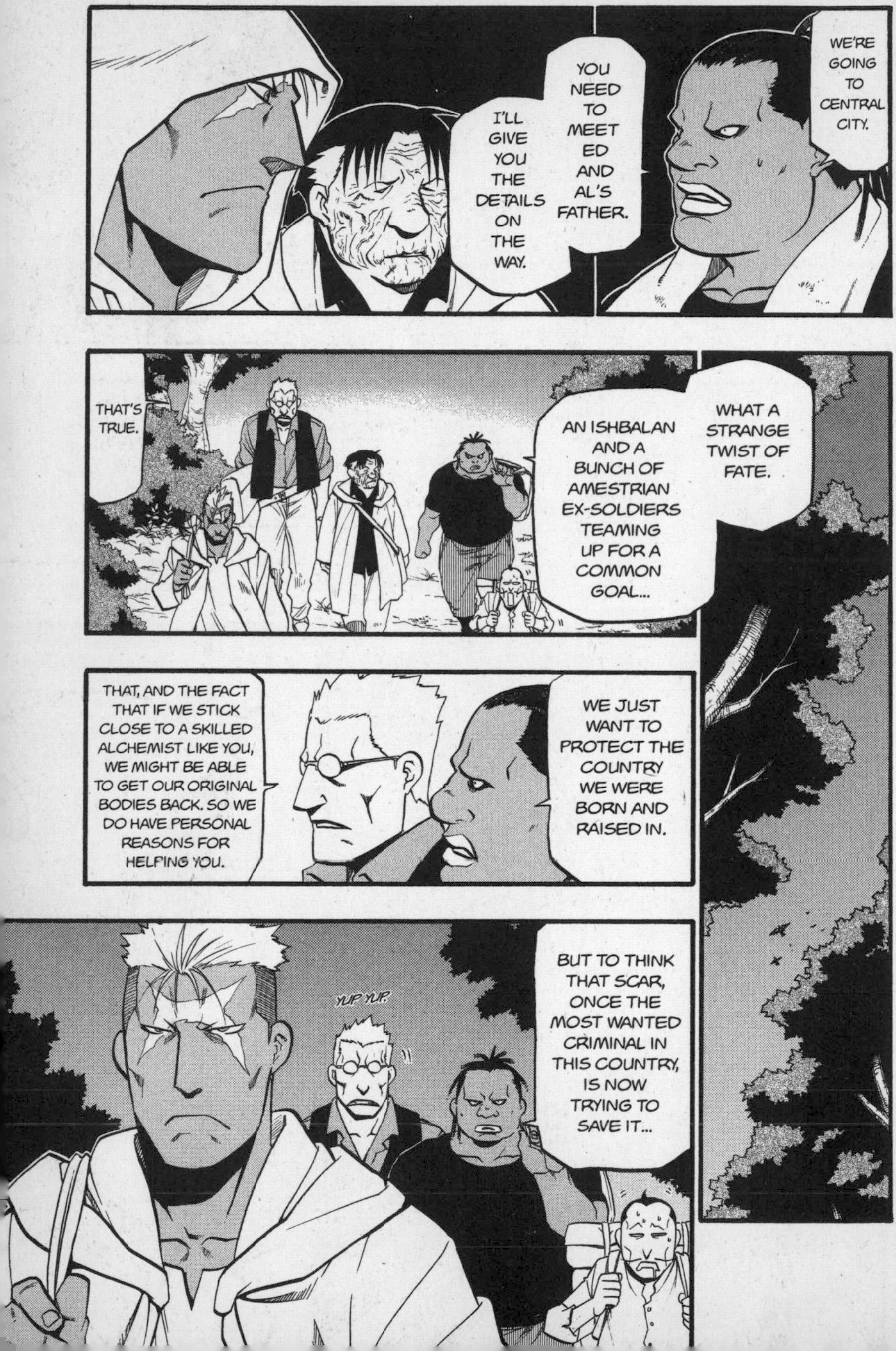
WE'RE GOING TO CENTRAL CITY.
YOU NEED TO MEET ED AND AL'S FATHER.
I'LL GIVE YOU THE DETAILS ON THE WAY.
WHAT A STRANGE TWIST OF FATE.
AN ISHBALAN AND A BUNCH OF AMESTRIAN EX-SOLDIERS TEAMING UP FOR A COMMON GOAL...
THAT'S TRUE.
WE JUST WANT TO PROTECT THE COUNTRY WE WERE BORN AND RAISED IN.
THAT, AND THE FACT THAT IF WE STICK CLOSE TO A SKILLED ALCHEMIST LIKE YOU, WE MIGHT BE ABLE TO GET OUR ORIGINAL BODIES BACK. SO WE DO HAVE PERSONAL REASONS FOR HELPING YOU.
BUT TO THINK THAT SCAR, ONCE THE MOST WANTED CRIMINAL IN THIS COUNTRY, IS NOW TRYING TO SAVE IT...
YUP YUP.

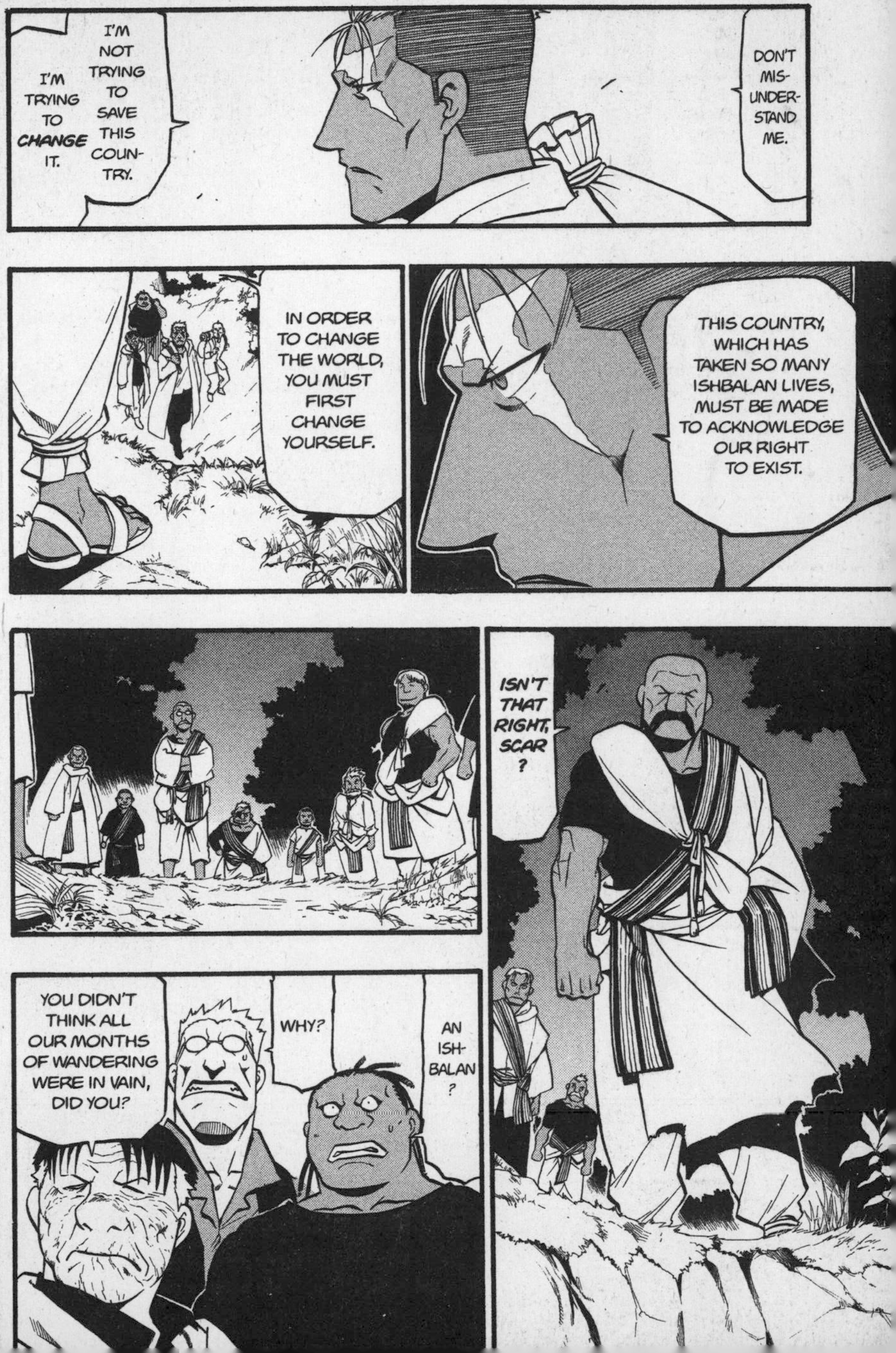
DON'T MIS-UNDER-STAND ME.
I'M NOT TRYING TO SAVE THIS COUN-TRY.
I'M TRYING TO *CHANGE* IT.
THIS COUNTRY, WHICH HAS TAKEN SO MANY ISHBALAN LIVES, MUST BE MADE TO ACKNOWLEDGE OUR RIGHT TO EXIST.
IN ORDER TO CHANGE THE WORLD, YOU MUST FIRST CHANGE YOURSELF.
ISN'T THAT RIGHT, SCAR?
AN ISH-BALAN?
WHY?
YOU DIDN'T THINK ALL OUR MONTHS OF WANDERING WERE IN VAIN, DID YOU?

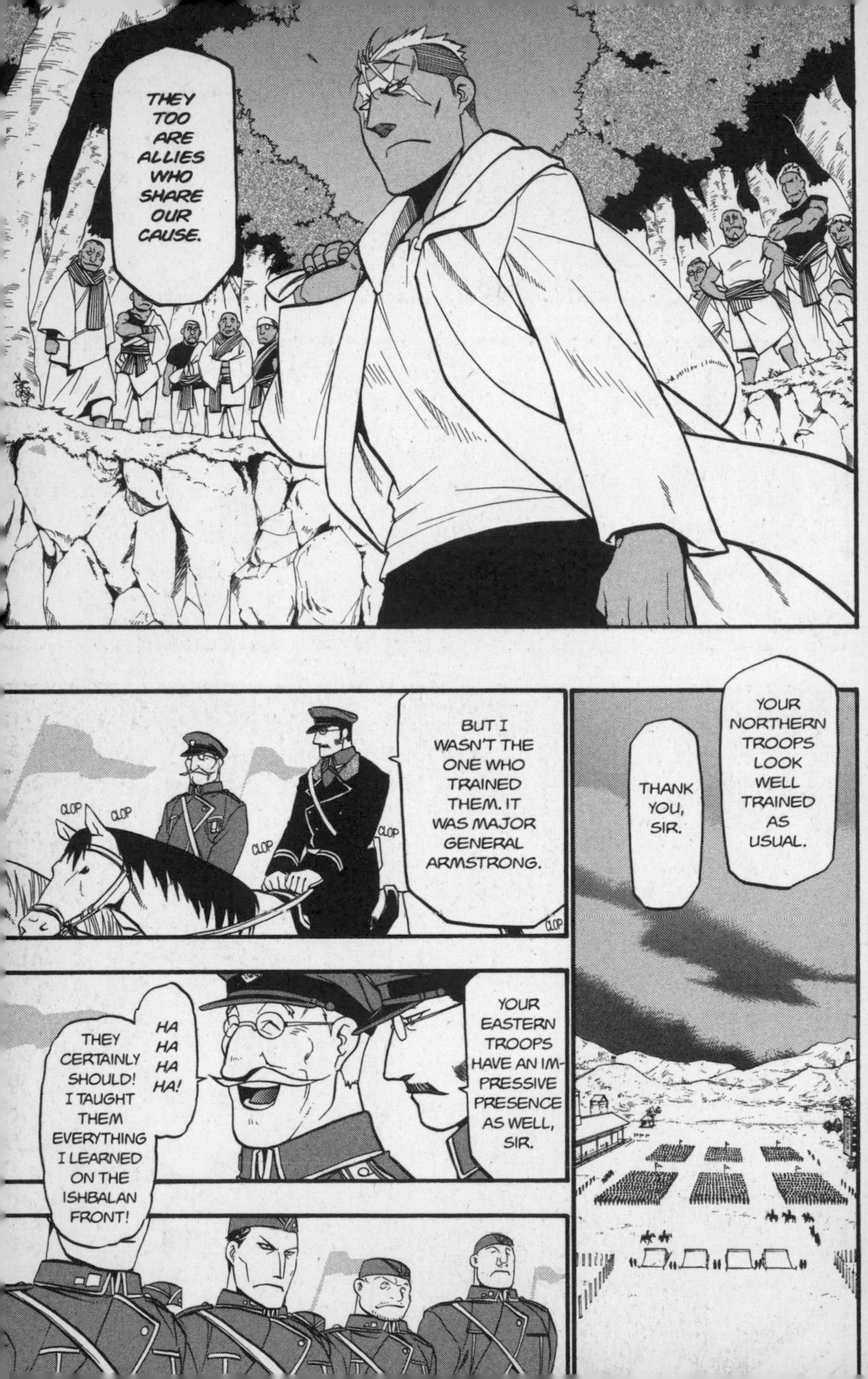
THEY TOO ARE ALLIES WHO SHARE OUR CAUSE.
YOUR NORTHERN TROOPS LOOK WELL TRAINED AS USUAL.
THANK YOU, SIR.
BUT I WASN'T THE ONE WHO TRAINED THEM. IT WAS MAJOR GENERAL ARMSTRONG.
CLOP
CLOP
CLOP
CLOP
CLOP
YOUR EASTERN TROOPS HAVE AN IM-PRESSIVE PRESENCE AS WELL, SIR.
HA HA HA HA!
THEY CERTAINLY SHOULD! I TAUGHT THEM EVERYTHING I LEARNED ON THE ISHBALAN FRONT!

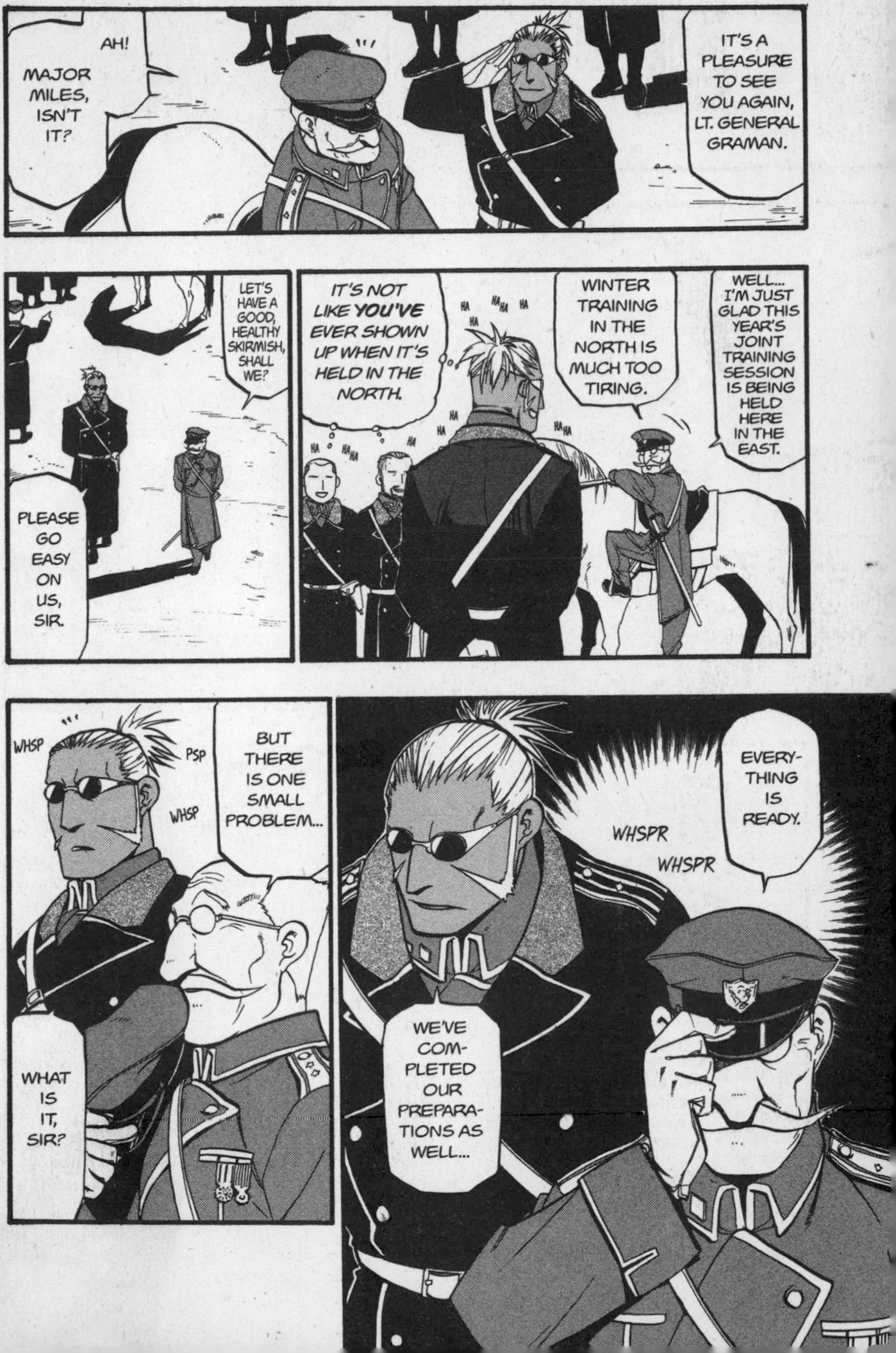
IT'S A PLEASURE TO SEE YOU AGAIN, LT. GENERAL GRAMAN.
AH!
MAJOR MILES, ISN'T IT?
WELL... I'M JUST GLAD THIS YEAR'S JOINT TRAINING SESSION IS BEING HELD HERE IN THE EAST.
WINTER TRAINING IN THE NORTH IS MUCH TOO TIRING.
HA HA HA HA HA
IT'S NOT LIKE **YOU'VE** EVER SHOWN UP WHEN IT'S HELD IN THE NORTH.
HA HA HA HA HA HA HA
LET'S HAVE A GOOD, HEALTHY SKIRMISH, SHALL WE?
PLEASE GO EASY ON US, SIR.
EVERY-THING IS READY.
WHSPR
WHSPR
WE'VE COM-PLETED OUR PREPARA-TIONS AS WELL...
.....
...
BUT THERE IS ONE SMALL PROBLEM...
WHSP
PSP
WHSP
WHAT IS IT, SIR?

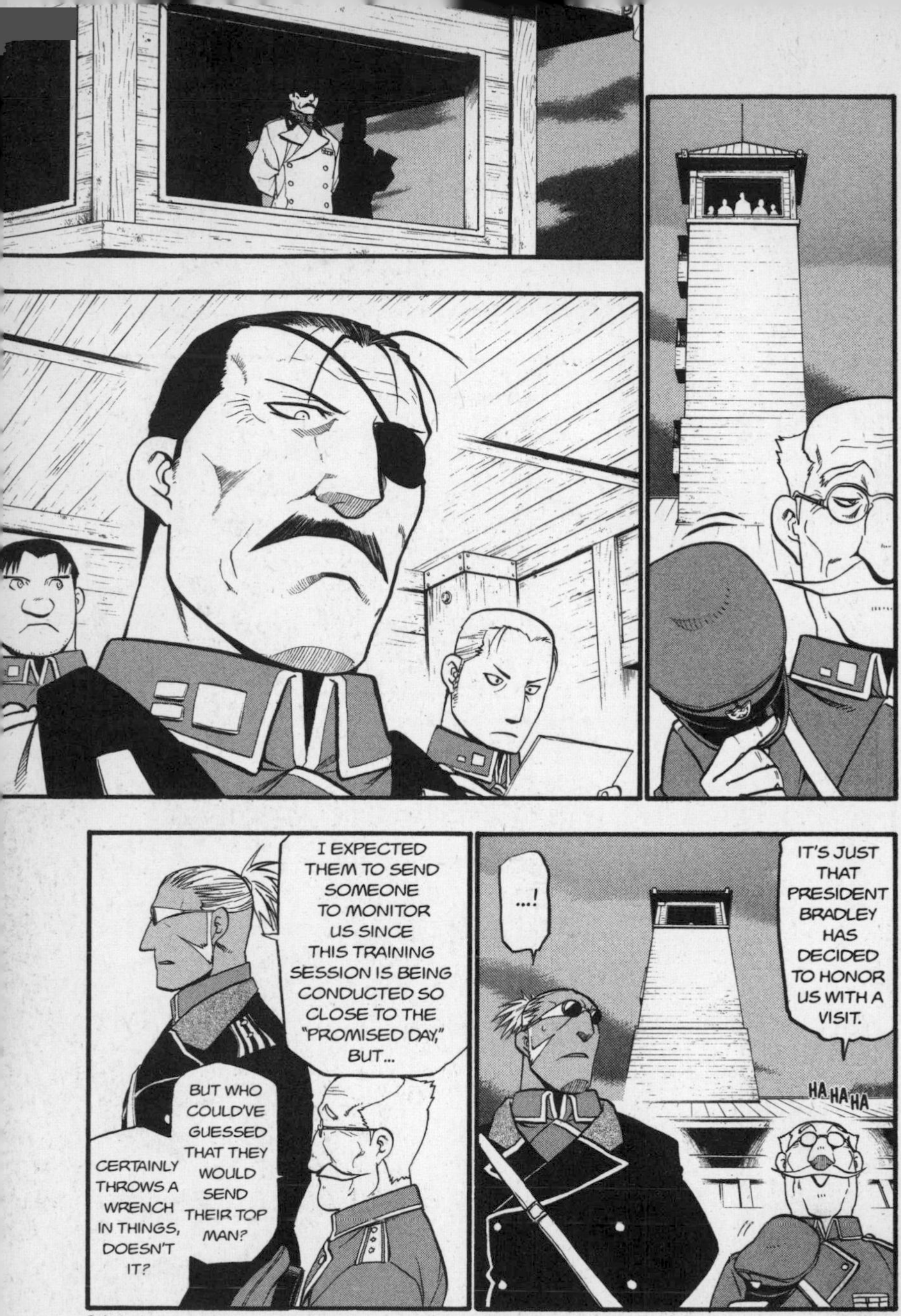
IT'S JUST THAT PRESIDENT BRADLEY HAS DECIDED TO HONOR US WITH A VISIT.
...!
HA HA HA
I EXPECTED THEM TO SEND SOMEONE TO MONITOR US SINCE THIS TRAINING SESSION IS BEING CONDUCTED SO CLOSE TO THE "PROMISED DAY," BUT...
BUT WHO COULD'VE GUESSED THAT THEY WOULD SEND THEIR TOP MAN?
CERTAINLY THROWS A WRENCH IN THINGS, DOESN'T IT?

I GUESS WE'LL JUST HAVE TO FIGURE SOMETHING OUT.

WELL.

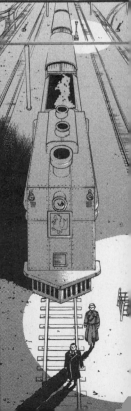

RRGH...

TWITCH

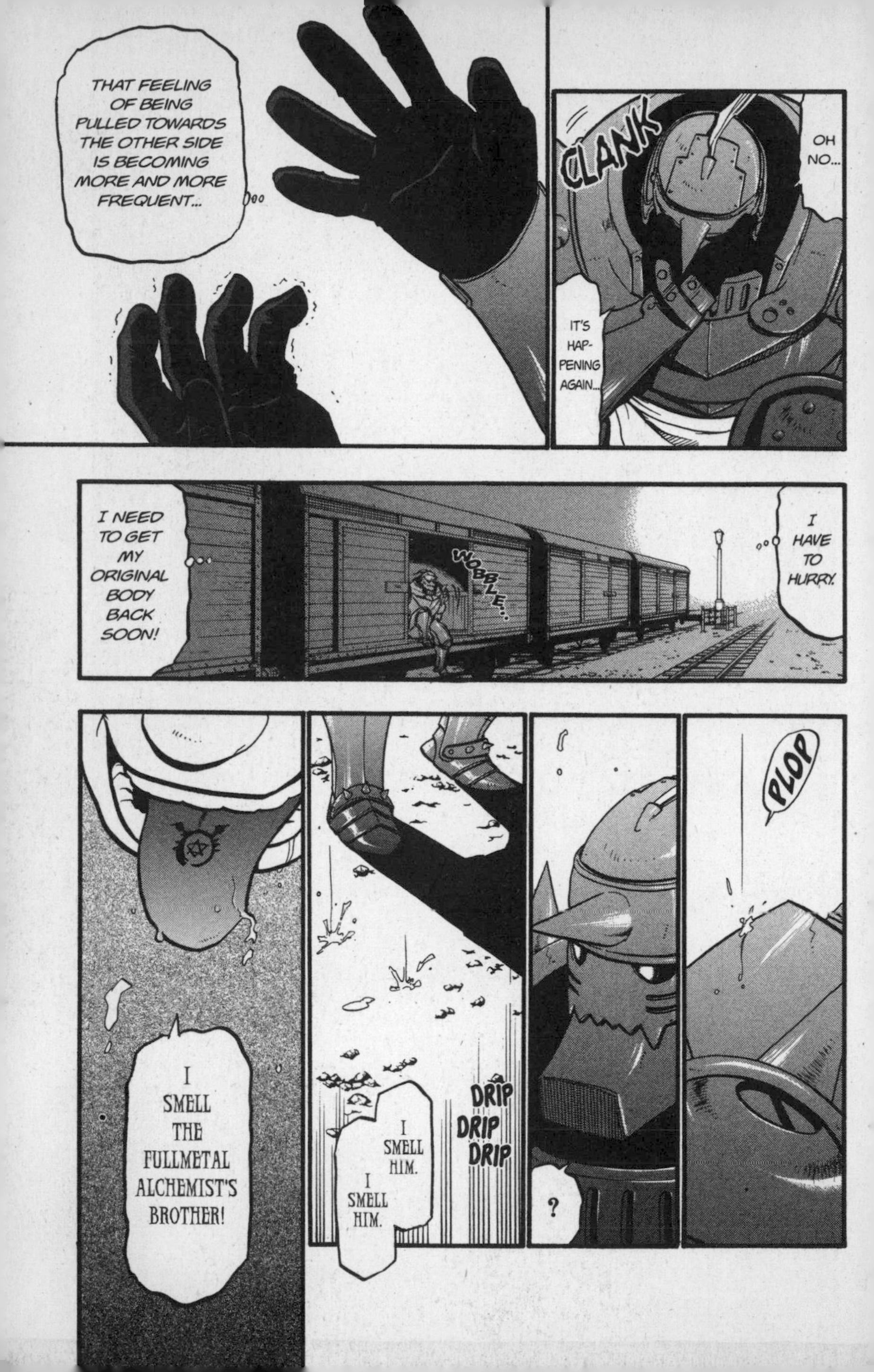
OH NO...
CLANK
IT'S HAPPENING AGAIN...
THAT FEELING OF BEING PULLED TOWARDS THE OTHER SIDE IS BECOMING MORE AND MORE FREQUENT...
I HAVE TO HURRY.
WOBBLE...
I NEED TO GET MY ORIGINAL BODY BACK SOON!
PLOP
?
DRIP DRIP DRIP
I SMELL HIM.
I SMELL HIM.
I SMELL THE FULLMETAL ALCHEMIST'S BROTHER!

!!
GRIIIN
OH NO...

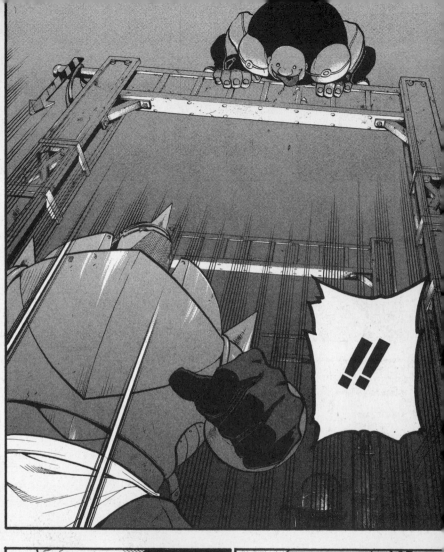

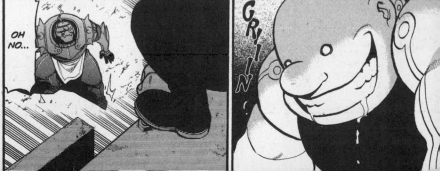

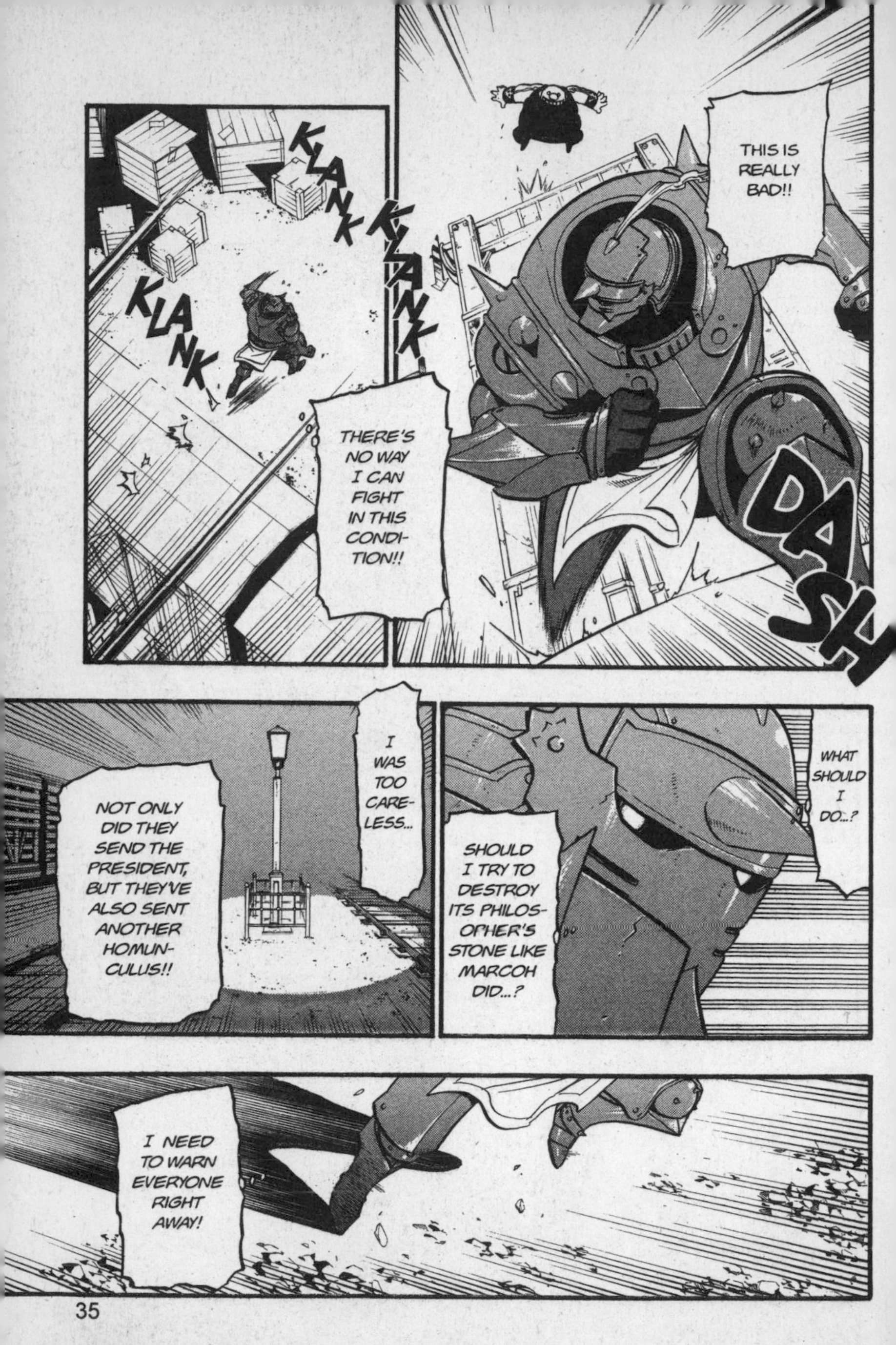
THIS IS REALLY BAD!!
THERE'S NO WAY I CAN FIGHT IN THIS CONDITION!!
DASH
KLANK
KLANK
KLANK
WHAT SHOULD I DO...?
SHOULD I TRY TO DESTROY ITS PHILOSOPHER'S STONE LIKE MARCOH DID...?
I WAS TOO CARELESS...
NOT ONLY DID THEY SEND THE PRESIDENT, BUT THEY'VE ALSO SENT ANOTHER HOMUNCULUS!!
I NEED TO WARN EVERYONE RIGHT AWAY!

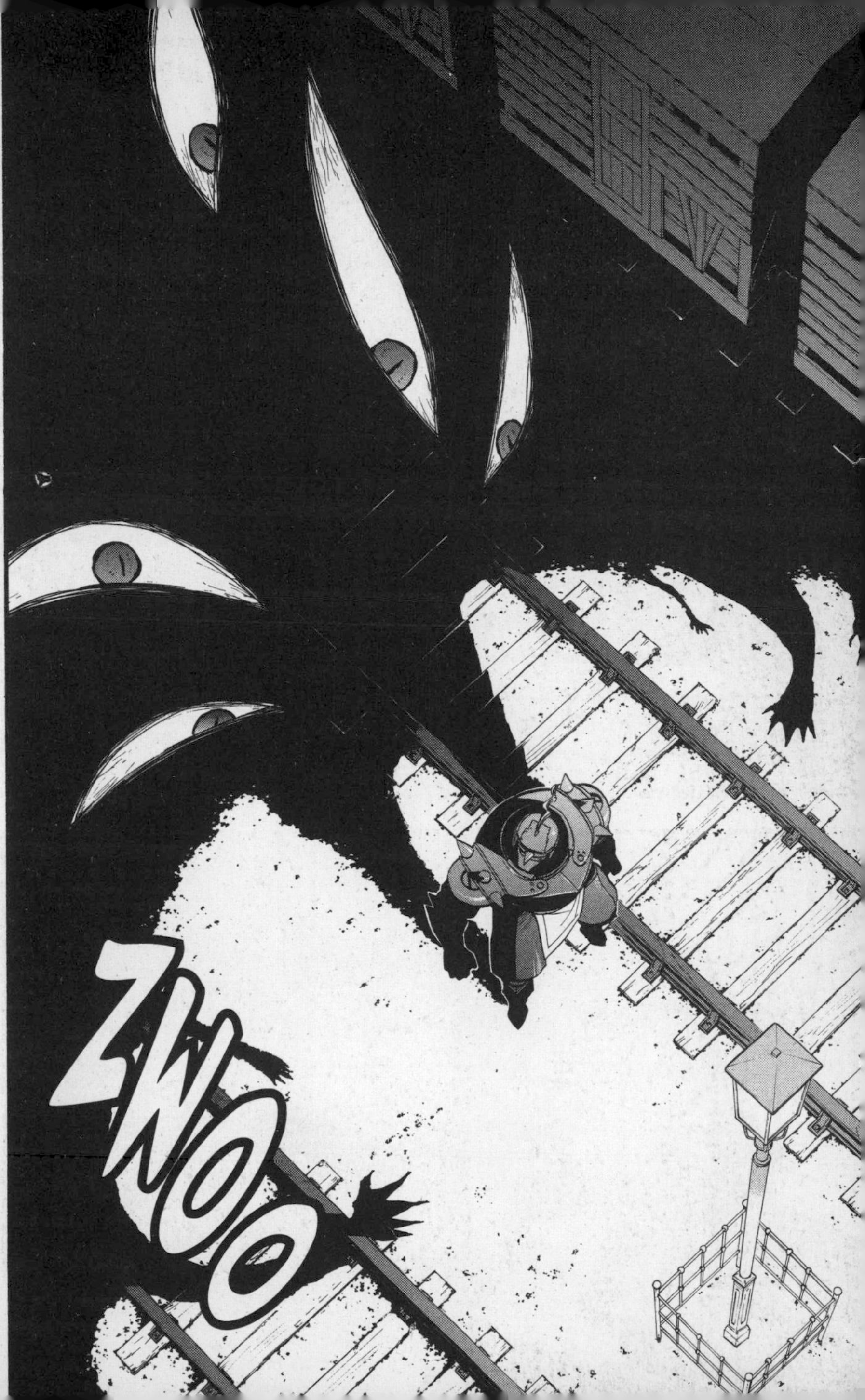
ZWOO

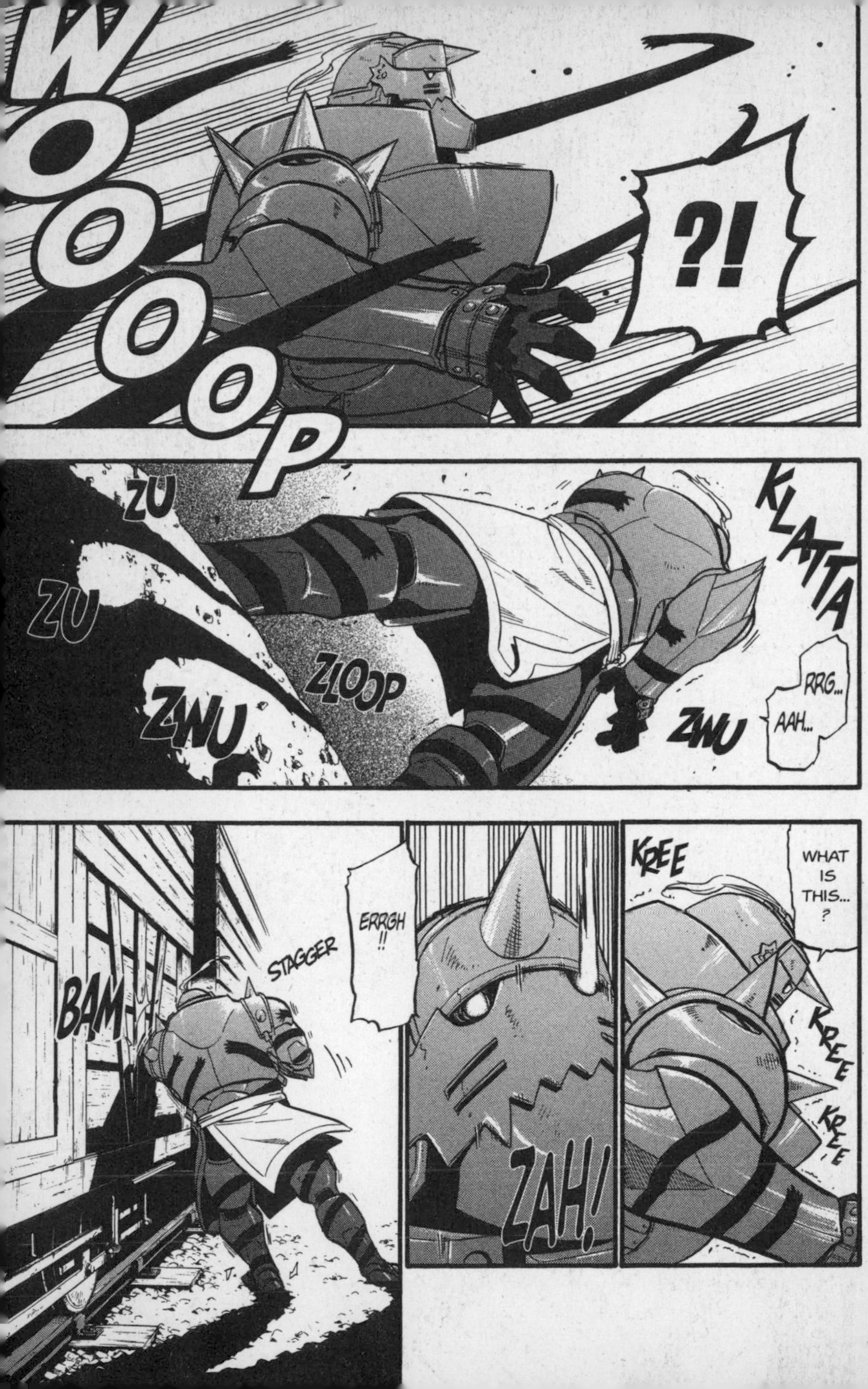
?!
WOOOOOP
KLATTA
RRG... AAH...
ZWU
ZLOOP
ZU
ZU
ZWU
WHAT IS THIS...?
KREE
KREE
KREE
ZAH!
ERRGH!!
STAGGER
BAM

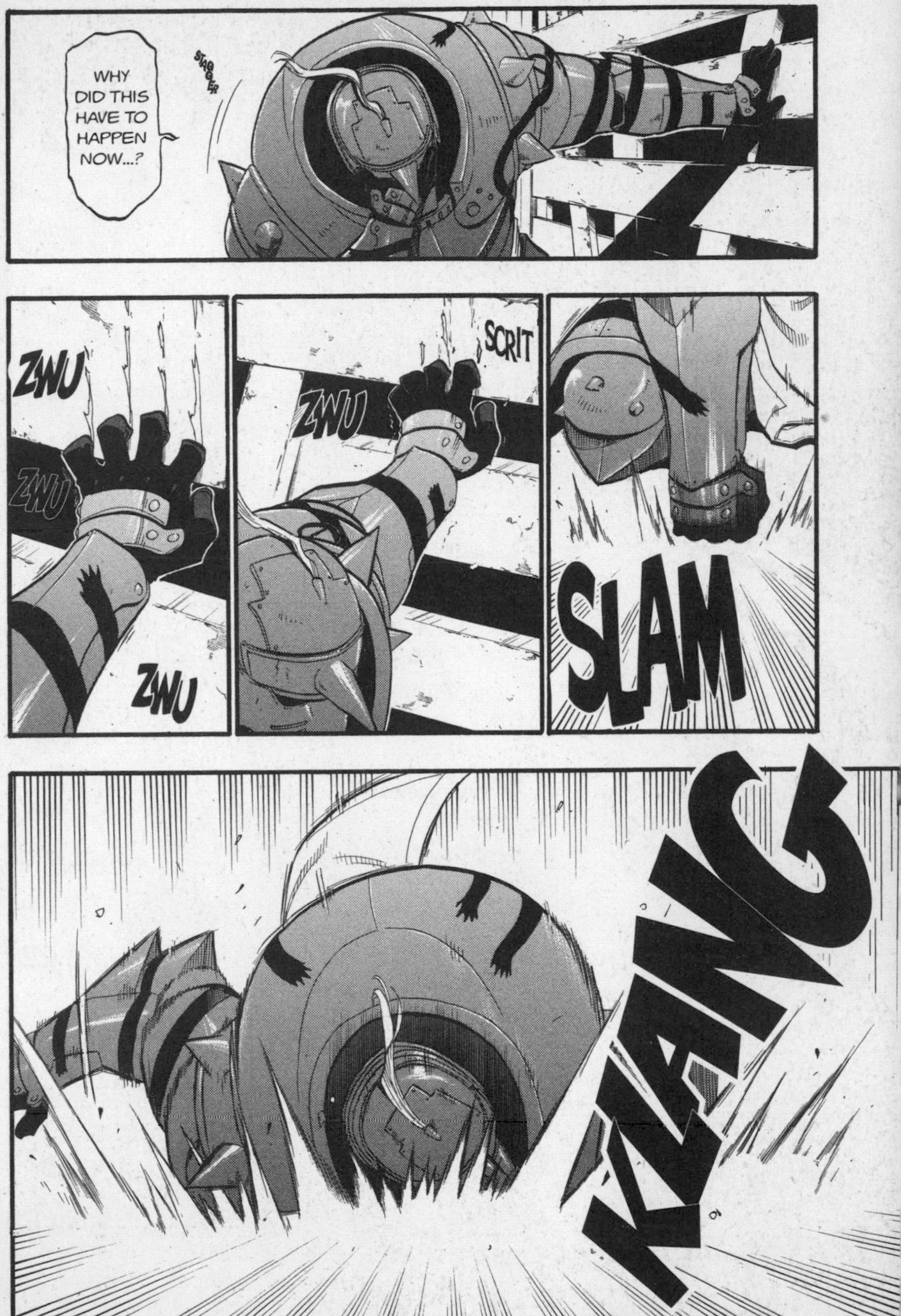
WHY DID THIS HAVE TO HAPPEN NOW...?
STAGGER
SLAM
SCRIT
ZWU
ZWU
ZWU
ZWU
KLANG

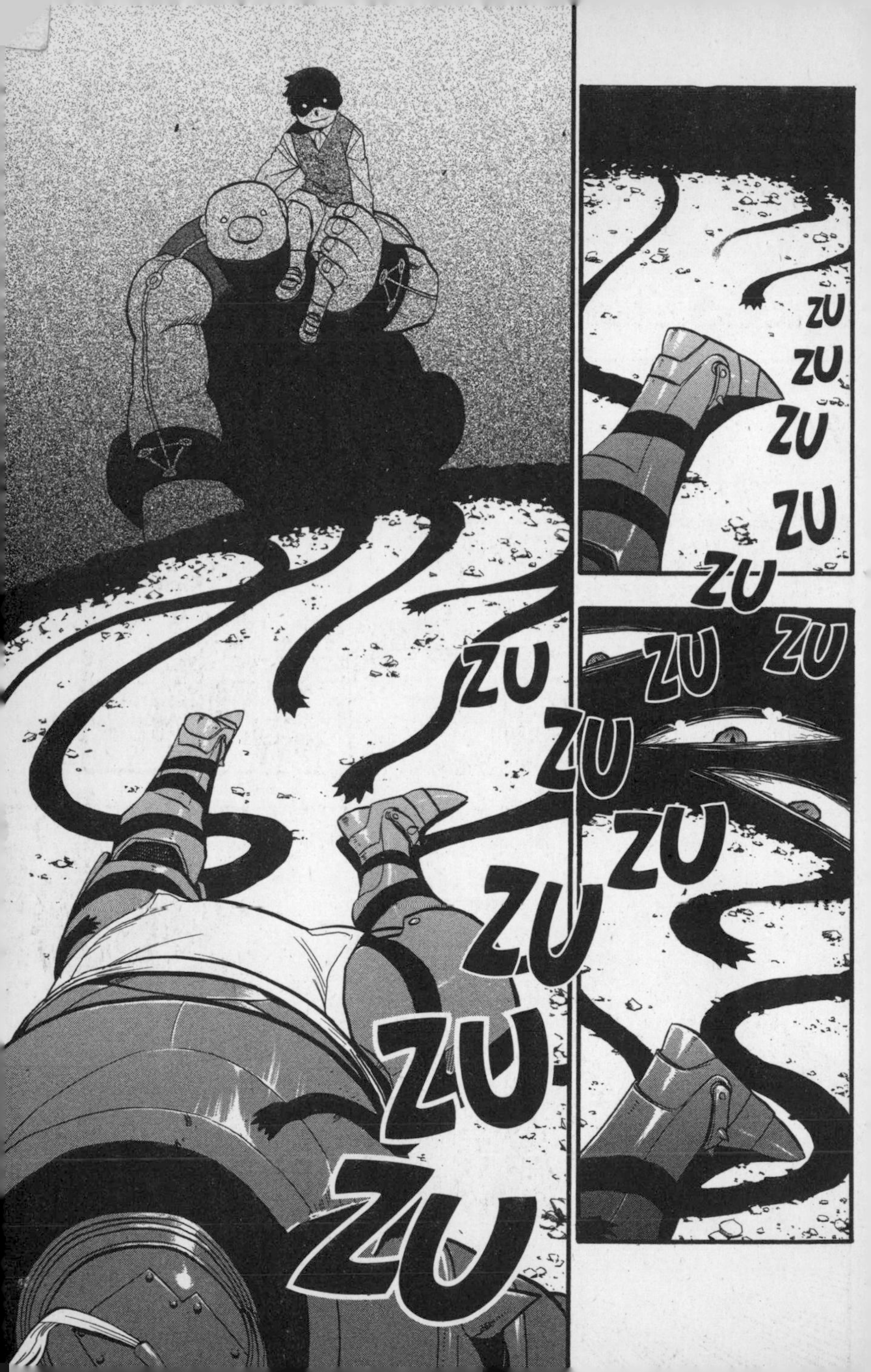
ZU
ZU
ZU
ZU
ZU-
ZU
ZU
ZU
ZU
ZU
ZU
ZU-
ZU

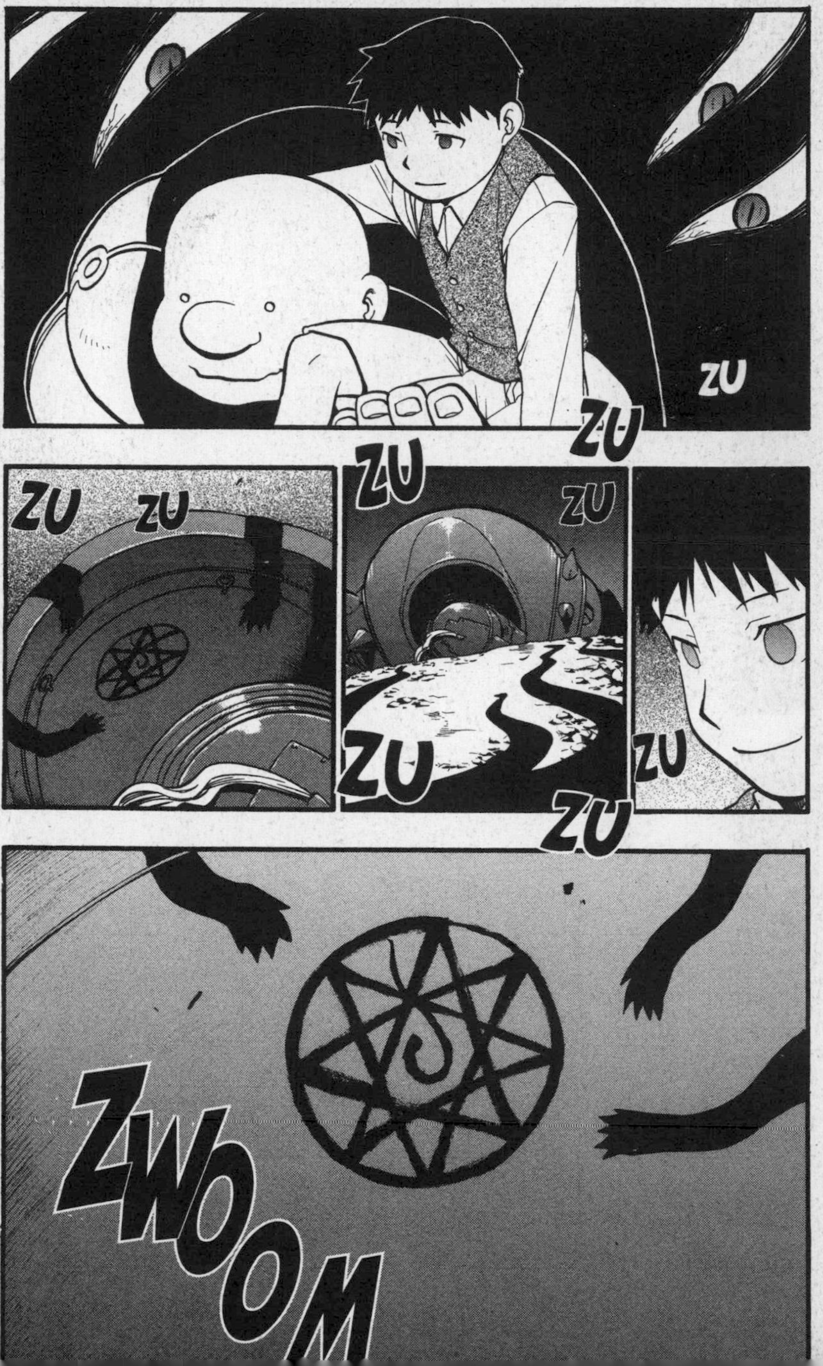
ZU
ZU
ZU
ZU
ZU
ZU
ZU
ZU
ZU
ZWOOM

FULLMETAL
ALCHEMIST

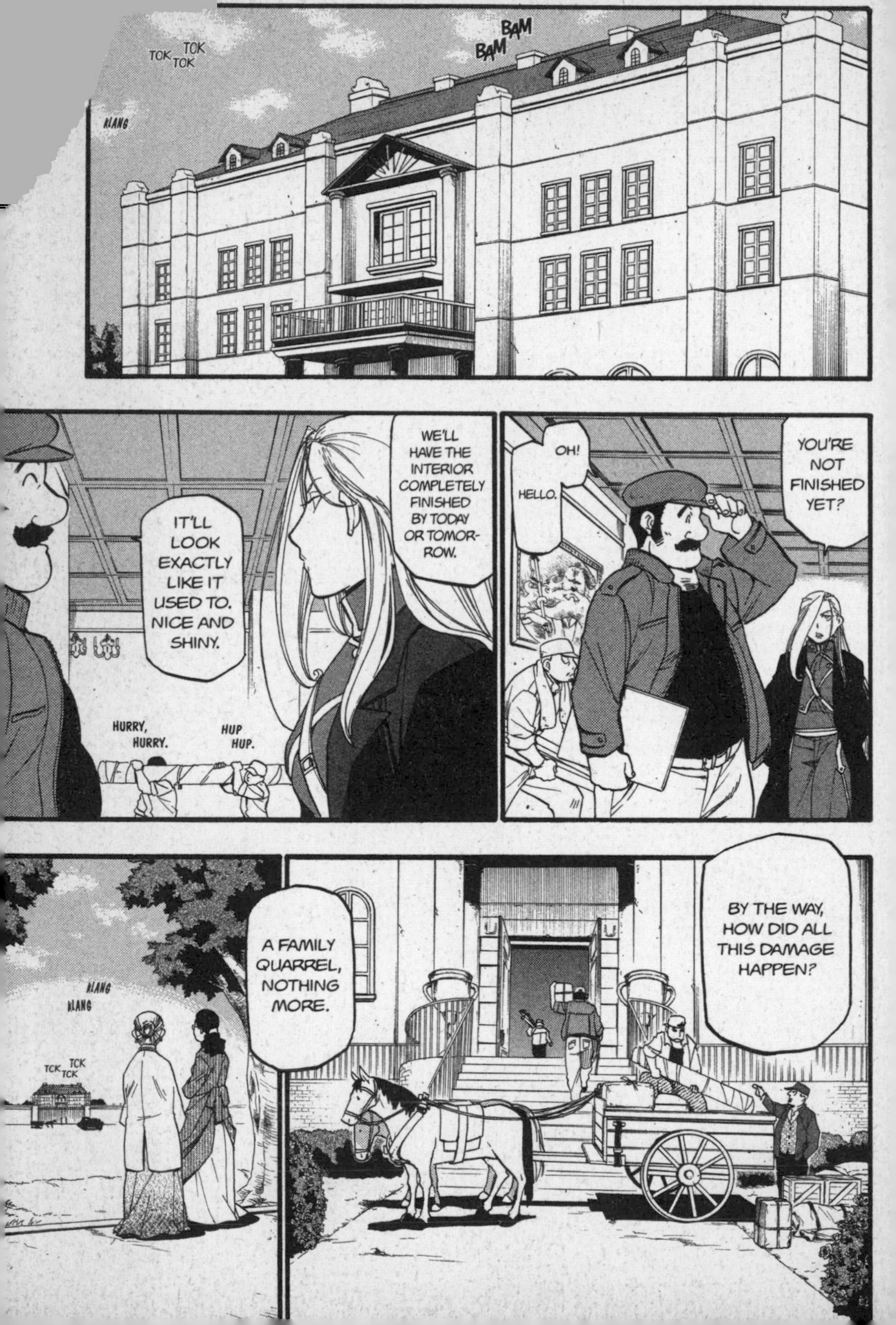
BAM BAM
TOK TOK TOK
KLANG
YOU'RE NOT FINISHED YET?
OH! HELLO.
WE'LL HAVE THE INTERIOR COMPLETELY FINISHED BY TODAY OR TOMORROW.
IT'LL LOOK EXACTLY LIKE IT USED TO. NICE AND SHINY.
HUP HUP.
HURRY, HURRY.
BY THE WAY, HOW DID ALL THIS DAMAGE HAPPEN?
A FAMILY QUARREL, NOTHING MORE.
KLANG KLANG
TCK TCK TCK

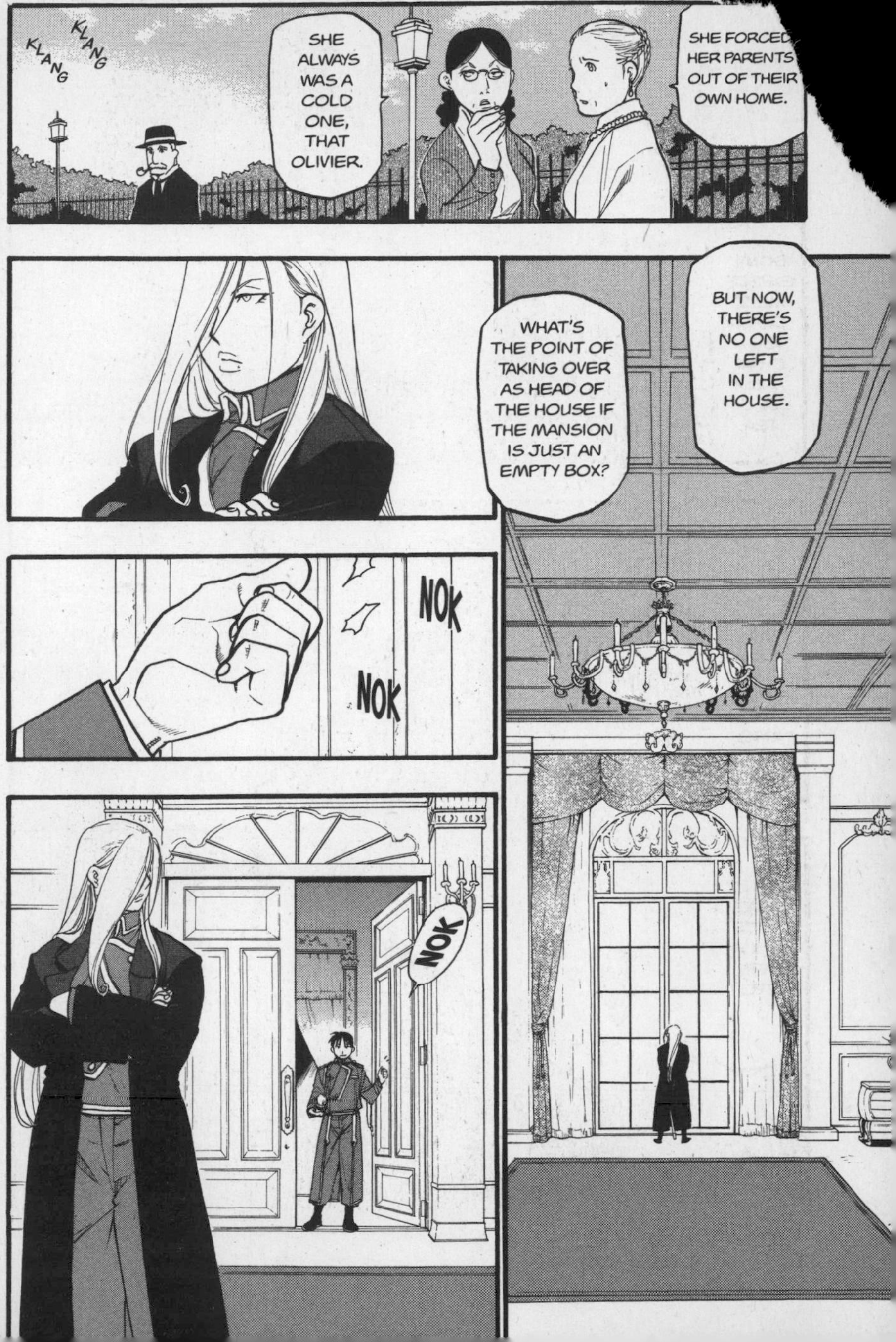
SHE FORCED HER PARENTS OUT OF THEIR OWN HOME.
SHE ALWAYS WAS A COLD ONE, THAT OLIVIER.
KLANG
KLANG
BUT NOW, THERE'S NO ONE LEFT IN THE HOUSE.
WHAT'S THE POINT OF TAKING OVER AS HEAD OF THE HOUSE IF THE MANSION IS JUST AN EMPTY BOX?
NOK
NOK
NOK

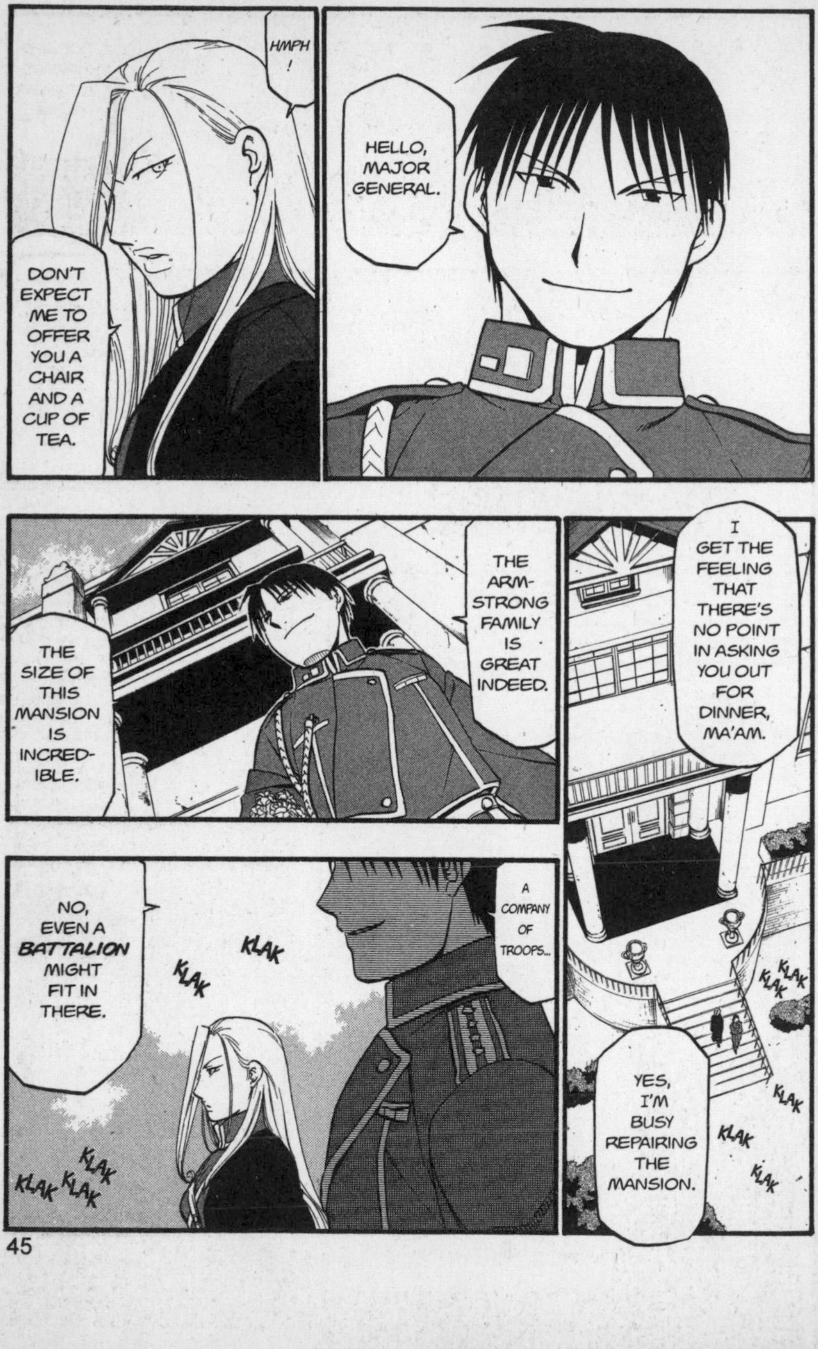
HELLO, MAJOR GENERAL.
HMPH!
DON'T EXPECT ME TO OFFER YOU A CHAIR AND A CUP OF TEA.
I GET THE FEELING THAT THERE'S NO POINT IN ASKING YOU OUT FOR DINNER, MA'AM.
KLAK KLAK
YES, I'M BUSY REPAIRING THE MANSION.
KLAK
KLAK
KLAK
THE ARMSTRONG FAMILY IS GREAT INDEED.
THE SIZE OF THIS MANSION IS INCREDIBLE.
A COMPANY OF TROOPS...
NO, EVEN A BATTALION MIGHT FIT IN THERE.
KLAK
KLAK
KLAK KLAK KLAK

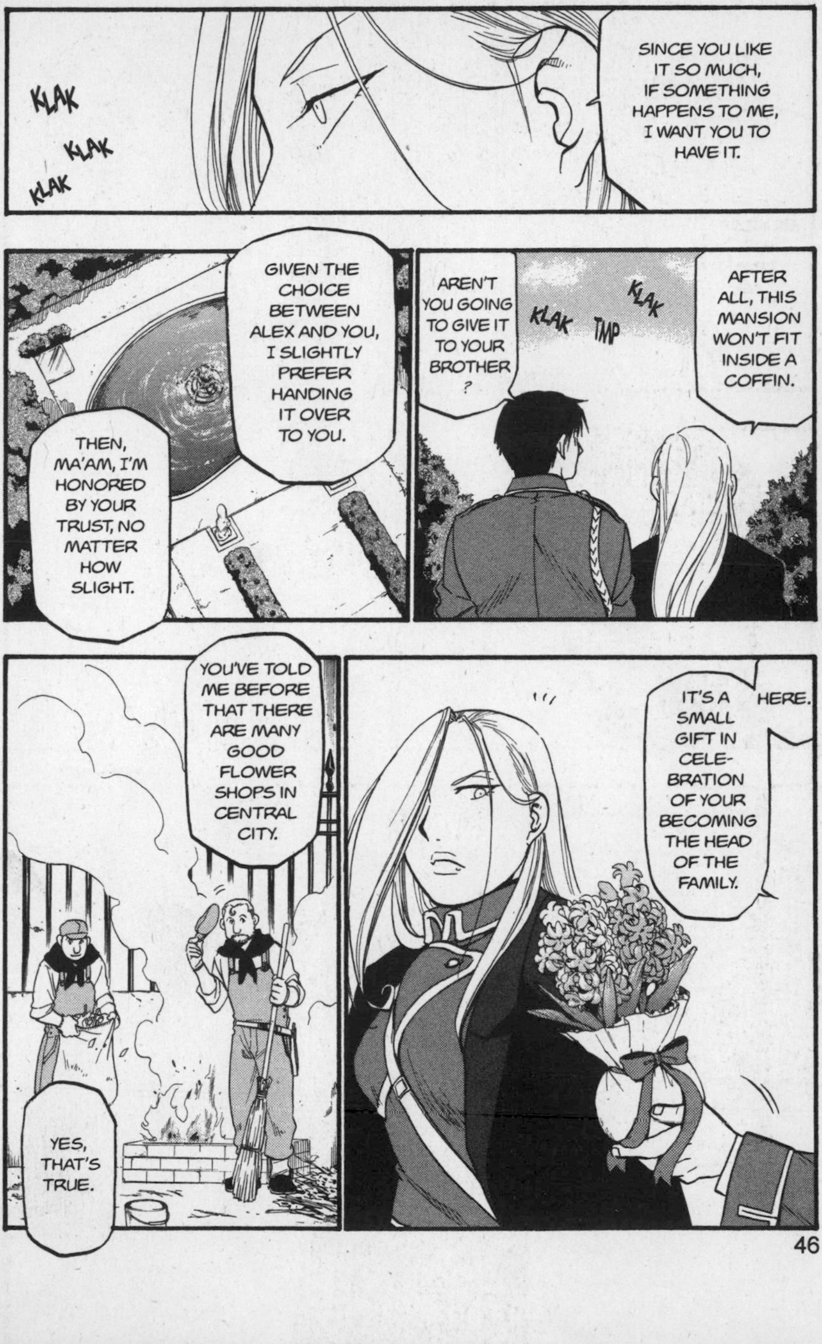
SINCE YOU LIKE IT SO MUCH, IF SOMETHING HAPPENS TO ME, I WANT YOU TO HAVE IT.
KLAK
KLAK
KLAK
AFTER ALL, THIS MANSION WON'T FIT INSIDE A COFFIN.
KLAK
TMP
KLAK
AREN'T YOU GOING TO GIVE IT TO YOUR BROTHER?
GIVEN THE CHOICE BETWEEN ALEX AND YOU, I SLIGHTLY PREFER HANDING IT OVER TO YOU.
THEN, MA'AM, I'M HONORED BY YOUR TRUST, NO MATTER HOW SLIGHT.
HERE.
IT'S A SMALL GIFT IN CELE-BRATION OF YOUR BECOMING THE HEAD OF THE FAMILY.
YOU'VE TOLD ME BEFORE THAT THERE ARE MANY GOOD FLOWER SHOPS IN CENTRAL CITY.
YES, THAT'S TRUE.

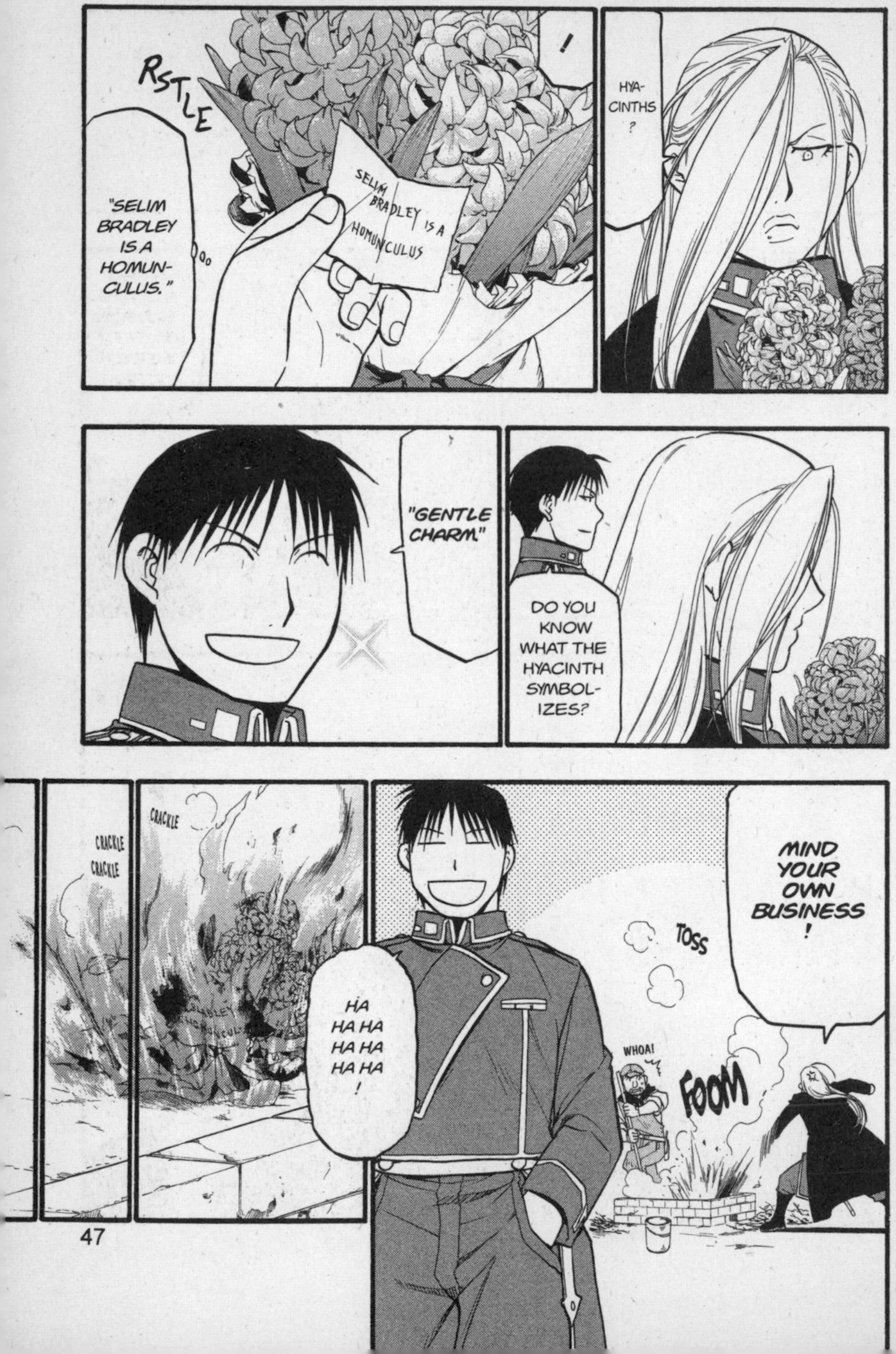
HYA-CINTHS?
!
RSTLE
SELIM BRADLEY IS A HOMUNCULUS
"SELIM BRADLEY IS A HOMUN-CULUS."
DO YOU KNOW WHAT THE HYACINTH SYMBOL-IZES?
"GENTLE CHARM."
MIND YOUR OWN BUSINESS!
TOSS
FOOM
WHOA!
HA HA HA HA HA HA HA HA!
CRACKLE
CRACKLE CRACKLE

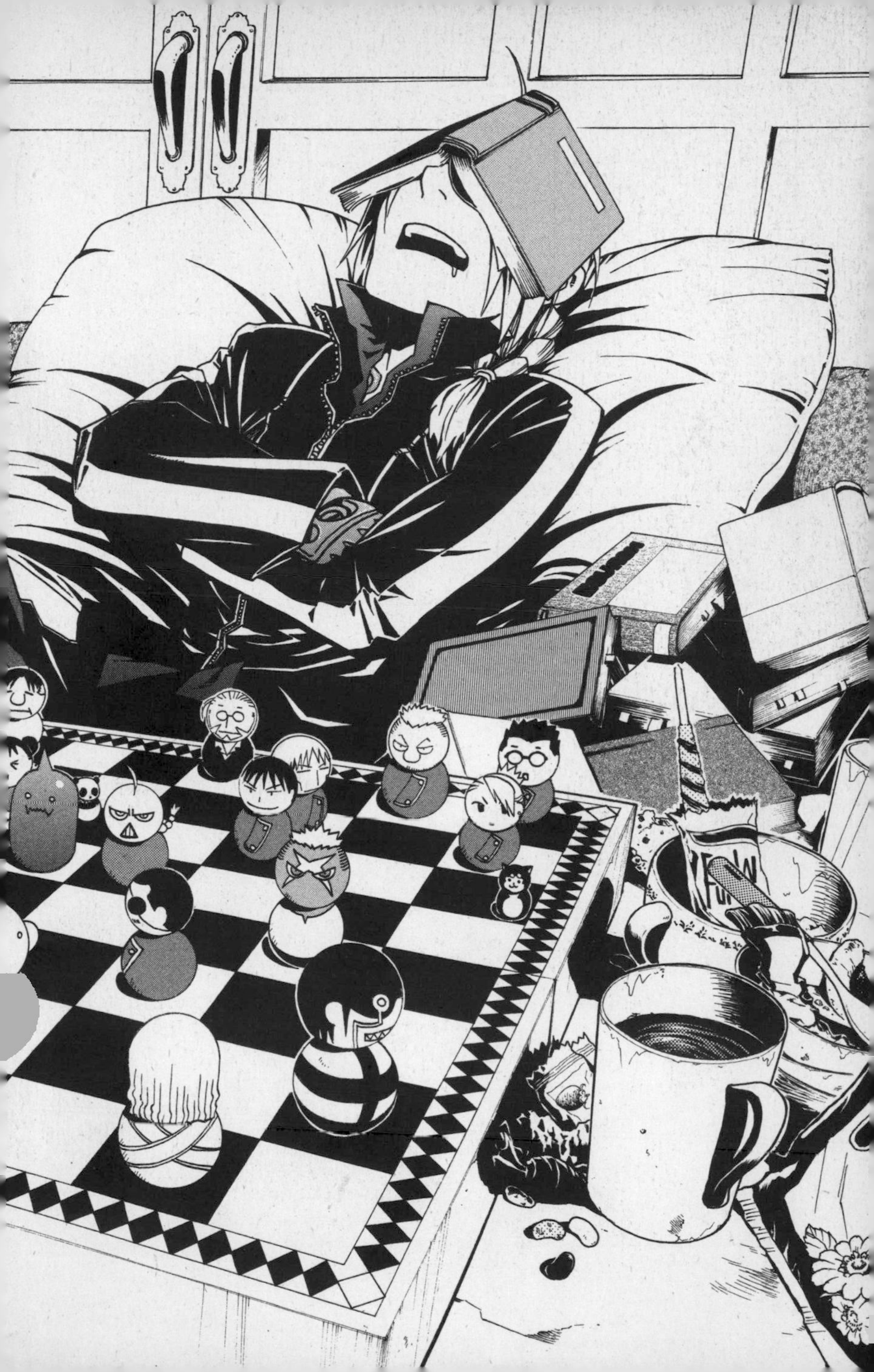

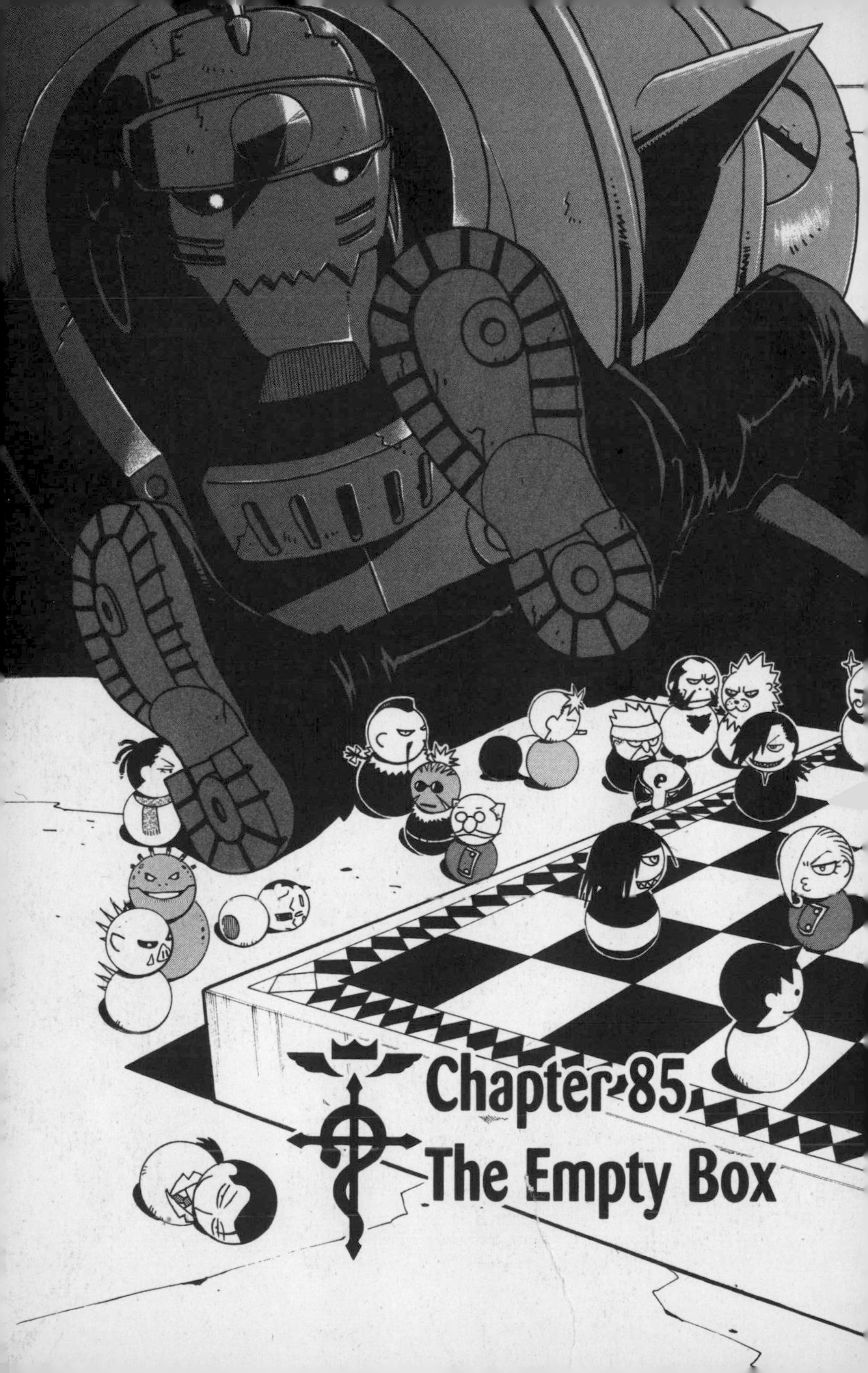
Chapter 85
The Empty Box

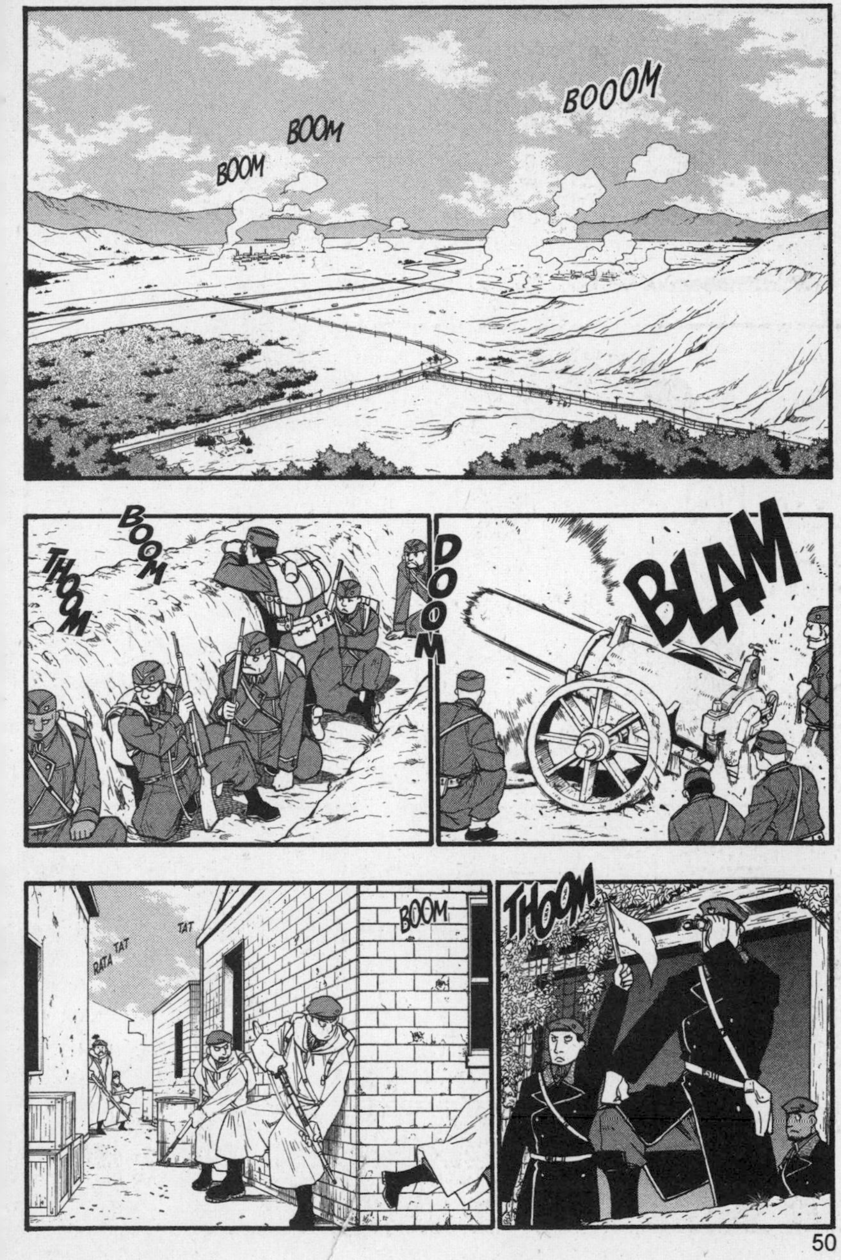
BOOOM
BOOM
BOOM
BLAM
DOOM
BOOM
THOOM
THOOM
BOOM
TAT
RATA TAT

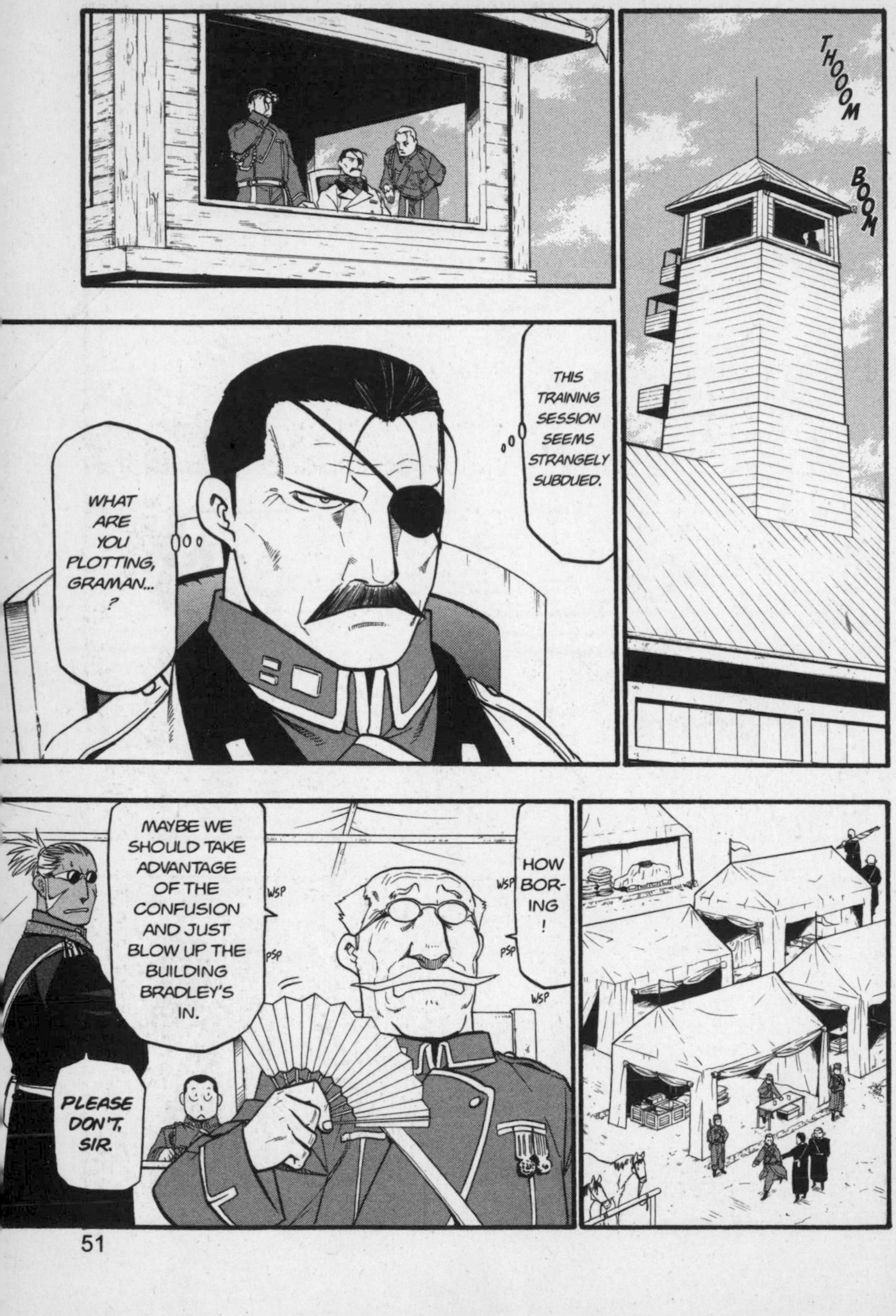
THOOOM
BOOM
THIS TRAINING SESSION SEEMS STRANGELY SUBDUED.
WHAT ARE YOU PLOTTING, GRAMAN...?
HOW BORING!
WSP
PSP
WSP
WSP
PSP
MAYBE WE SHOULD TAKE ADVANTAGE OF THE CONFUSION AND JUST BLOW UP THE BUILDING BRADLEY'S IN.
PLEASE DON'T, SIR.

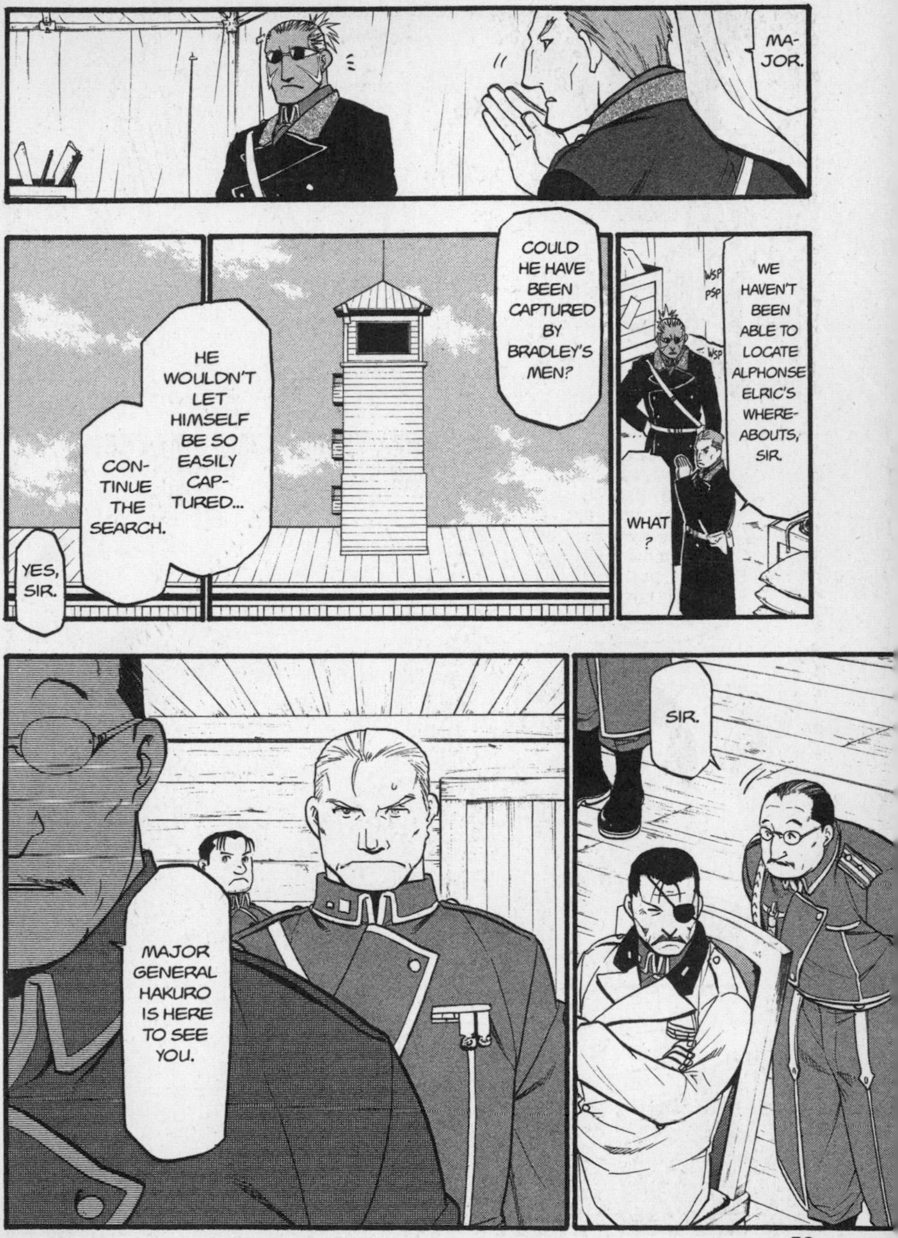
MAJOR.
WE HAVEN'T BEEN ABLE TO LOCATE ALPHONSE ELRIC'S WHEREABOUTS, SIR.
WHAT?
COULD HE HAVE BEEN CAPTURED BY BRADLEY'S MEN?
HE WOULDN'T LET HIMSELF BE SO EASILY CAPTURED...
CONTINUE THE SEARCH.
YES, SIR.
SIR.
MAJOR GENERAL HAKURO IS HERE TO SEE YOU.

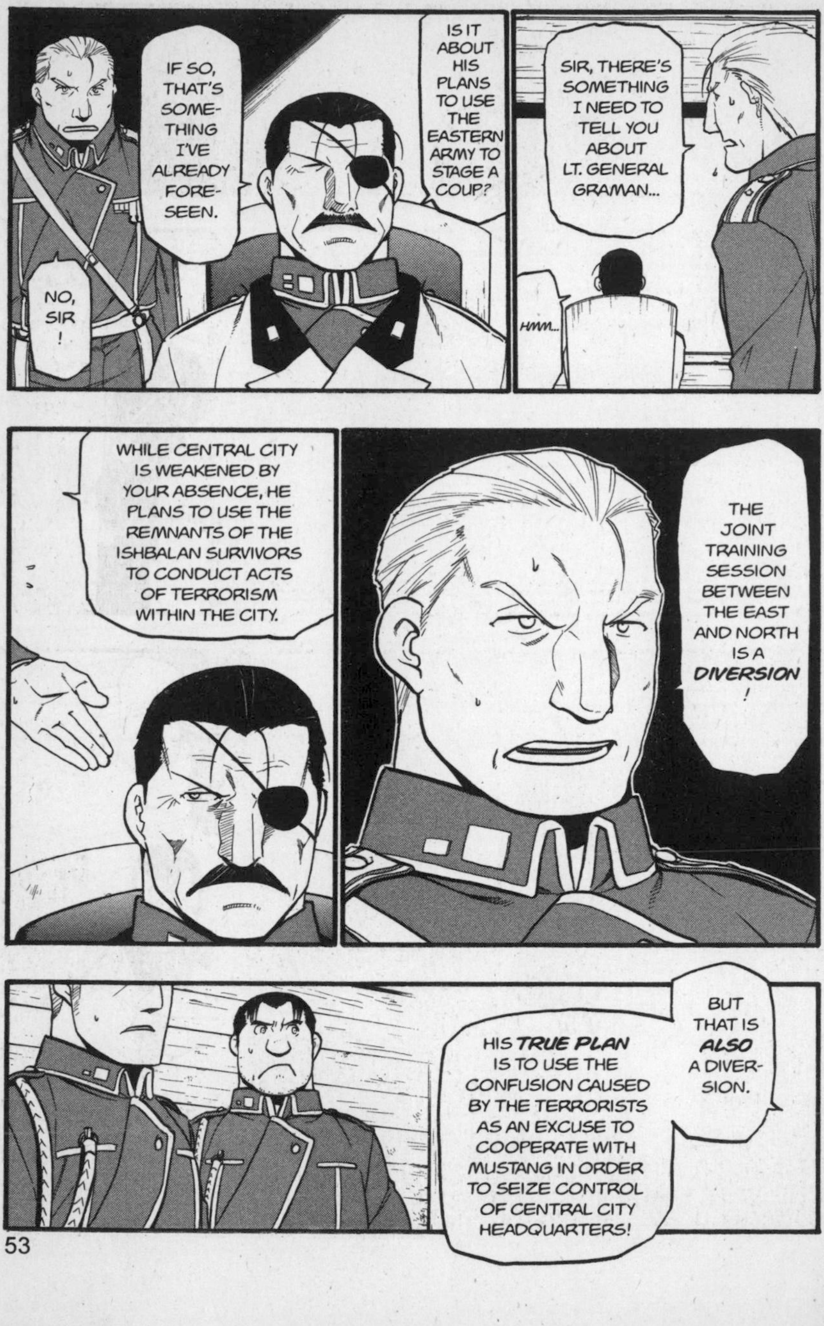
SIR, THERE'S SOMETHING I NEED TO TELL YOU ABOUT LT. GENERAL GRAMAN...
HMM...
IS IT ABOUT HIS PLANS TO USE THE EASTERN ARMY TO STAGE A COUP?
IF SO, THAT'S SOMETHING I'VE ALREADY FORESEEN.
NO, SIR!
THE JOINT TRAINING SESSION BETWEEN THE EAST AND NORTH IS A DIVERSION!
WHILE CENTRAL CITY IS WEAKENED BY YOUR ABSENCE, HE PLANS TO USE THE REMNANTS OF THE ISHBALAN SURVIVORS TO CONDUCT ACTS OF TERRORISM WITHIN THE CITY.
BUT THAT IS ALSO A DIVERSION.
HIS TRUE PLAN IS TO USE THE CONFUSION CAUSED BY THE TERRORISTS AS AN EXCUSE TO COOPERATE WITH MUSTANG IN ORDER TO SEIZE CONTROL OF CENTRAL CITY HEADQUARTERS!

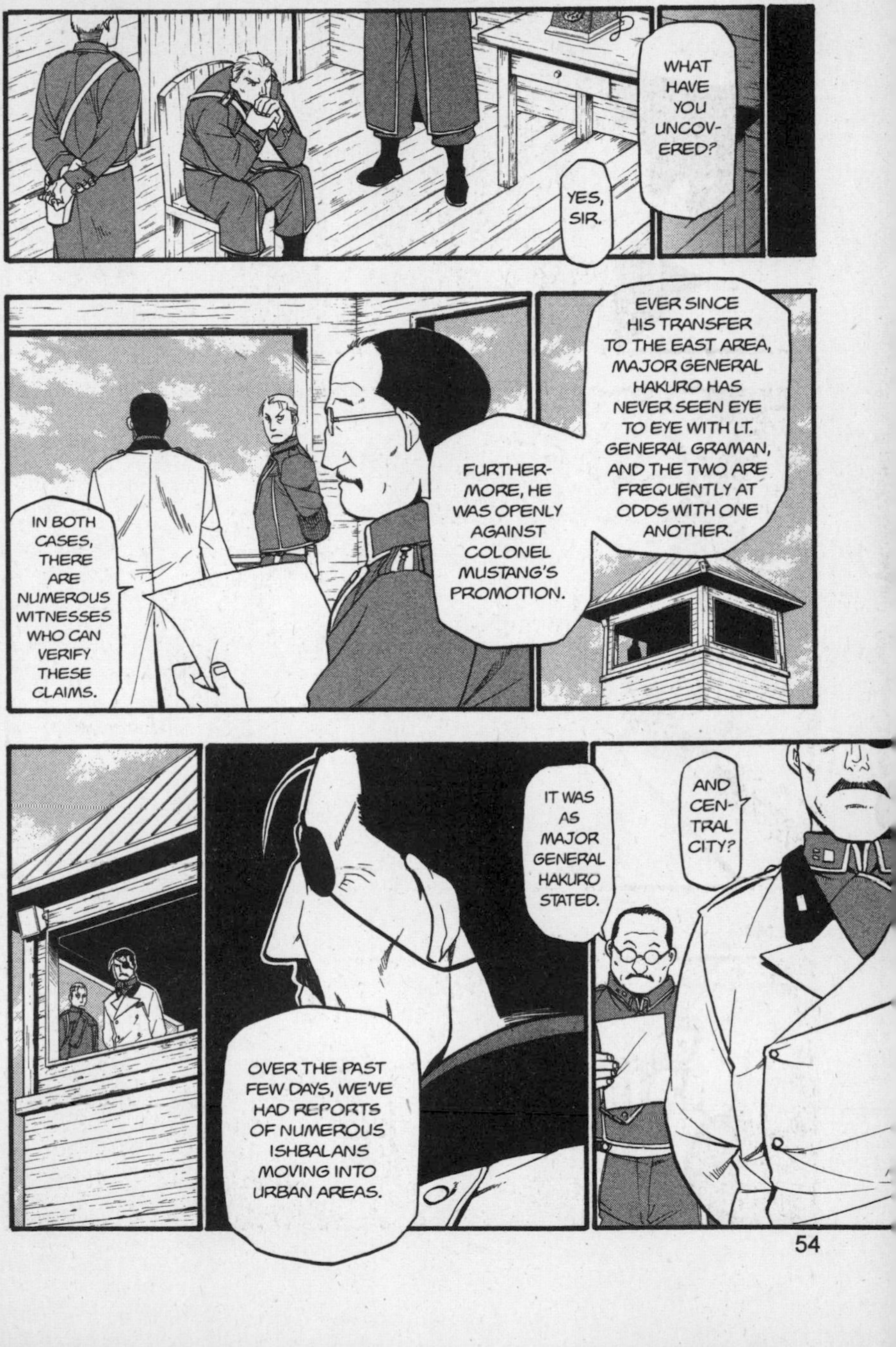
WHAT HAVE YOU UNCOVERED?
YES, SIR.
EVER SINCE HIS TRANSFER TO THE EAST AREA, MAJOR GENERAL HAKURO HAS NEVER SEEN EYE TO EYE WITH LT. GENERAL GRAMAN, AND THE TWO ARE FREQUENTLY AT ODDS WITH ONE ANOTHER.
FURTHERMORE, HE WAS OPENLY AGAINST COLONEL MUSTANG'S PROMOTION.
IN BOTH CASES, THERE ARE NUMEROUS WITNESSES WHO CAN VERIFY THESE CLAIMS.
AND CENTRAL CITY?
IT WAS AS MAJOR GENERAL HAKURO STATED.
OVER THE PAST FEW DAYS, WE'VE HAD REPORTS OF NUMEROUS ISHBALANS MOVING INTO URBAN AREAS.

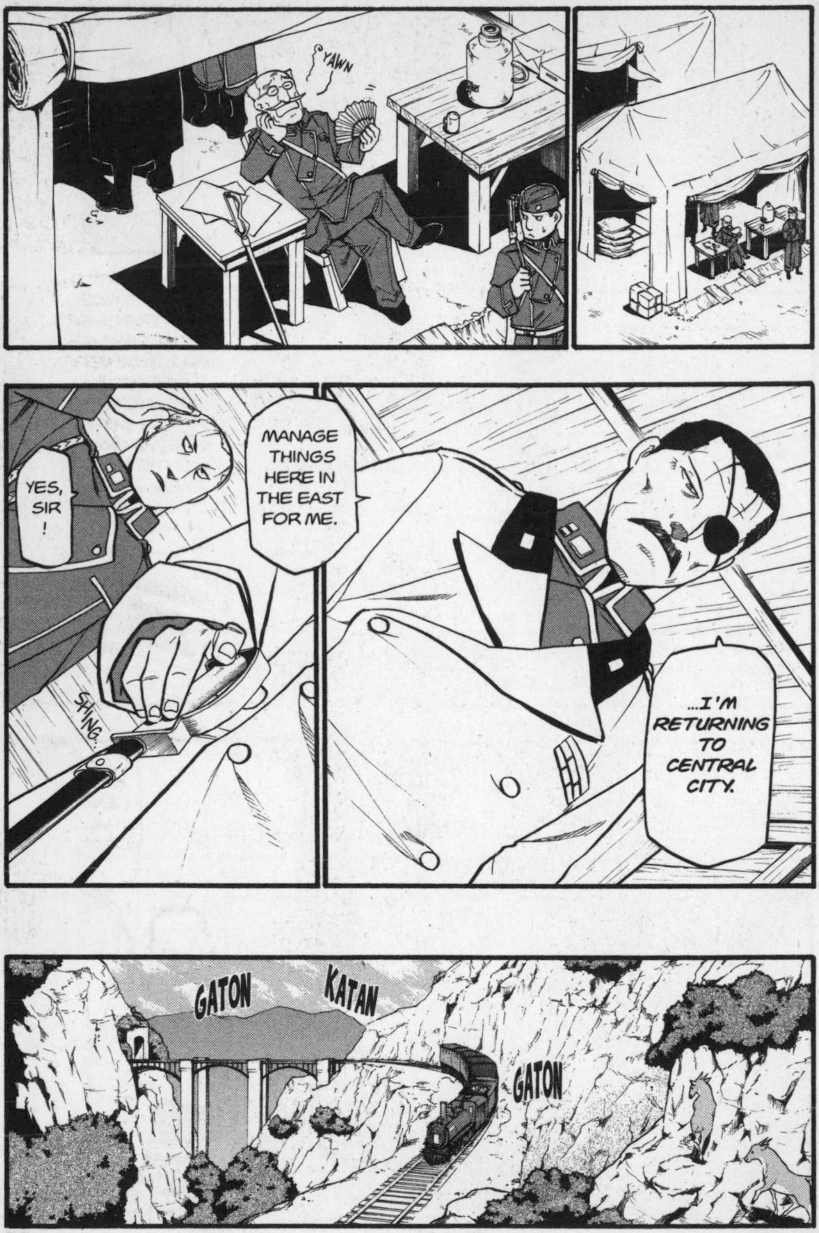
YAWN
...I'M RETURNING TO CENTRAL CITY.
MANAGE THINGS HERE IN THE EAST FOR ME.
YES, SIR!
SHING...
GATON
KATAN
GATON

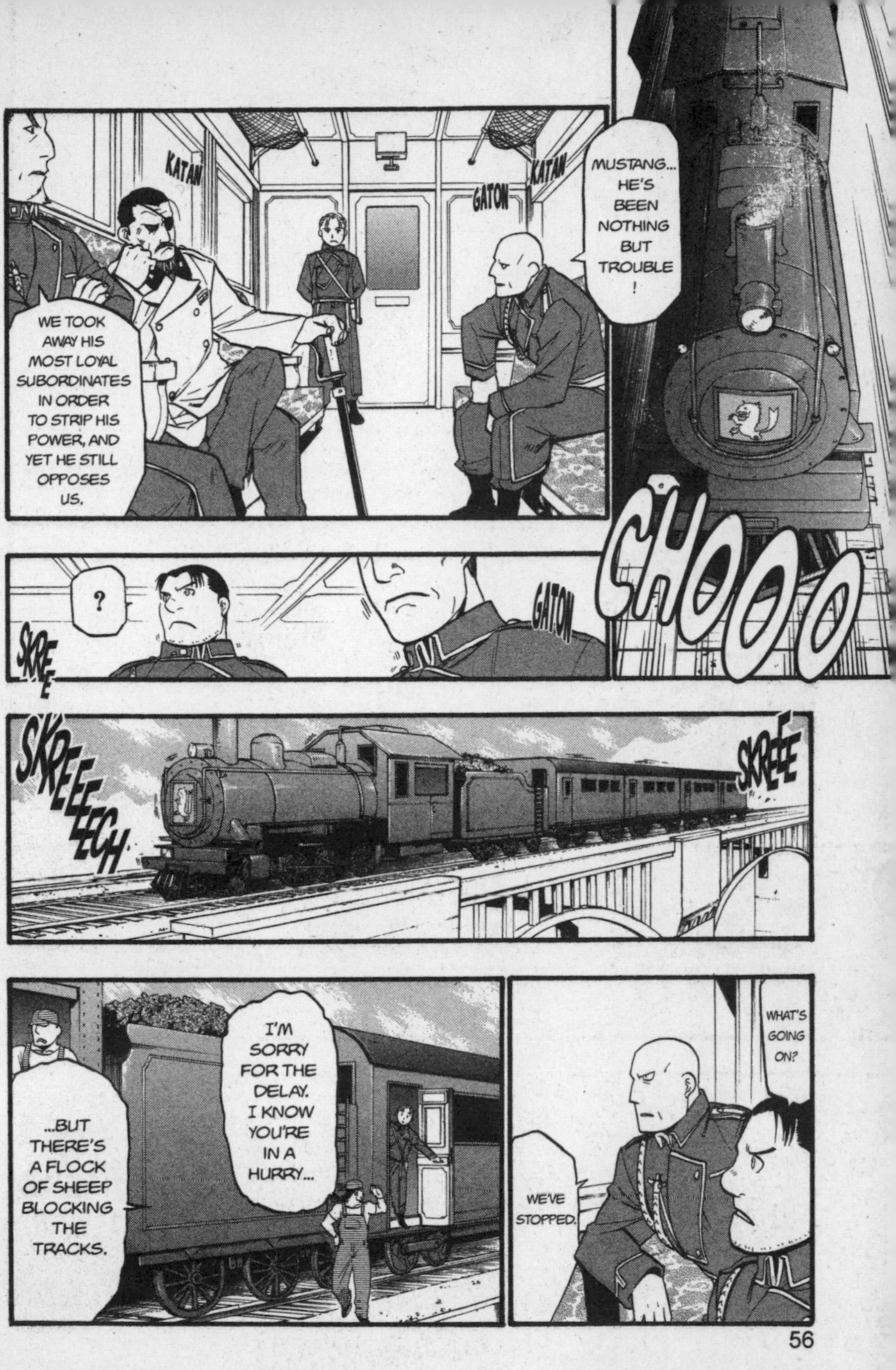
CHOOOO
KATAN
GATON
MUSTANG... HE'S BEEN NOTHING BUT TROUBLE!
KATAN
WE TOOK AWAY HIS MOST LOYAL SUBORDINATES IN ORDER TO STRIP HIS POWER, AND YET HE STILL OPPOSES US.
GATON
?
SKREE
SKREEE
SKREEEEECH
WHAT'S GOING ON?
WE'VE STOPPED.
I'M SORRY FOR THE DELAY. I KNOW YOU'RE IN A HURRY...
...BUT THERE'S A FLOCK OF SHEEP BLOCKING THE TRACKS.

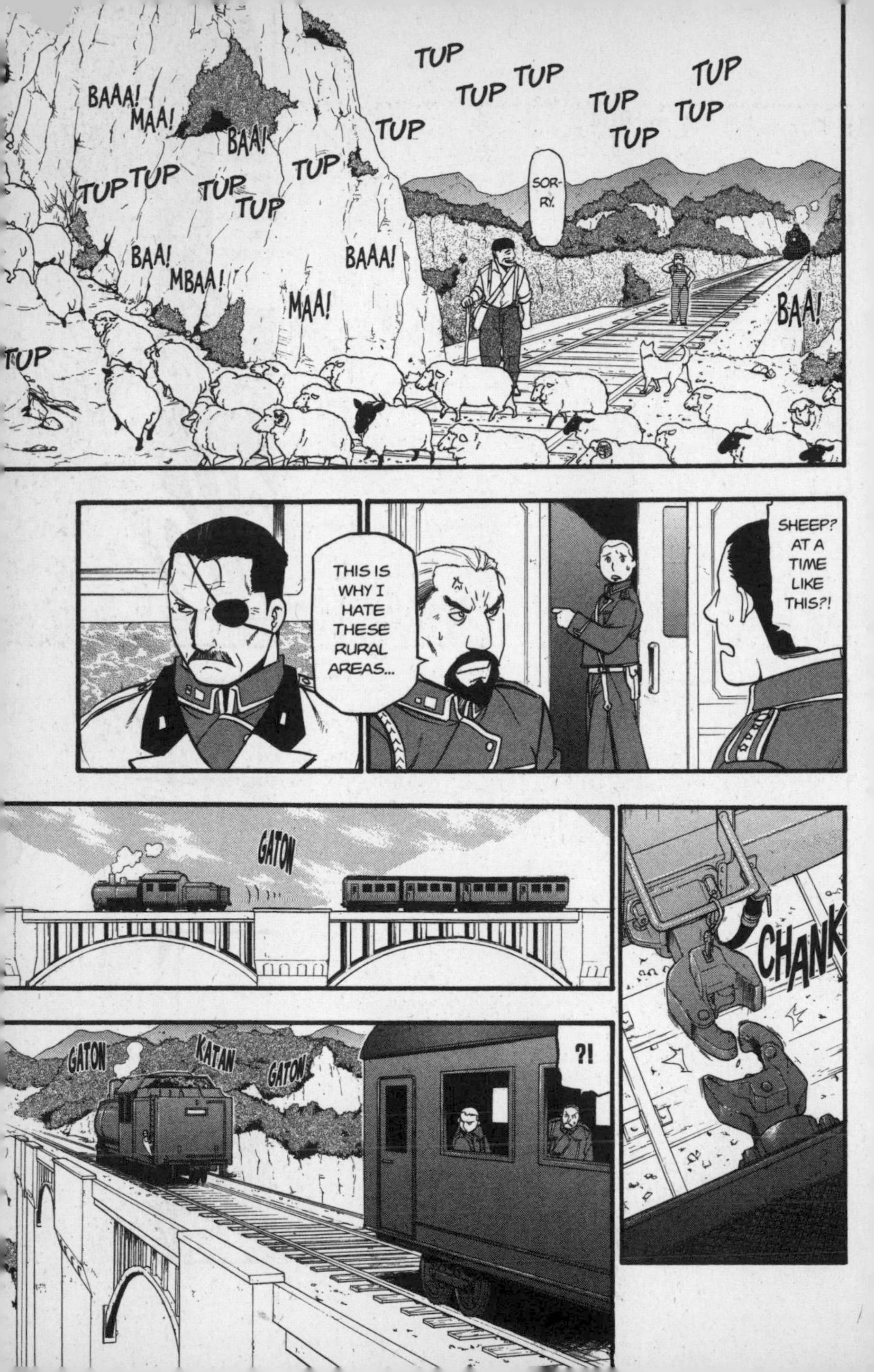
TUP
TUP
TUP TUP
TUP
TUP
TUP
TUP
TUP
SOR-RY.
BAA!
BAAA!
MAA!
BAAA!
MAA!
BAA!
TUP
TUP
TUP
TUP TUP
BAA!
MBAA!
TUP
SHEEP? AT A TIME LIKE THIS?!
THIS IS WHY I HATE THESE RURAL AREAS...
CHANK
GATON
?!
GATON
KATAN
GATON

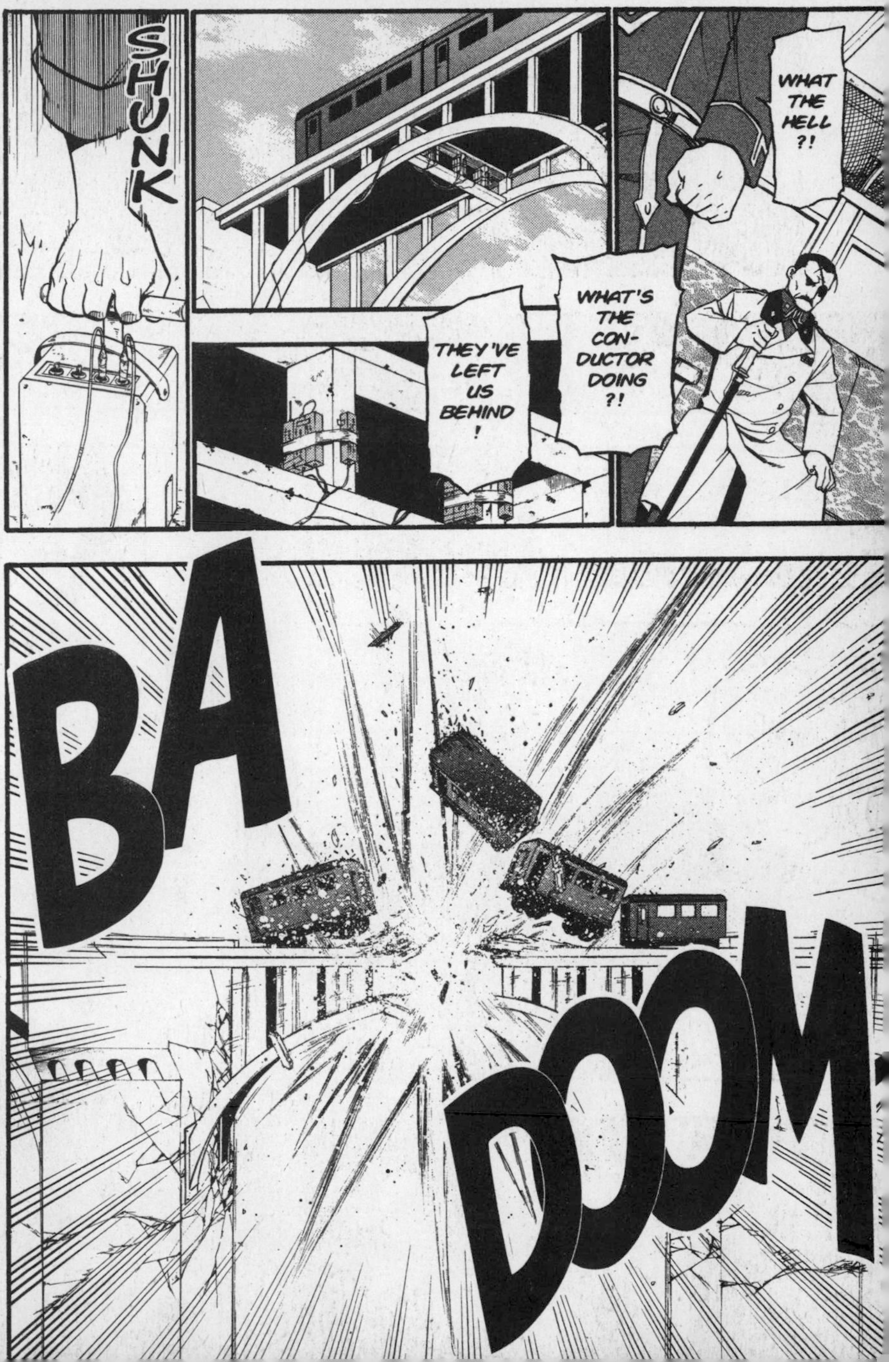
WHAT THE HELL ?!
WHAT'S THE CON-DUCTOR DOING ?!
THEY'VE LEFT US BEHIND !
SHUNK
BA
DOOM

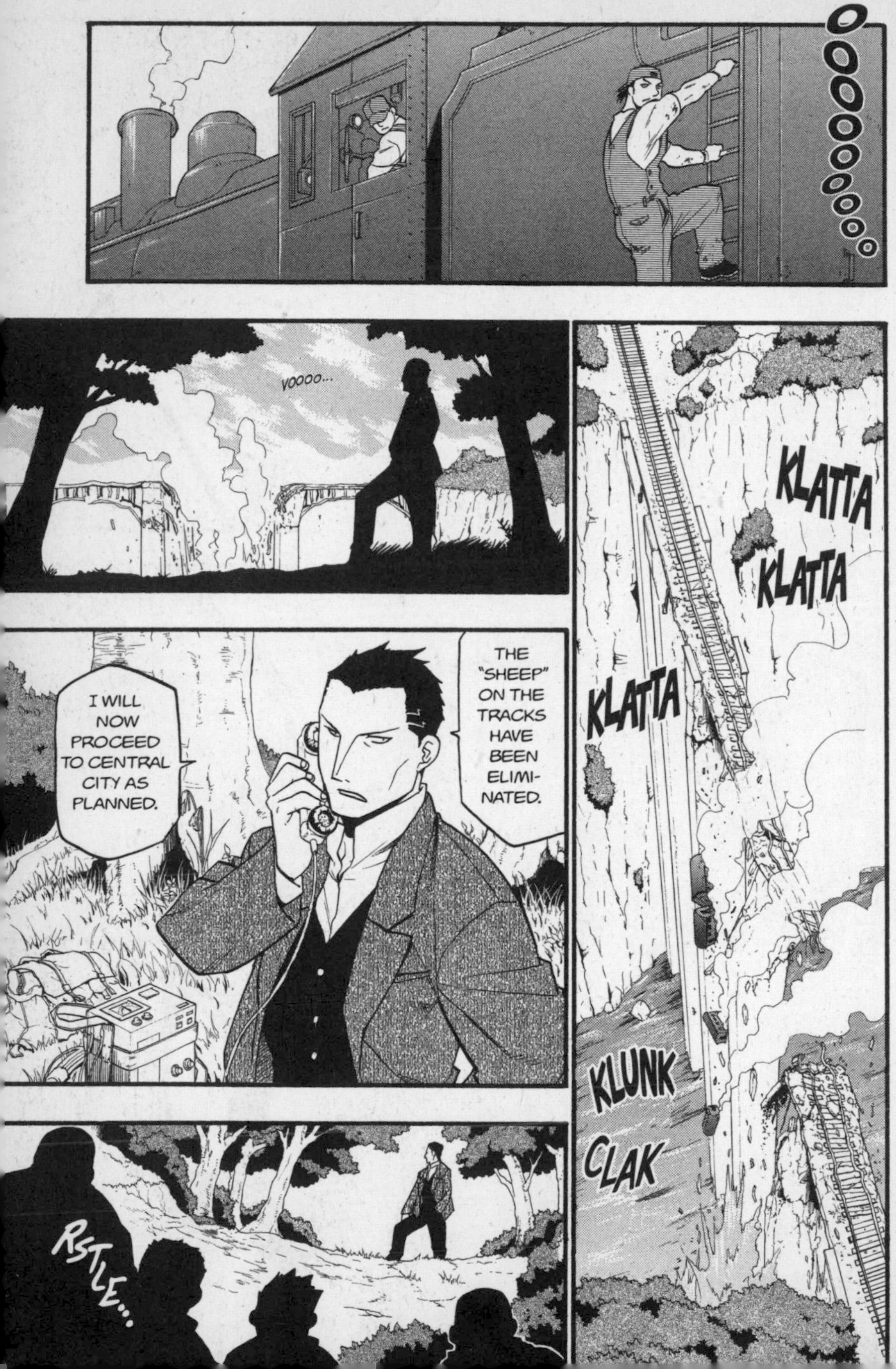
OOOOOOOOOOOO
KLATTA
KLATTA
KLATTA
KLUNK
CLAK
VOOOO...
THE "SHEEP" ON THE TRACKS HAVE BEEN ELIMI-NATED.
I WILL NOW PROCEED TO CENTRAL CITY AS PLANNED.
RSTLE...

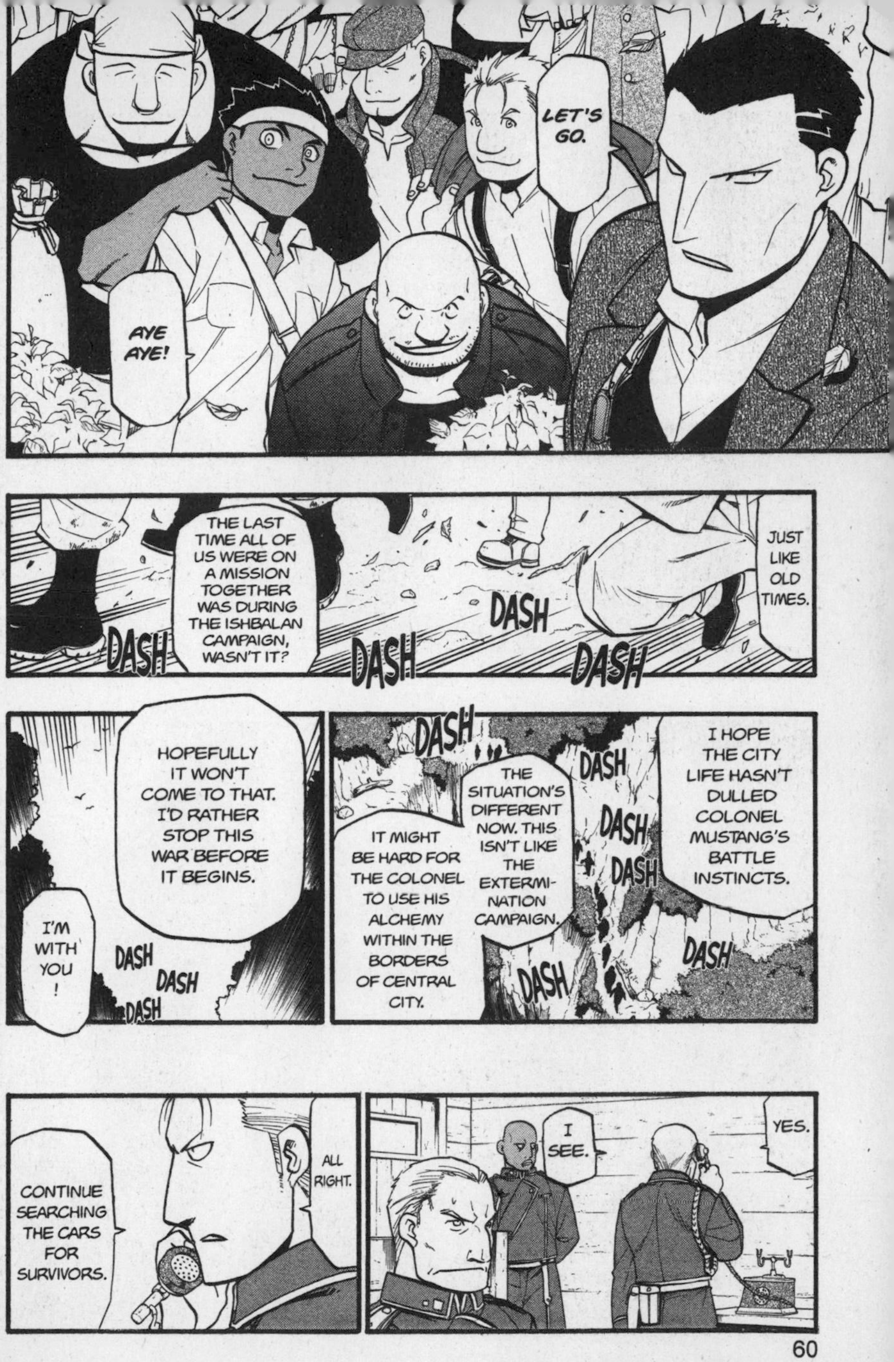

LET'S GO.
AYE AYE!
JUST LIKE OLD TIMES.
DASH
DASH
THE LAST TIME ALL OF US WERE ON A MISSION TOGETHER WAS DURING THE ISHBALAN CAMPAIGN, WASN'T IT?
DASH
DASH
I HOPE THE CITY LIFE HASN'T DULLED COLONEL MUSTANG'S BATTLE INSTINCTS.
DASH
DASH DASH DASH
THE SITUATION'S DIFFERENT NOW. THIS ISN'T LIKE THE EXTERMINATION CAMPAIGN.
IT MIGHT BE HARD FOR THE COLONEL TO USE HIS ALCHEMY WITHIN THE BORDERS OF CENTRAL CITY.
DASH
DASH
HOPEFULLY IT WON'T COME TO THAT. I'D RATHER STOP THIS WAR BEFORE IT BEGINS.
DASH DASH DASH
I'M WITH YOU!
YES.
I SEE.
ALL RIGHT.
CONTINUE SEARCHING THE CARS FOR SURVIVORS.

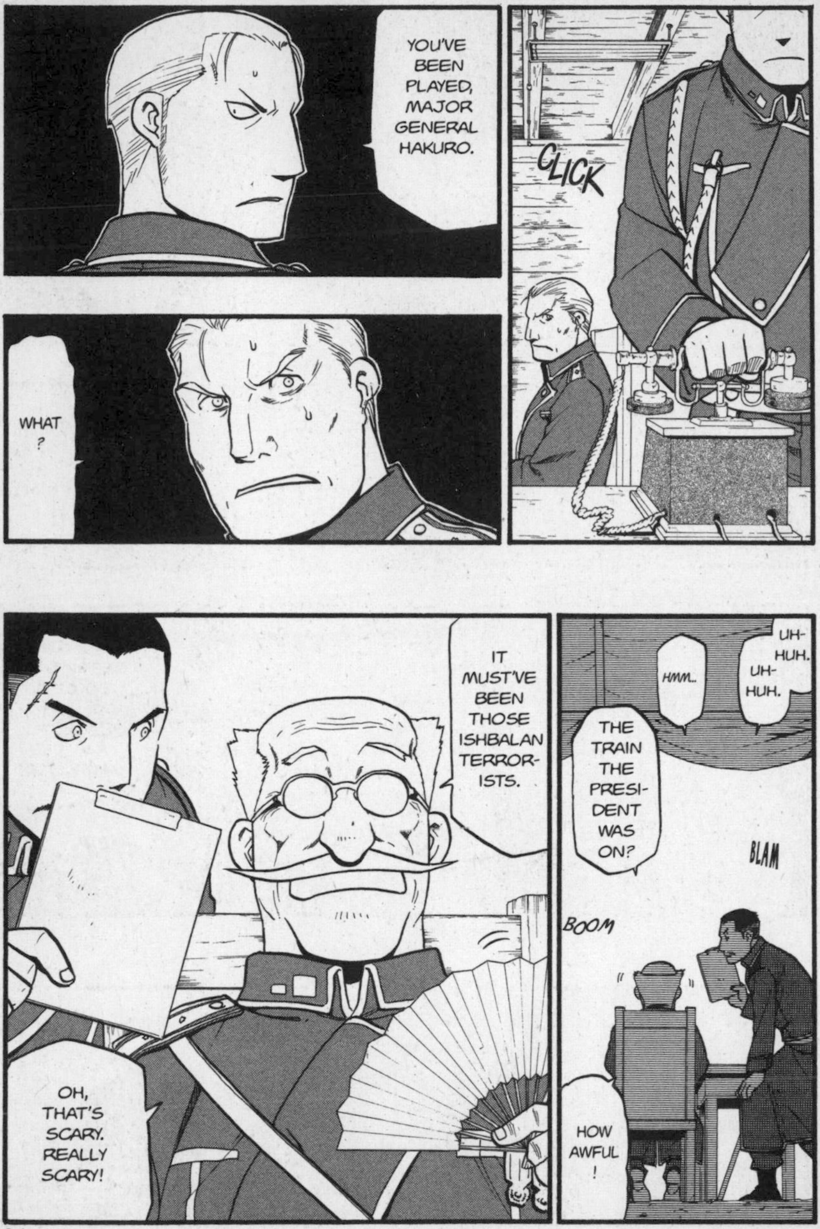
CLICK
YOU'VE BEEN PLAYED, MAJOR GENERAL HAKURO.
WHAT?
UH-HUH. UH-HUH.
HMM..
THE TRAIN THE PRESIDENT WAS ON?
BLAM
BOOM
HOW AWFUL!
IT MUST'VE BEEN THOSE ISHBALAN TERRORISTS.
OH, THAT'S SCARY. REALLY SCARY!

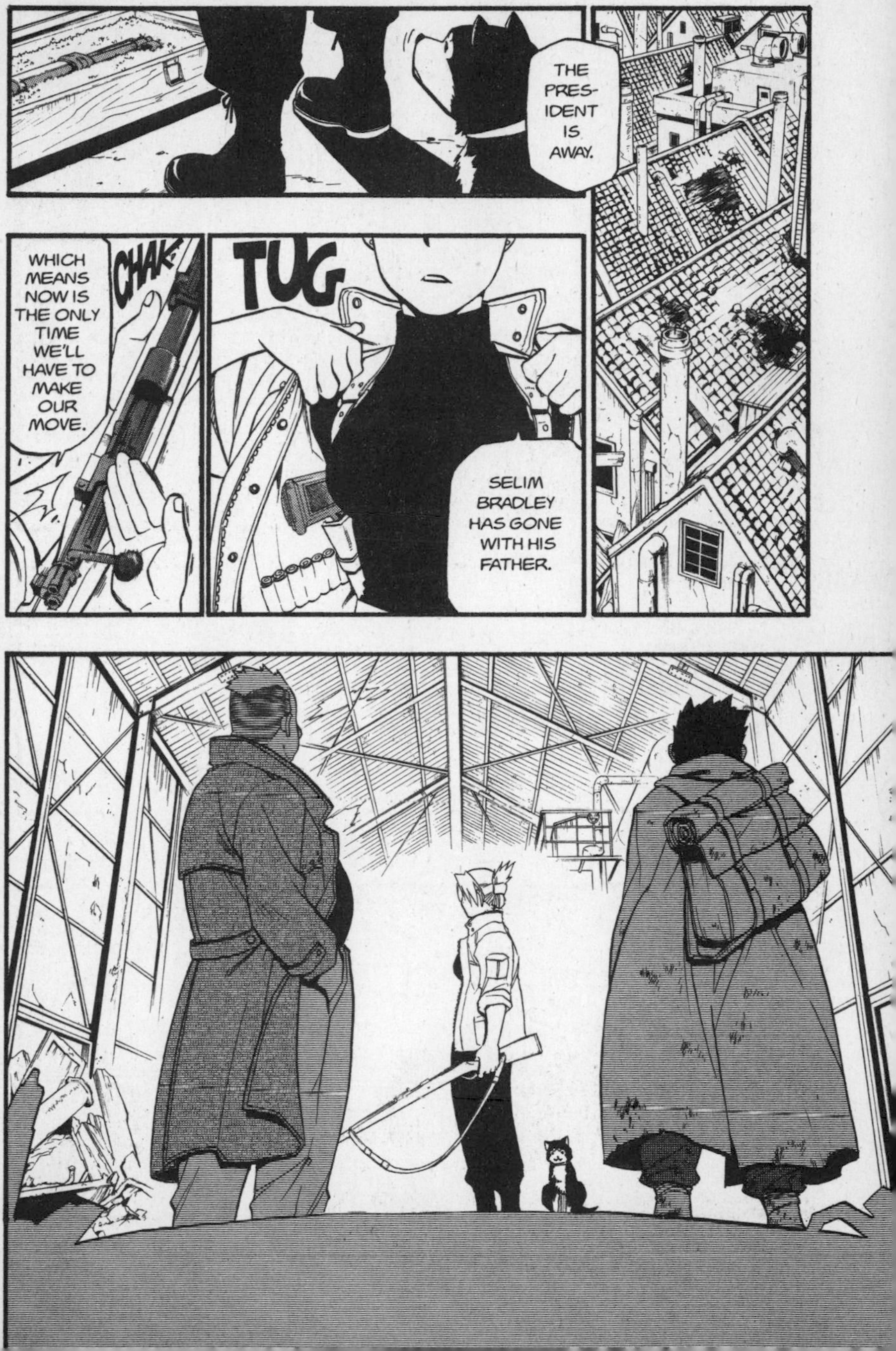
THE PRESIDENT IS AWAY.
TUG
SELIM BRADLEY HAS GONE WITH HIS FATHER.
CHAK
WHICH MEANS NOW IS THE ONLY TIME WE'LL HAVE TO MAKE OUR MOVE.

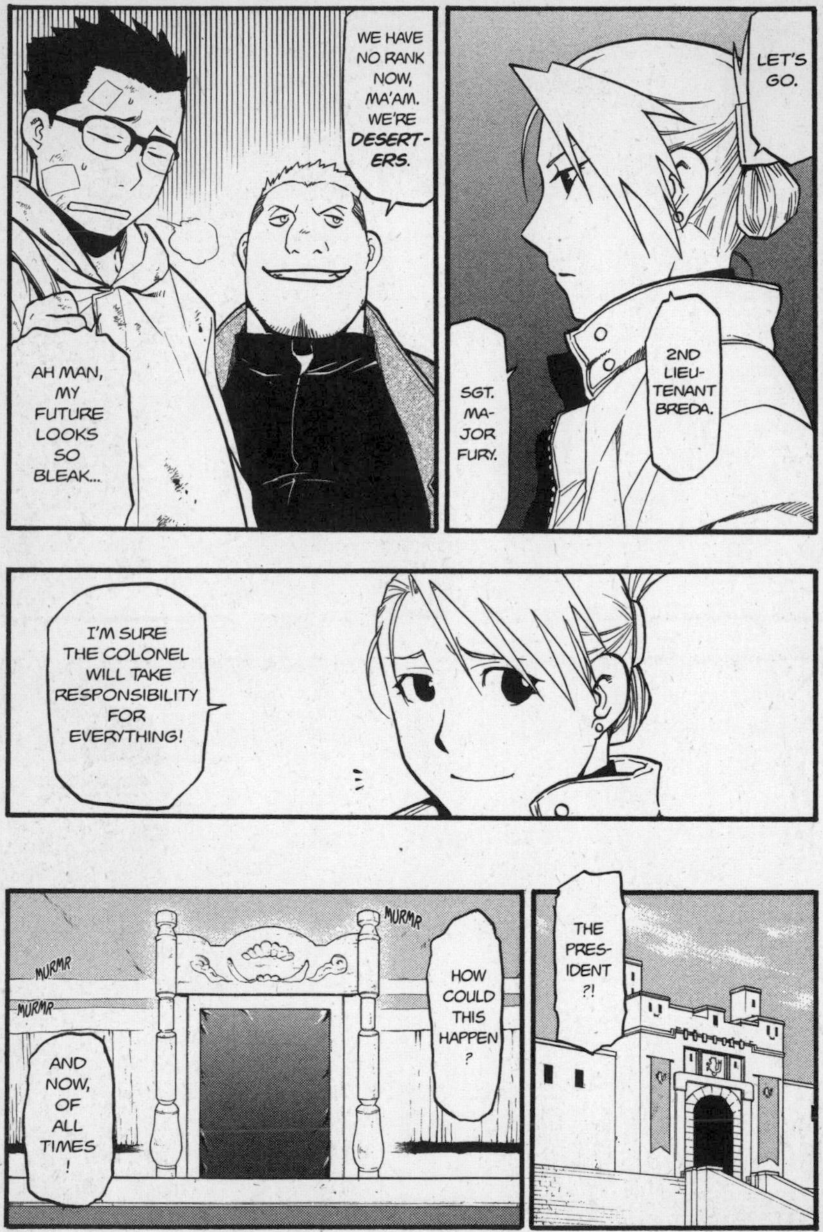
LET'S GO.
2ND LIEUTENANT BREDA.
SGT. MAJOR FURY.
WE HAVE NO RANK NOW, MA'AM. WE'RE *DESERTERS*.
AH MAN, MY FUTURE LOOKS SO BLEAK...
I'M SURE THE COLONEL WILL TAKE RESPONSIBILITY FOR EVERYTHING!
THE PRESIDENT?!
MURMR
HOW COULD THIS HAPPEN?
MURMR
MURMR
AND NOW, OF ALL TIMES!

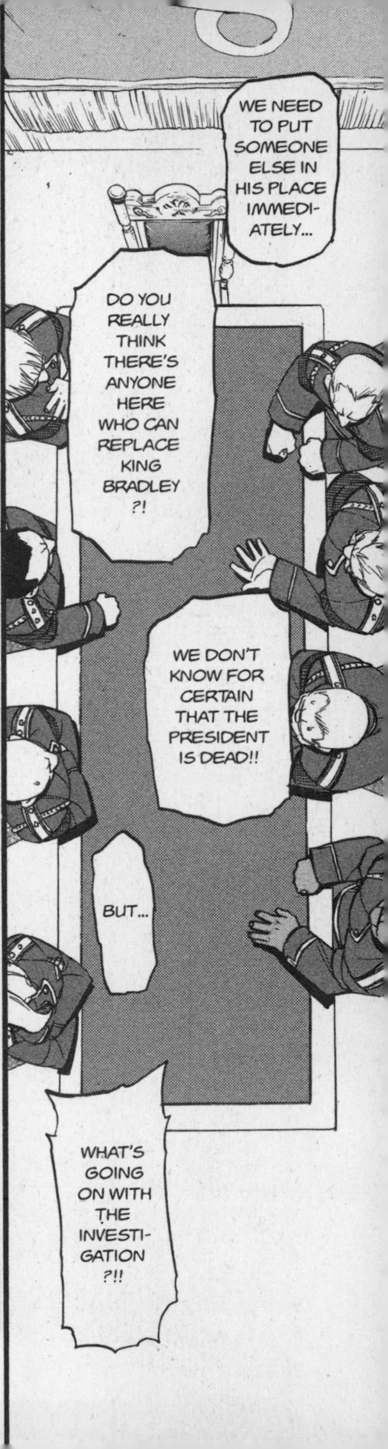
WE NEED TO PUT SOMEONE ELSE IN HIS PLACE IMMEDIATELY...
DO YOU REALLY THINK THERE'S ANYONE HERE WHO CAN REPLACE KING BRADLEY?!
WE DON'T KNOW FOR CERTAIN THAT THE PRESIDENT IS DEAD!!
BUT...
WHAT'S GOING ON WITH THE INVESTIGATION?!!
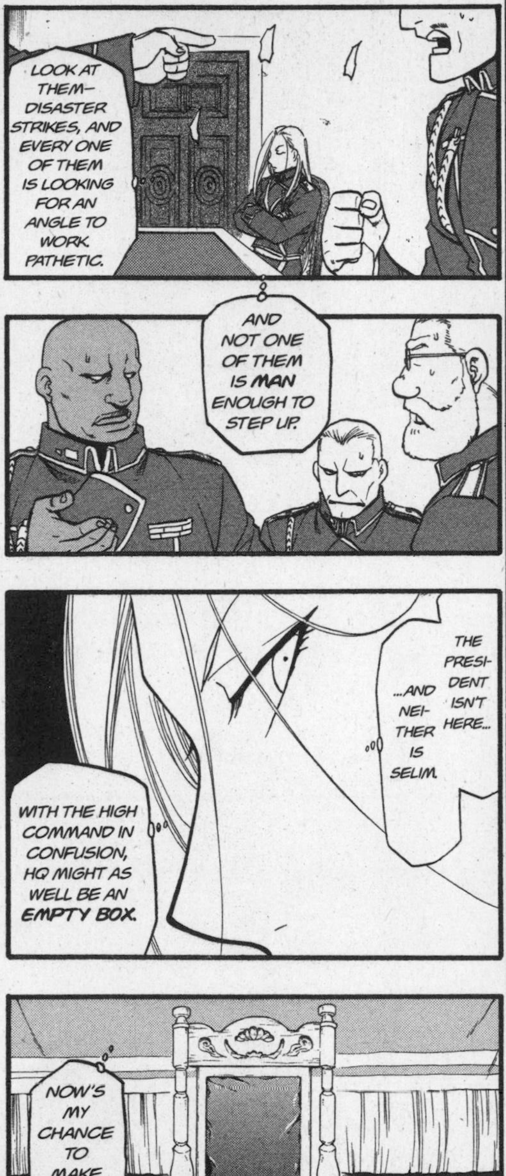
LOOK AT THEM— DISASTER STRIKES, AND EVERY ONE OF THEM IS LOOKING FOR AN ANGLE TO WORK. PATHETIC.
AND NOT ONE OF THEM IS MAN ENOUGH TO STEP UP.
THE PRESIDENT ISN'T HERE...
...AND NEITHER IS SELIM.
WITH THE HIGH COMMAND IN CONFUSION, HQ MIGHT AS WELL BE AN EMPTY BOX.
NOW'S MY CHANCE TO MAKE A MOVE...

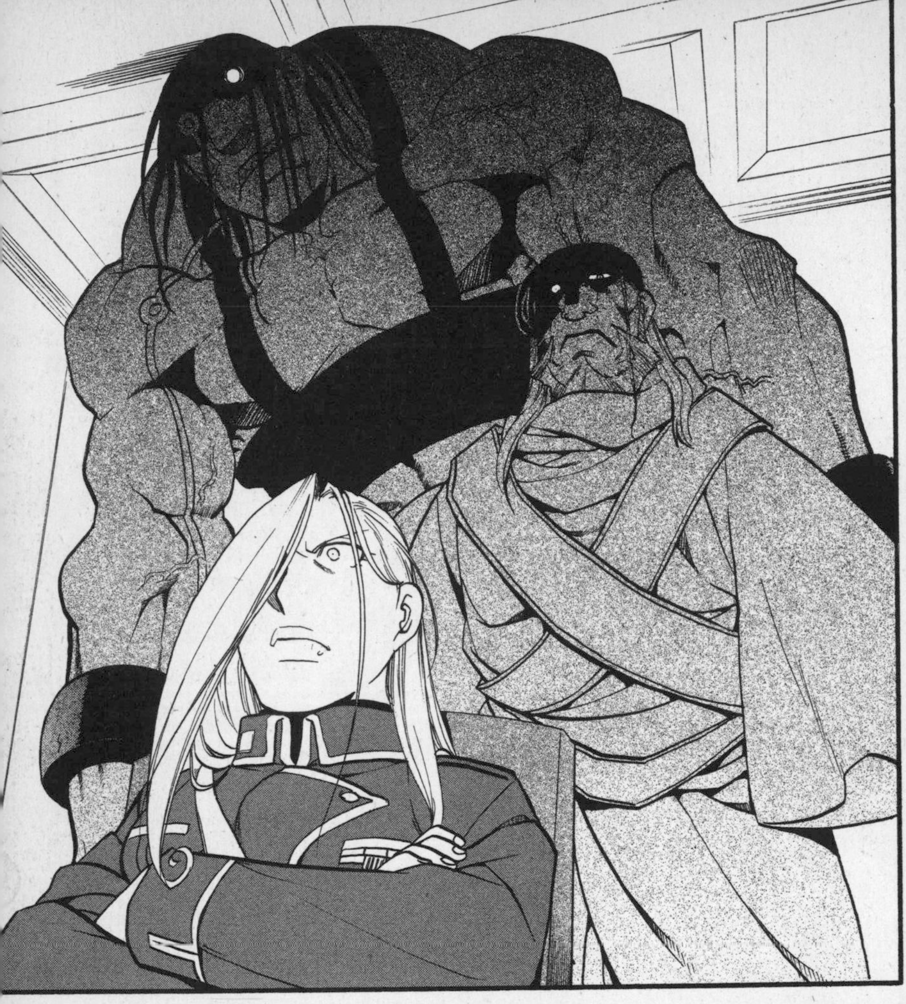

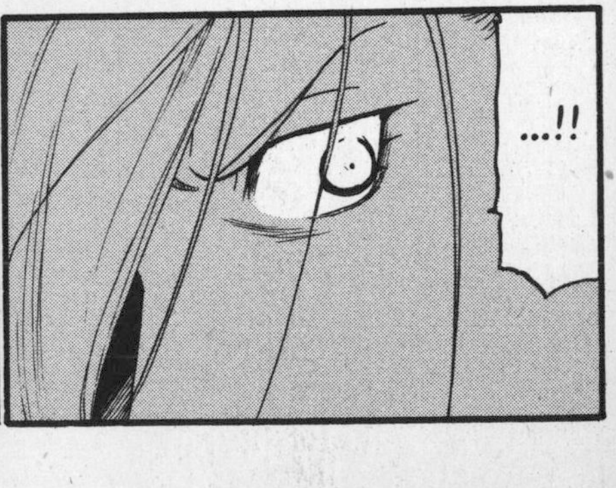
...!!

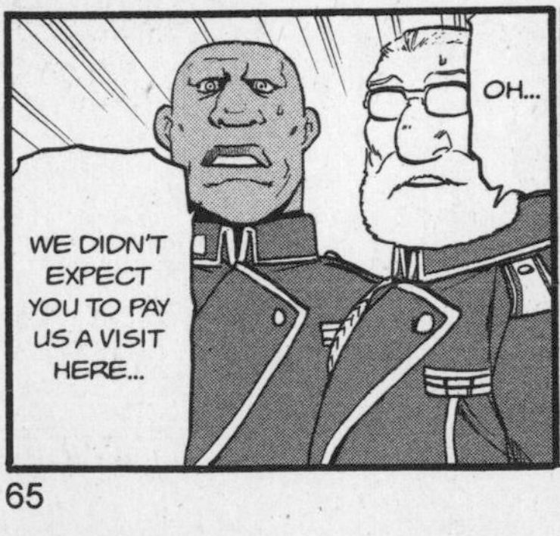
OH...
WE DIDN'T EXPECT YOU TO PAY US A VISIT HERE...

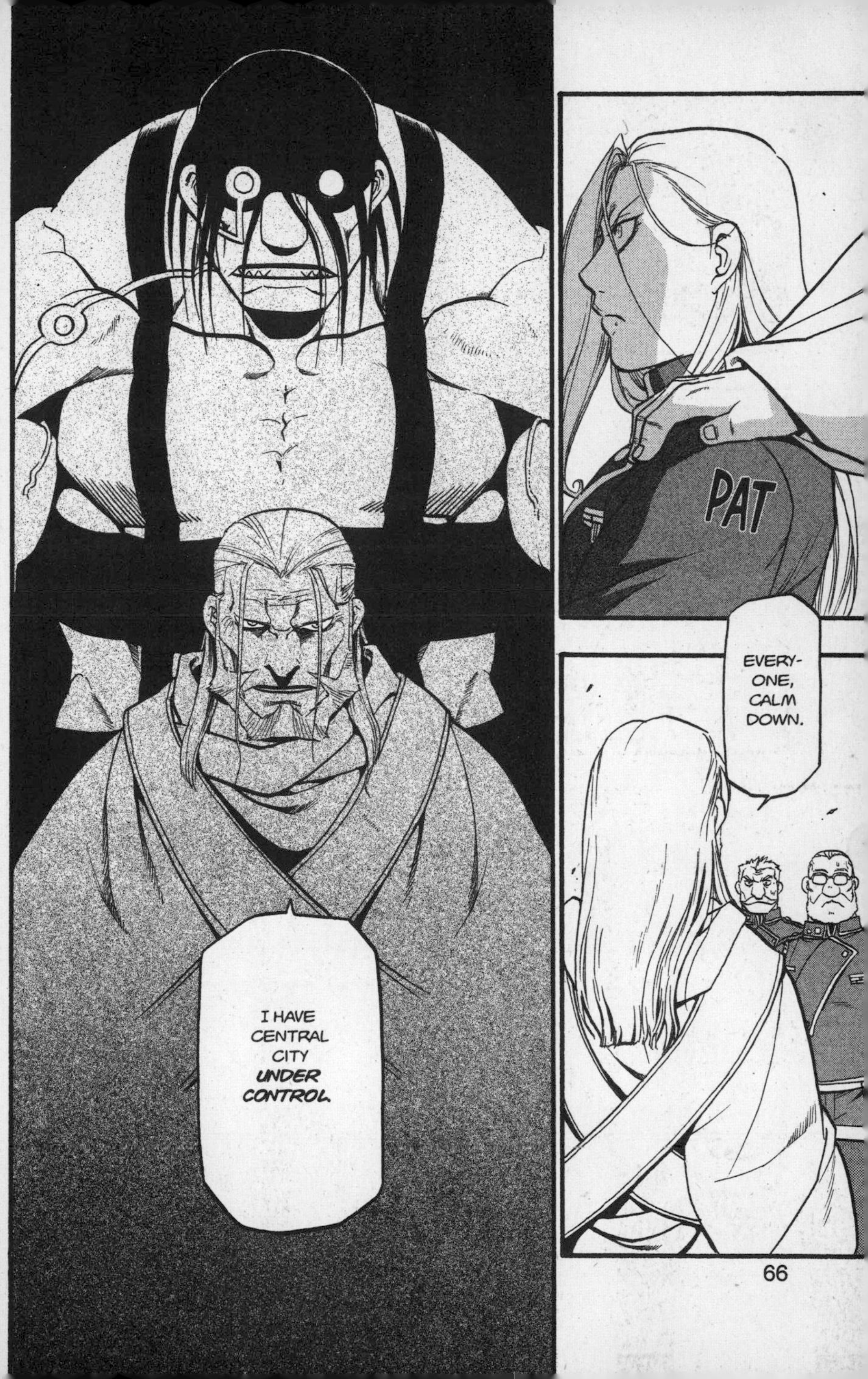
PAT
EVERY-ONE, CALM DOWN.
I HAVE CENTRAL CITY UNDER CONTROL.

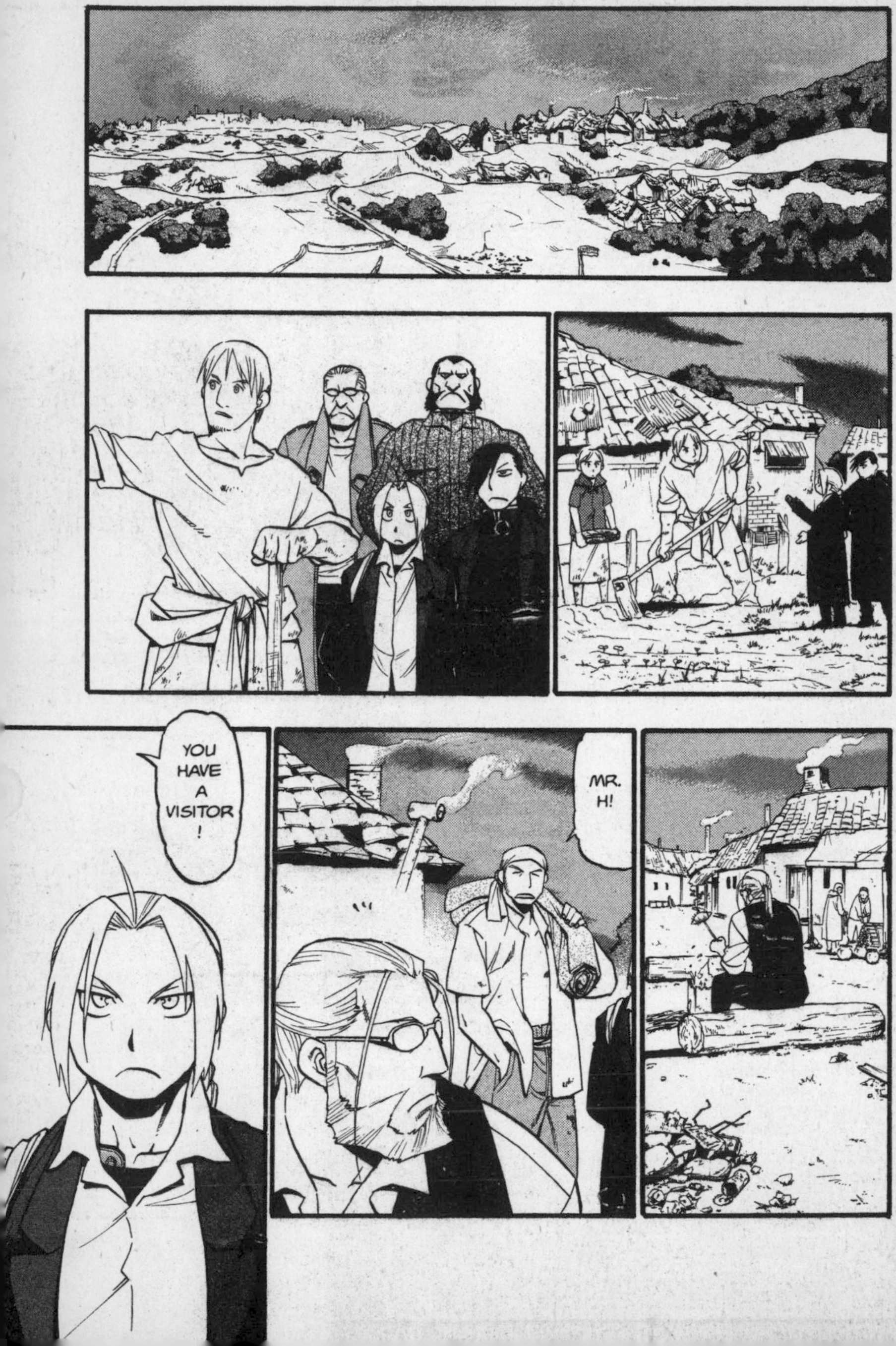
MR. H!
YOU HAVE A VISITOR!

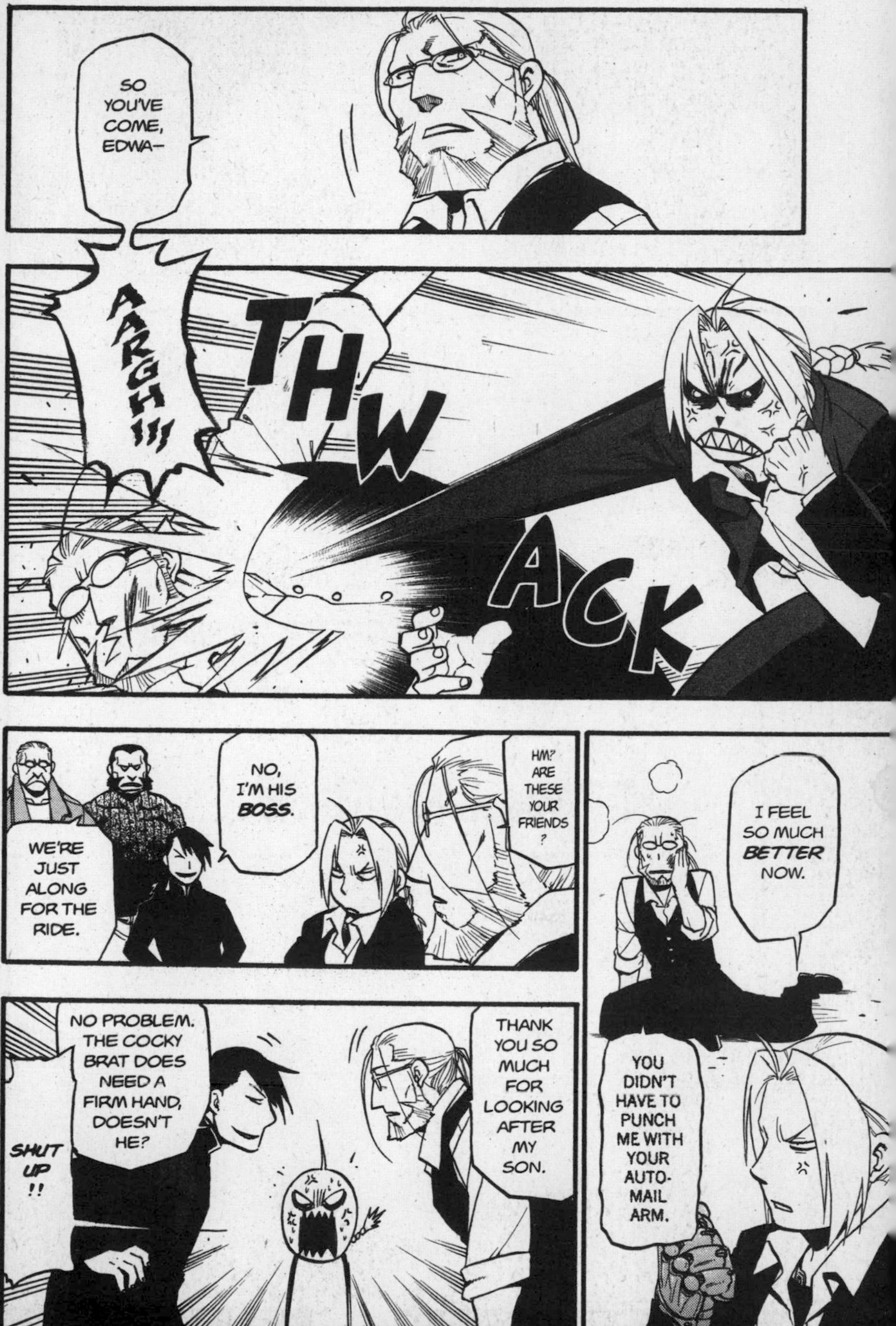
SO YOU'VE COME, EDWA—
THWACK
AARGH!!!
I FEEL SO MUCH *BETTER* NOW.
YOU DIDN'T HAVE TO PUNCH ME WITH YOUR AUTO-MAIL ARM.
HM? ARE THESE YOUR FRIENDS?
NO, I'M HIS *BOSS*.
WE'RE JUST ALONG FOR THE RIDE.
THANK YOU SO MUCH FOR LOOKING AFTER MY SON.
NO PROBLEM. THE COCKY BRAT DOES NEED A FIRM HAND, DOESN'T HE?
SHUT UP!!

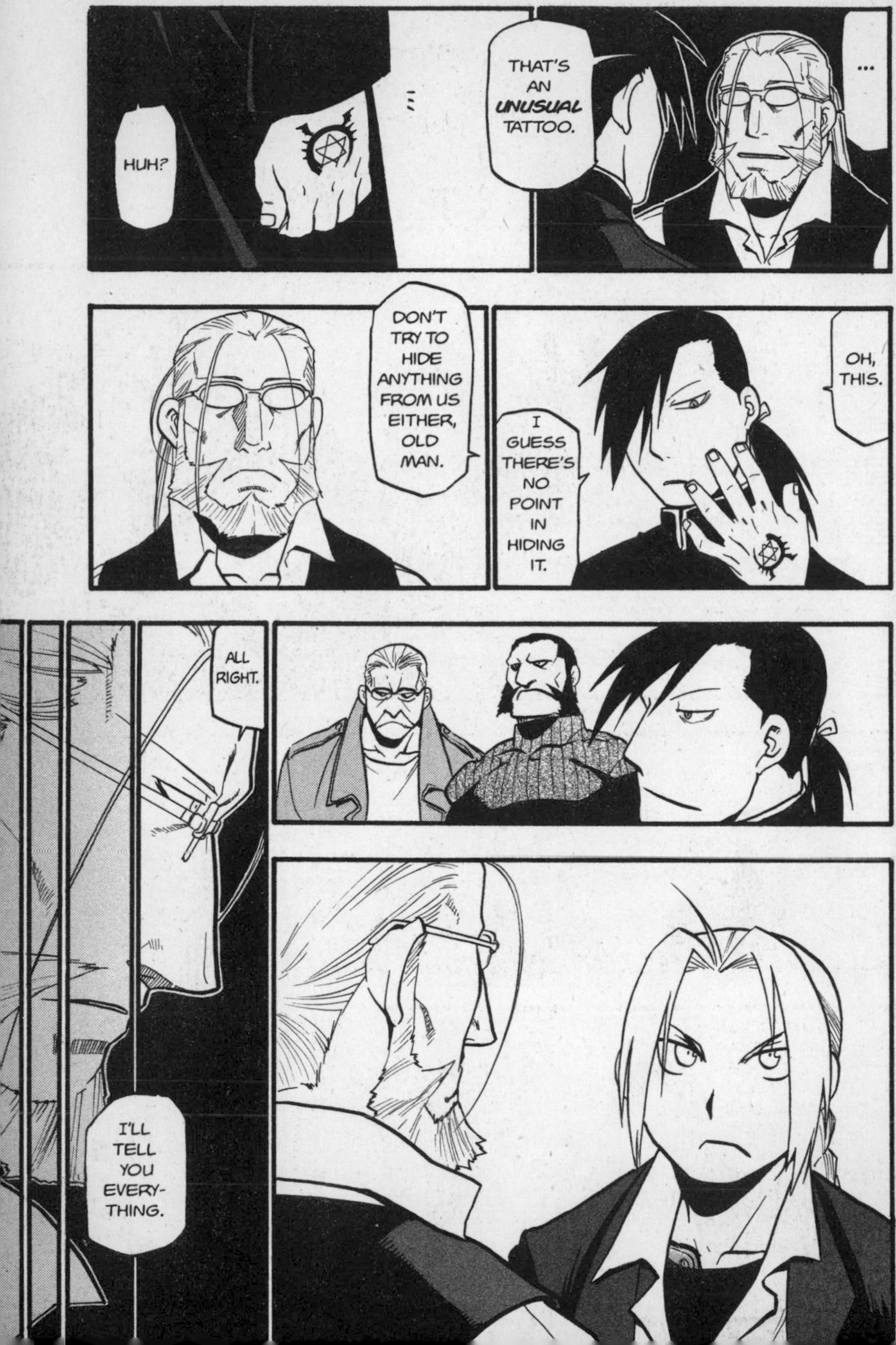
...
THAT'S AN *UNUSUAL* TATTOO.
HUH?
OH, THIS.
I GUESS THERE'S NO POINT IN HIDING IT.
DON'T TRY TO HIDE ANYTHING FROM US EITHER, OLD MAN.
ALL RIGHT.
I'LL TELL YOU EVERYTHING.

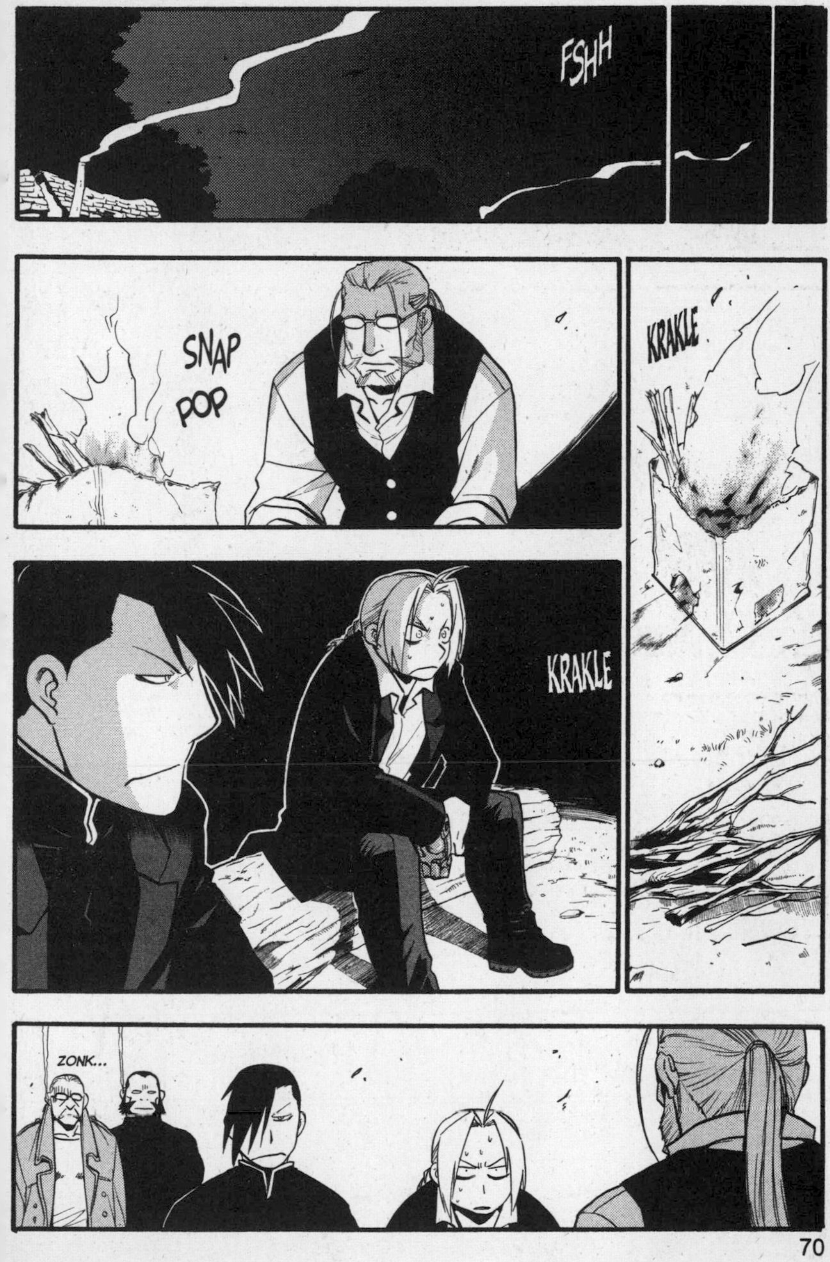
FSHH
KRAKLE
SNAP
POP
KRAKLE
ZONK...

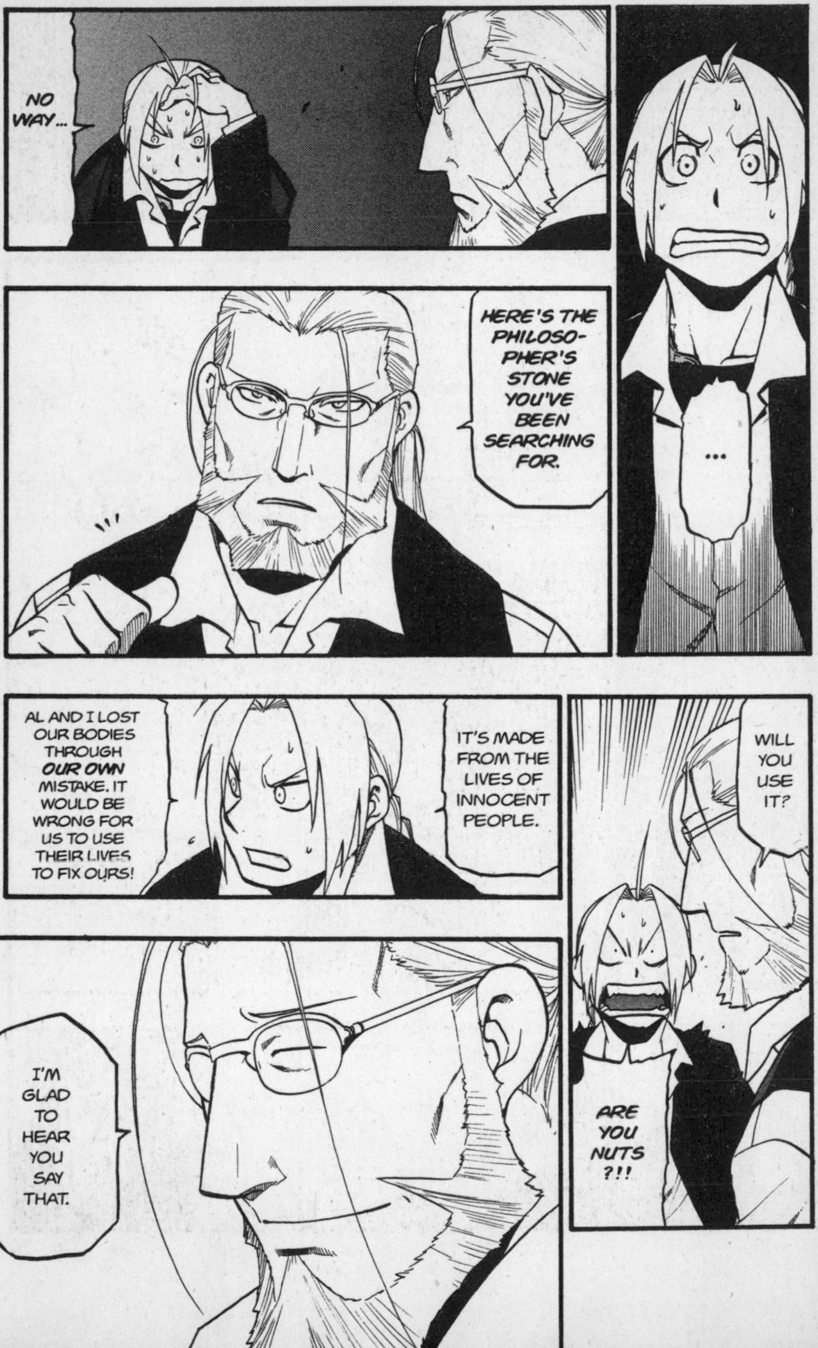
...
NO WAY...
HERE'S THE PHILOSO-PHER'S STONE YOU'VE BEEN SEARCHING FOR.
WILL YOU USE IT?
ARE YOU NUTS?!!
IT'S MADE FROM THE LIVES OF INNOCENT PEOPLE.
AL AND I LOST OUR BODIES THROUGH OUR OWN MISTAKE. IT WOULD BE WRONG FOR US TO USE THEIR LIVES TO FIX OURS!
I'M GLAD TO HEAR YOU SAY THAT.

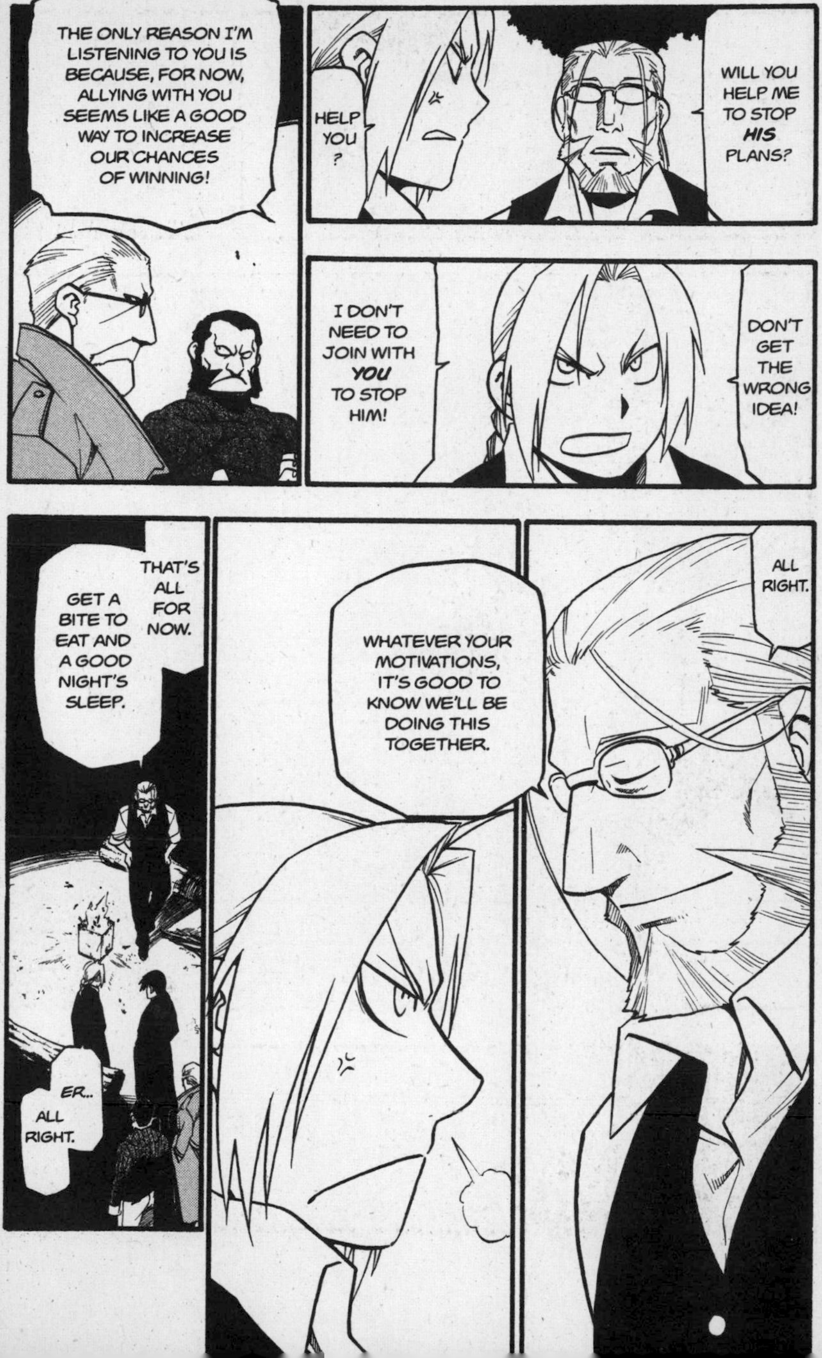
WILL YOU HELP ME TO STOP **HIS** PLANS?
HELP YOU?
DON'T GET THE WRONG IDEA!
I DON'T NEED TO JOIN WITH **YOU** TO STOP HIM!
THE ONLY REASON I'M LISTENING TO YOU IS BECAUSE, FOR NOW, ALLYING WITH YOU SEEMS LIKE A GOOD WAY TO INCREASE OUR CHANCES OF WINNING!
ALL RIGHT.
WHATEVER YOUR MOTIVATIONS, IT'S GOOD TO KNOW WE'LL BE DOING THIS TOGETHER.
THAT'S ALL FOR NOW.
GET A BITE TO EAT AND A GOOD NIGHT'S SLEEP.
ER... ALL RIGHT.

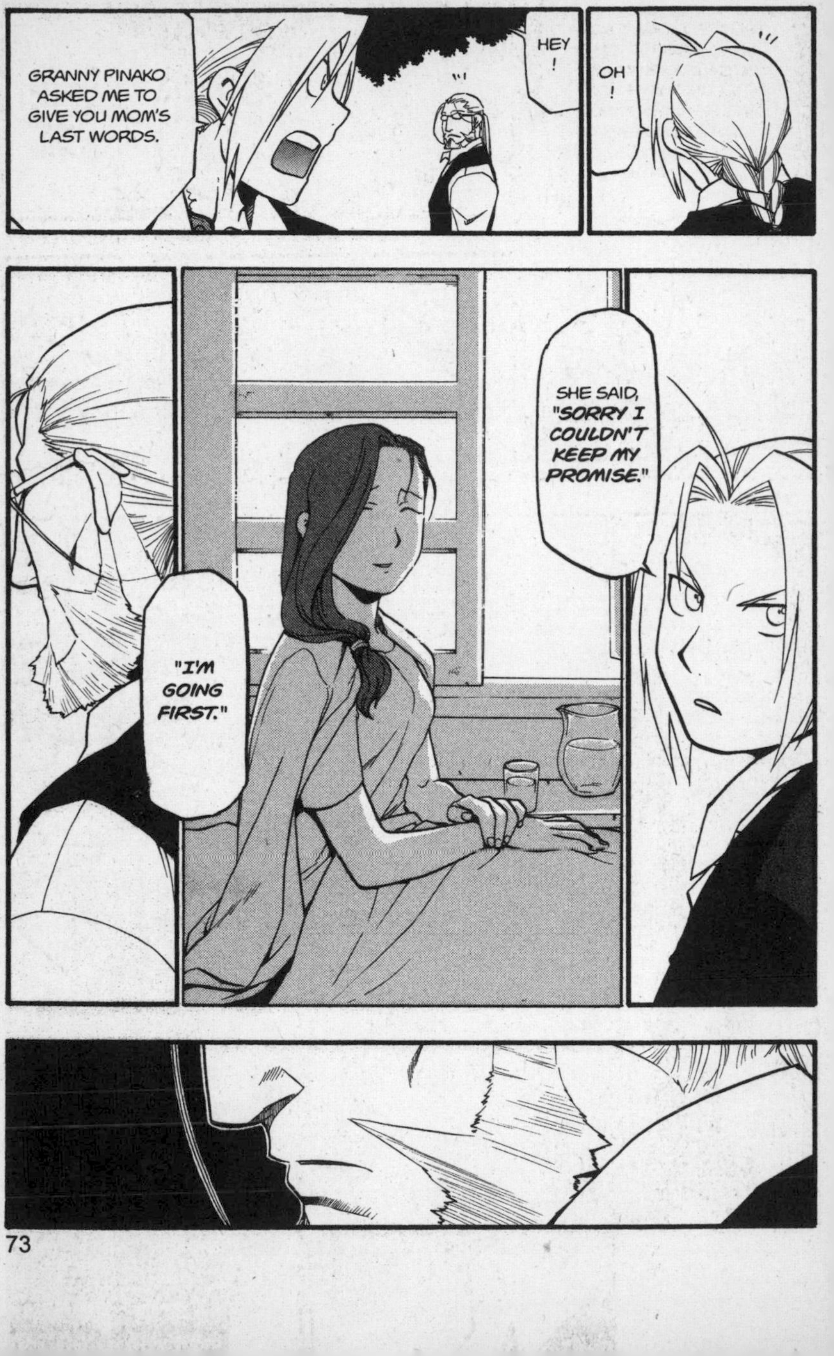
OH!
HEY!
GRANNY PINAKO ASKED ME TO GIVE YOU MOM'S LAST WORDS.
SHE SAID, "SORRY I COULDN'T KEEP MY PROMISE."
"I'M GOING FIRST."

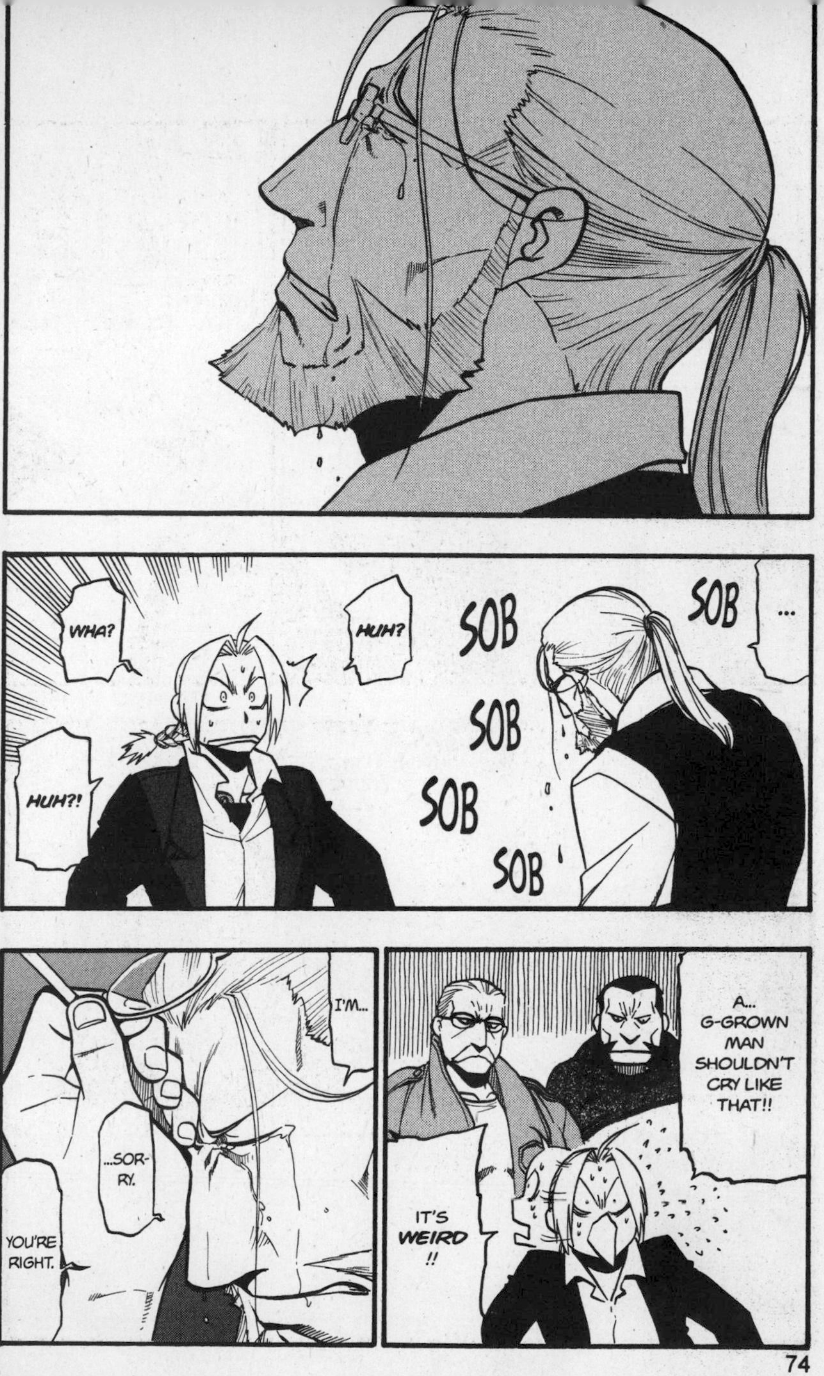
...
SOB
SOB
SOB
SOB
SOB
HUH?
WHA?
HUH?!
A... G-GROWN MAN SHOULDN'T CRY LIKE THAT!!
IT'S WEIRD !!
I'M...
...SOR-RY.
YOU'RE RIGHT.

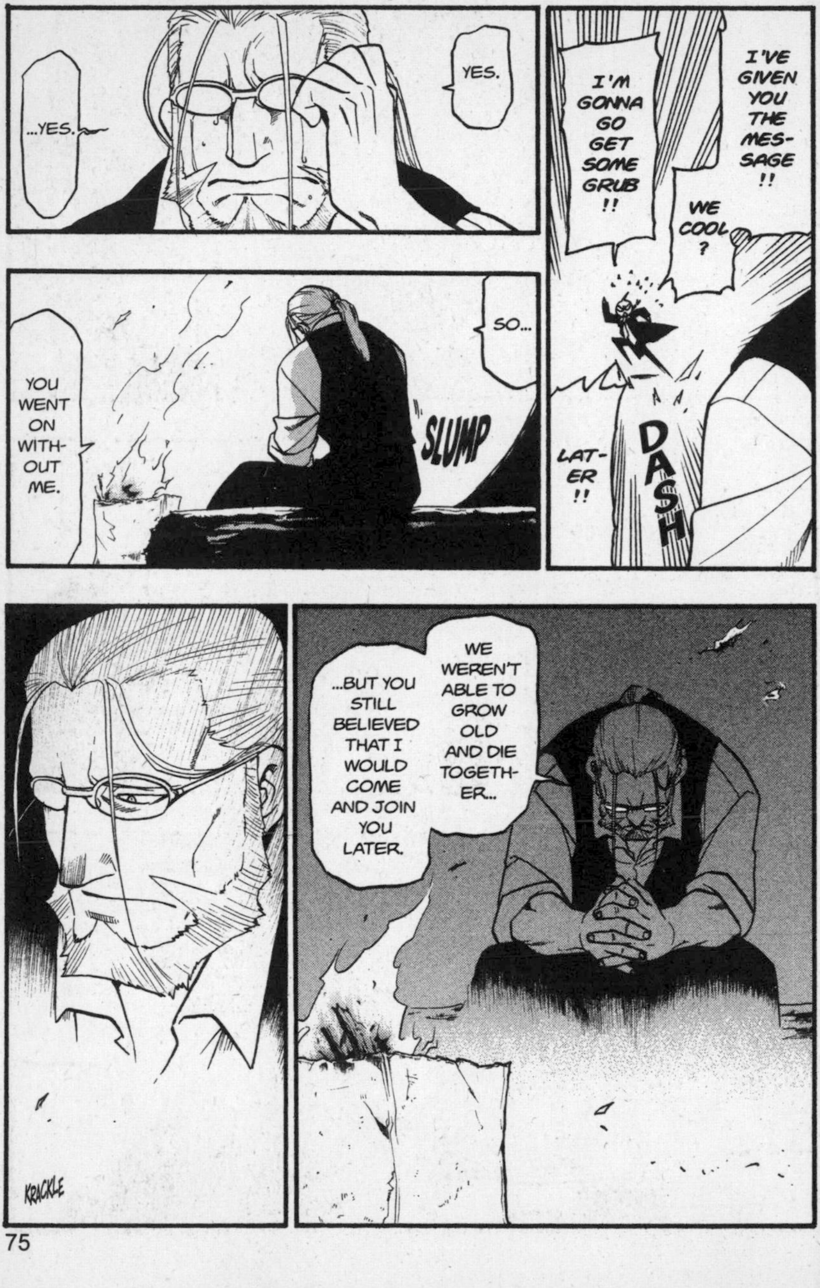
I'VE GIVEN YOU THE MES-SAGE!!
I'M GONNA GO GET SOME GRUB!!
WE COOL?
DASH
LATER!!
YES.
...YES.
SO...
SLUMP
YOU WENT ON WITH-OUT ME.
WE WEREN'T ABLE TO GROW OLD AND DIE TOGETH-ER...
...BUT YOU STILL BELIEVED THAT I WOULD COME AND JOIN YOU LATER.
KRACKLE

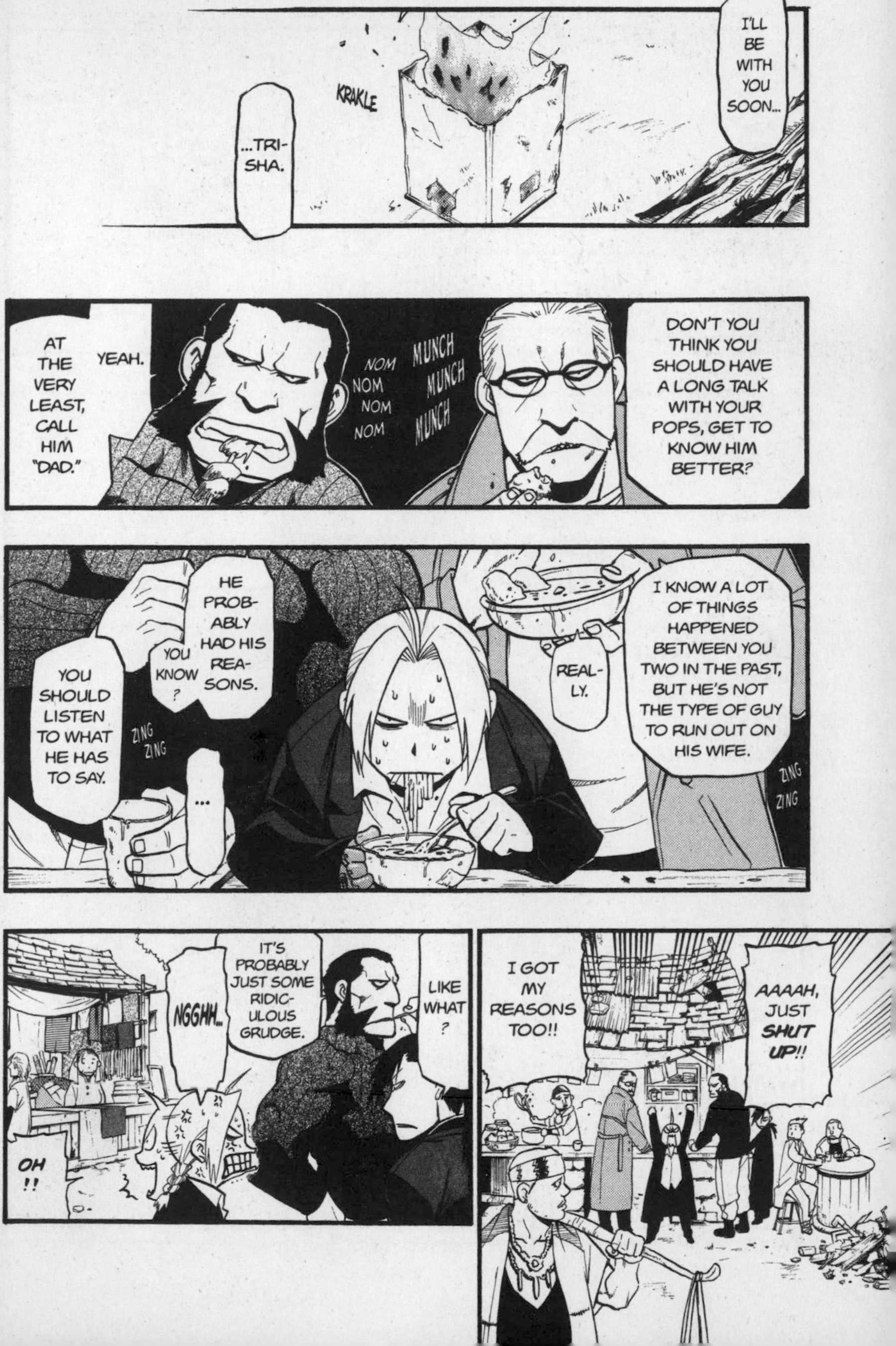
I'LL BE WITH YOU SOON...
KRAKLE
...TRI-SHA.
DON'T YOU THINK YOU SHOULD HAVE A LONG TALK WITH YOUR POPS, GET TO KNOW HIM BETTER?
MUNCH MUNCH MUNCH
NOM NOM NOM NOM
YEAH.
AT THE VERY LEAST, CALL HIM "DAD."
I KNOW A LOT OF THINGS HAPPENED BETWEEN YOU TWO IN THE PAST, BUT HE'S NOT THE TYPE OF GUY TO RUN OUT ON HIS WIFE.
ZING ZING
REAL-LY.
HE PROB-ABLY HAD HIS REA-SONS.
YOU KNOW?
YOU SHOULD LISTEN TO WHAT HE HAS TO SAY.
ZING ZING
...
AAAAH, JUST SHUT UP!!
I GOT MY REASONS TOO!!
LIKE WHAT?
IT'S PROBABLY JUST SOME RIDIC-ULOUS GRUDGE.
NGGHH...
OH!!

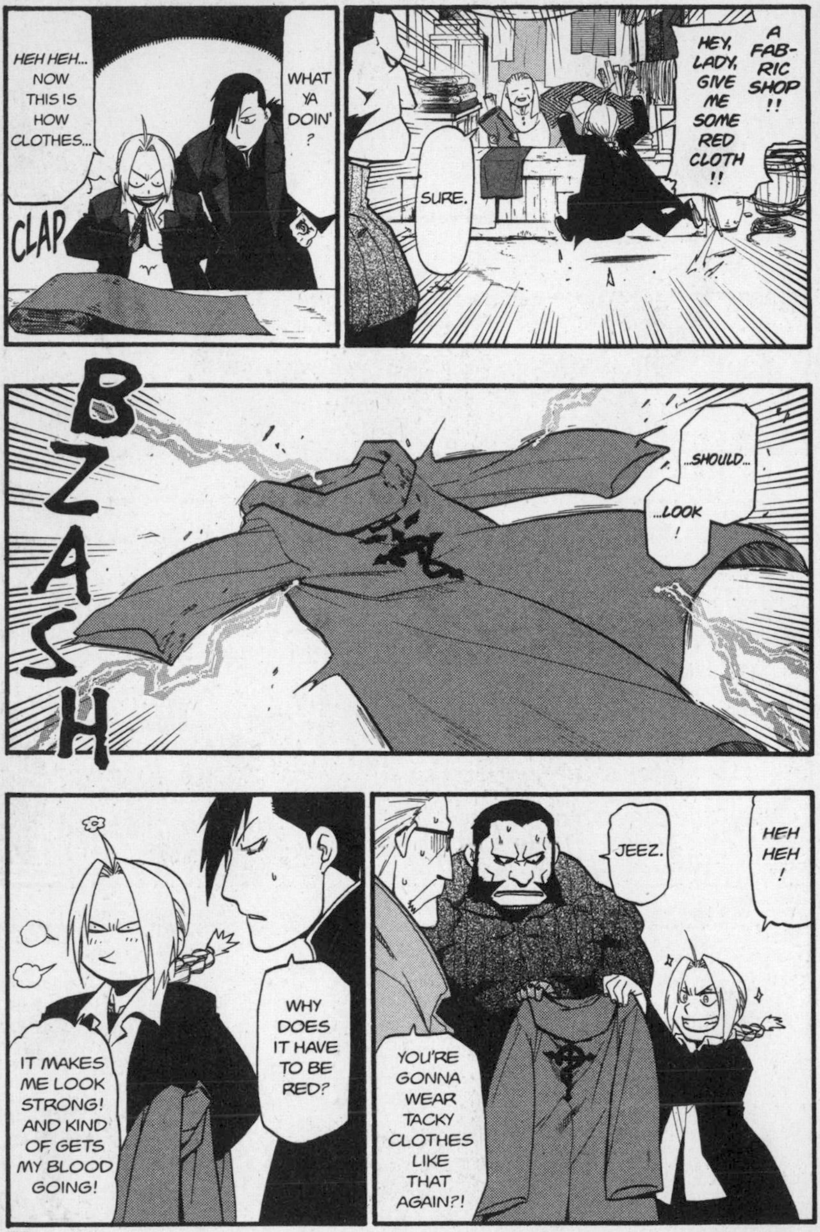
A FABRIC SHOP!!
HEY, LADY, GIVE ME SOME RED CLOTH!!
SURE.
WHAT YA DOIN'?
HEH HEH... NOW THIS IS HOW CLOTHES...
CLAP
...SHOULD... ...LOOK!
BZASH
HEH HEH!
JEEZ.
YOU'RE GONNA WEAR TACKY CLOTHES LIKE THAT AGAIN?!
WHY DOES IT HAVE TO BE RED?
IT MAKES ME LOOK STRONG! AND KIND OF GETS MY BLOOD GOING!

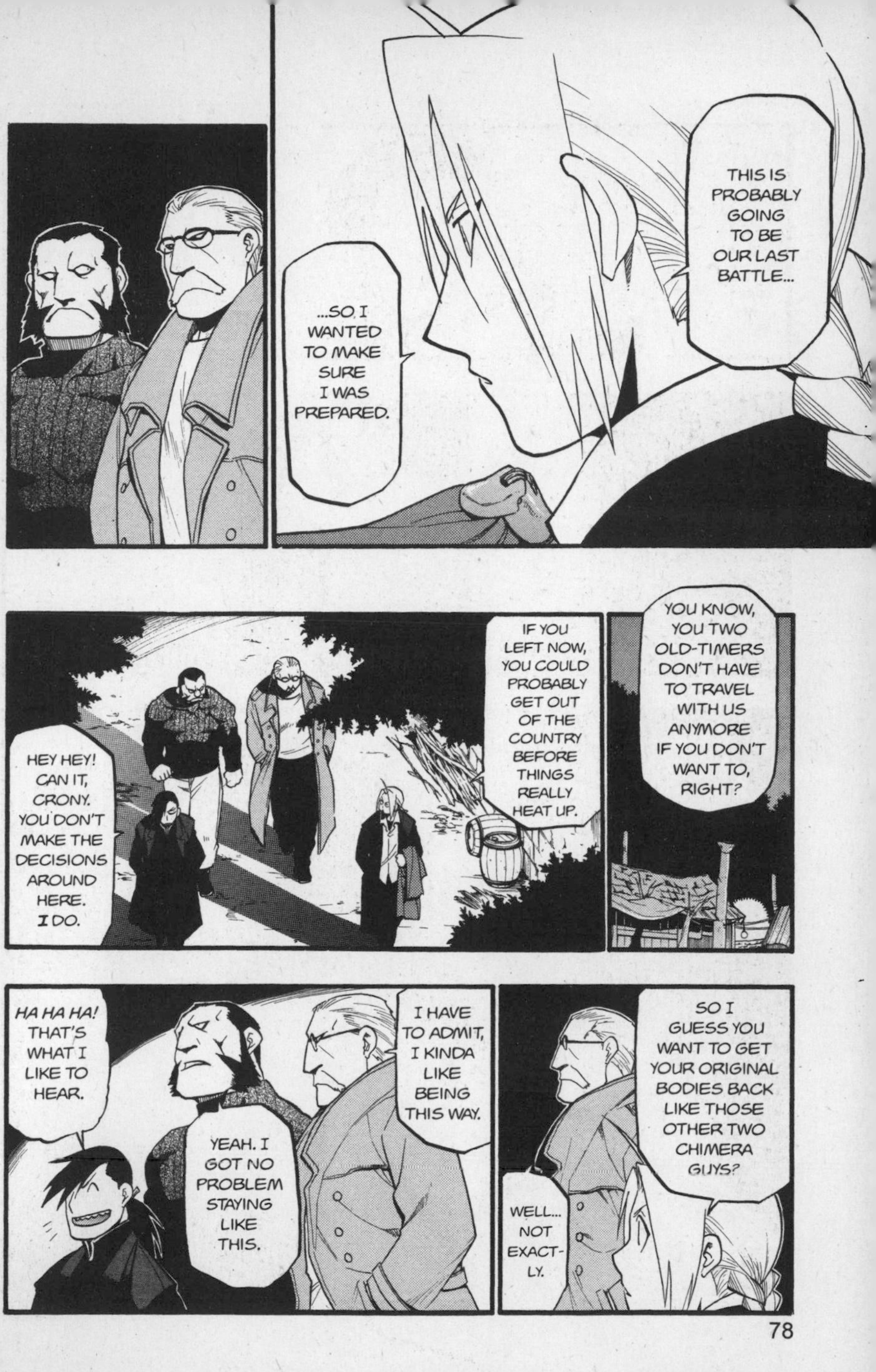
THIS IS PROBABLY GOING TO BE OUR LAST BATTLE...
...SO I WANTED TO MAKE SURE I WAS PREPARED.
YOU KNOW, YOU TWO OLD-TIMERS DON'T HAVE TO TRAVEL WITH US ANYMORE IF YOU DON'T WANT TO, RIGHT?
IF YOU LEFT NOW, YOU COULD PROBABLY GET OUT OF THE COUNTRY BEFORE THINGS REALLY HEAT UP.
HEY HEY! CAN IT, CRONY. YOU DON'T MAKE THE DECISIONS AROUND HERE. I DO.
SO I GUESS YOU WANT TO GET YOUR ORIGINAL BODIES BACK LIKE THOSE OTHER TWO CHIMERA GUYS?
WELL... NOT EXACT-LY.
I HAVE TO ADMIT, I KINDA LIKE BEING THIS WAY.
YEAH. I GOT NO PROBLEM STAYING LIKE THIS.
HA HA HA! THAT'S WHAT I LIKE TO HEAR.

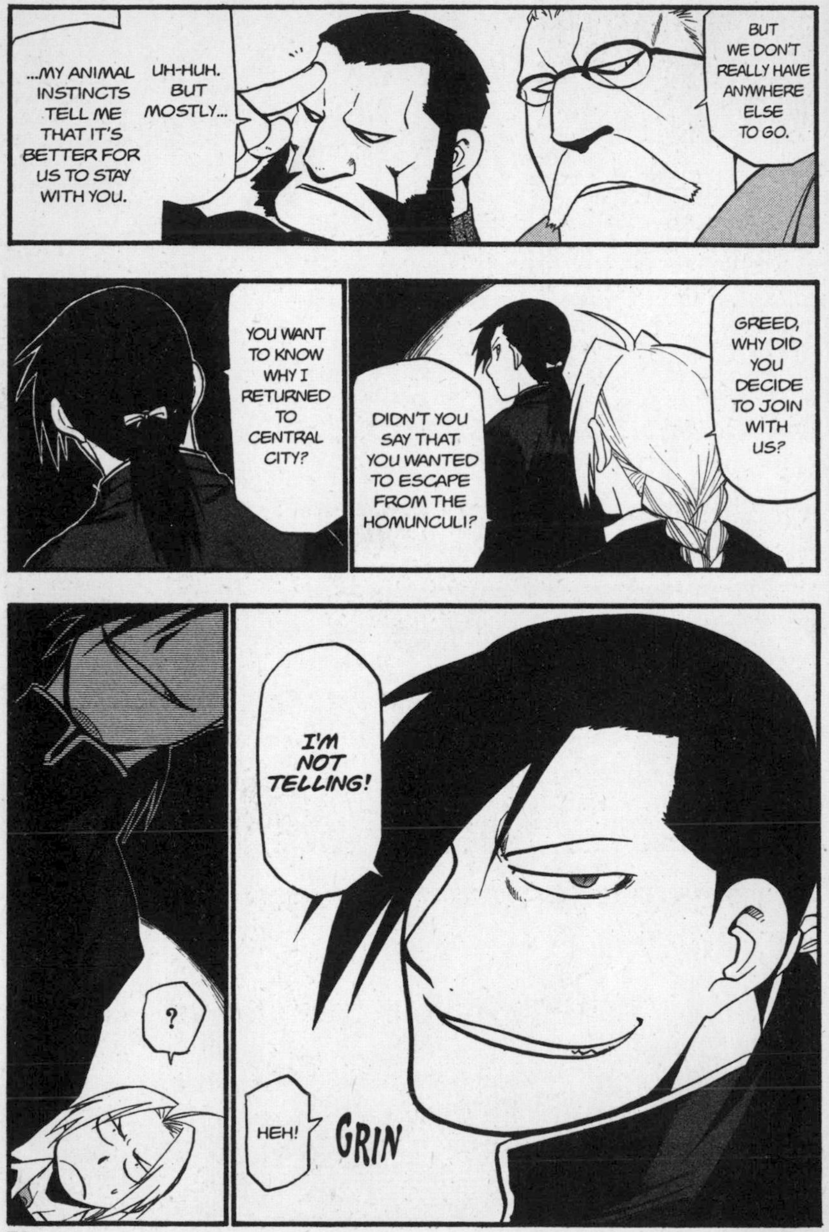
BUT WE DON'T REALLY HAVE ANYWHERE ELSE TO GO.
UH-HUH. BUT MOSTLY...
...MY ANIMAL INSTINCTS TELL ME THAT IT'S BETTER FOR US TO STAY WITH YOU.
GREED, WHY DID YOU DECIDE TO JOIN WITH US?
DIDN'T YOU SAY THAT YOU WANTED TO ESCAPE FROM THE HOMUNCULI?
YOU WANT TO KNOW WHY I RETURNED TO CENTRAL CITY?
I'M NOT TELLING!
HEH!
GRIN
?

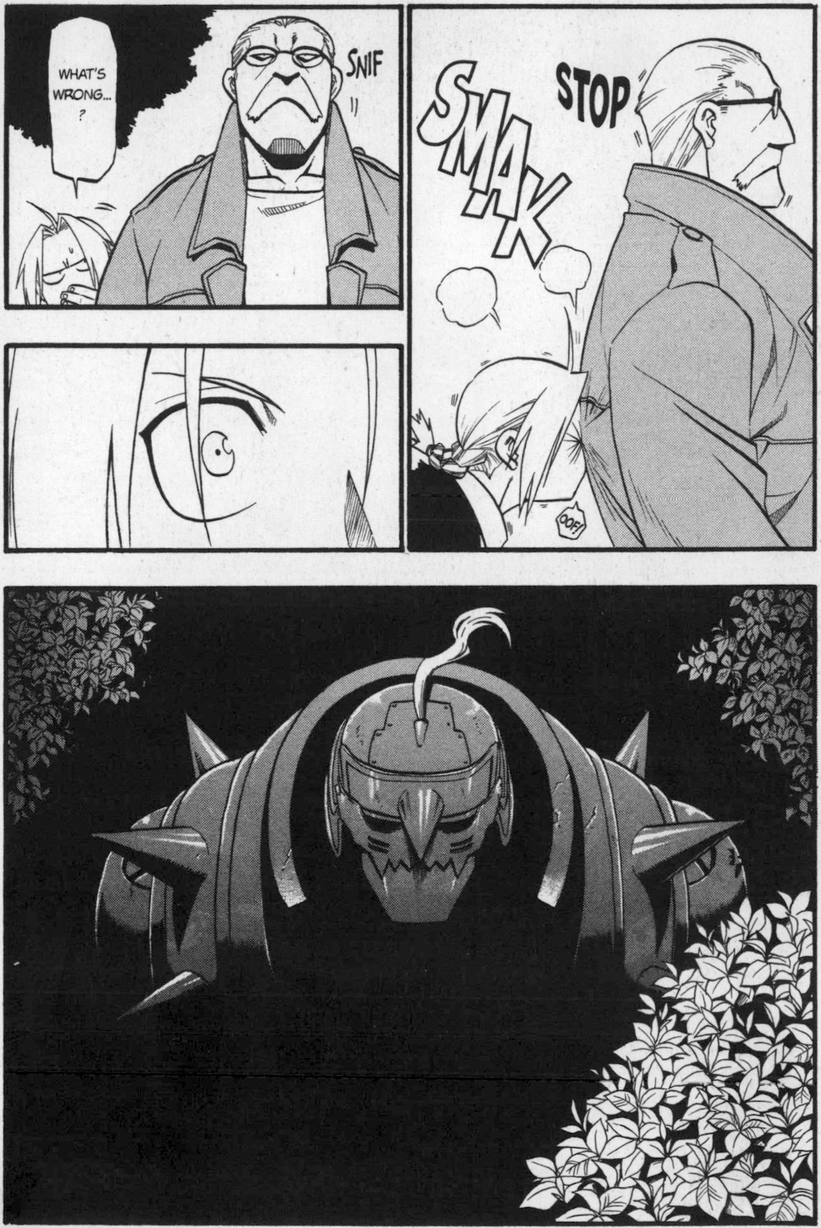
STOP
SMAK
OOF!
SNIF
WHAT'S WRONG... ?

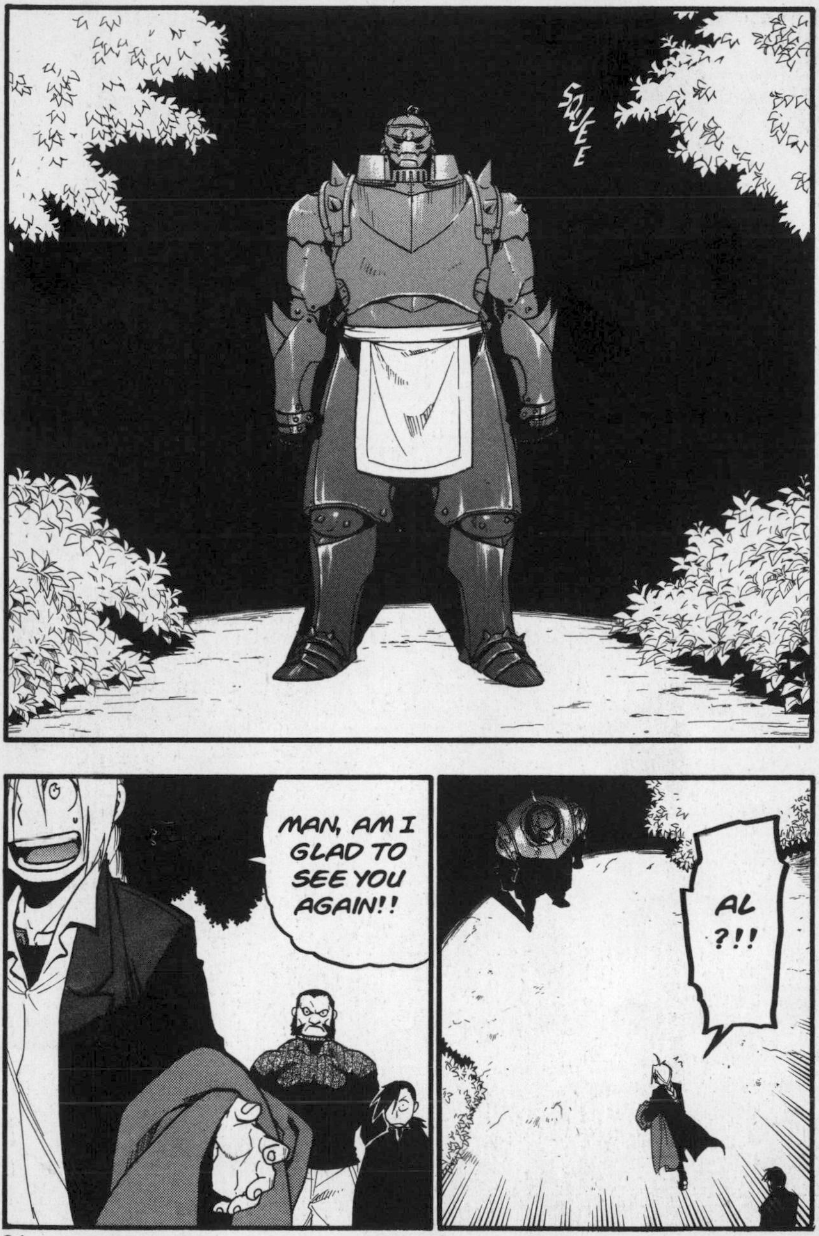
SQUEEE
AL ?!!
MAN, AM I GLAD TO SEE YOU AGAIN!!

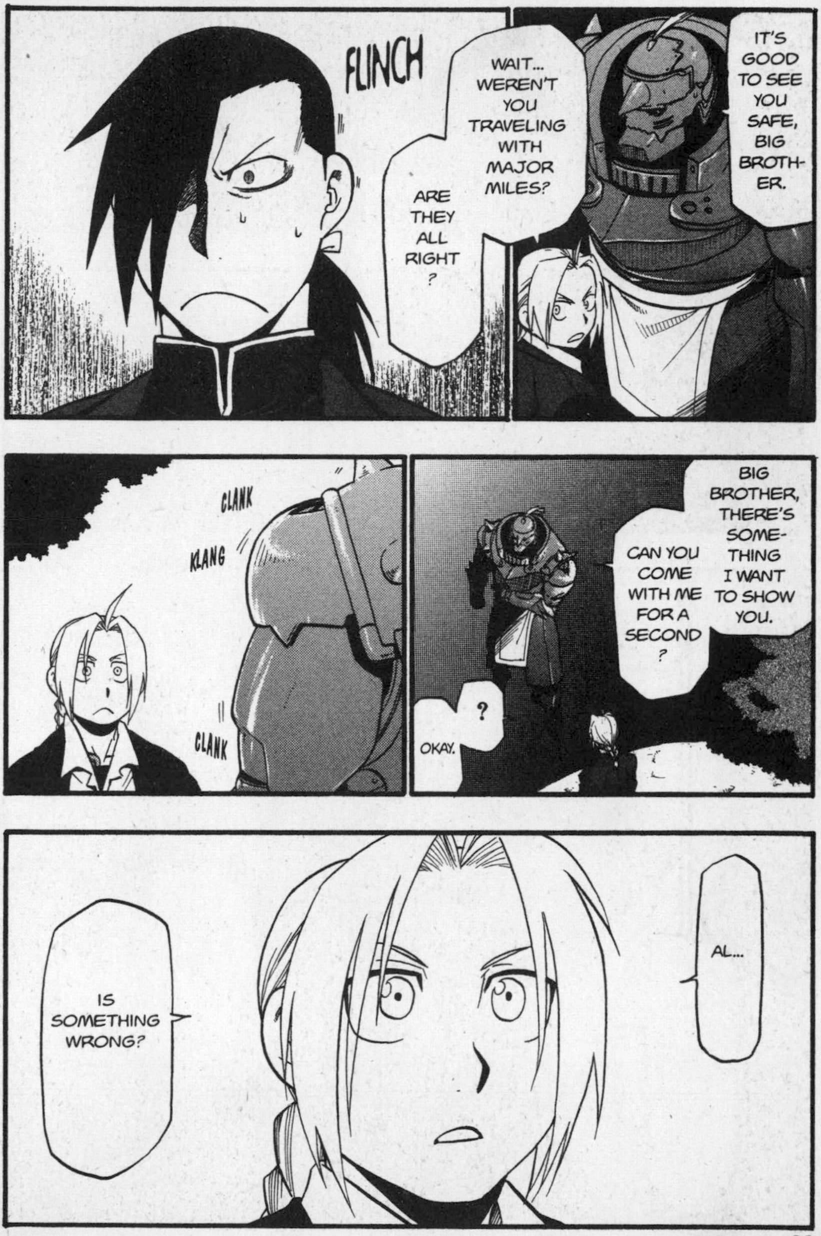
IT'S GOOD TO SEE YOU SAFE, BIG BROTHER.
FLINCH
WAIT... WEREN'T YOU TRAVELING WITH MAJOR MILES?
ARE THEY ALL RIGHT?
BIG BROTHER, THERE'S SOMETHING I WANT TO SHOW YOU.
CAN YOU COME WITH ME FOR A SECOND?
?
OKAY.
CLANK
KLANG
CLANK
AL...
IS SOMETHING WRONG?

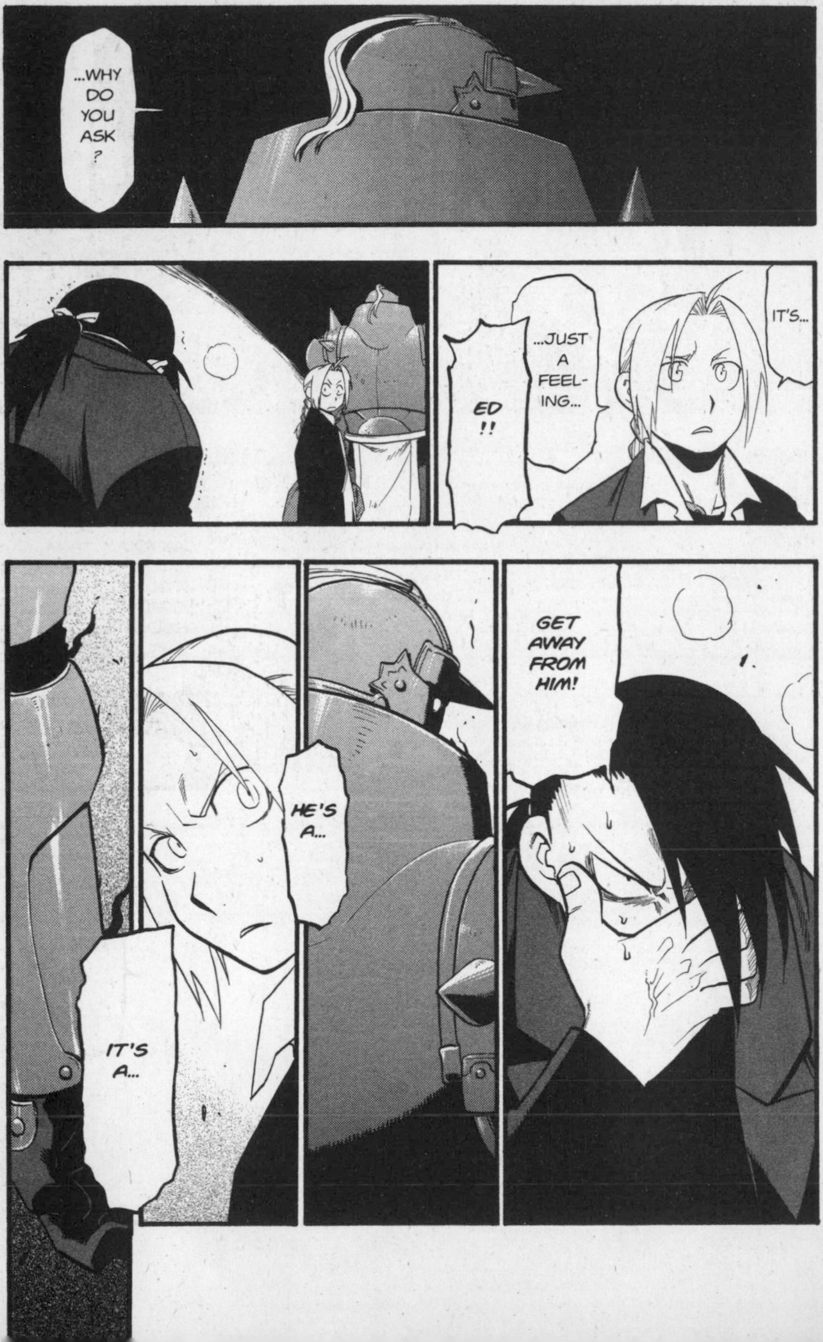
...WHY DO YOU ASK ?
IT'S...
...JUST A FEEL- ING...
ED !!
GET AWAY FROM HIM!
HE'S A...
IT'S A...

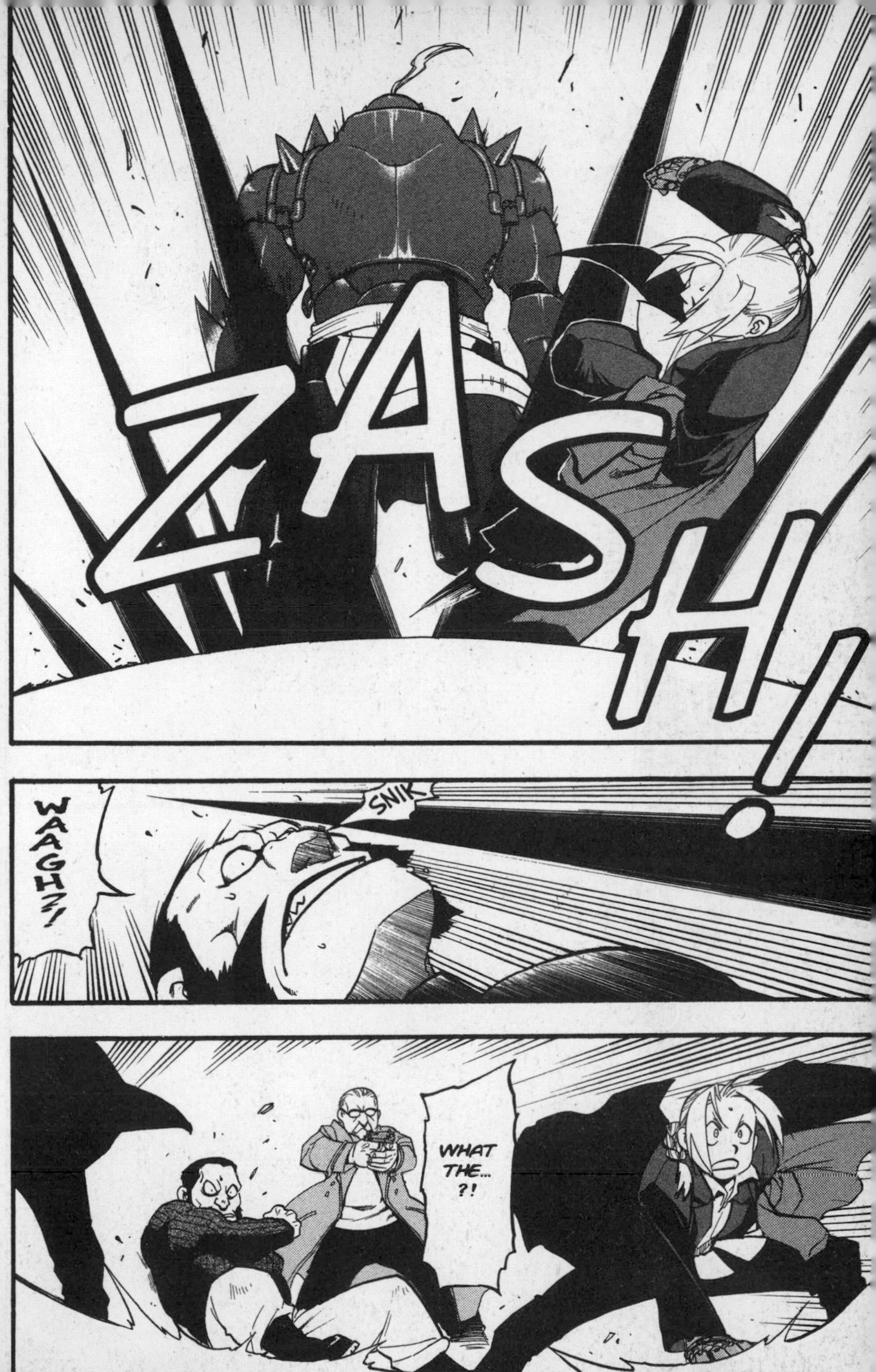
ZASH!!
SNIK
WAAGH?!
WHAT THE... ?!

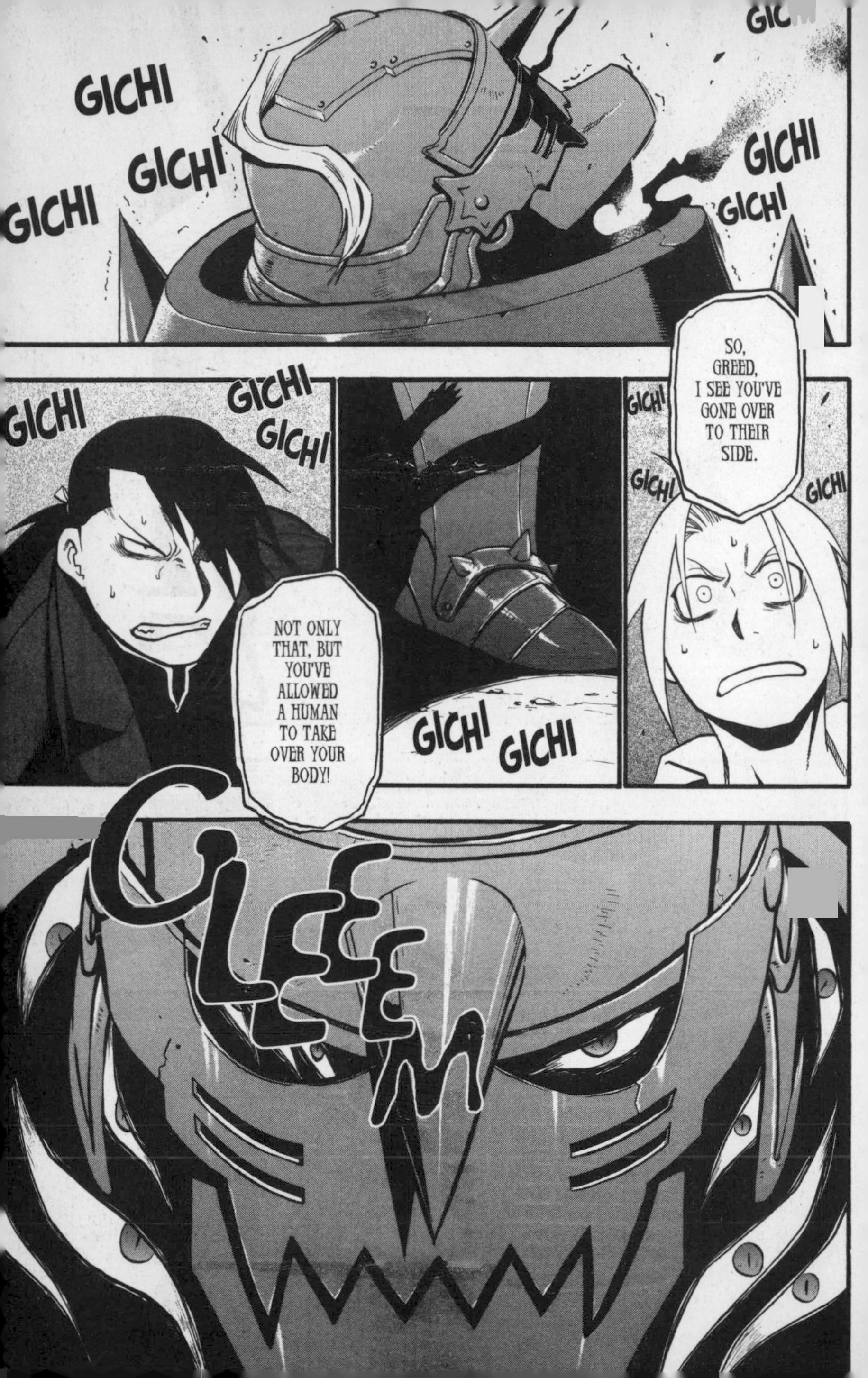
GICHI
GICHI
GICHI
GICHI
GICHI
GICHI
SO, GREED, I SEE YOU'VE GONE OVER TO THEIR SIDE.
GICHI
GICHI
GICHI
GICHI
GICHI
GICHI
GICHI
GICHI
NOT ONLY THAT, BUT YOU'VE ALLOWED A HUMAN TO TAKE OVER YOUR BODY!
GLEEEM

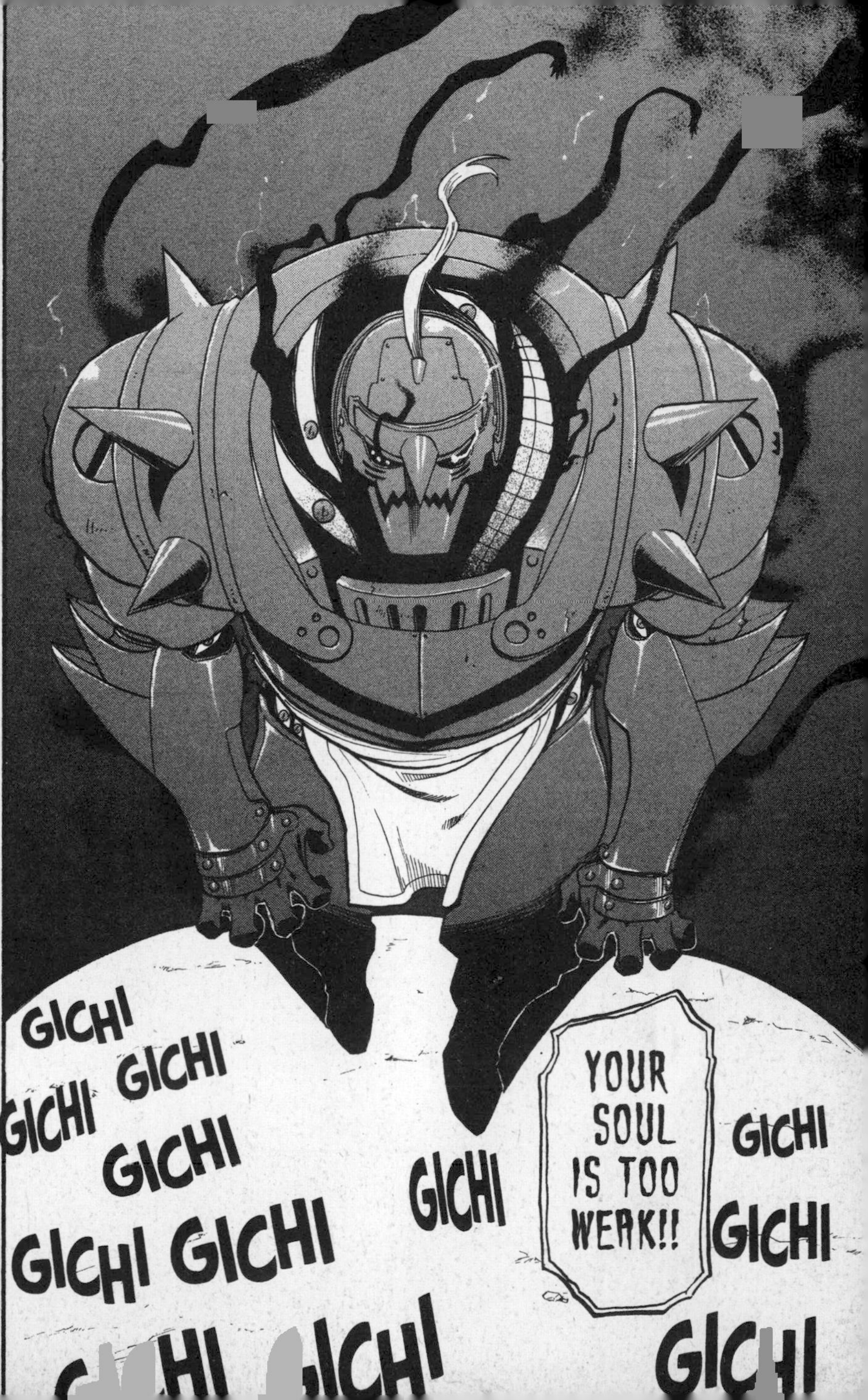
GICHI
GICHI
GICHI
YOUR SOUL IS TOO WEAK!!
GICHI
GICHI
GICHI
GICHI
GICHI
GICHI
GICHI

FULLMETAL
ALCHEMIST

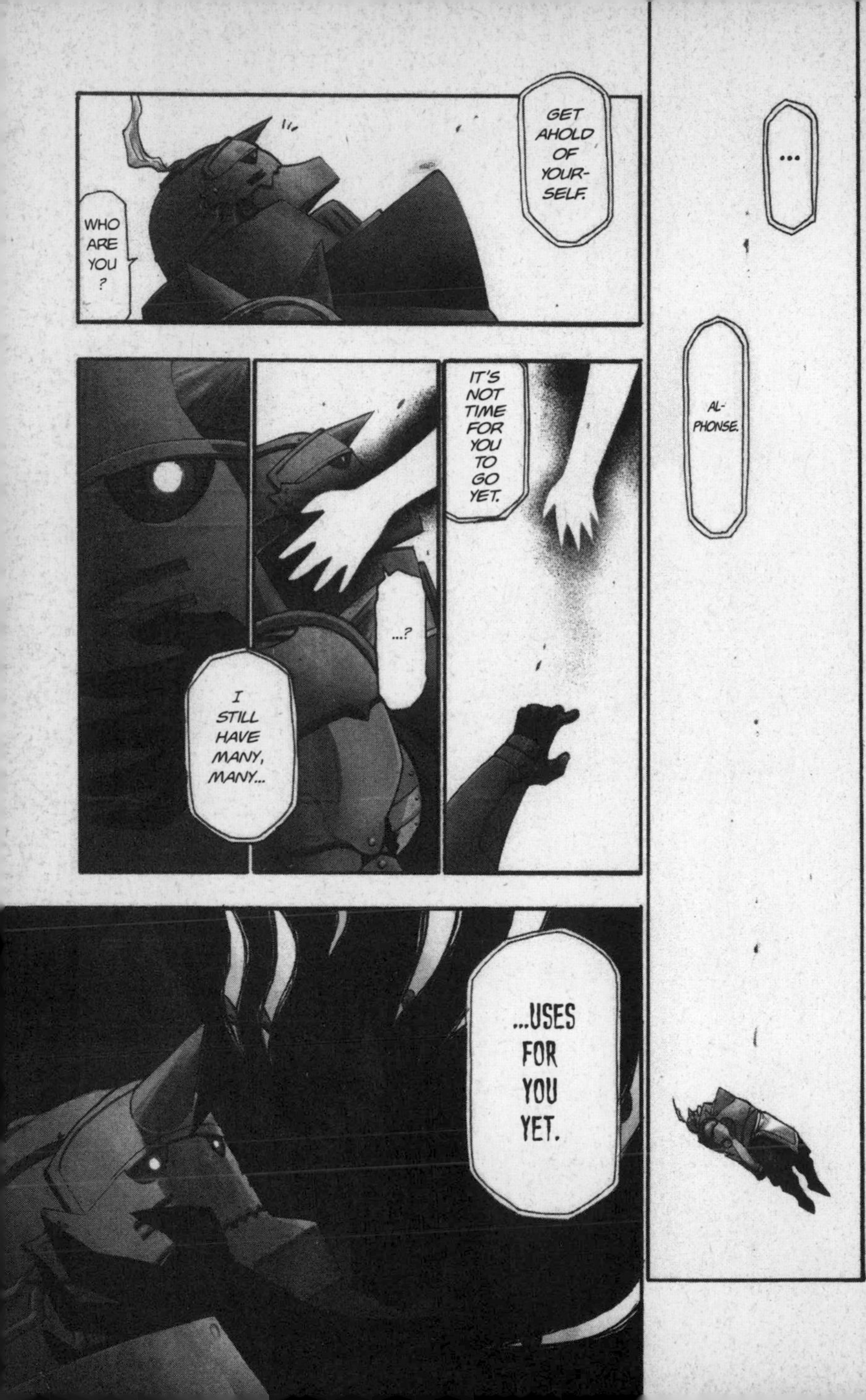
...
AL-PHONSE.
GET AHOLD OF YOUR-SELF.
WHO ARE YOU?
IT'S NOT TIME FOR YOU TO GO YET.
...?
I STILL HAVE MANY, MANY...
...USES FOR YOU YET.

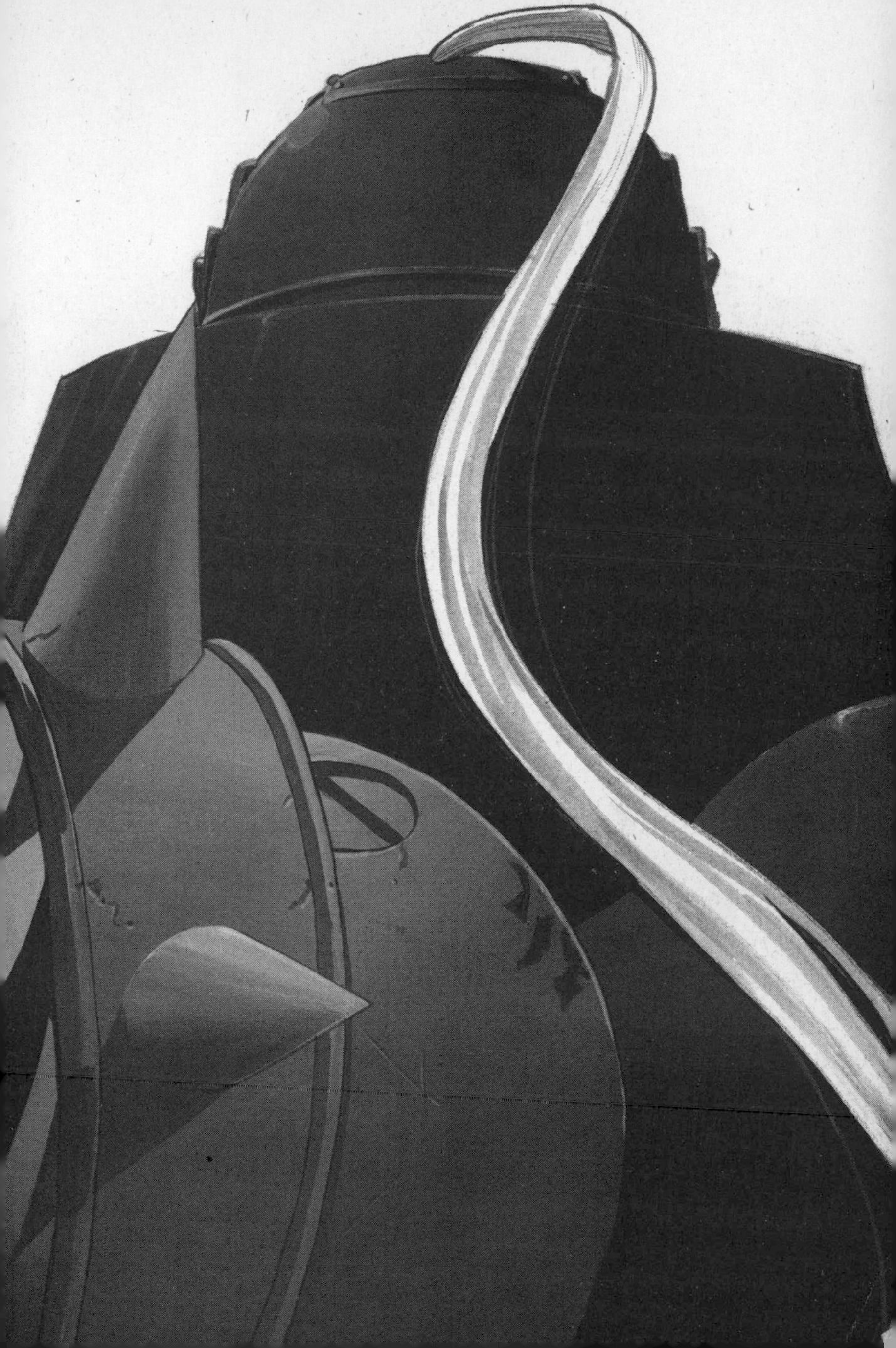

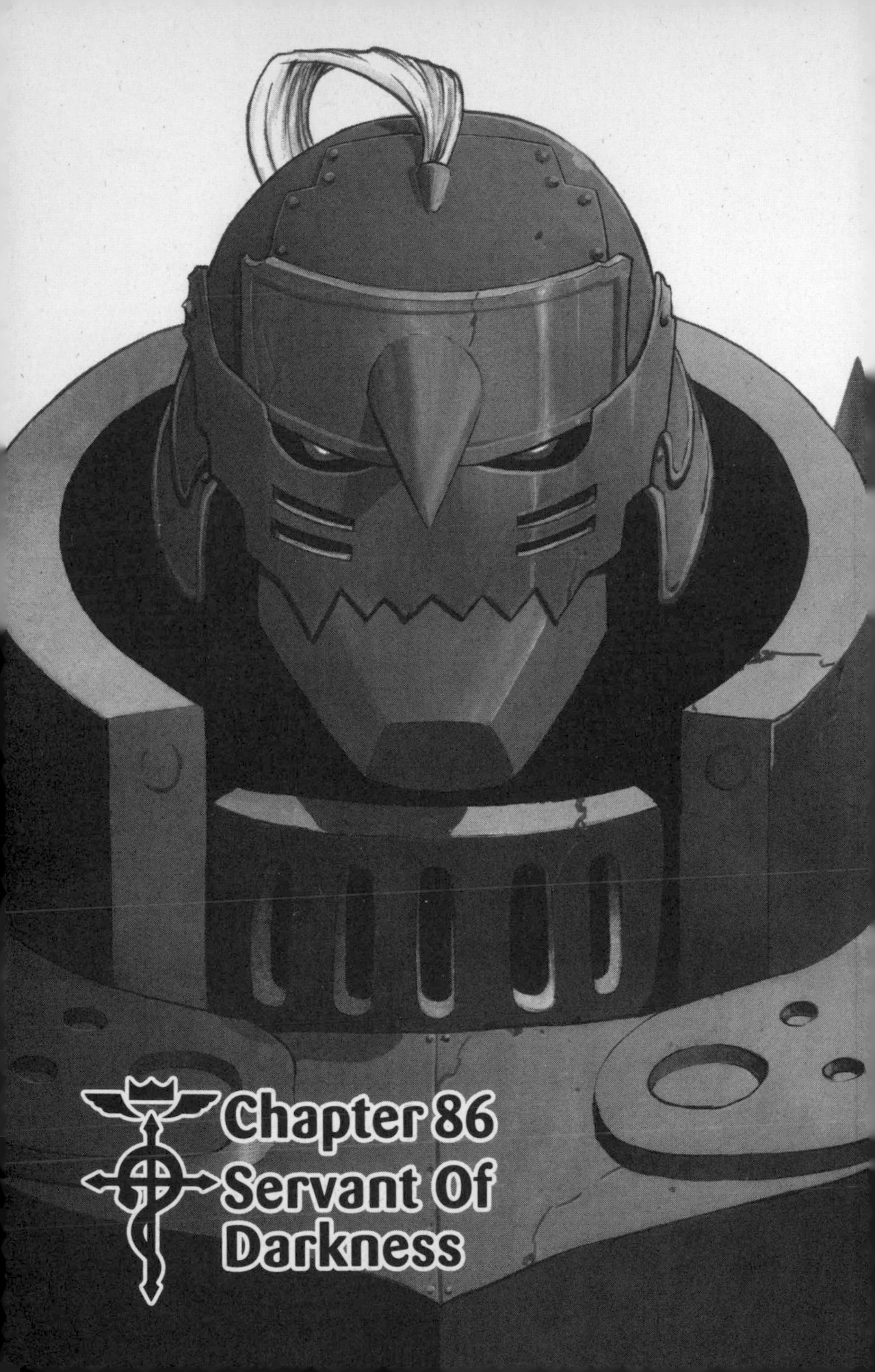
Chapter 86
Servant Of
Darkness

FULLMETAL
ALCHEMIST

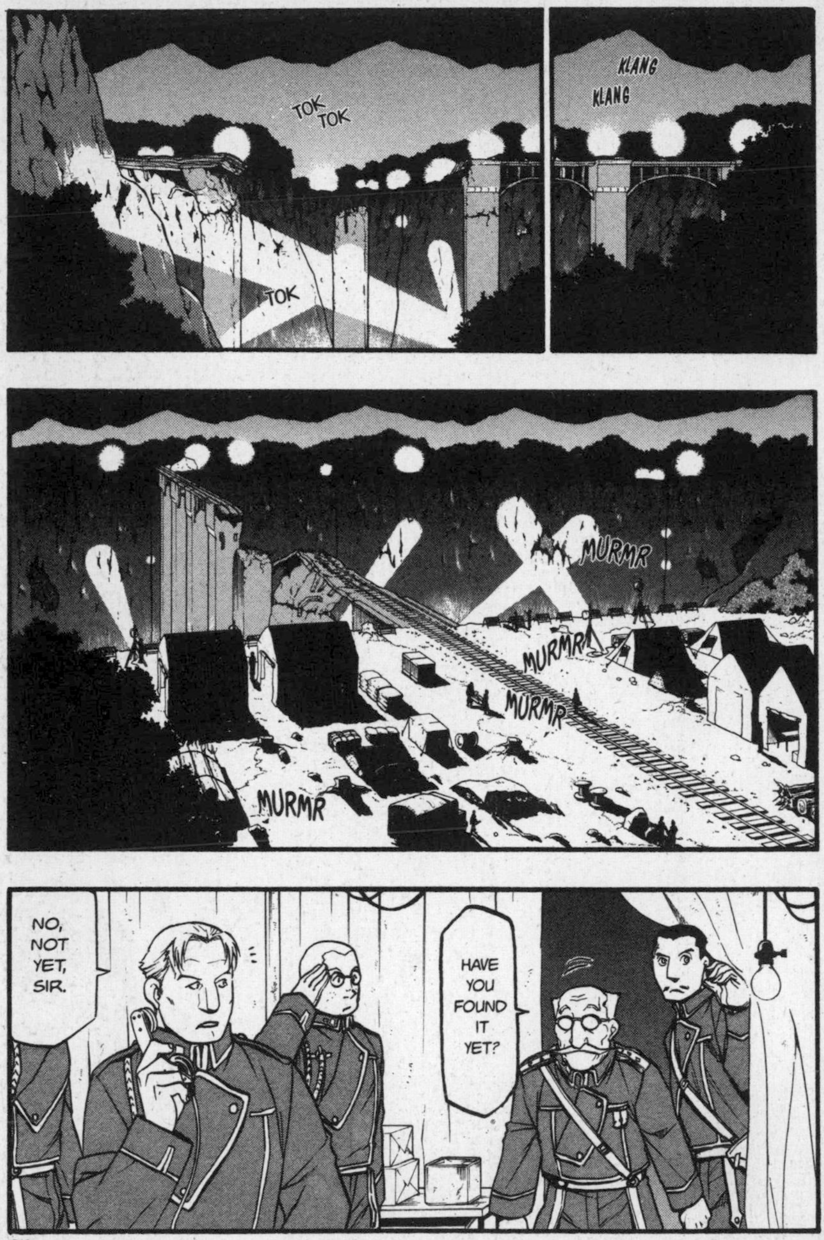
KLANG
KLANG
TOK TOK
TOK
MURMR
MURMR
MURMR
MURMR
HAVE YOU FOUND IT YET?
NO, NOT YET, SIR.

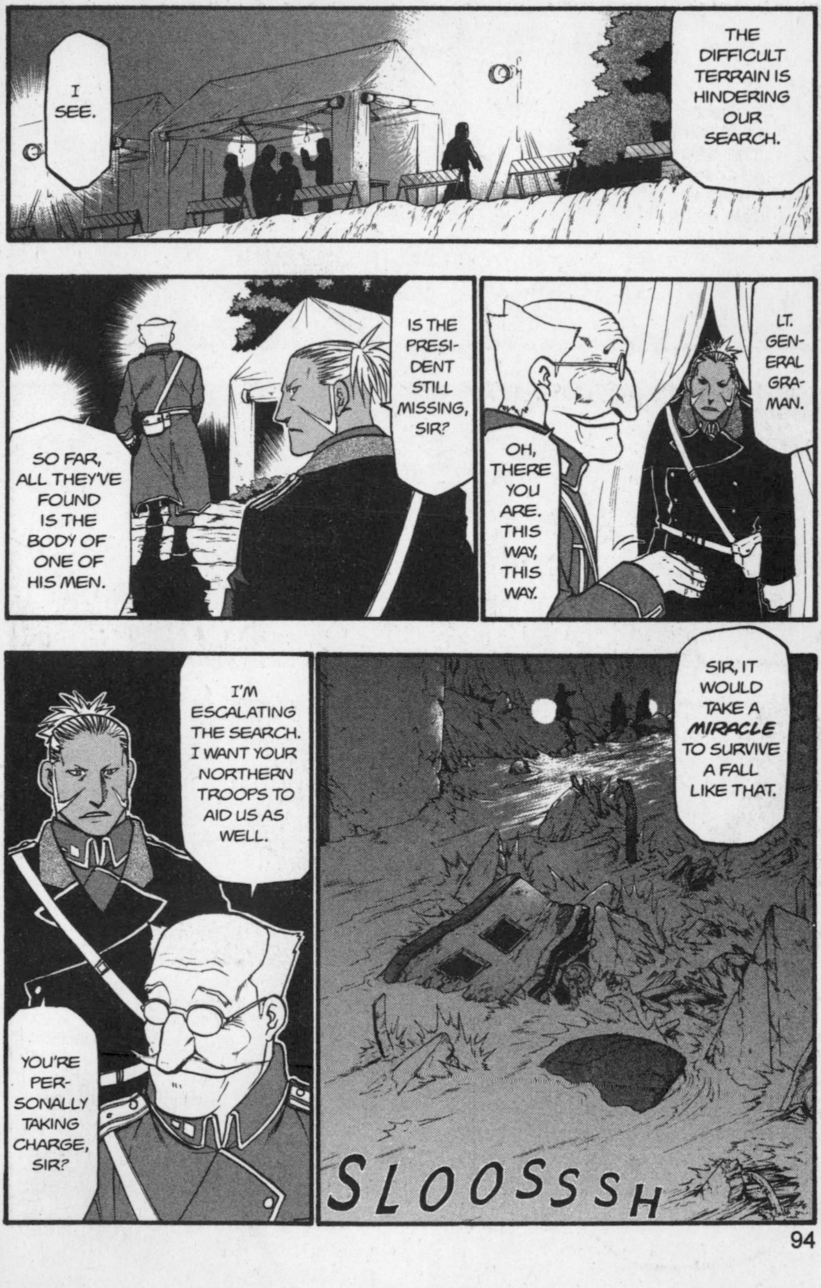
THE DIFFICULT TERRAIN IS HINDERING OUR SEARCH.
I SEE.
LT. GENERAL GRAMAN.
OH, THERE YOU ARE. THIS WAY, THIS WAY.
IS THE PRESIDENT STILL MISSING, SIR?
SO FAR, ALL THEY'VE FOUND IS THE BODY OF ONE OF HIS MEN.
SIR, IT WOULD TAKE A *MIRACLE* TO SURVIVE A FALL LIKE THAT.
SLOOSSSH
I'M ESCALATING THE SEARCH. I WANT YOUR NORTHERN TROOPS TO AID US AS WELL.
YOU'RE PERSONALLY TAKING CHARGE, SIR?

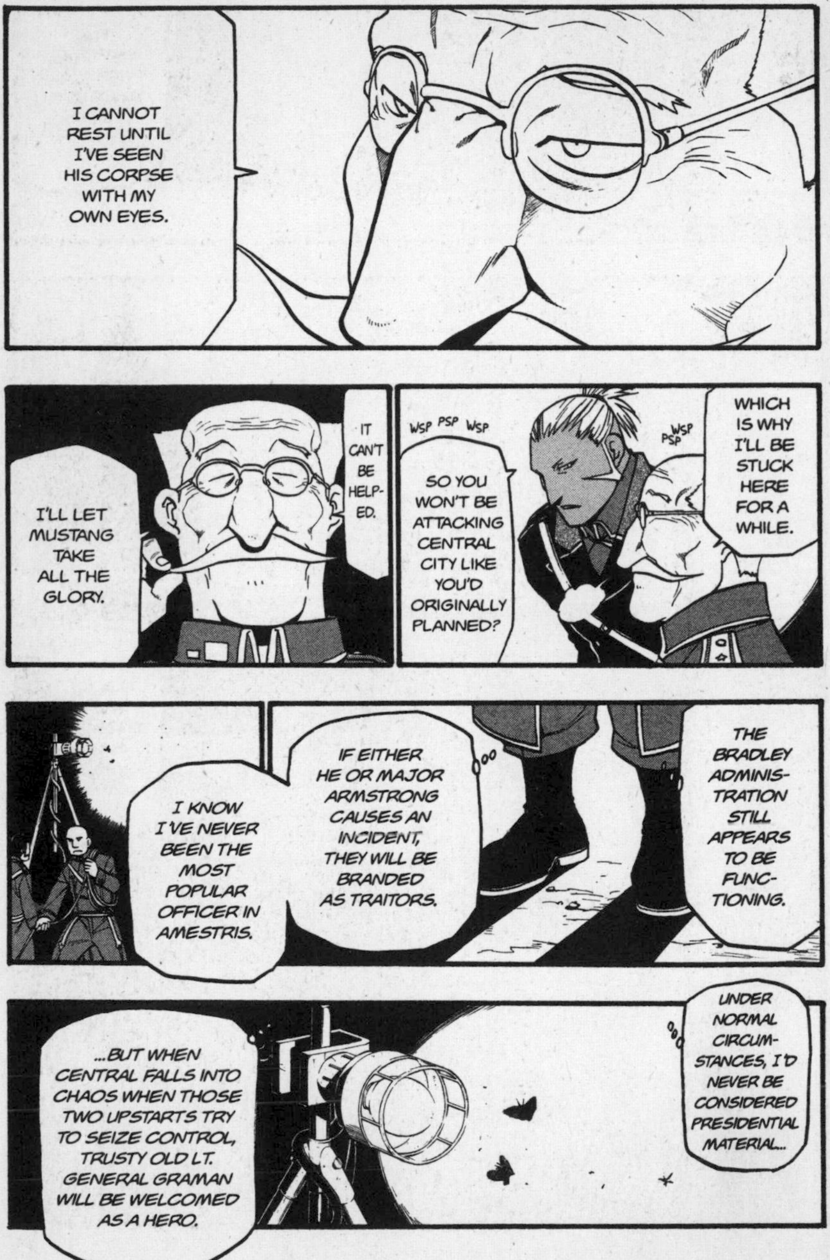
I CANNOT REST UNTIL I'VE SEEN HIS CORPSE WITH MY OWN EYES.
PSP WSP
WHICH IS WHY I'LL BE STUCK HERE FOR A WHILE.
WSP PSP WSP
SO YOU WON'T BE ATTACKING CENTRAL CITY LIKE YOU'D ORIGINALLY PLANNED?
IT CAN'T BE HELP-ED.
I'LL LET MUSTANG TAKE ALL THE GLORY.
THE BRADLEY ADMINIS-TRATION STILL APPEARS TO BE FUNC-TIONING.
IF EITHER HE OR MAJOR ARMSTRONG CAUSES AN INCIDENT, THEY WILL BE BRANDED AS TRAITORS.
I KNOW I'VE NEVER BEEN THE MOST POPULAR OFFICER IN AMESTRIS.
UNDER NORMAL CIRCUM-STANCES, I'D NEVER BE CONSIDERED PRESIDENTIAL MATERIAL...
...BUT WHEN CENTRAL FALLS INTO CHAOS WHEN THOSE TWO UPSTARTS TRY TO SEIZE CONTROL, TRUSTY OLD LT. GENERAL GRAMAN WILL BE WELCOMED AS A HERO.

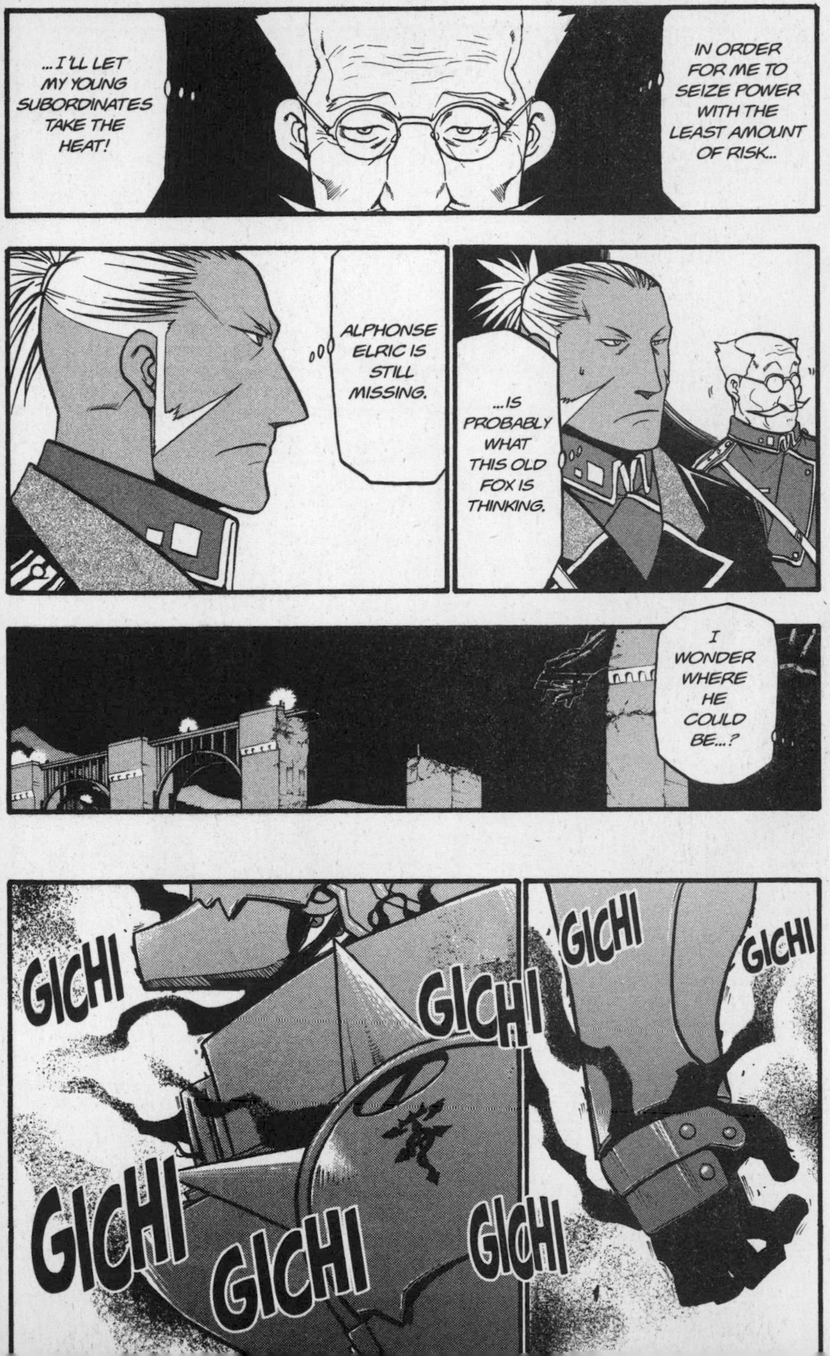
IN ORDER FOR ME TO SEIZE POWER WITH THE LEAST AMOUNT OF RISK..
...I'LL LET MY YOUNG SUBORDINATES TAKE THE HEAT!
...IS PROBABLY WHAT THIS OLD FOX IS THINKING.
ALPHONSE ELRIC IS STILL MISSING.
I WONDER WHERE HE COULD BE...?
GICHI
GICHI
GICHI
GICHI
GICHI
GICHI
GICHI

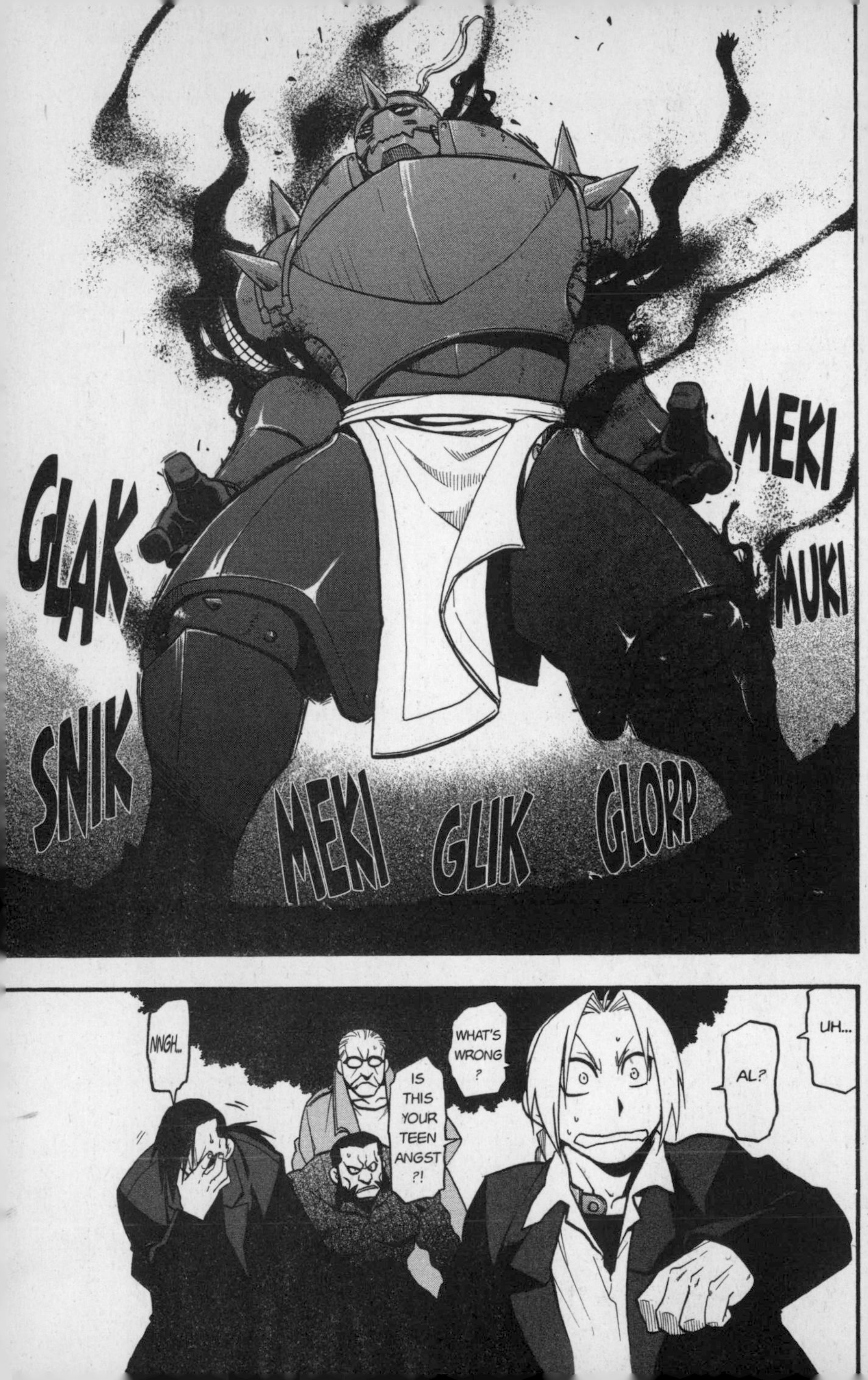
MEKI
MUKI
GLAK
SNIK
GLORP
GLIK
MEKI
UH...
AL?
WHAT'S WRONG?
IS THIS YOUR TEEN ANGST?!
NNGH...

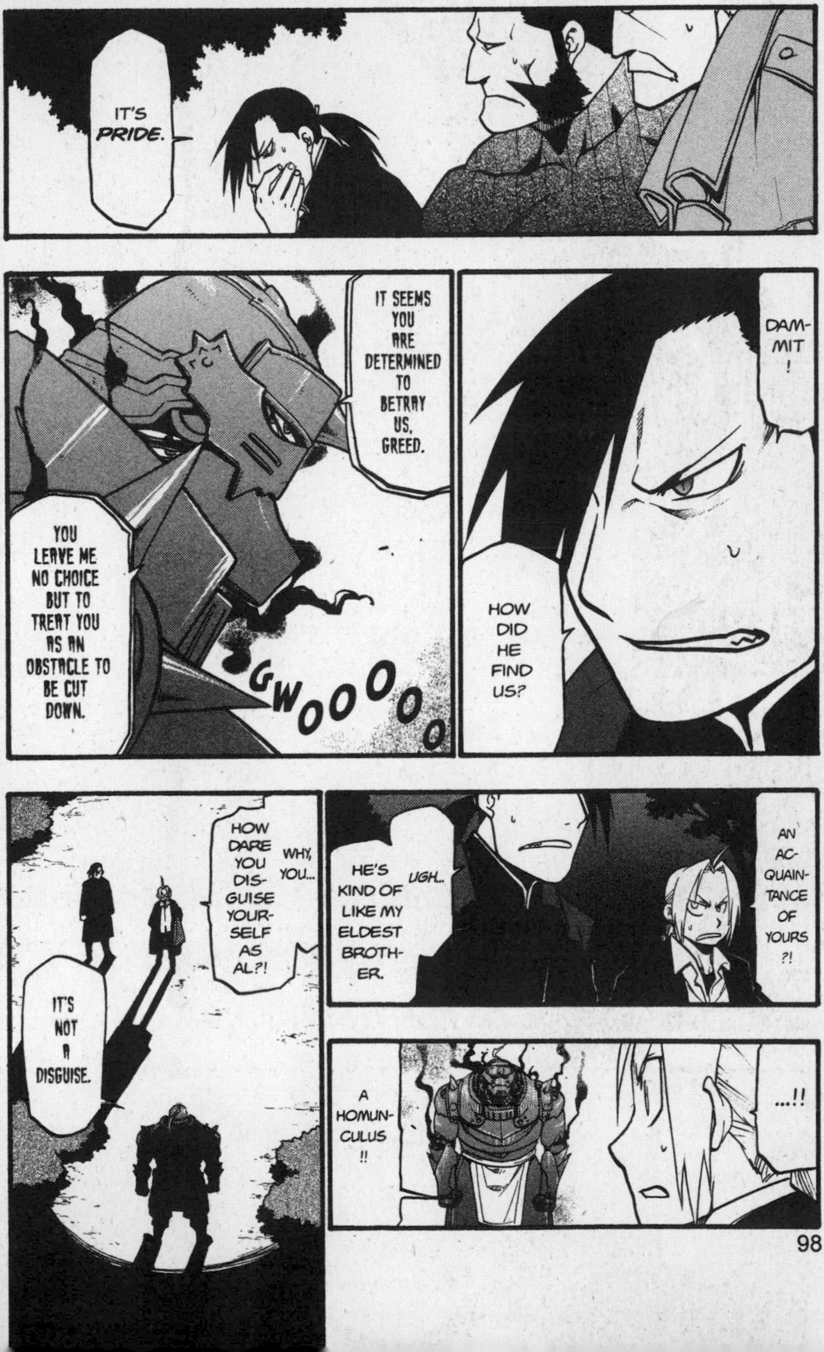
IT'S PRIDE.
DAM-MIT!
HOW DID HE FIND US?
IT SEEMS YOU ARE DETERMINED TO BETRAY US, GREED.
YOU LEAVE ME NO CHOICE BUT TO TREAT YOU AS AN OBSTACLE TO BE CUT DOWN.
GWOOOOOO
AN AC-QUAIN-TANCE OF YOURS?!
UGH...
HE'S KIND OF LIKE MY ELDEST BROTH-ER.
...!!
A HOMUN-CULUS!!
WHY, YOU...
HOW DARE YOU DIS-GUISE YOUR-SELF AS AL?!
IT'S NOT A DISGUISE.

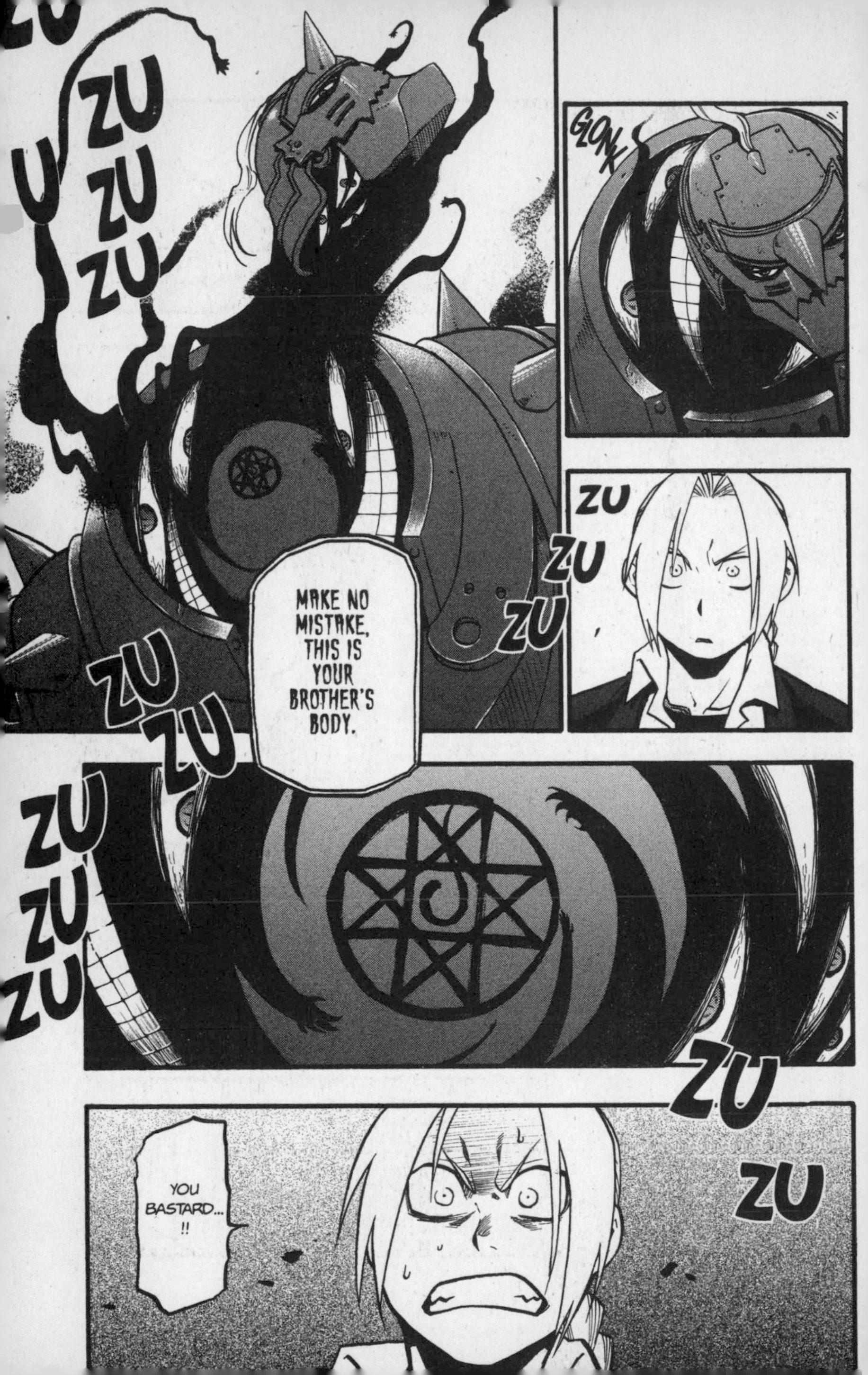
GLONK
ZU
ZU
ZU
ZU
ZU
ZU
ZU
U
MAKE NO MISTAKE, THIS IS YOUR BROTHER'S BODY.
ZU
ZU
ZU
ZU
ZU
ZU
ZU
ZU
YOU BASTARD... !!

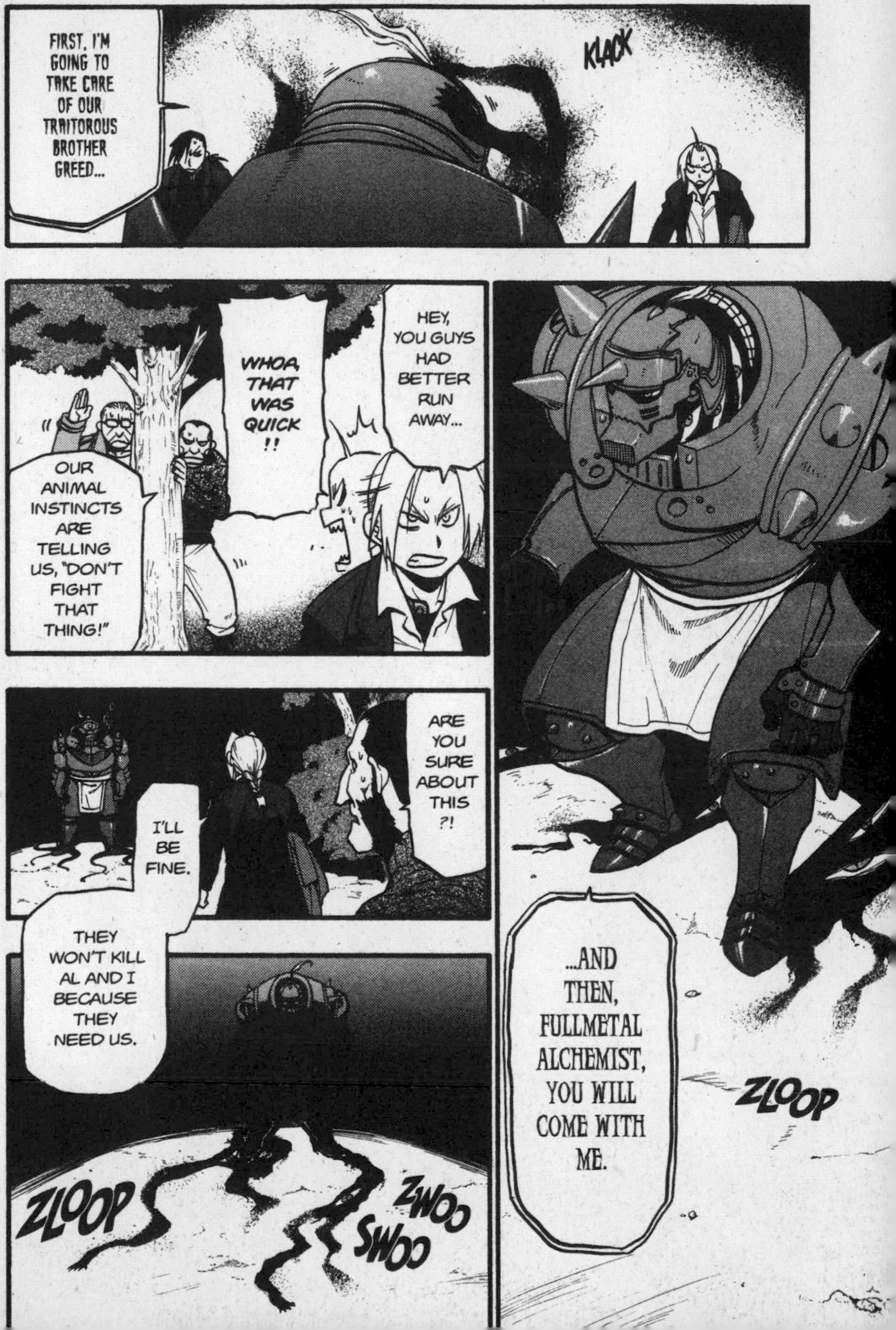
KLACK
FIRST, I'M GOING TO TAKE CARE OF OUR TRAITOROUS BROTHER GREED...
...AND THEN, FULLMETAL ALCHEMIST, YOU WILL COME WITH ME.
ZLOOP
HEY, YOU GUYS HAD BETTER RUN AWAY...
WHOA, THAT WAS QUICK!!
OUR ANIMAL INSTINCTS ARE TELLING US, "DON'T FIGHT THAT THING!"
ARE YOU SURE ABOUT THIS?!
I'LL BE FINE.
THEY WON'T KILL AL AND I BECAUSE THEY NEED US.
ZWOO
SWOO
ZLOOP

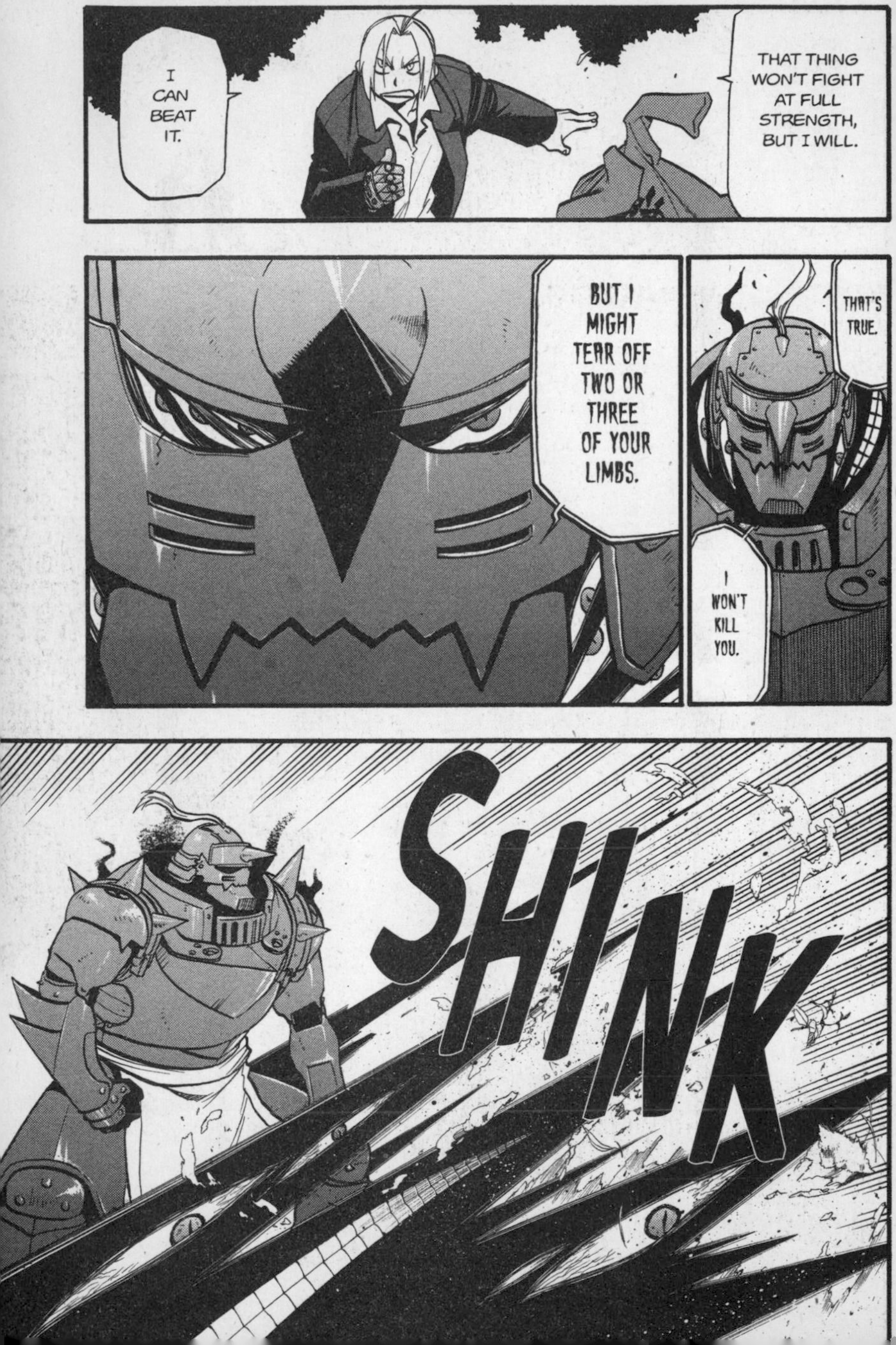
THAT THING WON'T FIGHT AT FULL STRENGTH, BUT I WILL.
I CAN BEAT IT.
THAT'S TRUE.
I WON'T KILL YOU.
BUT I MIGHT TEAR OFF TWO OR THREE OF YOUR LIMBS.
SHINK

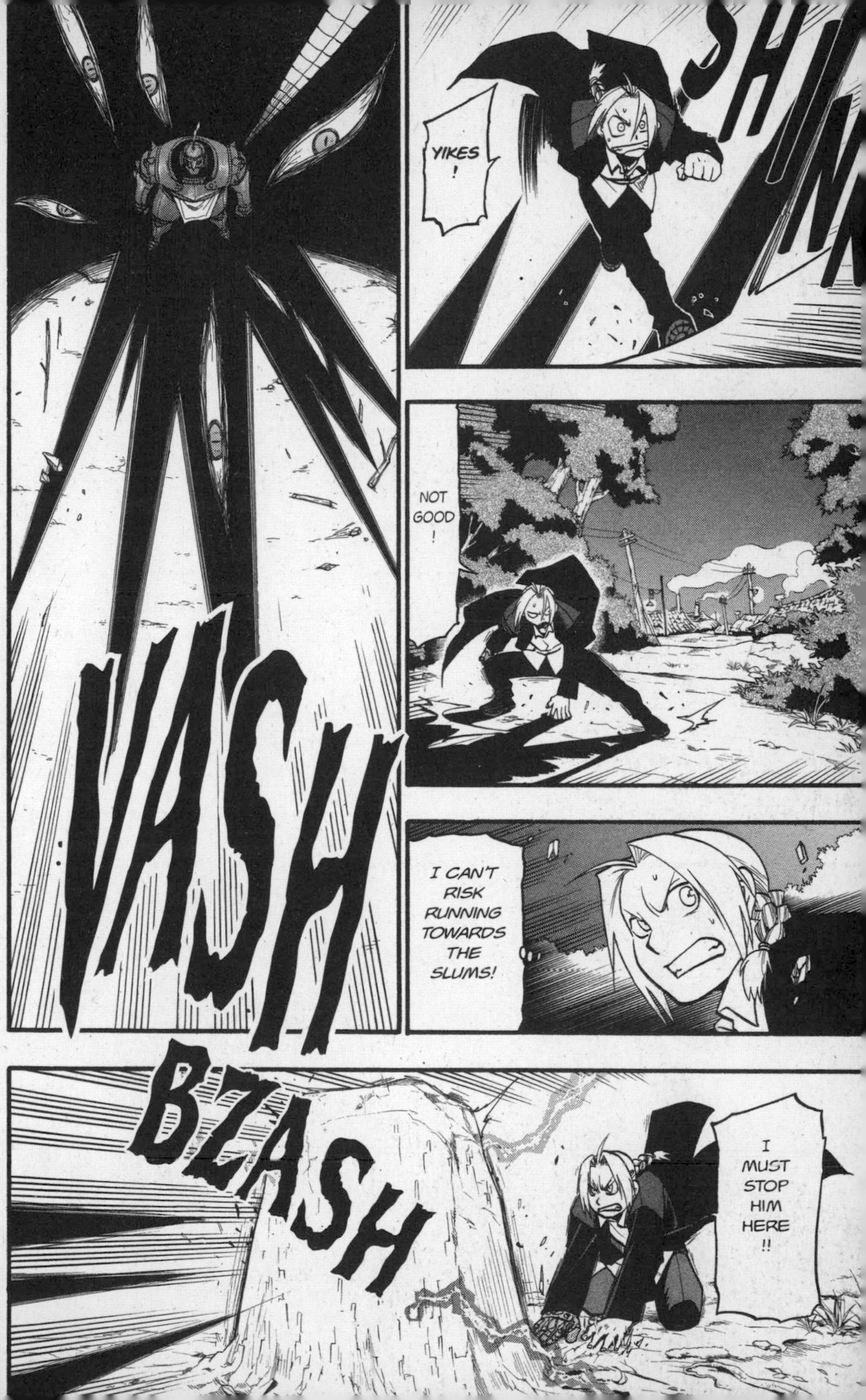
YIKES!
NOT GOOD!
I CAN'T RISK RUNNING TOWARDS THE SLUMS!
VASH
I MUST STOP HIM HERE!!
BZASH

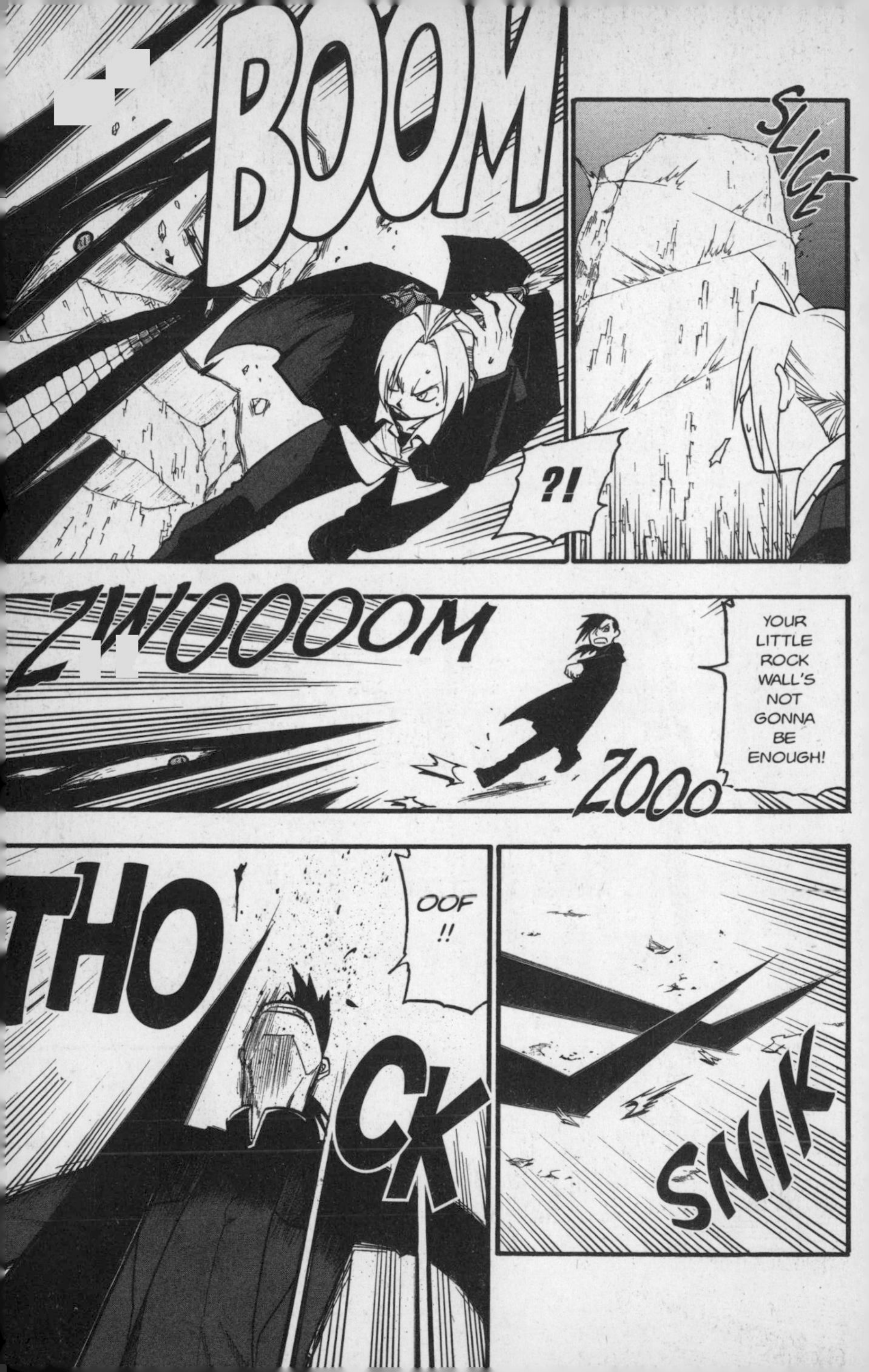
SLICE
BOOM
?!
YOUR LITTLE ROCK WALL'S NOT GONNA BE ENOUGH!
ZOOO
ZWOOOOOM
SNIK
OOF!!
THOCK

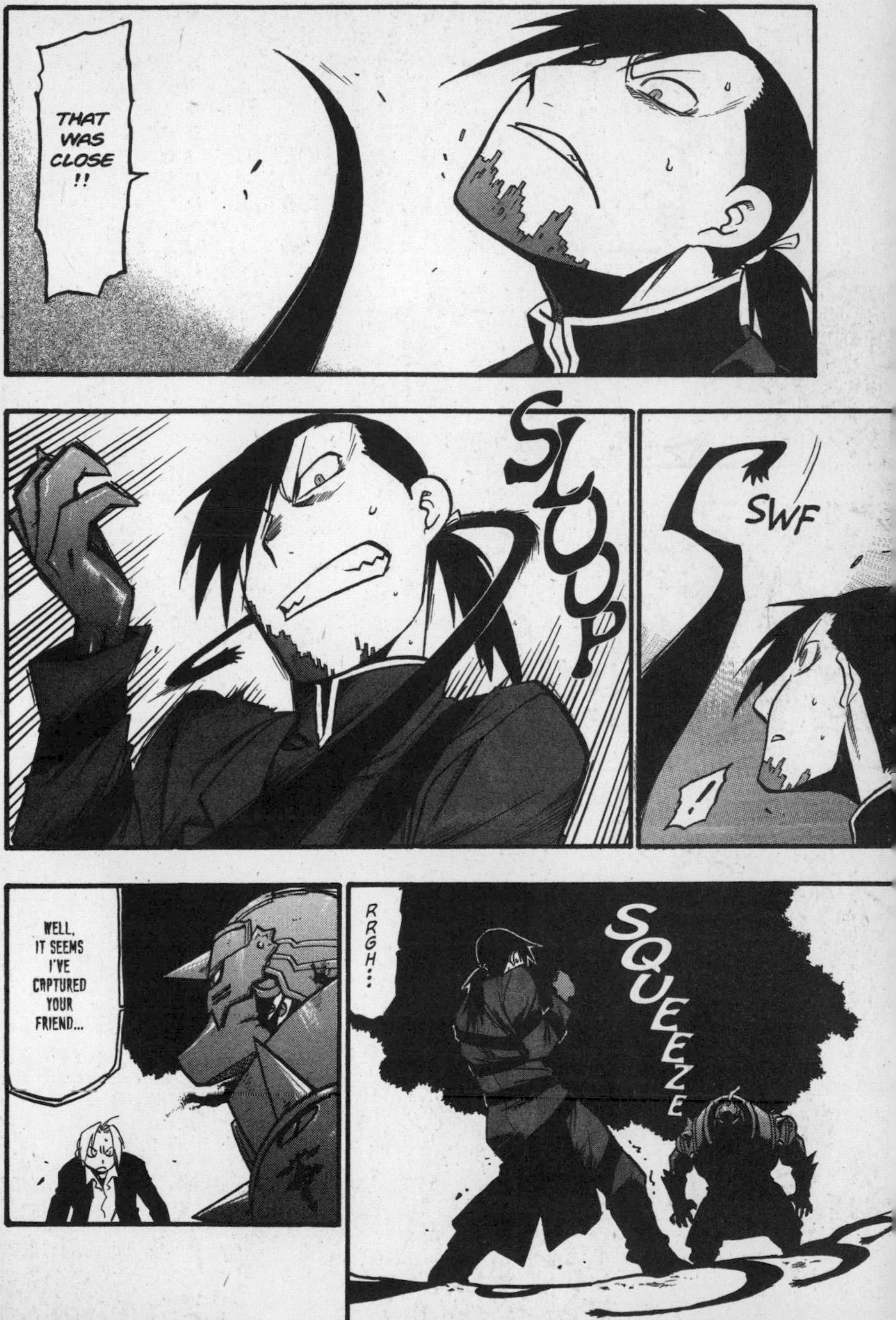
THAT WAS CLOSE !!
SWF
!
SLOOP
RRGH...
SQUEEZE
WELL, IT SEEMS I'VE CAPTURED YOUR FRIEND...

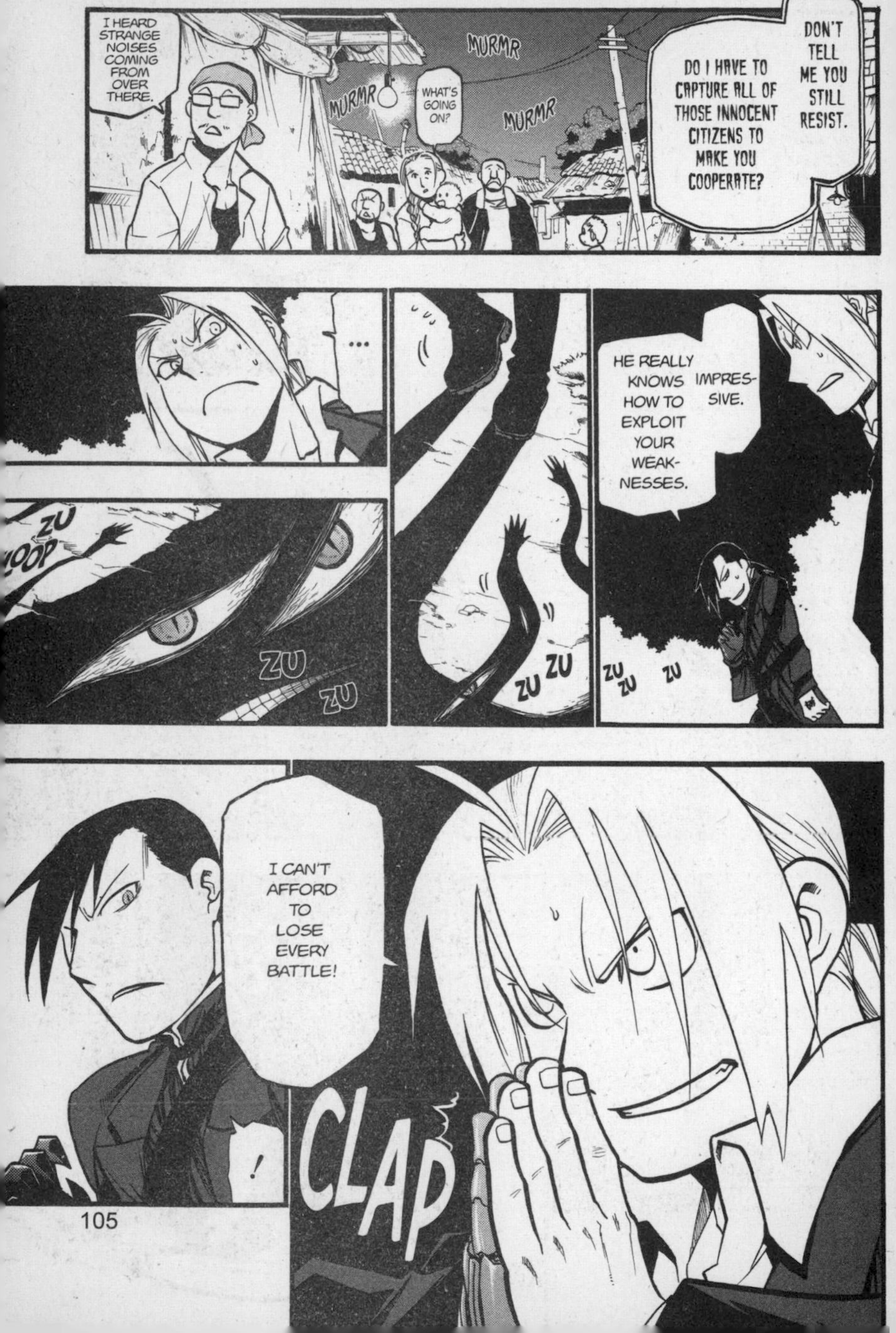
DON'T TELL ME YOU STILL RESIST.
DO I HAVE TO CAPTURE ALL OF THOSE INNOCENT CITIZENS TO MAKE YOU COOPERATE?
MURMR
WHAT'S GOING ON?
MURMR
MURMR
I HEARD STRANGE NOISES COMING FROM OVER THERE.
IMPRESSIVE.
HE REALLY KNOWS HOW TO EXPLOIT YOUR WEAKNESSES.
ZU ZU ZU
ZU ZU
ZU ZU
...
ZU
ZU
ZU
CLAP
I CAN'T AFFORD TO LOSE EVERY BATTLE!
!

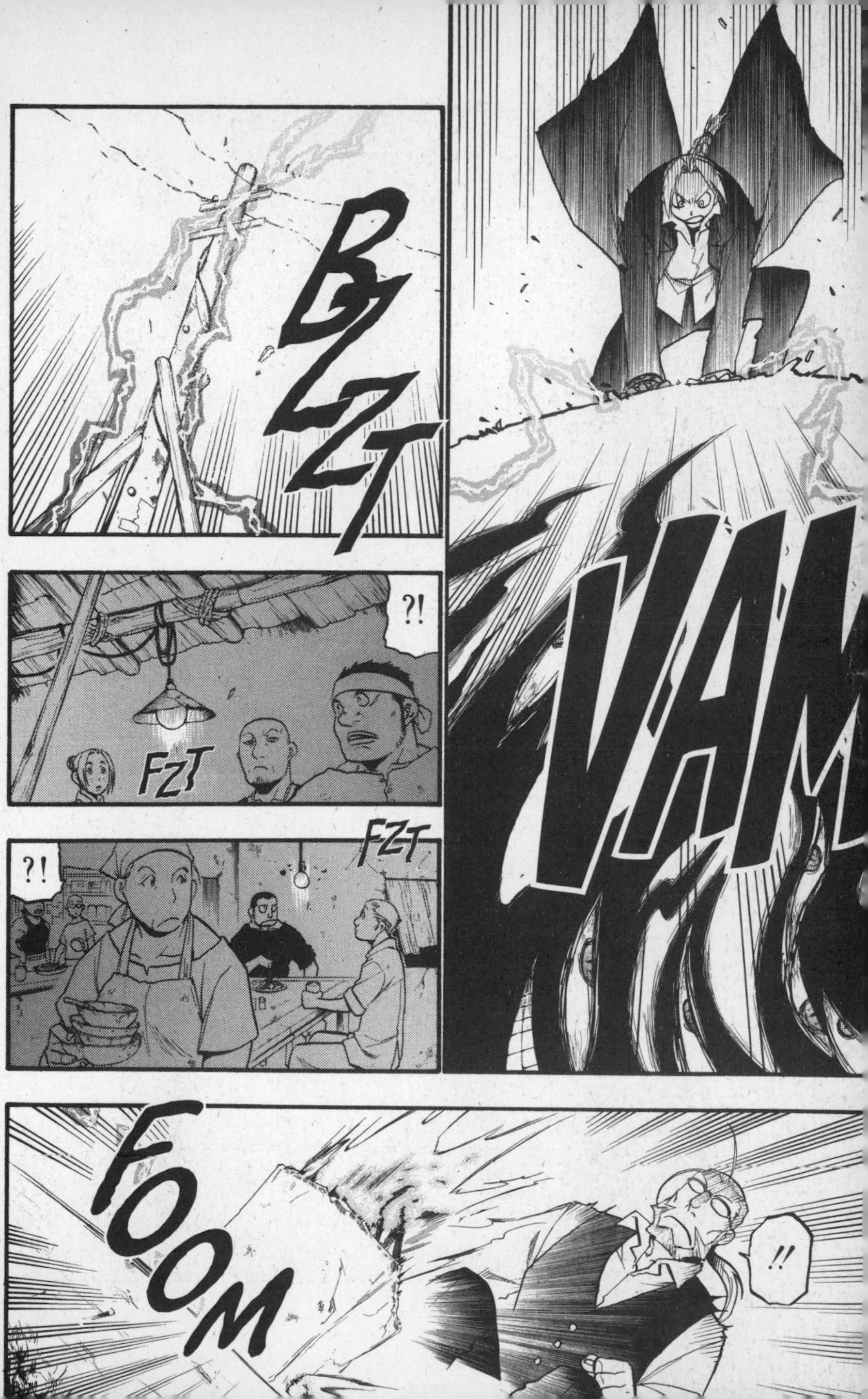
VAM
BZZT
?!
FZT
FZT
?!
!!
FOOM

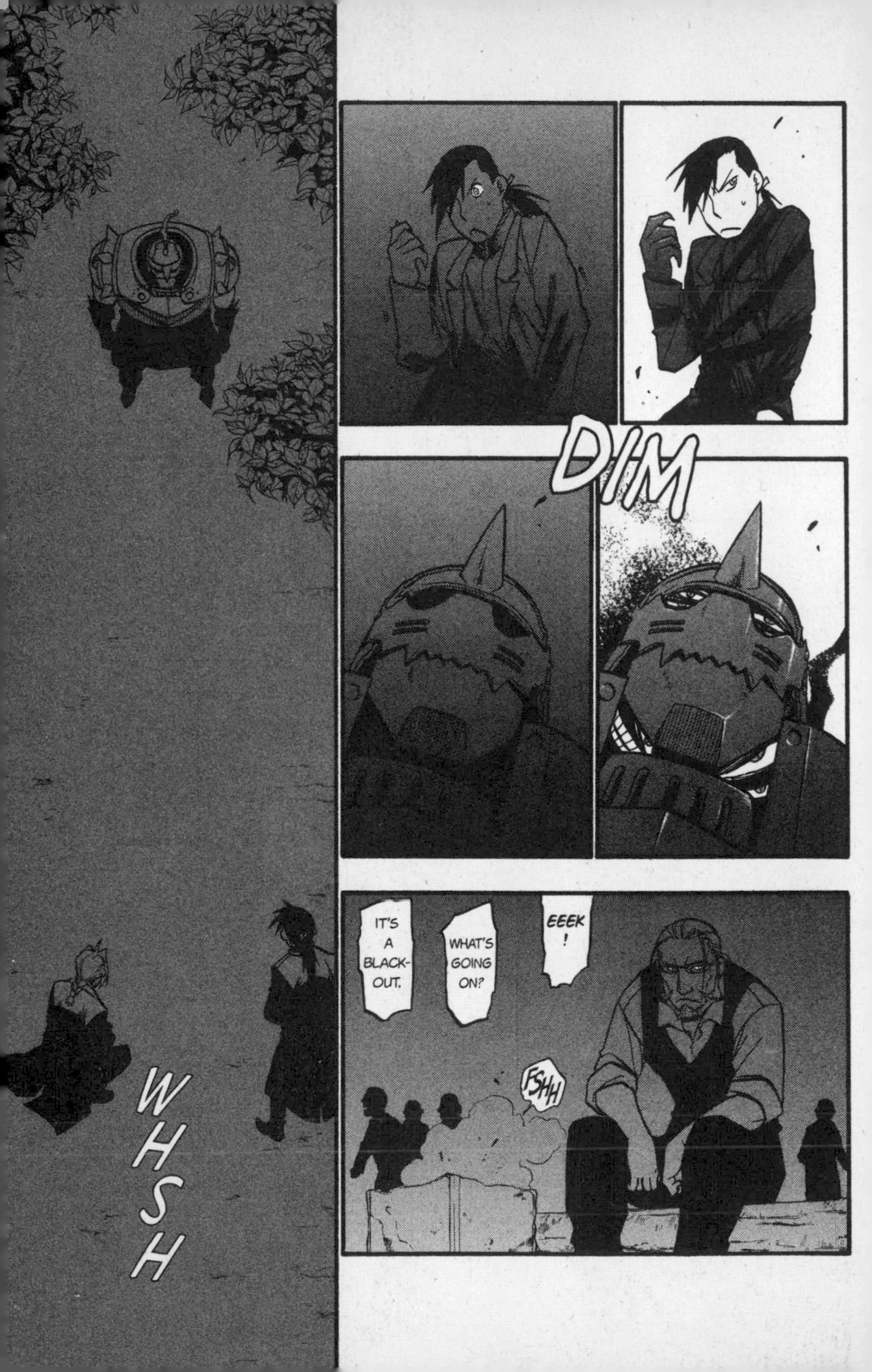
DIM
EEEK!
WHAT'S GOING ON?
IT'S A BLACK-OUT.
FSHH
WHSH

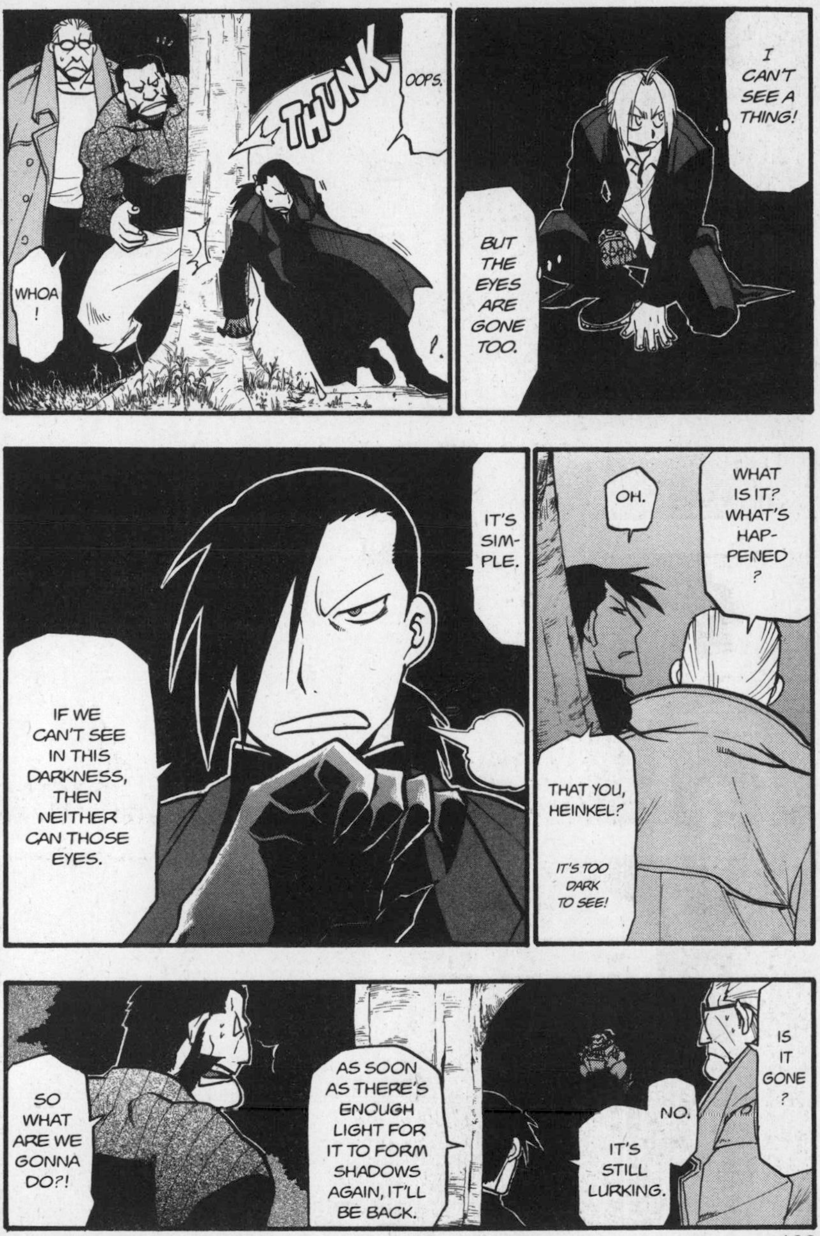
I CAN'T SEE A THING!
BUT THE EYES ARE GONE TOO.
THUNK
OOPS.
WHOA!
WHAT IS IT? WHAT'S HAPPENED?
OH.
THAT YOU, HEINKEL?
IT'S TOO DARK TO SEE!
IT'S SIMPLE.
IF WE CAN'T SEE IN THIS DARKNESS, THEN NEITHER CAN THOSE EYES.
IS IT GONE?
NO.
IT'S STILL LURKING.
AS SOON AS THERE'S ENOUGH LIGHT FOR IT TO FORM SHADOWS AGAIN, IT'LL BE BACK.
SO WHAT ARE WE GONNA DO?!

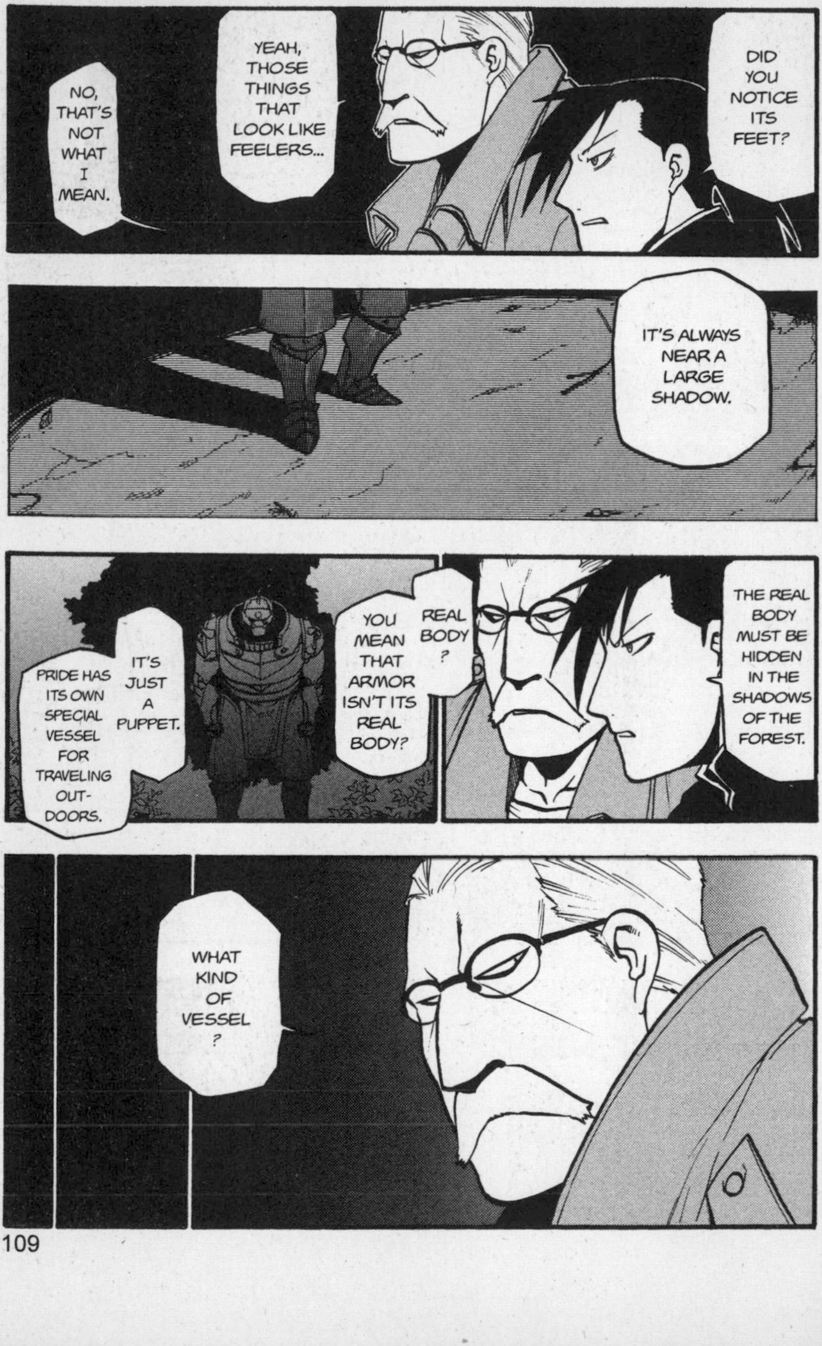
DID YOU NOTICE ITS FEET?
YEAH, THOSE THINGS THAT LOOK LIKE FEELERS...
NO, THAT'S NOT WHAT I MEAN.
IT'S ALWAYS NEAR A LARGE SHADOW.
THE REAL BODY MUST BE HIDDEN IN THE SHADOWS OF THE FOREST.
REAL BODY?
YOU MEAN THAT ARMOR ISN'T ITS REAL BODY?
IT'S JUST A PUPPET.
PRIDE HAS ITS OWN SPECIAL VESSEL FOR TRAVELING OUT-DOORS.
WHAT KIND OF VESSEL?

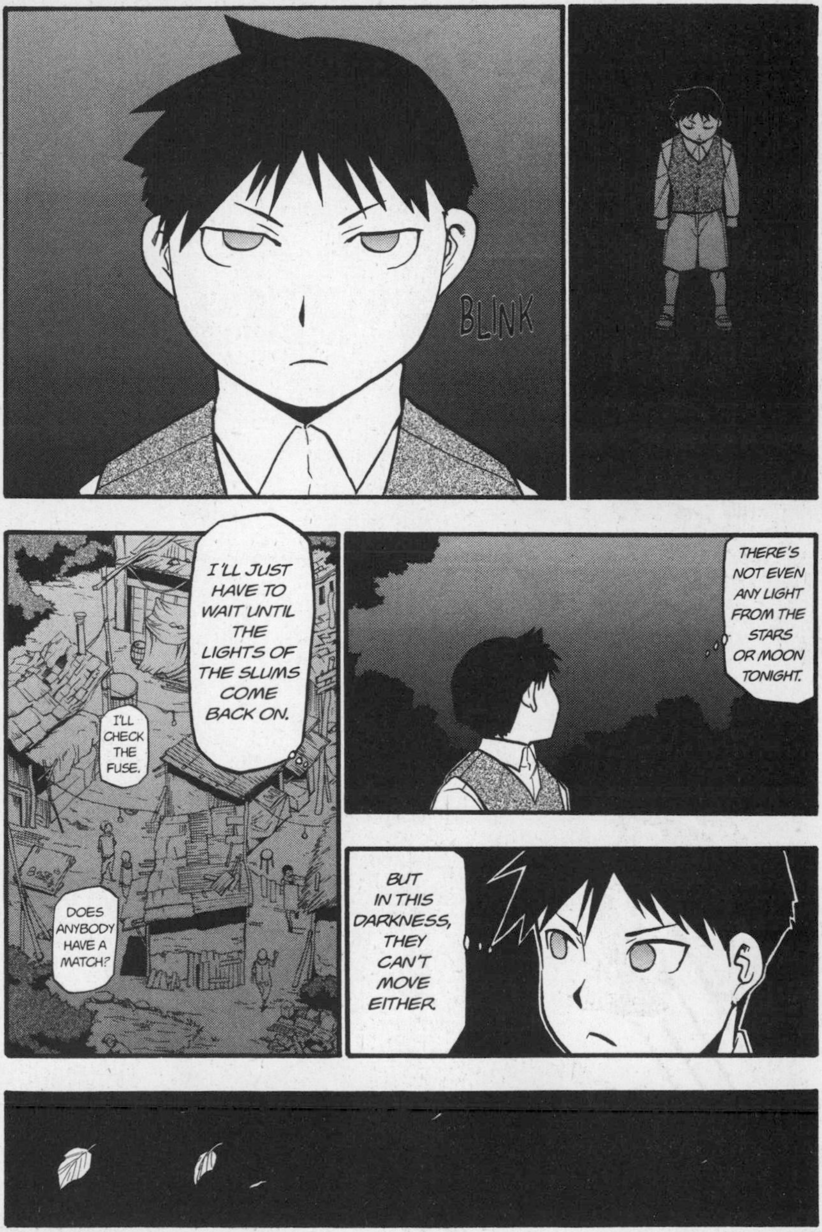
BLINK
THERE'S NOT EVEN ANY LIGHT FROM THE STARS OR MOON TONIGHT.
BUT IN THIS DARKNESS, THEY CAN'T MOVE EITHER.
I'LL JUST HAVE TO WAIT UNTIL THE LIGHTS OF THE SLUMS COME BACK ON.
I'LL CHECK THE FUSE.
DOES ANYBODY HAVE A MATCH?

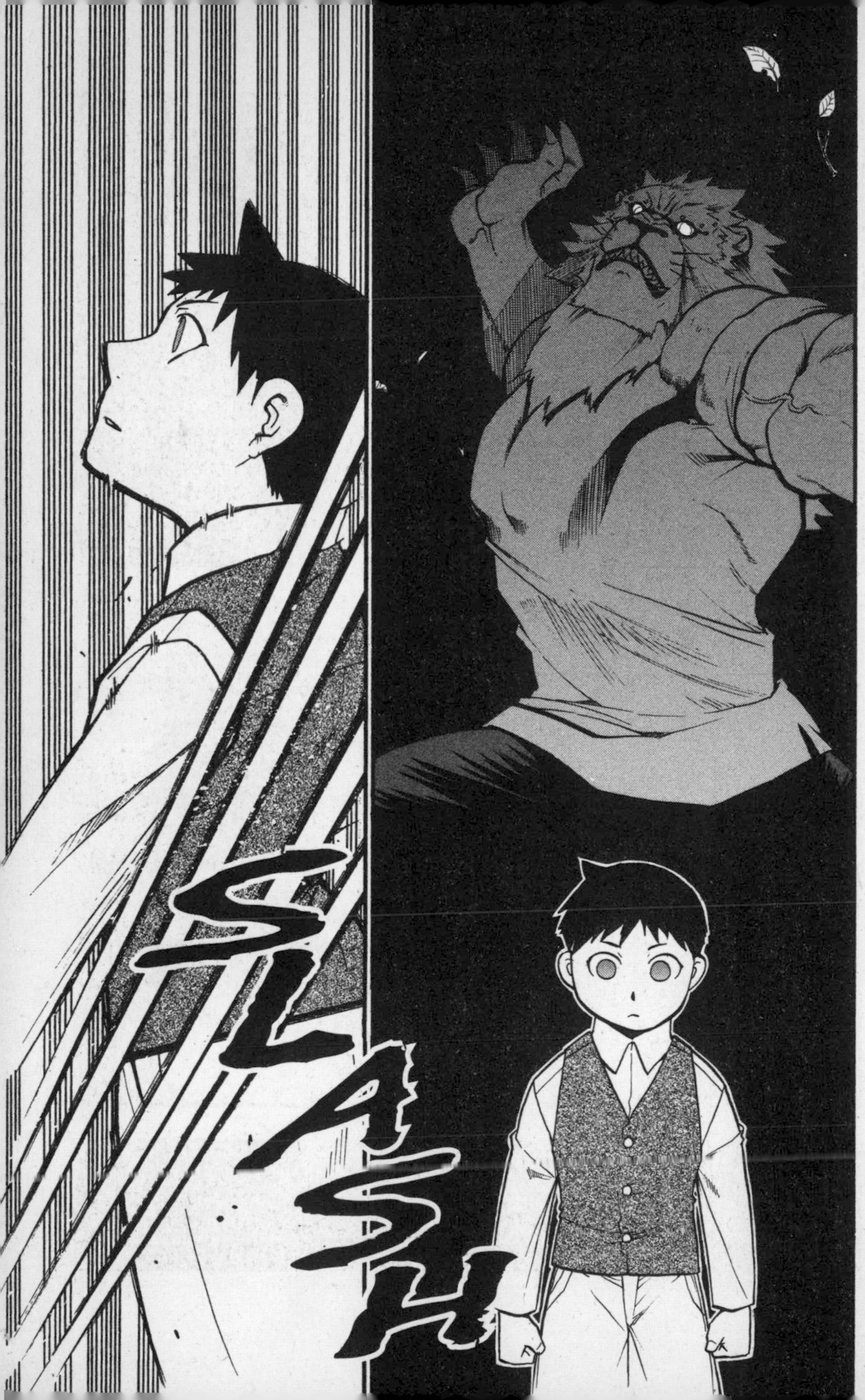
SLASH

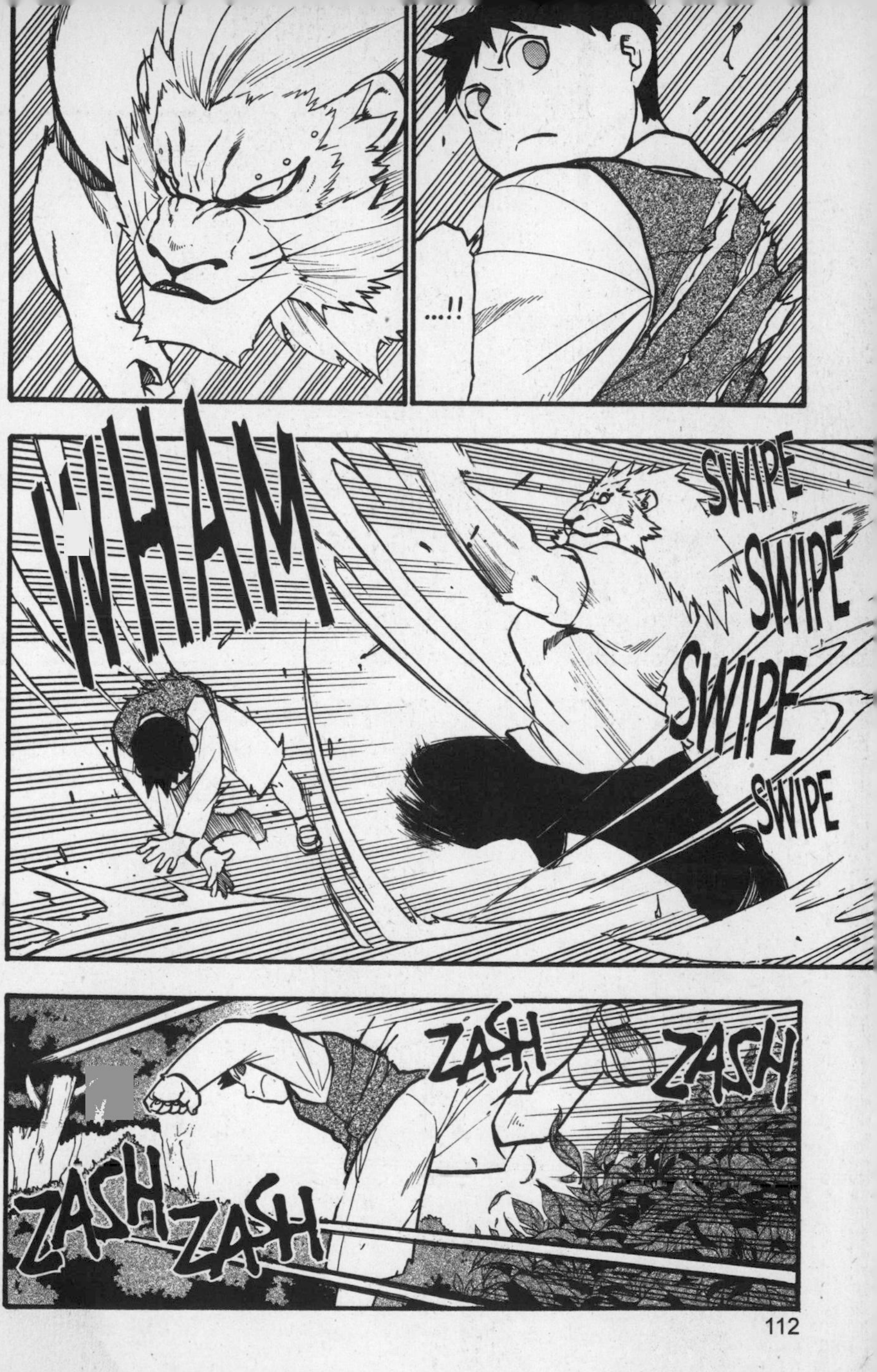
...!!
SWIPE
SWIPE
SWIPE
SWIPE
WHAM
ZASH
ZASH
ZASH
ZASH

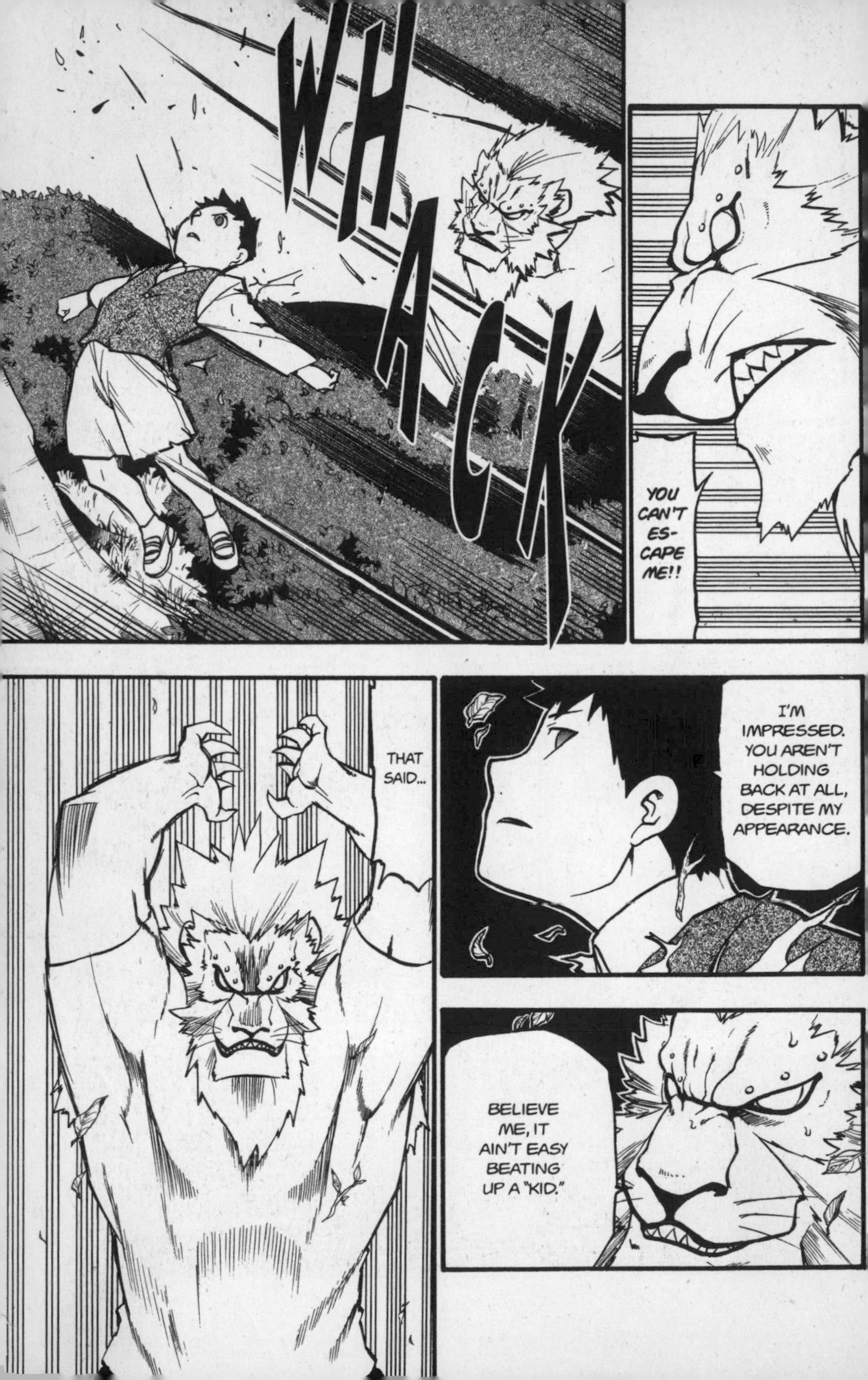
YOU CAN'T ES-CAPE ME!!
WHACK
I'M IMPRESSED. YOU AREN'T HOLDING BACK AT ALL, DESPITE MY APPEARANCE.
BELIEVE ME, IT AIN'T EASY BEATING UP A "KID."
THAT SAID...

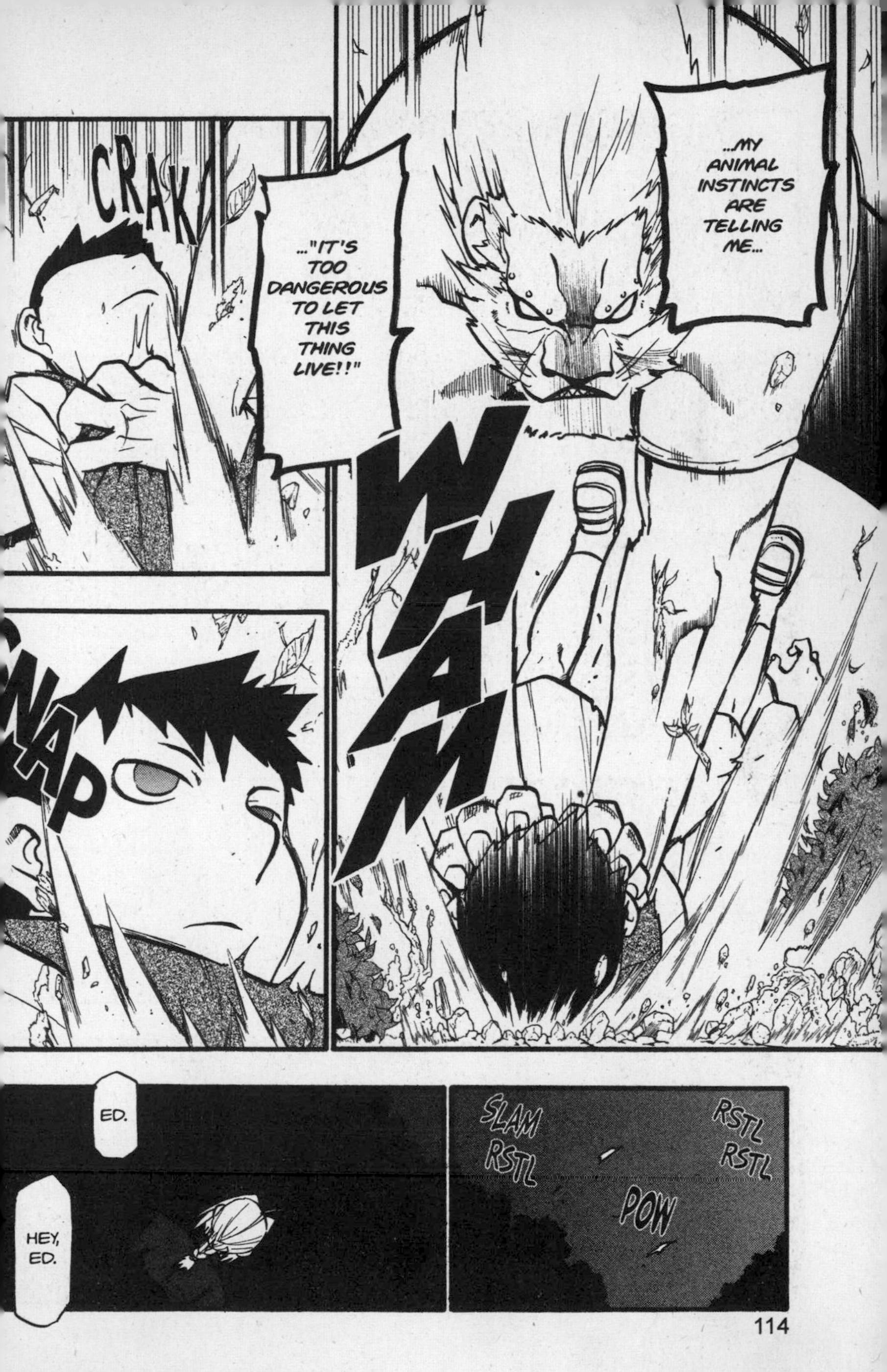
...MY ANIMAL INSTINCTS ARE TELLING ME...
..."IT'S TOO DANGEROUS TO LET THIS THING LIVE!!"
WHAM
CRAK
SNAP
RSTL RSTL
SLAM RSTL
POW
ED.
HEY, ED.

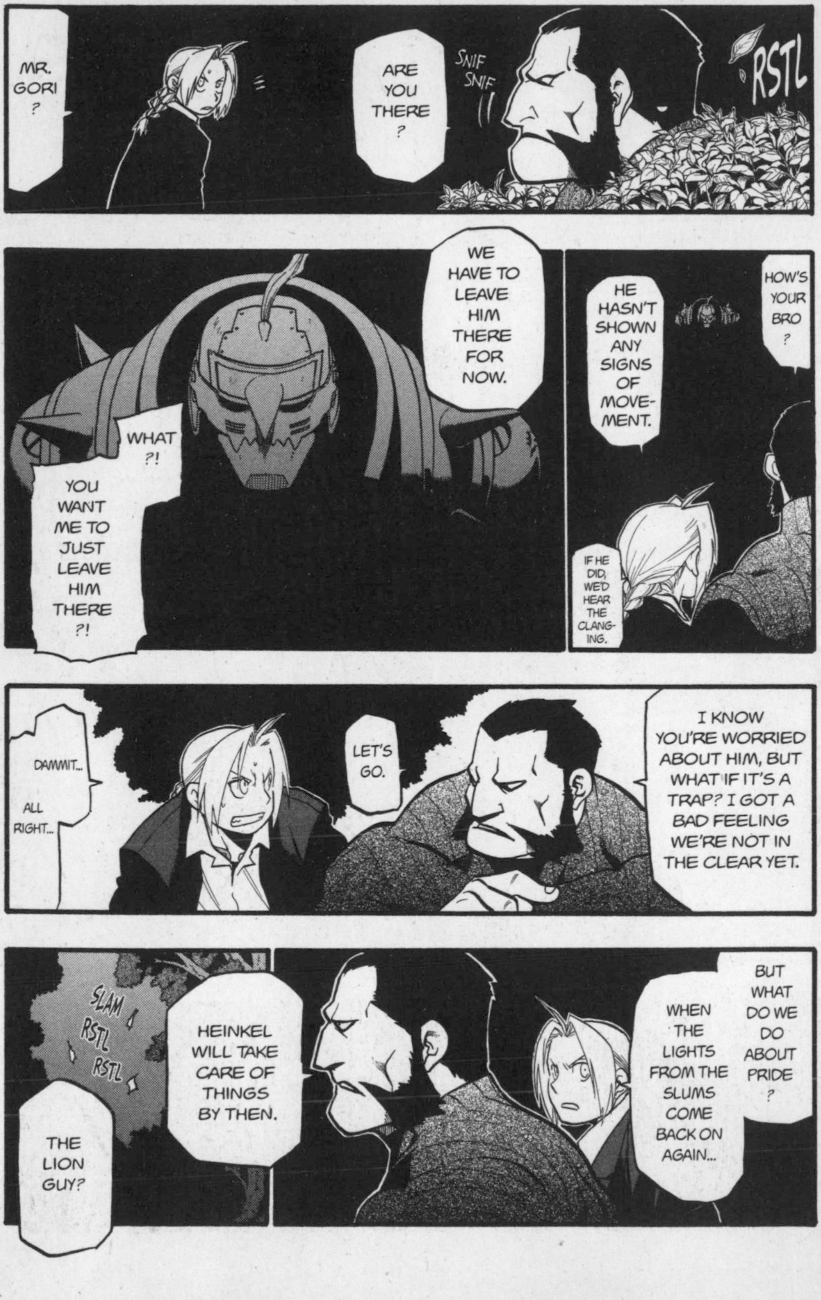
RSTL
SNIF SNIF
ARE YOU THERE?
MR. GORI?
HOW'S YOUR BRO?
HE HASN'T SHOWN ANY SIGNS OF MOVEMENT.
IF HE DID, WE'D HEAR THE CLANGING.
WE HAVE TO LEAVE HIM THERE FOR NOW.
WHAT?!
YOU WANT ME TO JUST LEAVE HIM THERE?!
I KNOW YOU'RE WORRIED ABOUT HIM, BUT WHAT IF IT'S A TRAP? I GOT A BAD FEELING WE'RE NOT IN THE CLEAR YET.
LET'S GO.
DAMMIT... ALL RIGHT...
BUT WHAT DO WE DO ABOUT PRIDE?
WHEN THE LIGHTS FROM THE SLUMS COME BACK ON AGAIN...
HEINKEL WILL TAKE CARE OF THINGS BY THEN.
SLAM RSTL RSTL
THE LION GUY?

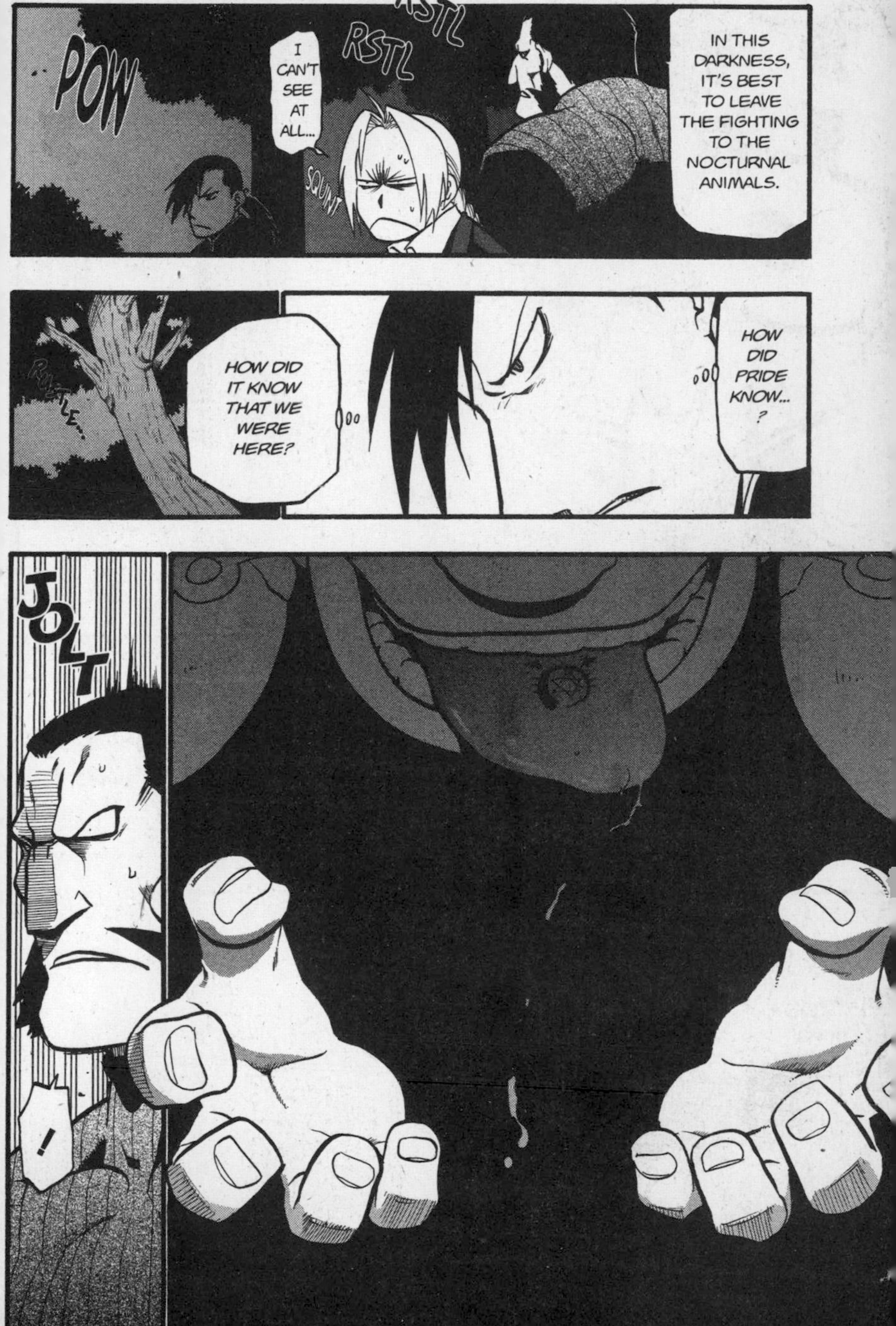
IN THIS DARKNESS, IT'S BEST TO LEAVE THE FIGHTING TO THE NOCTURNAL ANIMALS.
RSTL
RSTL
I CAN'T SEE AT ALL...
SQUINT
POW
HOW DID PRIDE KNOW...?
HOW DID IT KNOW THAT WE WERE HERE?
RUSTLE...
JOLT
!

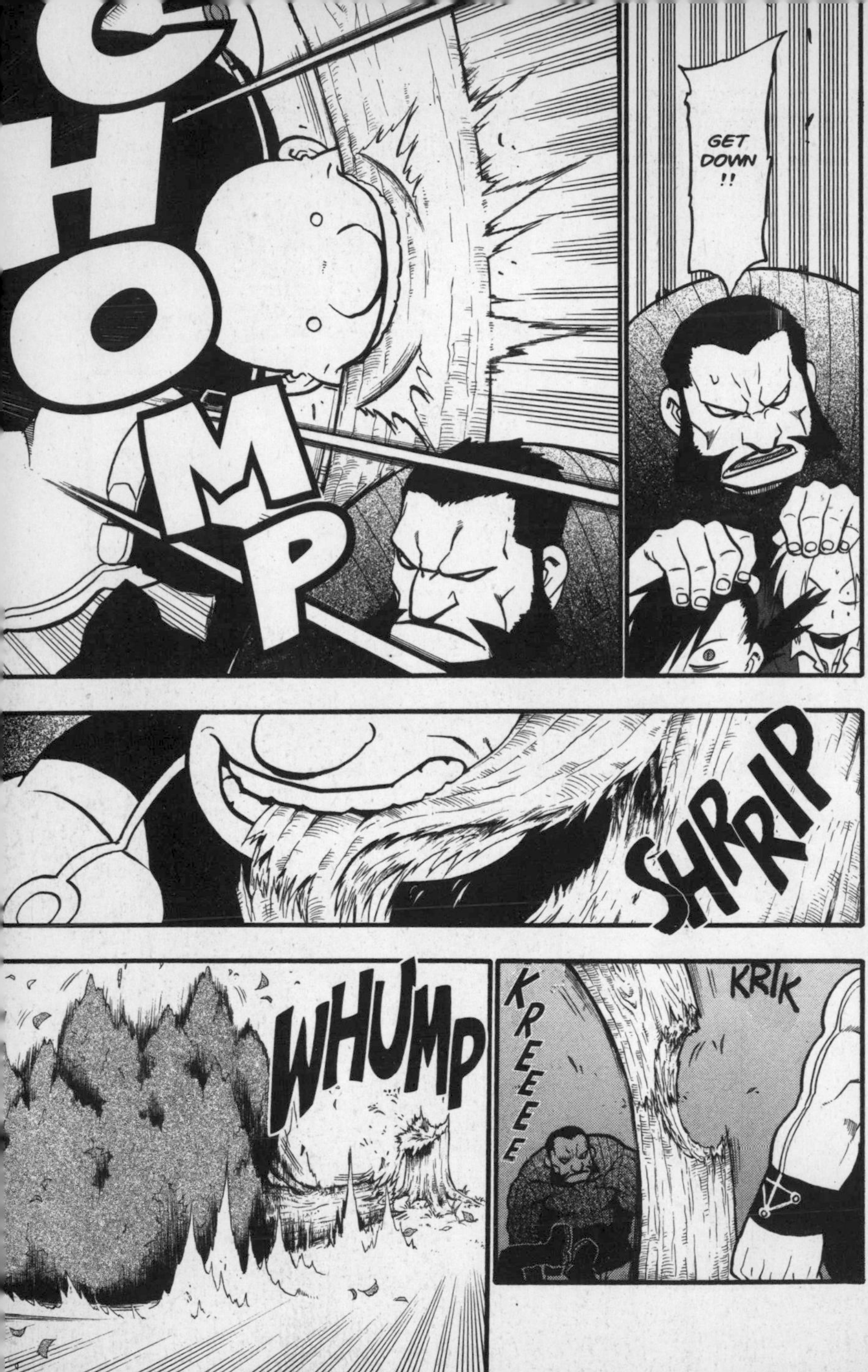
GET DOWN !!
CHOMP
SHRIP
KRIK
KREEEEE
WHUMP

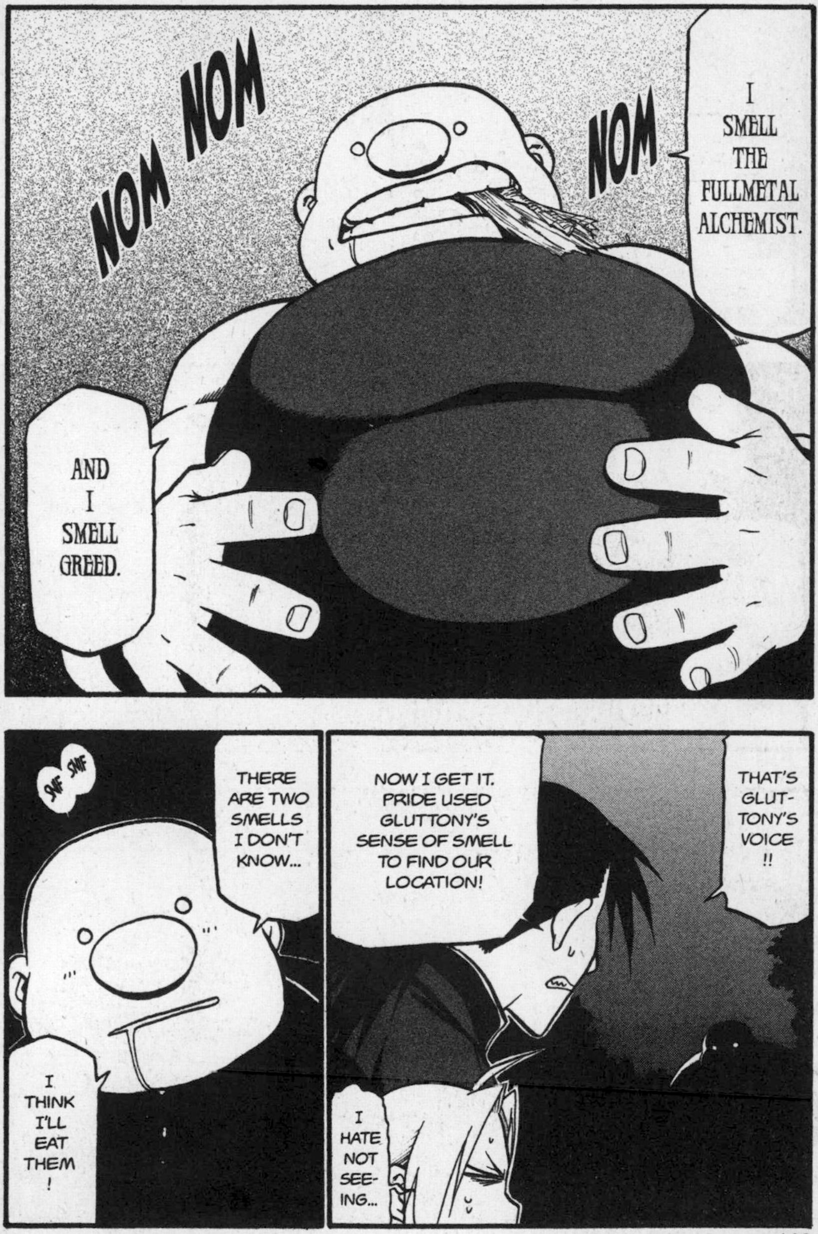

I SMELL THE FULLMETAL ALCHEMIST.
NOM
NOM NOM
AND I SMELL GREED.
THAT'S GLUT-TONY'S VOICE!!
NOW I GET IT. PRIDE USED GLUTTONY'S SENSE OF SMELL TO FIND OUR LOCATION!
I HATE NOT SEE-ING...
SNIF SNIF
THERE ARE TWO SMELLS I DON'T KNOW...
I THINK I'LL EAT THEM!

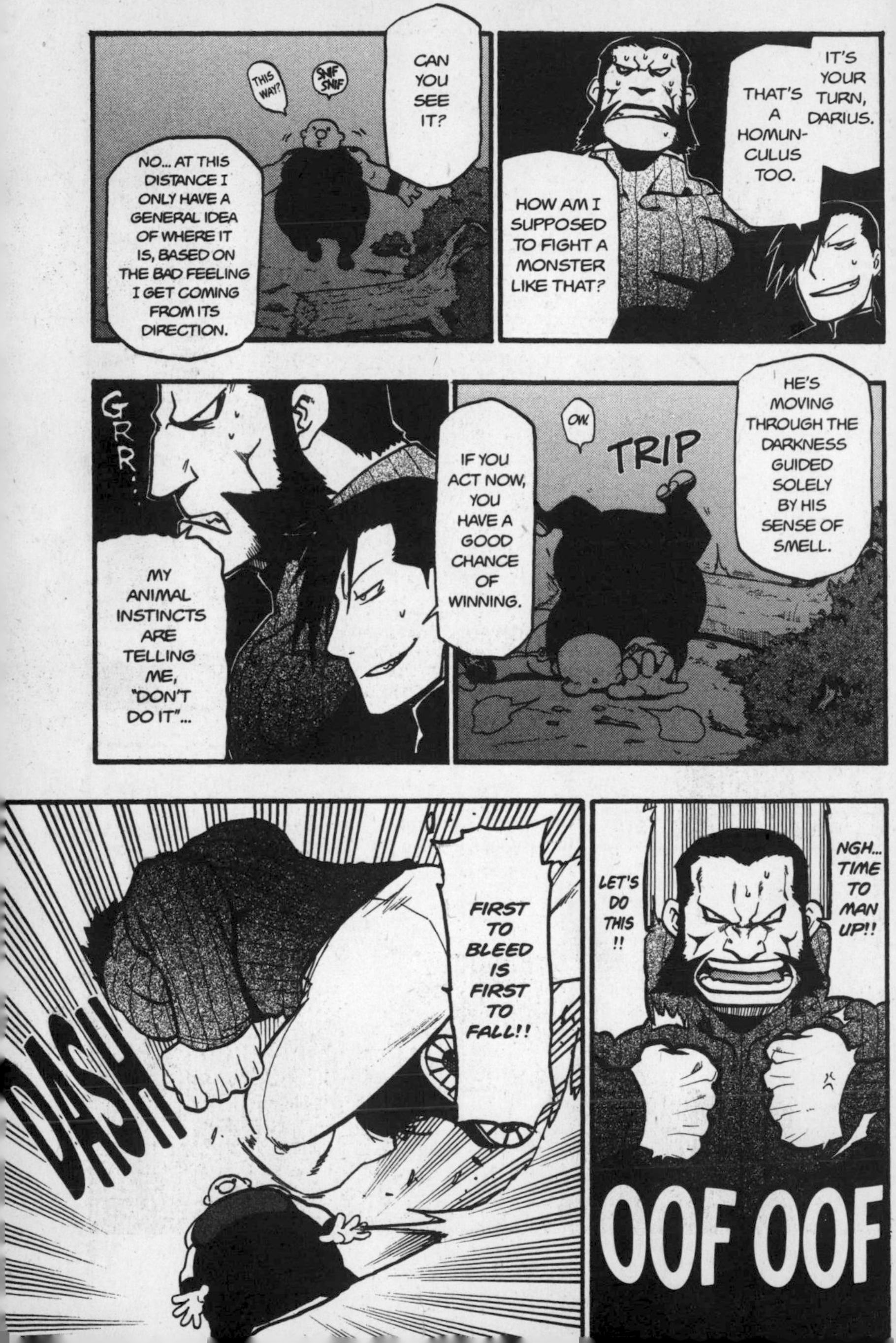
IT'S YOUR TURN, DARIUS.
THAT'S A HOMUNCULUS TOO.
HOW AM I SUPPOSED TO FIGHT A MONSTER LIKE THAT?
CAN YOU SEE IT?
SNIF SNIF
THIS WAY?
NO... AT THIS DISTANCE I ONLY HAVE A GENERAL IDEA OF WHERE IT IS, BASED ON THE BAD FEELING I GET COMING FROM ITS DIRECTION.
HE'S MOVING THROUGH THE DARKNESS GUIDED SOLELY BY HIS SENSE OF SMELL.
TRIP
OW.
IF YOU ACT NOW, YOU HAVE A GOOD CHANCE OF WINNING.
GRR...
MY ANIMAL INSTINCTS ARE TELLING ME, "DON'T DO IT"...
NGH... TIME TO MAN UP!!
LET'S DO THIS!!
OOF OOF
FIRST TO BLEED IS FIRST TO FALL!!
DASH

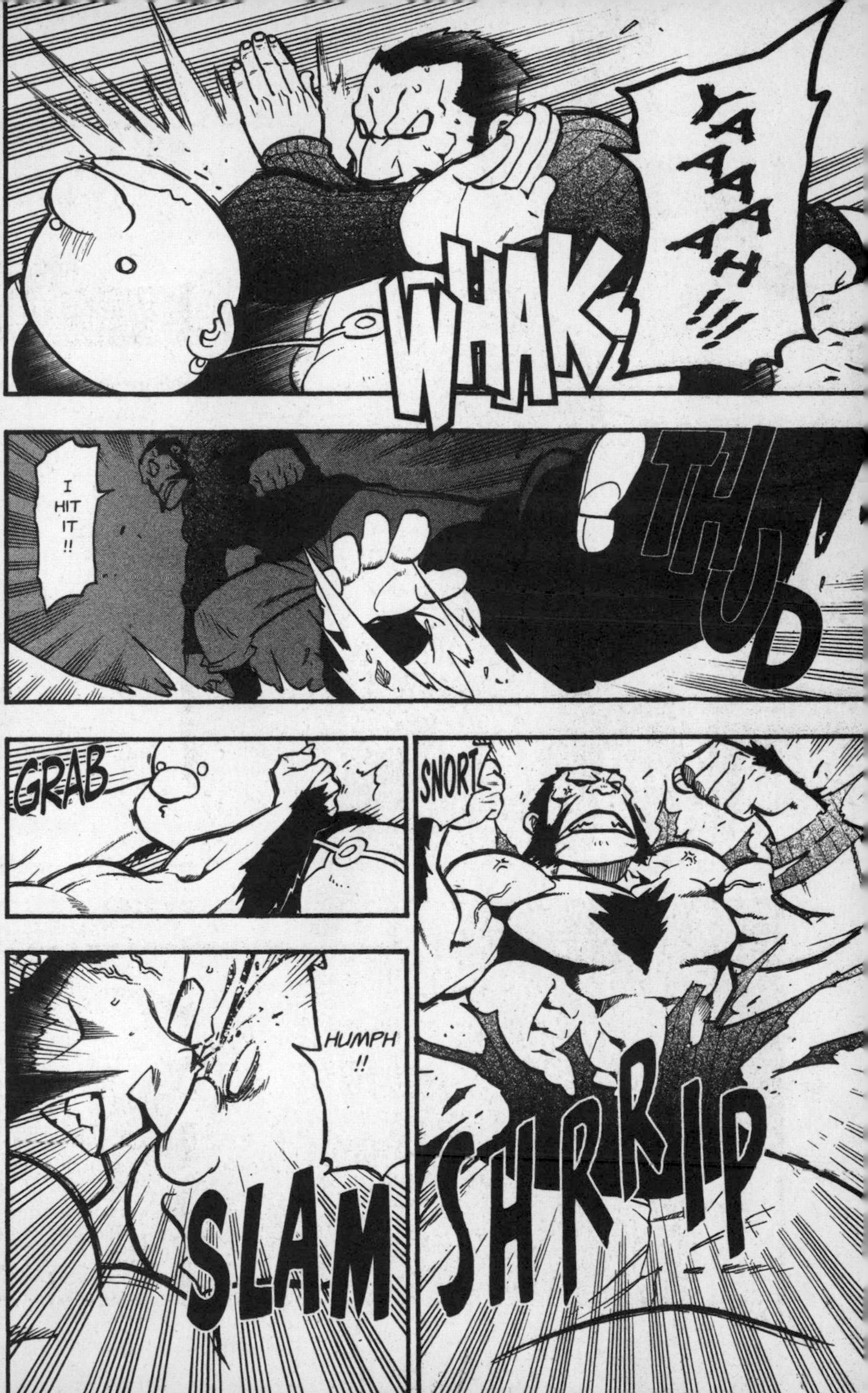
YAAAAAH!!!
WHAK
THUD
I HIT IT!!
SNORT
SHRRIP
GRAB
HUMPH!!
SLAM

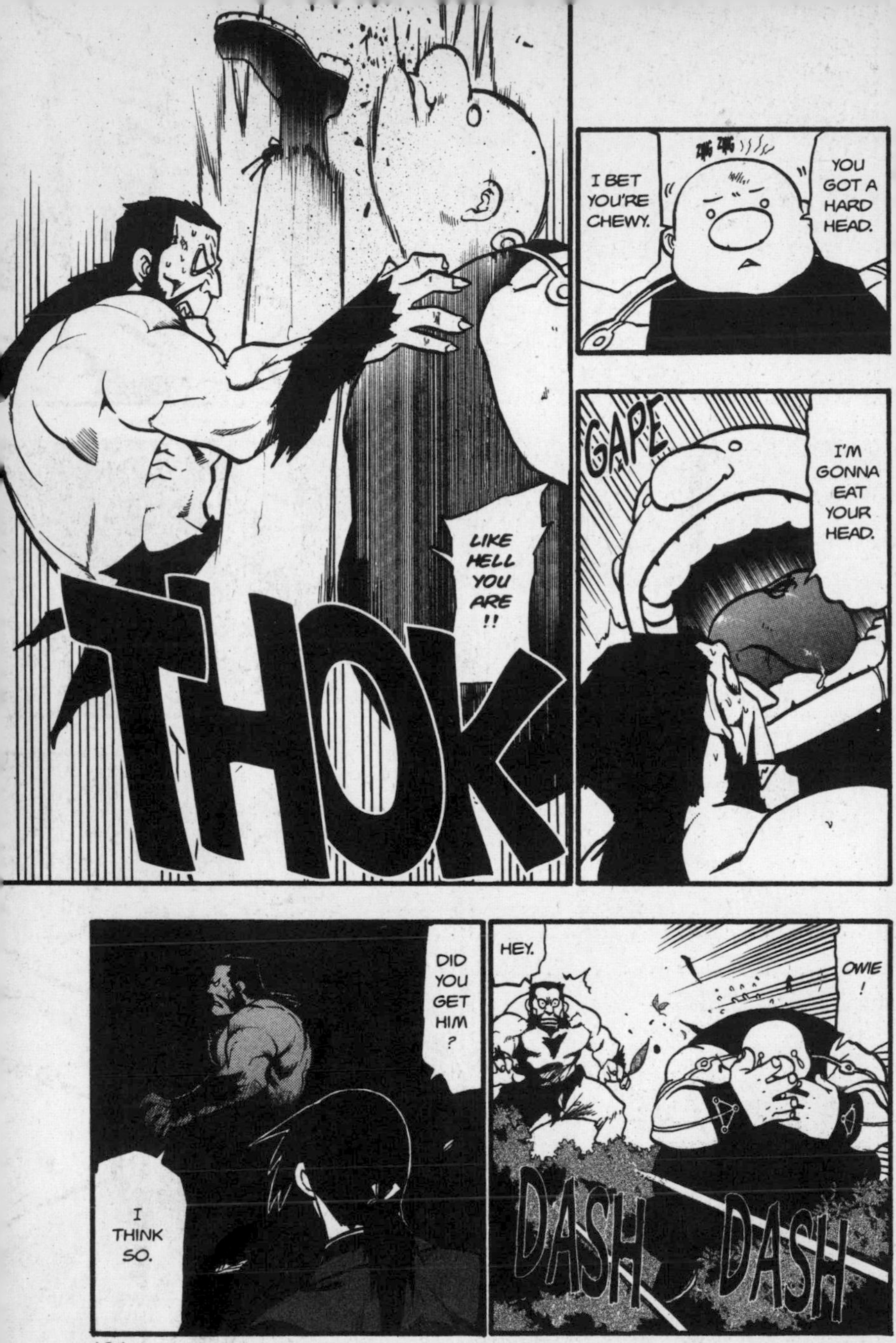
YOU GOT A HARD HEAD.
I BET YOU'RE CHEWY.
GAPE
I'M GONNA EAT YOUR HEAD.
LIKE HELL YOU ARE!!
THOK
OWIE!
HEY.
DASH
DASH
DID YOU GET HIM?
I THINK SO.

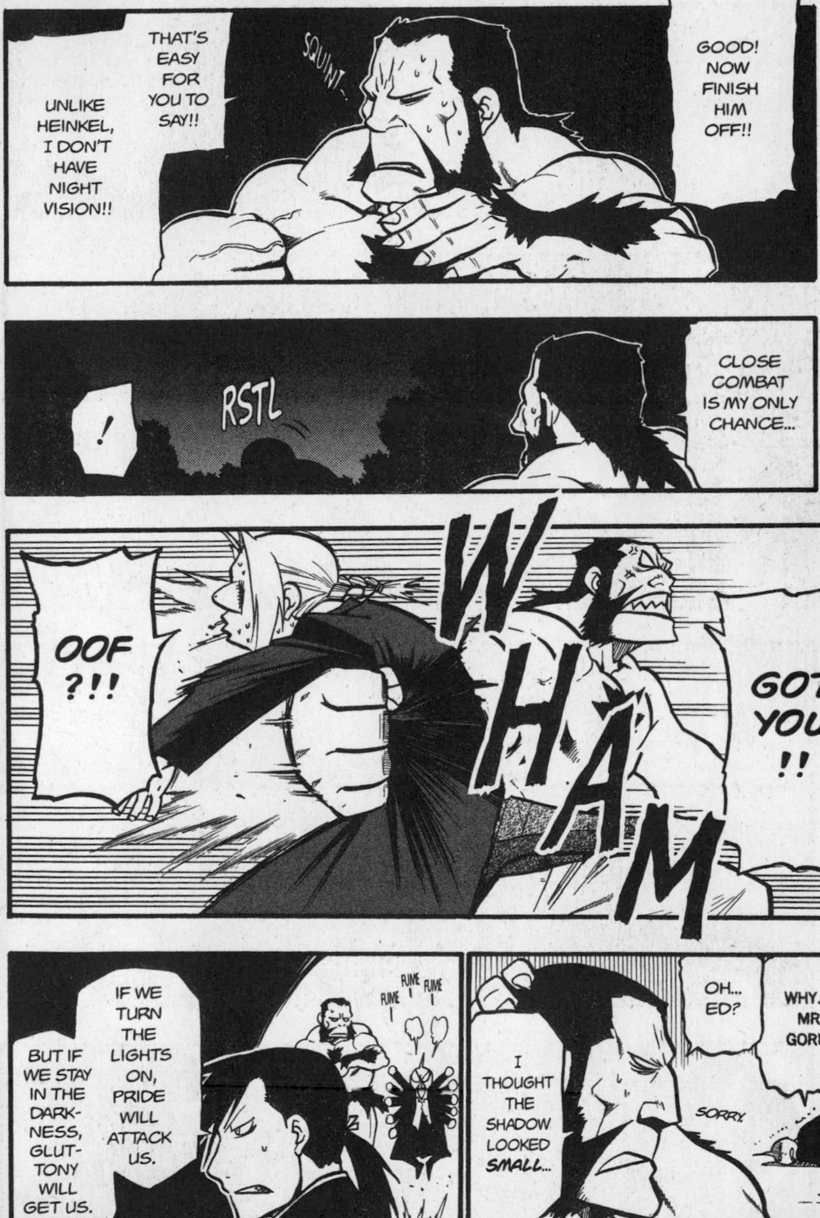
GOOD! NOW FINISH HIM OFF!!
SQUINT
THAT'S EASY FOR YOU TO SAY!!
UNLIKE HEINKEL, I DON'T HAVE NIGHT VISION!!
CLOSE COMBAT IS MY ONLY CHANCE...
RSTL
!
GOT YOU!!
WHAM
OOF?!!
WHY...? MR. GORI...
OH... ED?
SORRY
I THOUGHT THE SHADOW LOOKED SMALL...
FUME FUME FUME
IF WE TURN THE LIGHTS ON, PRIDE WILL ATTACK US.
BUT IF WE STAY IN THE DARKNESS, GLUTTONY WILL GET US.

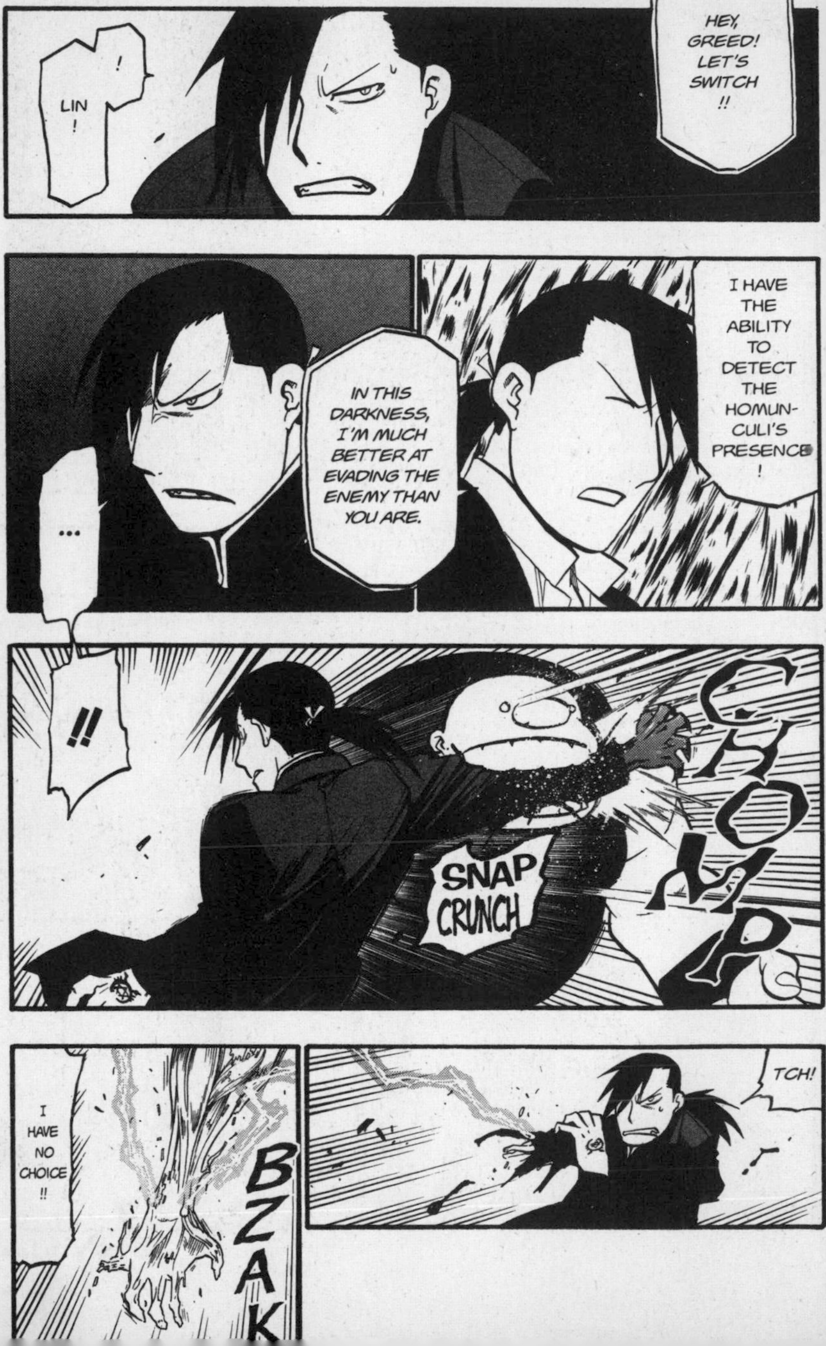
HEY, GREED! LET'S SWITCH !!
! LIN !
I HAVE THE ABILITY TO DETECT THE HOMUNCULI'S PRESENCE !
IN THIS DARKNESS, I'M MUCH BETTER AT EVADING THE ENEMY THAN YOU ARE.
...
CHOMP
SNAP CRUNCH
!!
TCH!
BZAK
I HAVE NO CHOICE !!

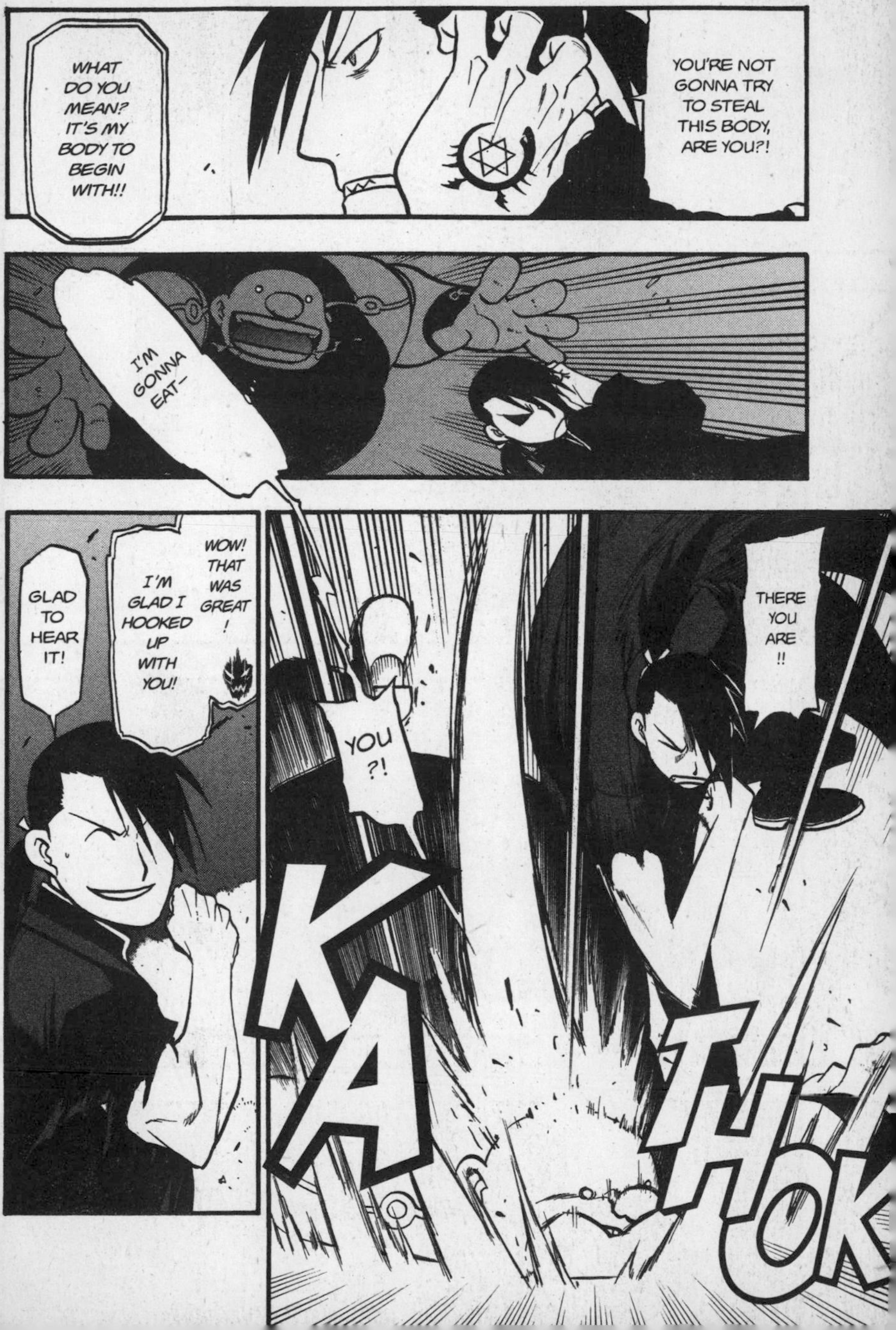
YOU'RE NOT GONNA TRY TO STEAL THIS BODY, ARE YOU?!
WHAT DO YOU MEAN? IT'S MY BODY TO BEGIN WITH!!
I'M GONNA EAT—
THERE YOU ARE!!
YOU?!
KA
THOK
WOW! THAT WAS GREAT!
I'M GLAD I HOOKED UP WITH YOU!
GLAD TO HEAR IT!

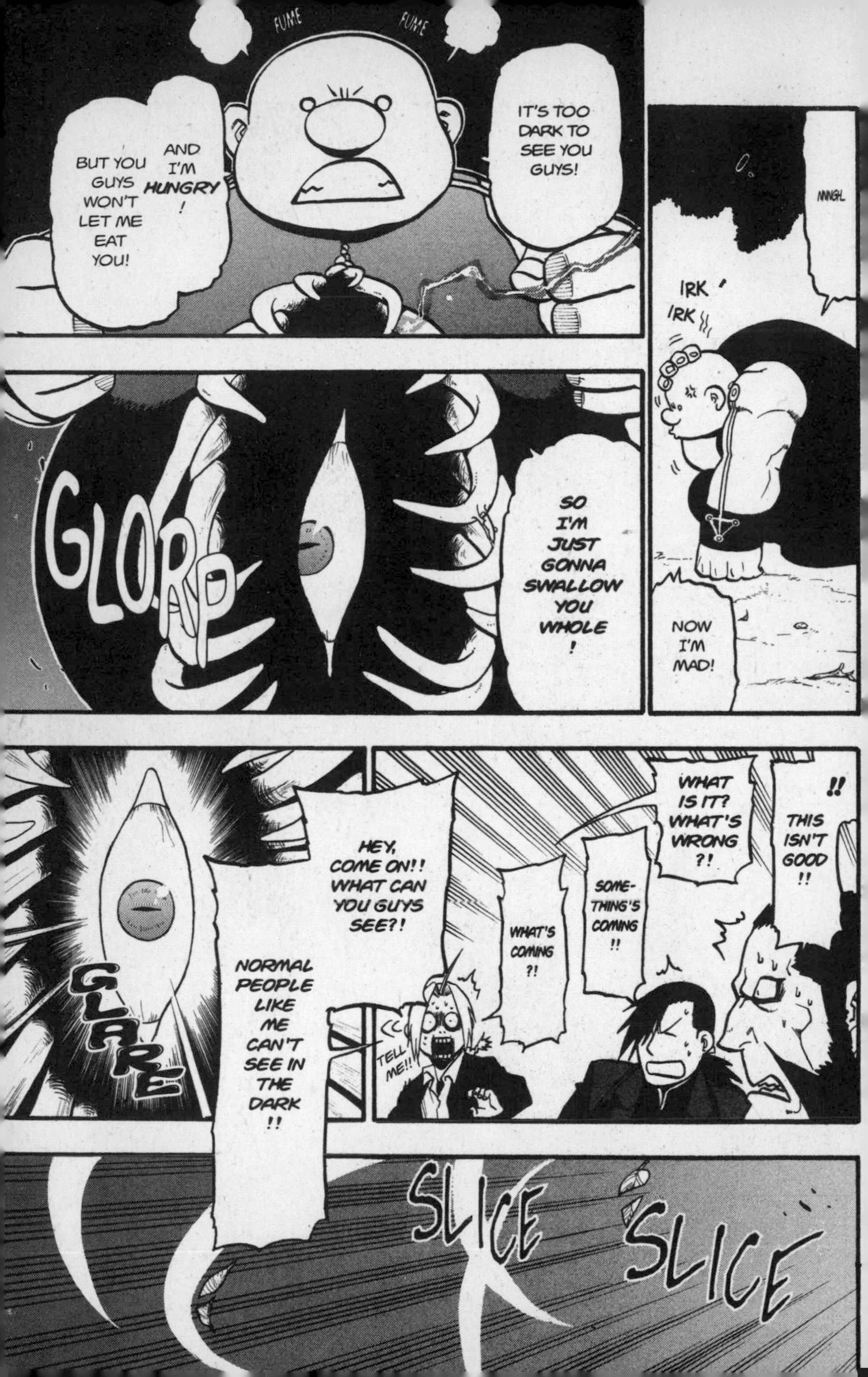
NNNGH
IRK IRK
NOW I'M MAD!
FUME FUME
IT'S TOO DARK TO SEE YOU GUYS!
AND I'M HUNGRY!
BUT YOU GUYS WON'T LET ME EAT YOU!
SO I'M JUST GONNA SWALLOW YOU WHOLE!
GLORP
!!
THIS ISN'T GOOD!!
WHAT IS IT? WHAT'S WRONG?!
SOME-THING'S COMING!!
WHAT'S COMING?!
HEY, COME ON!! WHAT CAN YOU GUYS SEE?!
TELL ME!!
NORMAL PEOPLE LIKE ME CAN'T SEE IN THE DARK!!
GLARE
SLICE
SLICE

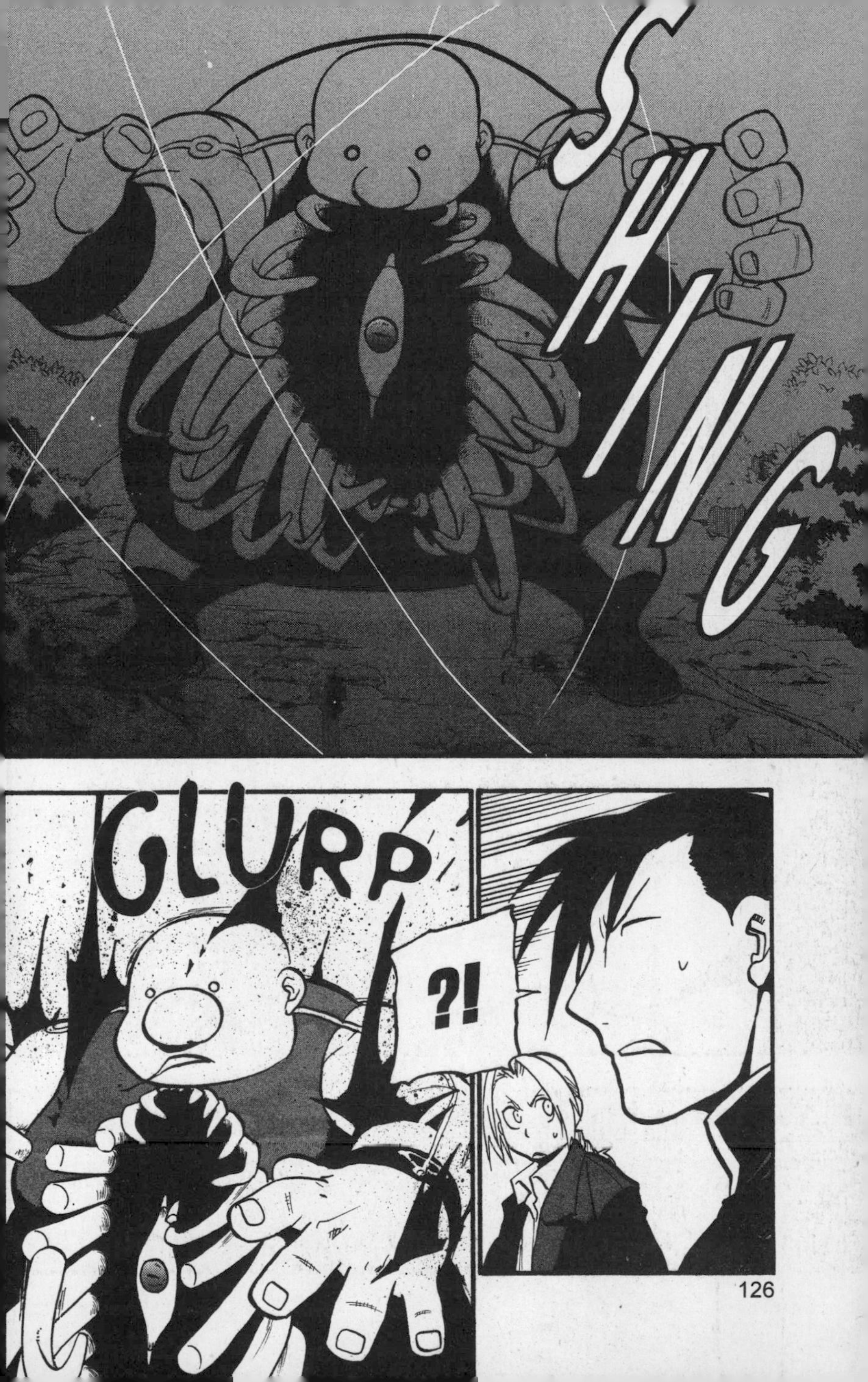
SHING
?!
GLURP

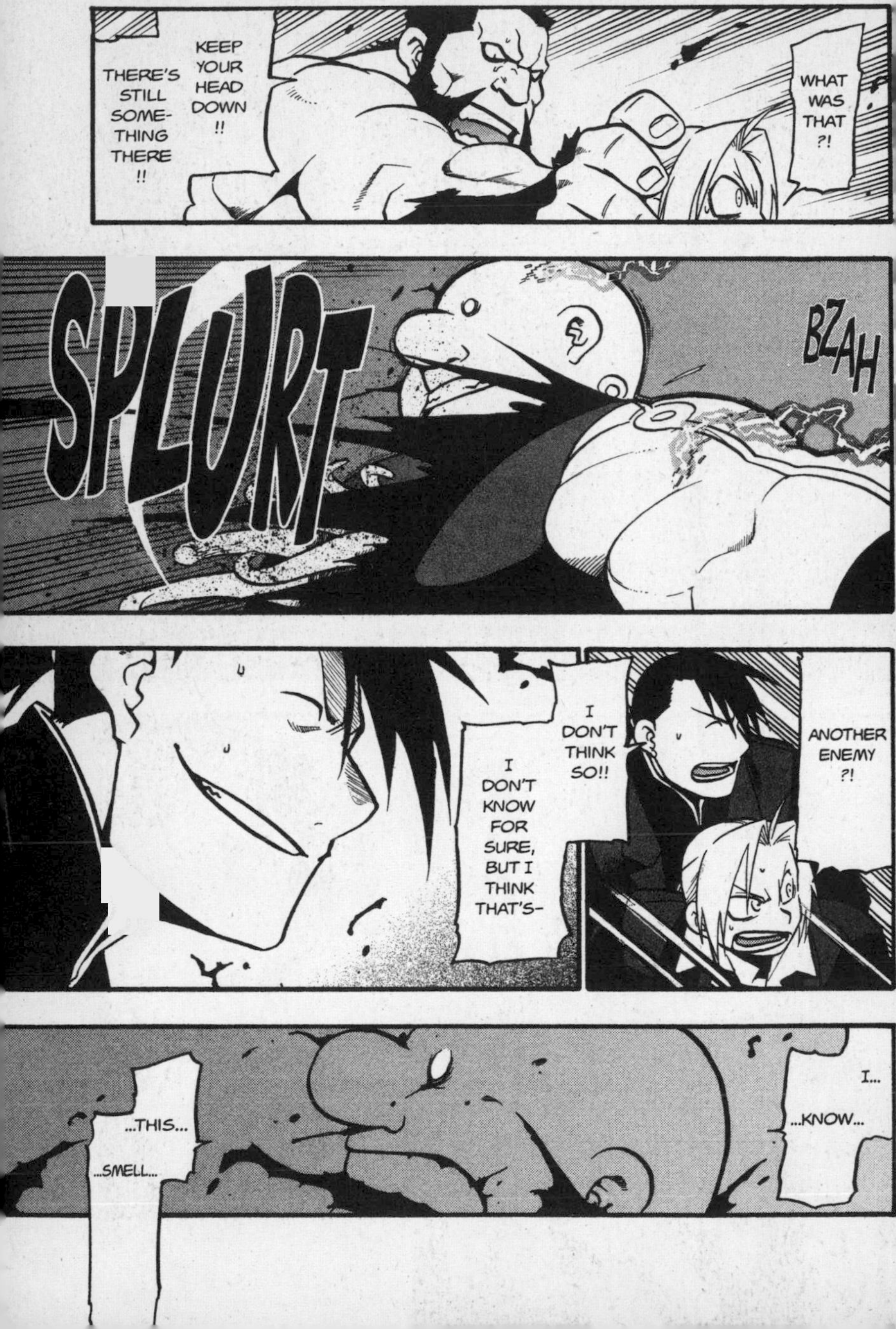
WHAT WAS THAT ?!
KEEP YOUR HEAD DOWN !!
THERE'S STILL SOME-THING THERE !!
BZAH
SPLURT
ANOTHER ENEMY ?!
I DON'T THINK SO!!
I DON'T KNOW FOR SURE, BUT I THINK THAT'S-
I...
...KNOW...
...THIS...
...SMELL...

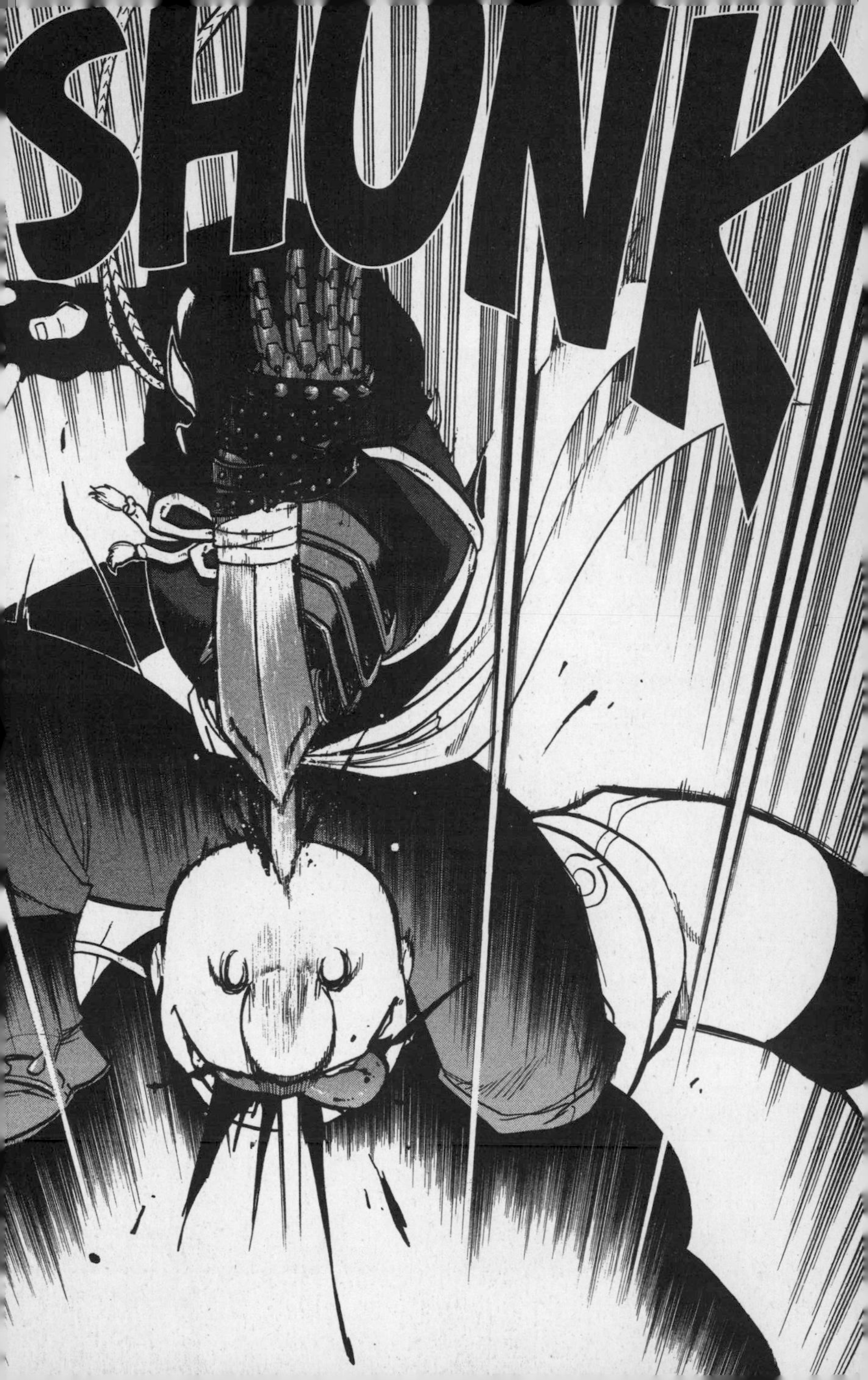
SHUNK

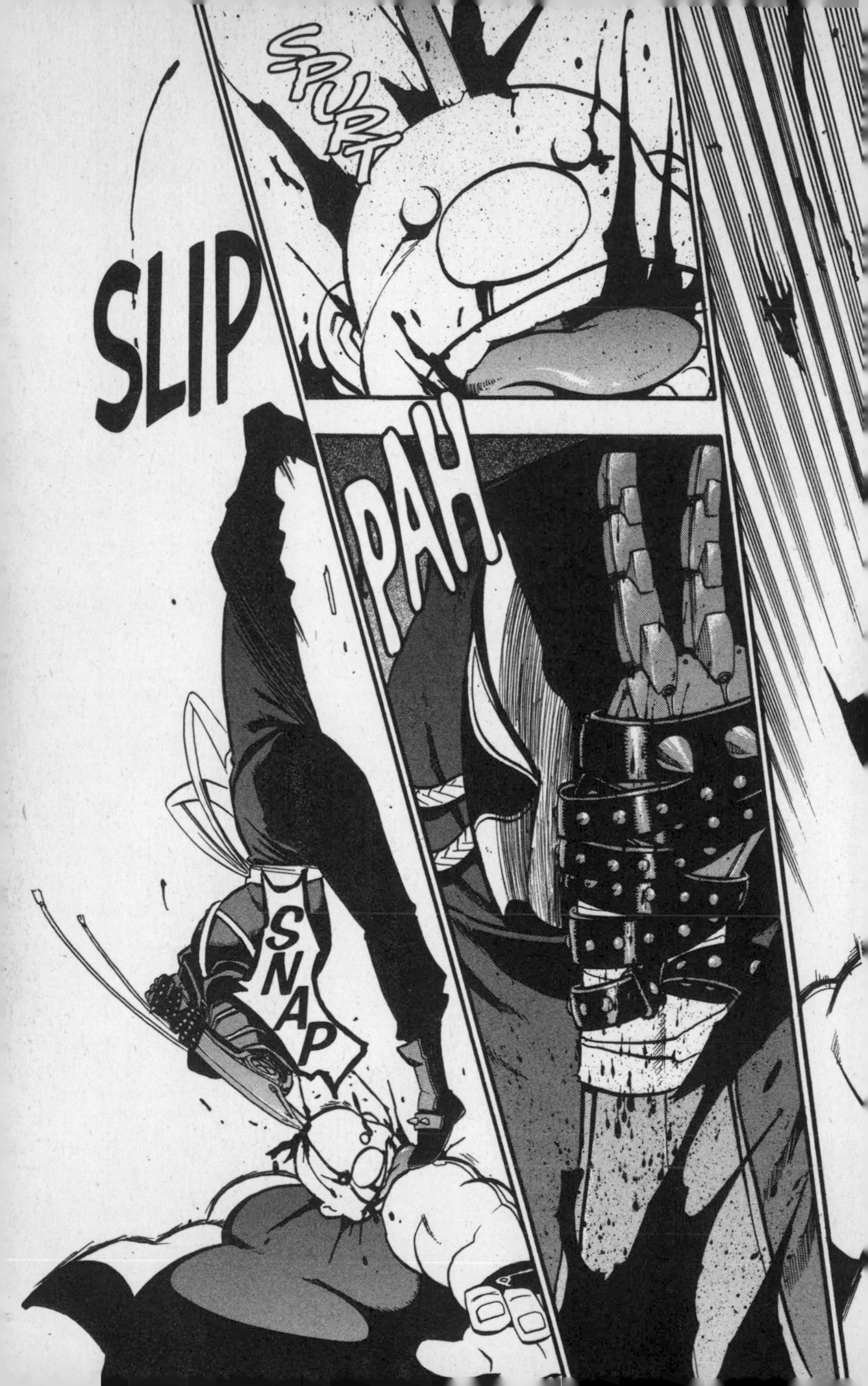
SPURT
PAH
SLIP
SNAP

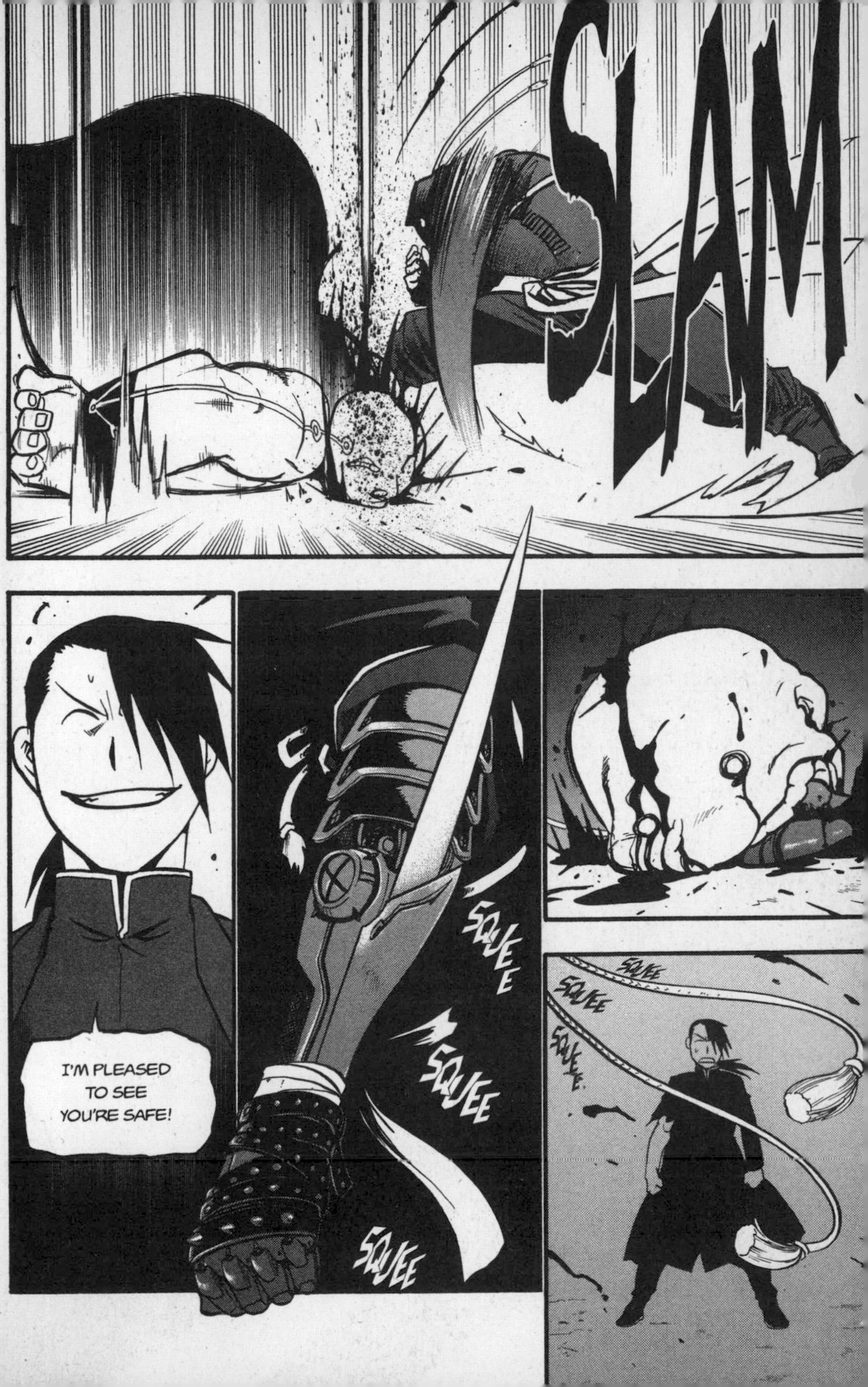
SLAM
SQUEE
SQUEE
SQUEE
SQUEE
SQUEE
SQUEE
I'M PLEASED TO SEE YOU'RE SAFE!

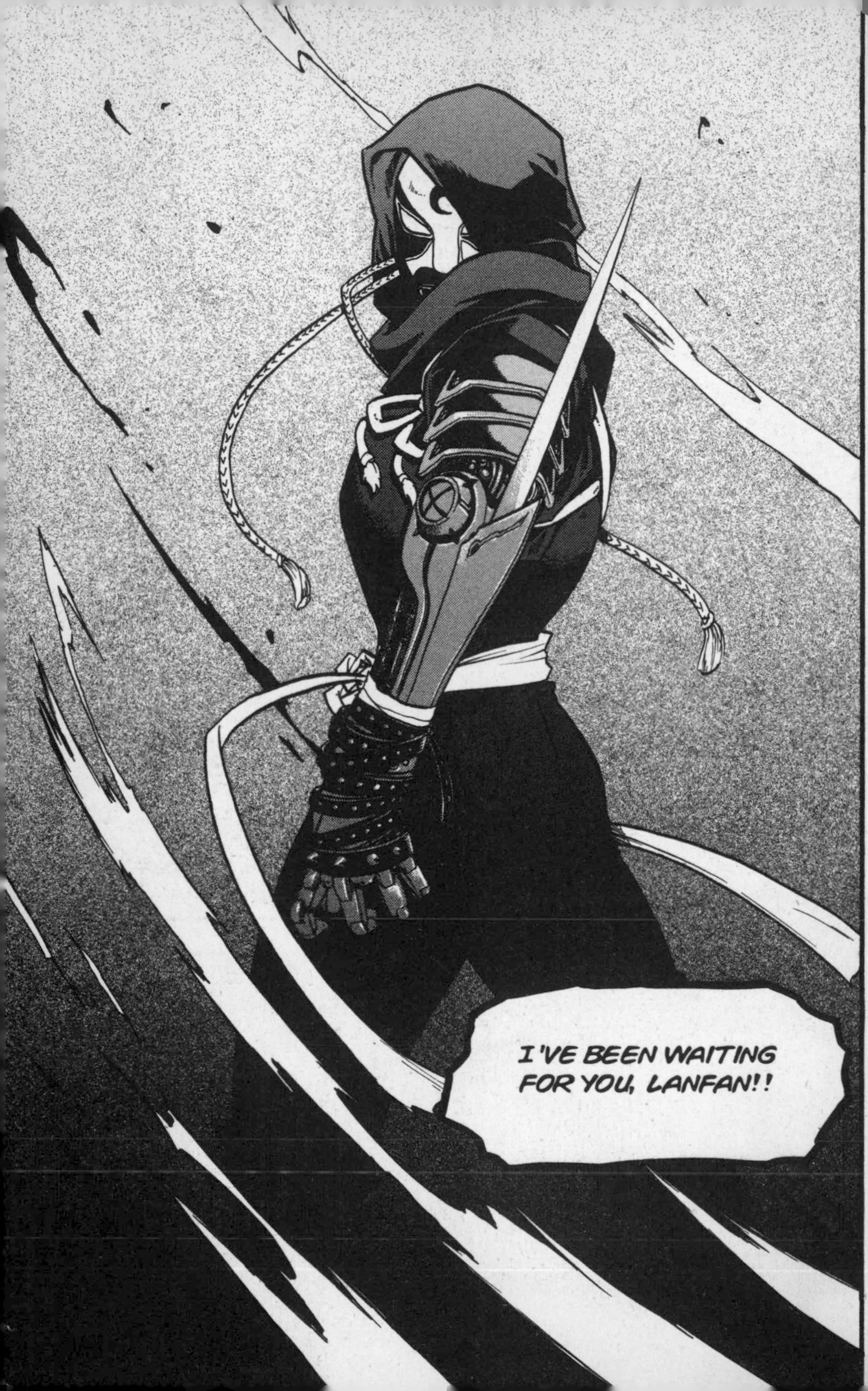
I'VE BEEN WAITING FOR YOU, LANFAN!!

FULLMETAL
ALCHEMIST

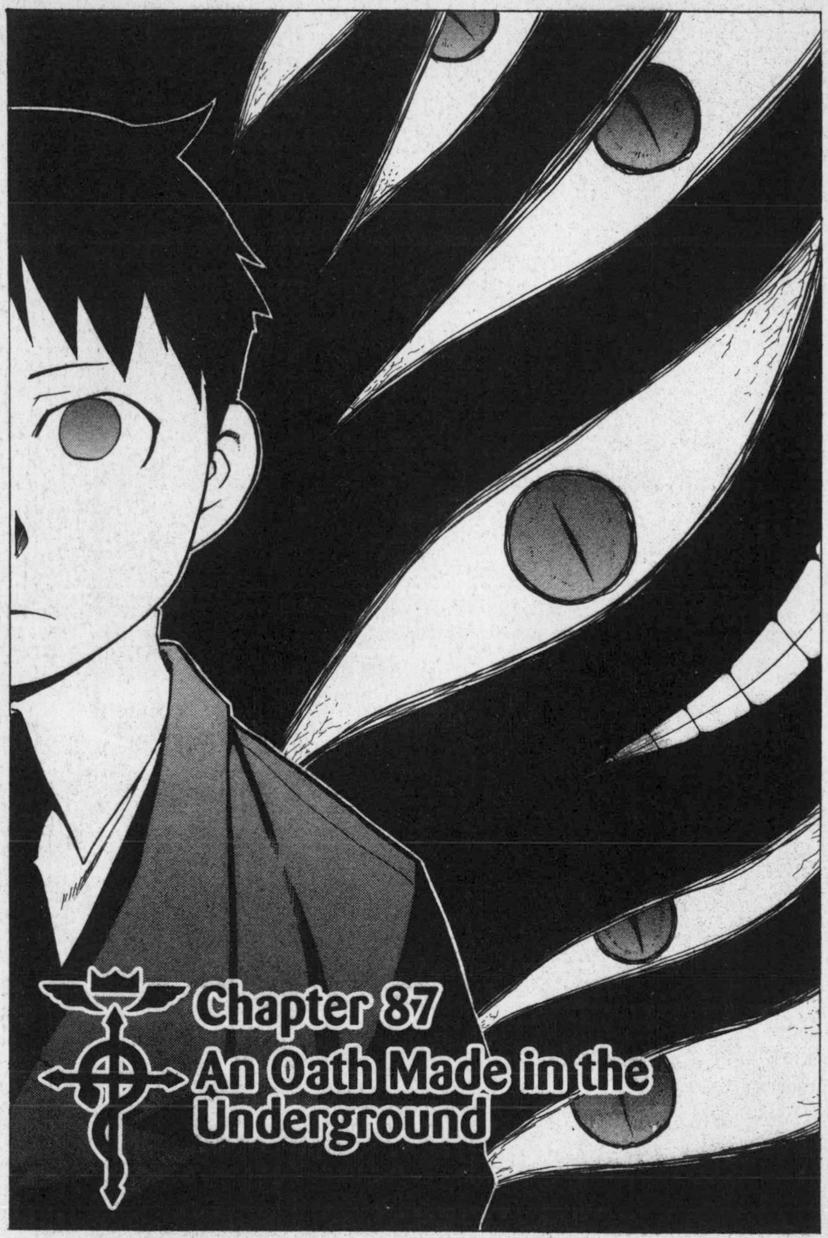
Chapter 87
An Oath Made in the Underground

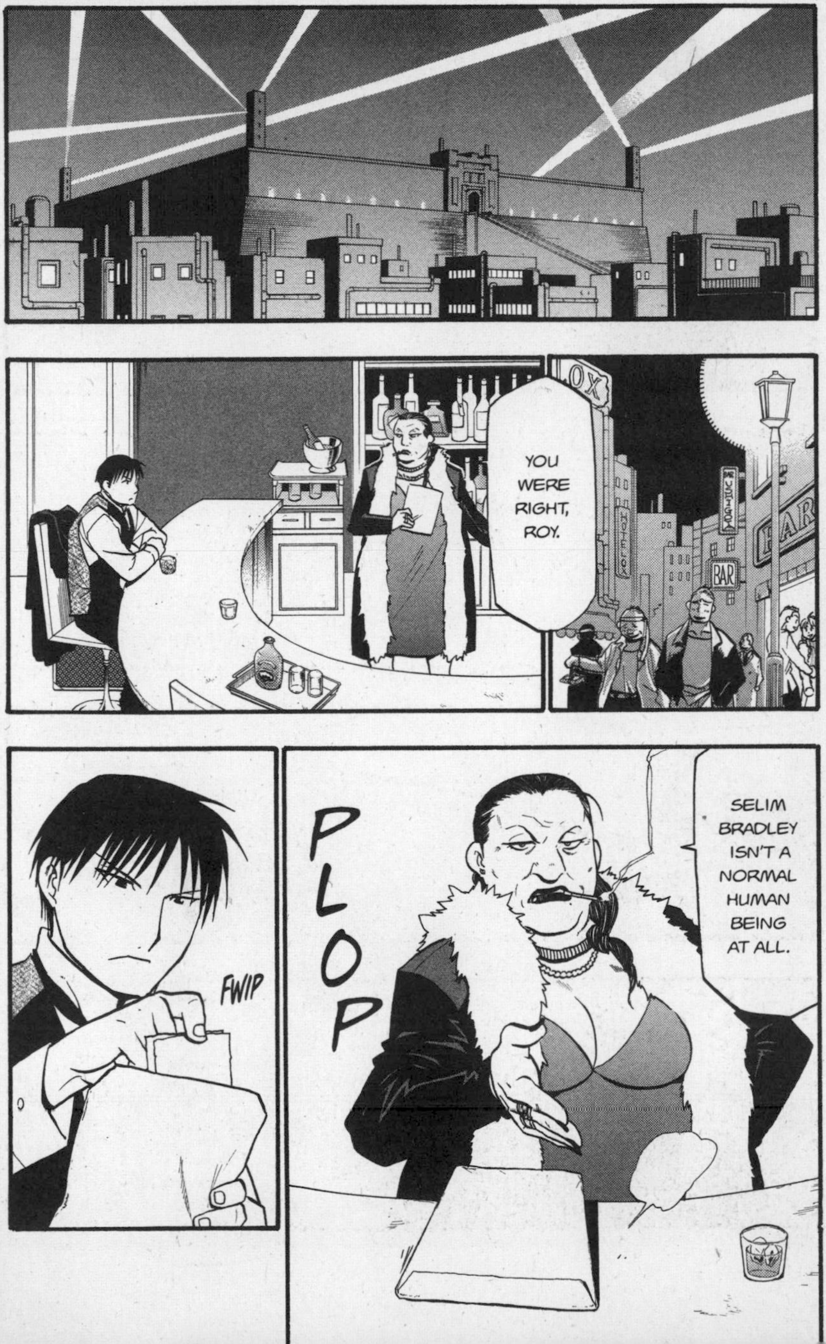
HOTEL OX
BAR
YOU WERE RIGHT, ROY.
SELIM BRADLEY ISN'T A NORMAL HUMAN BEING AT ALL.
PLOP
FWIP

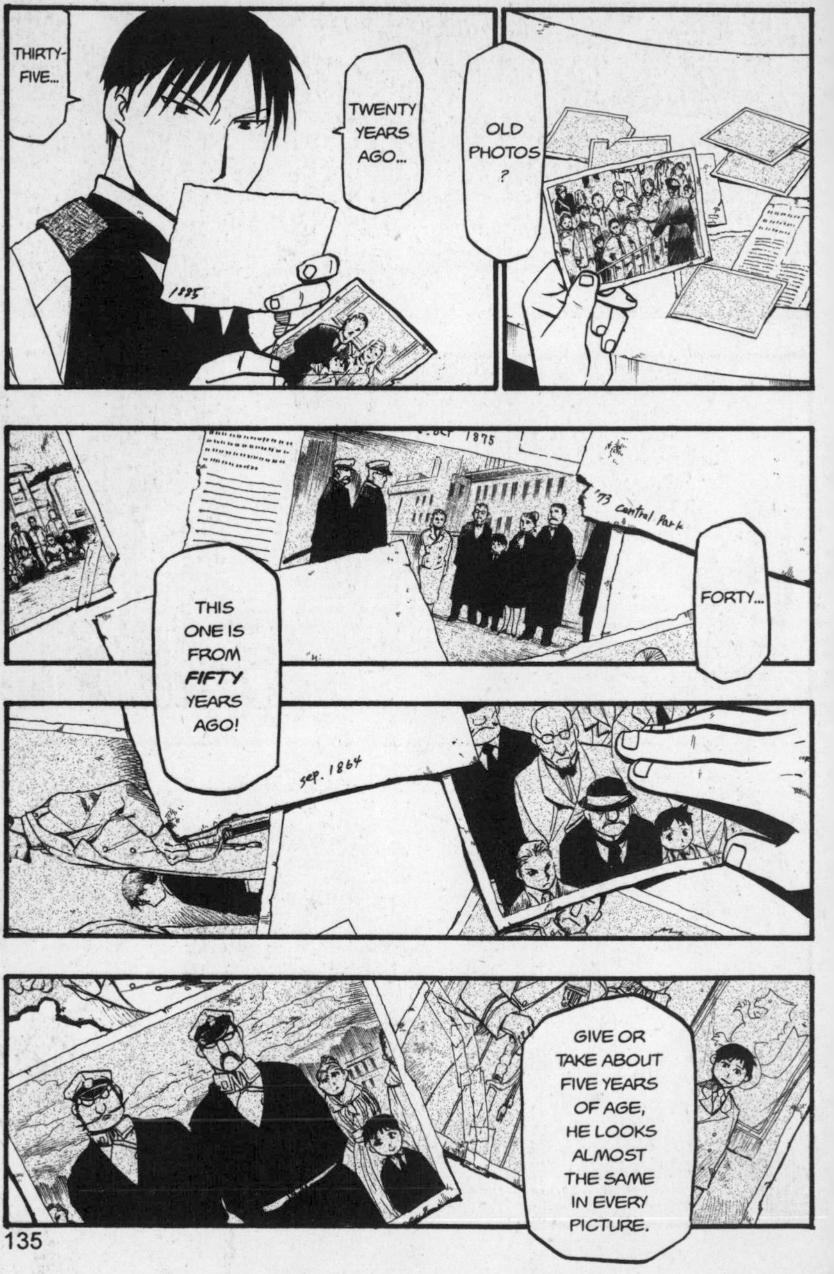
OLD PHOTOS ?
TWENTY YEARS AGO...
THIRTY-FIVE...
1885
FORTY...
'73 Central Park
1875
THIS ONE IS FROM *FIFTY* YEARS AGO!
sep. 1864
GIVE OR TAKE ABOUT FIVE YEARS OF AGE, HE LOOKS ALMOST THE SAME IN EVERY PICTURE.

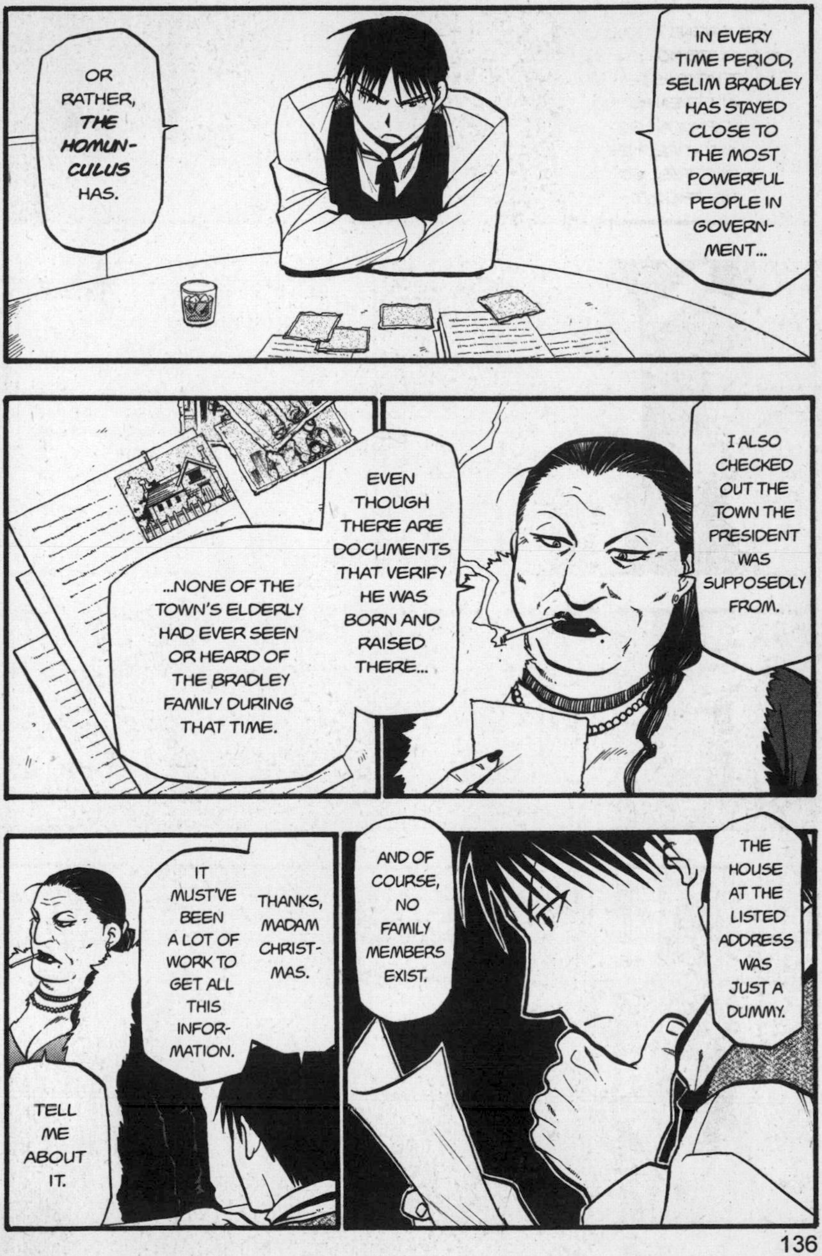
IN EVERY TIME PERIOD, SELIM BRADLEY HAS STAYED CLOSE TO THE MOST POWERFUL PEOPLE IN GOVERNMENT...
OR RATHER, *THE HOMUNCULUS* HAS.
I ALSO CHECKED OUT THE TOWN THE PRESIDENT WAS SUPPOSEDLY FROM.
EVEN THOUGH THERE ARE DOCUMENTS THAT VERIFY HE WAS BORN AND RAISED THERE...
...NONE OF THE TOWN'S ELDERLY HAD EVER SEEN OR HEARD OF THE BRADLEY FAMILY DURING THAT TIME.
THE HOUSE AT THE LISTED ADDRESS WAS JUST A DUMMY.
AND OF COURSE, NO FAMILY MEMBERS EXIST.
THANKS, MADAM CHRISTMAS.
IT MUST'VE BEEN A LOT OF WORK TO GET ALL THIS INFORMATION.
TELL ME ABOUT IT.

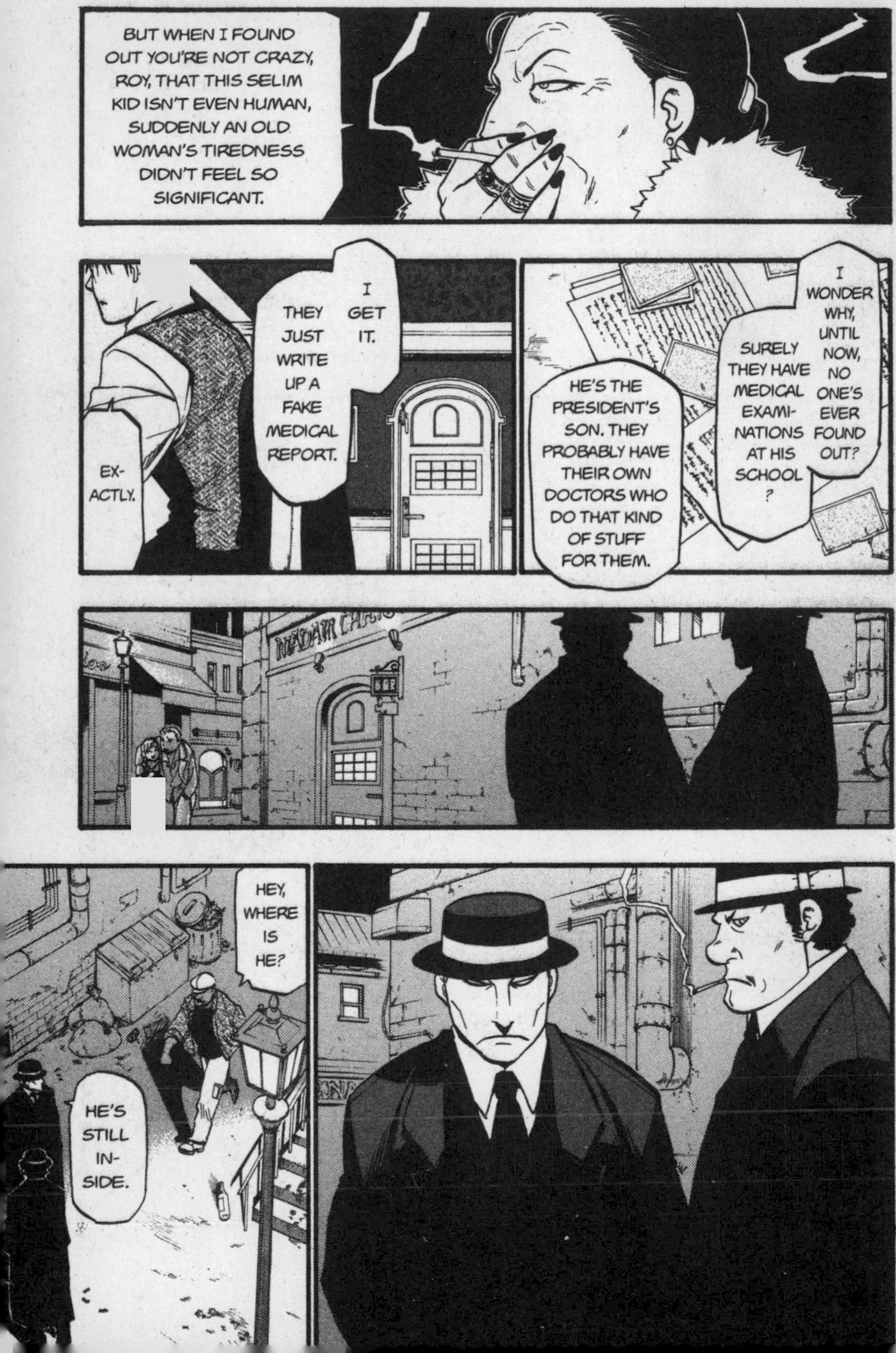
BUT WHEN I FOUND OUT YOU'RE NOT CRAZY, ROY, THAT THIS SELIM KID ISN'T EVEN HUMAN, SUDDENLY AN OLD WOMAN'S TIREDNESS DIDN'T FEEL SO SIGNIFICANT.
I WONDER WHY, UNTIL NOW, NO ONE'S EVER FOUND OUT?
SURELY THEY HAVE MEDICAL EXAMI-NATIONS AT HIS SCHOOL?
HE'S THE PRESIDENT'S SON. THEY PROBABLY HAVE THEIR OWN DOCTORS WHO DO THAT KIND OF STUFF FOR THEM.
I GET IT.
THEY JUST WRITE UP A FAKE MEDICAL REPORT.
EX-ACTLY.
HEY, WHERE IS HE?
HE'S STILL IN-SIDE.

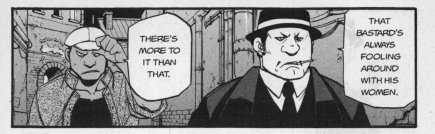

THAT BASTARD'S ALWAYS FOOLING AROUND WITH HIS WOMEN.
THERE'S MORE TO IT THAN THAT.
!
YOU FIGURED SOME-THING OUT?!
THE WOMAN THEY CALL MADAM CHRIST-MAS...
HER REAL NAME IS CHRIS MUSTANG.
SHE'S COLONEL MUSTANG'S ADOPTIVE MOTHER.
!!
BAM

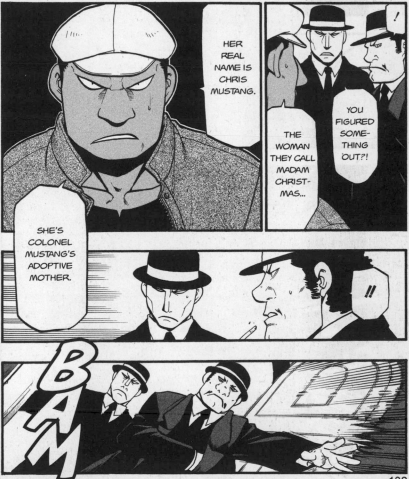

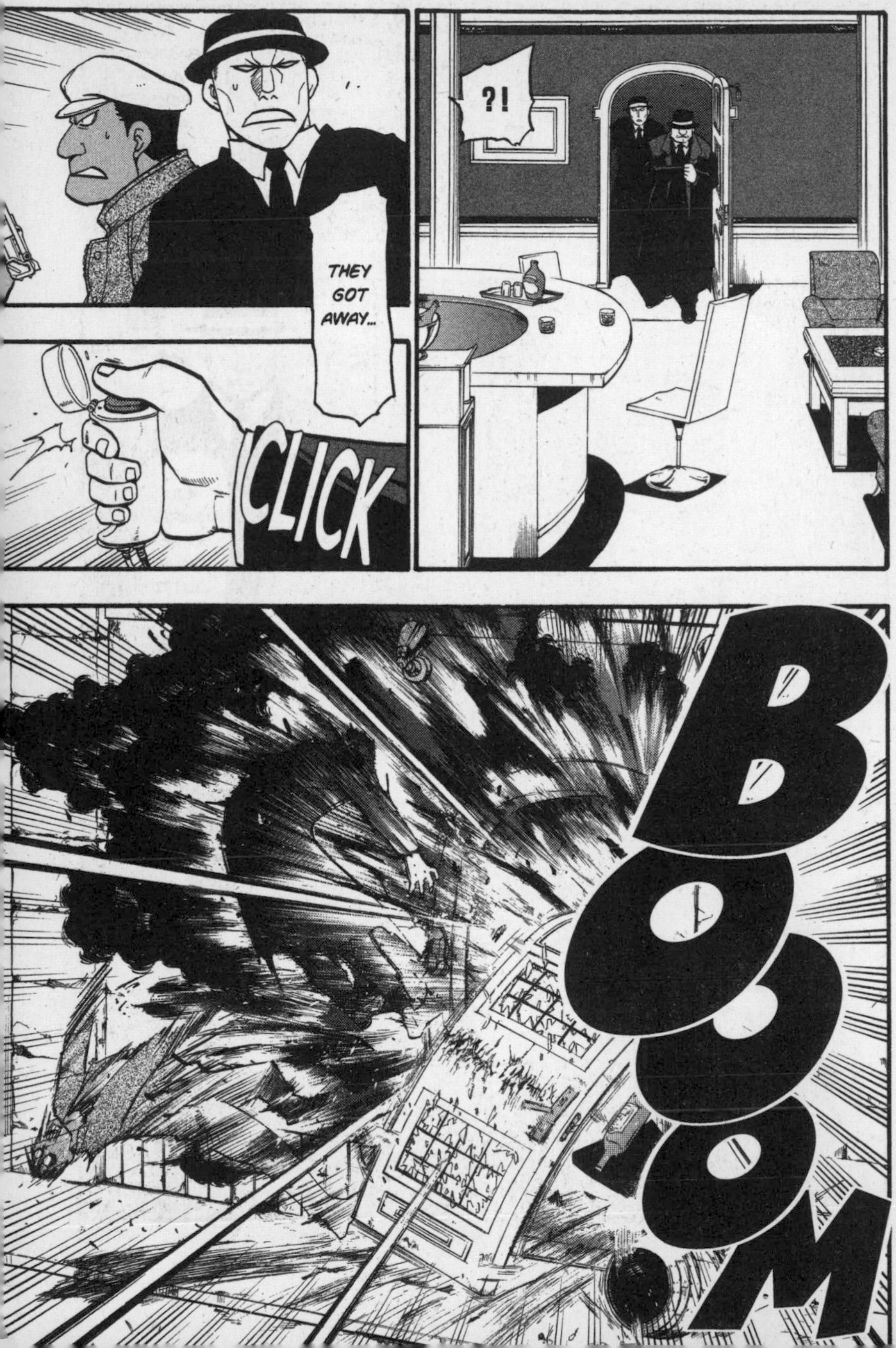

?!
THEY GOT AWAY...
CLICK
BOOOOM

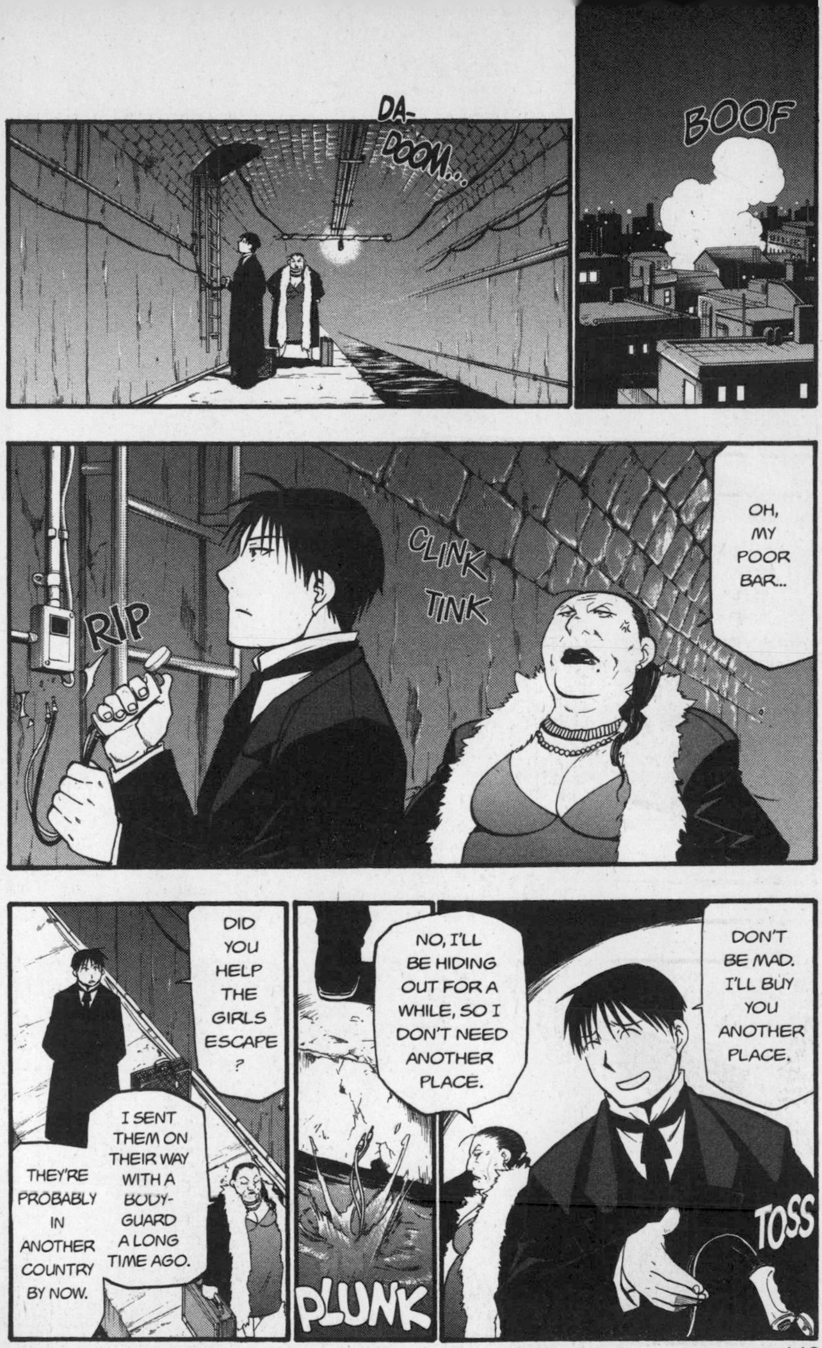
BOOF
DA-DOOM...
OH, MY POOR BAR...
CLINK TINK
RIP
DON'T BE MAD. I'LL BUY YOU ANOTHER PLACE.
TOSS
NO, I'LL BE HIDING OUT FOR A WHILE, SO I DON'T NEED ANOTHER PLACE.
PLUNK
DID YOU HELP THE GIRLS ESCAPE?
I SENT THEM ON THEIR WAY WITH A BODY-GUARD A LONG TIME AGO.
THEY'RE PROBABLY IN ANOTHER COUNTRY BY NOW.

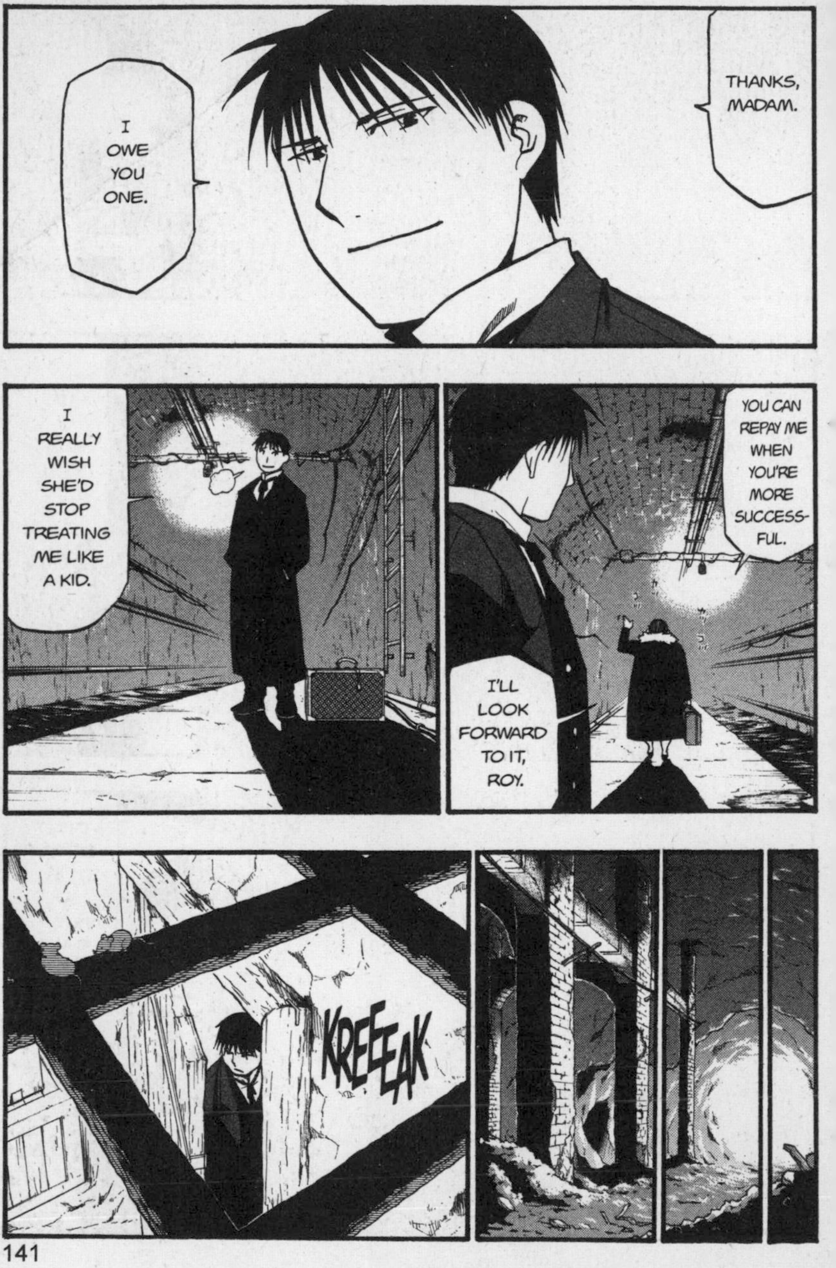
THANKS, MADAM.
I OWE YOU ONE.
YOU CAN REPAY ME WHEN YOU'RE MORE SUCCESS-FUL.
I'LL LOOK FORWARD TO IT, ROY.
I REALLY WISH SHE'D STOP TREATING ME LIKE A KID.
KREEEAK

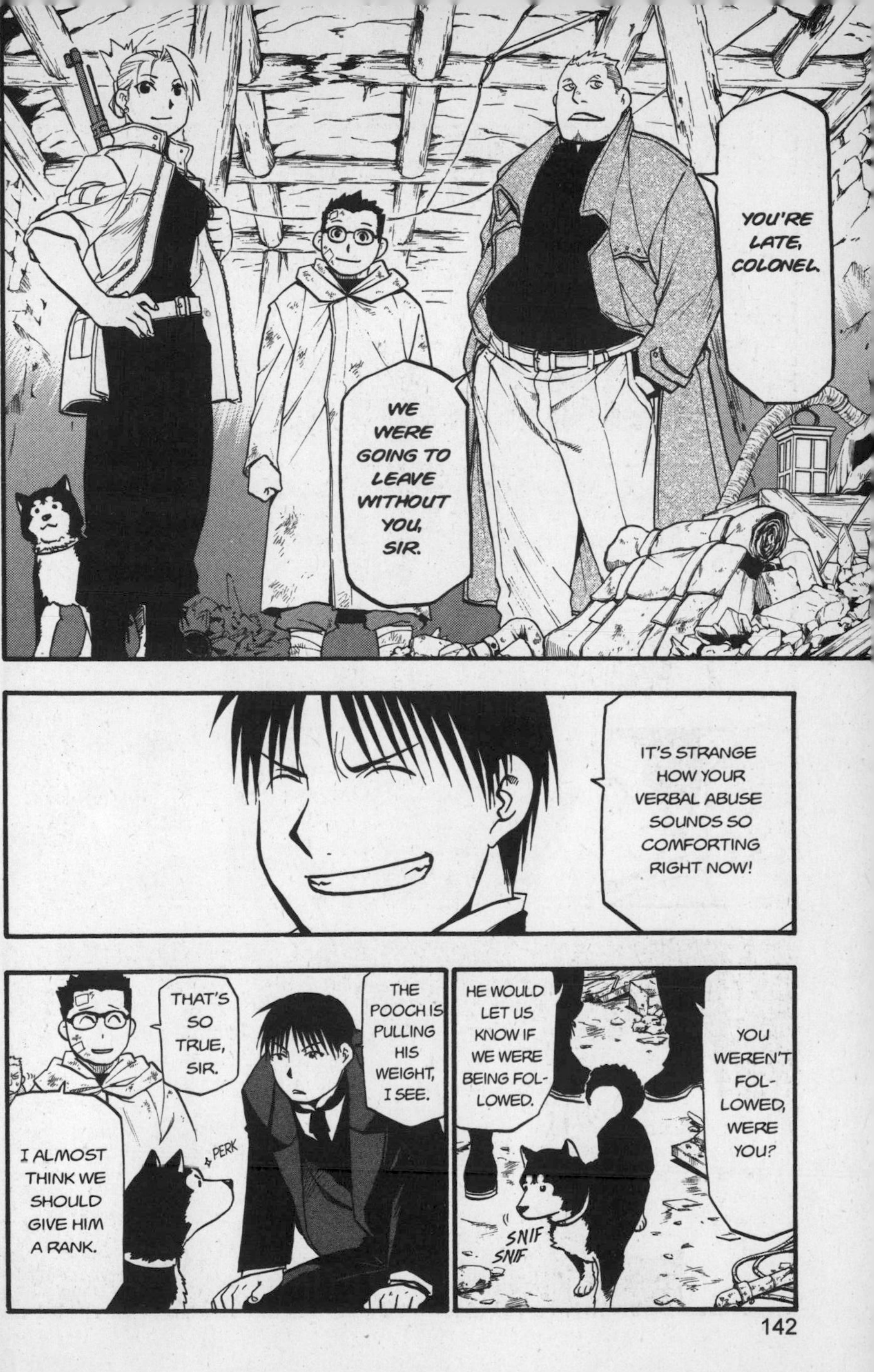
YOU'RE LATE, COLONEL.
WE WERE GOING TO LEAVE WITHOUT YOU, SIR.
IT'S STRANGE HOW YOUR VERBAL ABUSE SOUNDS SO COMFORTING RIGHT NOW!
YOU WEREN'T FOL-LOWED, WERE YOU?
HE WOULD LET US KNOW IF WE WERE BEING FOL-LOWED.
SNIF SNIF
THE POOCH IS PULLING HIS WEIGHT, I SEE.
THAT'S SO TRUE, SIR.
PERK
I ALMOST THINK WE SHOULD GIVE HIM A RANK.

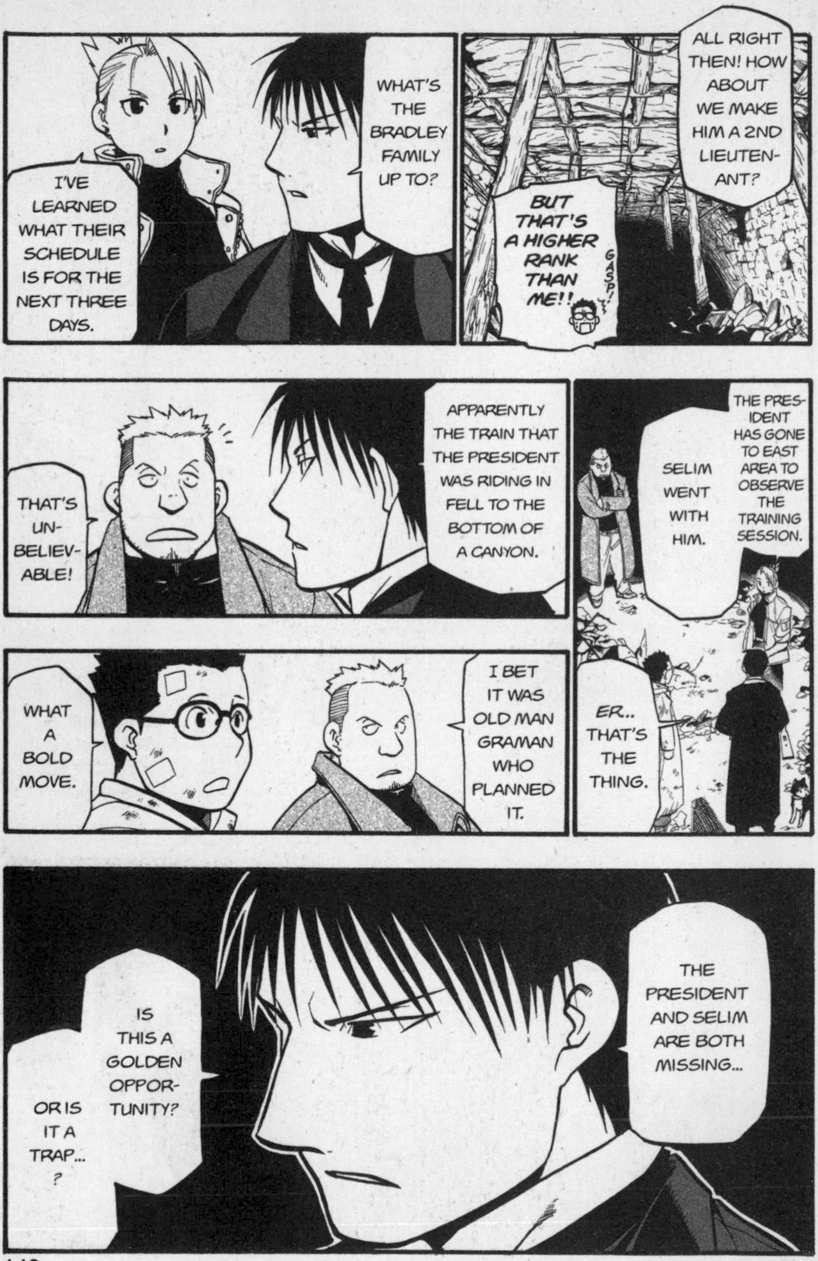
ALL RIGHT THEN! HOW ABOUT WE MAKE HIM A 2ND LIEUTENANT?
BUT THAT'S A HIGHER RANK THAN ME!!
GASP!
WHAT'S THE BRADLEY FAMILY UP TO?
I'VE LEARNED WHAT THEIR SCHEDULE IS FOR THE NEXT THREE DAYS.
THE PRESIDENT HAS GONE TO EAST AREA TO OBSERVE THE TRAINING SESSION.
SELIM WENT WITH HIM.
ER... THAT'S THE THING.
APPARENTLY THE TRAIN THAT THE PRESIDENT WAS RIDING IN FELL TO THE BOTTOM OF A CANYON.
THAT'S UNBELIEVABLE!
I BET IT WAS OLD MAN GRAMAN WHO PLANNED IT.
WHAT A BOLD MOVE.
THE PRESIDENT AND SELIM ARE BOTH MISSING...
IS THIS A GOLDEN OPPORTUNITY?
OR IS IT A TRAP...?

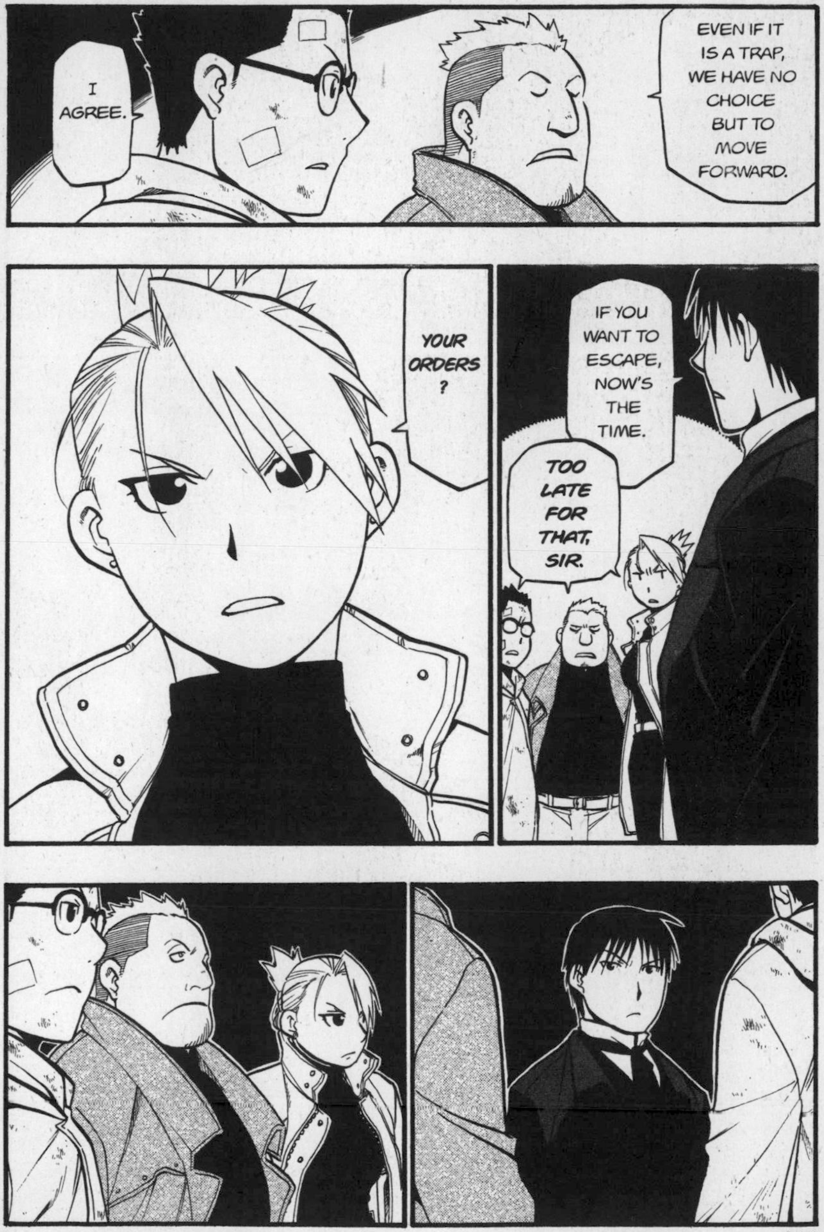
EVEN IF IT IS A TRAP, WE HAVE NO CHOICE BUT TO MOVE FORWARD.
I AGREE.
IF YOU WANT TO ESCAPE, NOW'S THE TIME.
TOO LATE FOR THAT, SIR.
YOUR ORDERS?

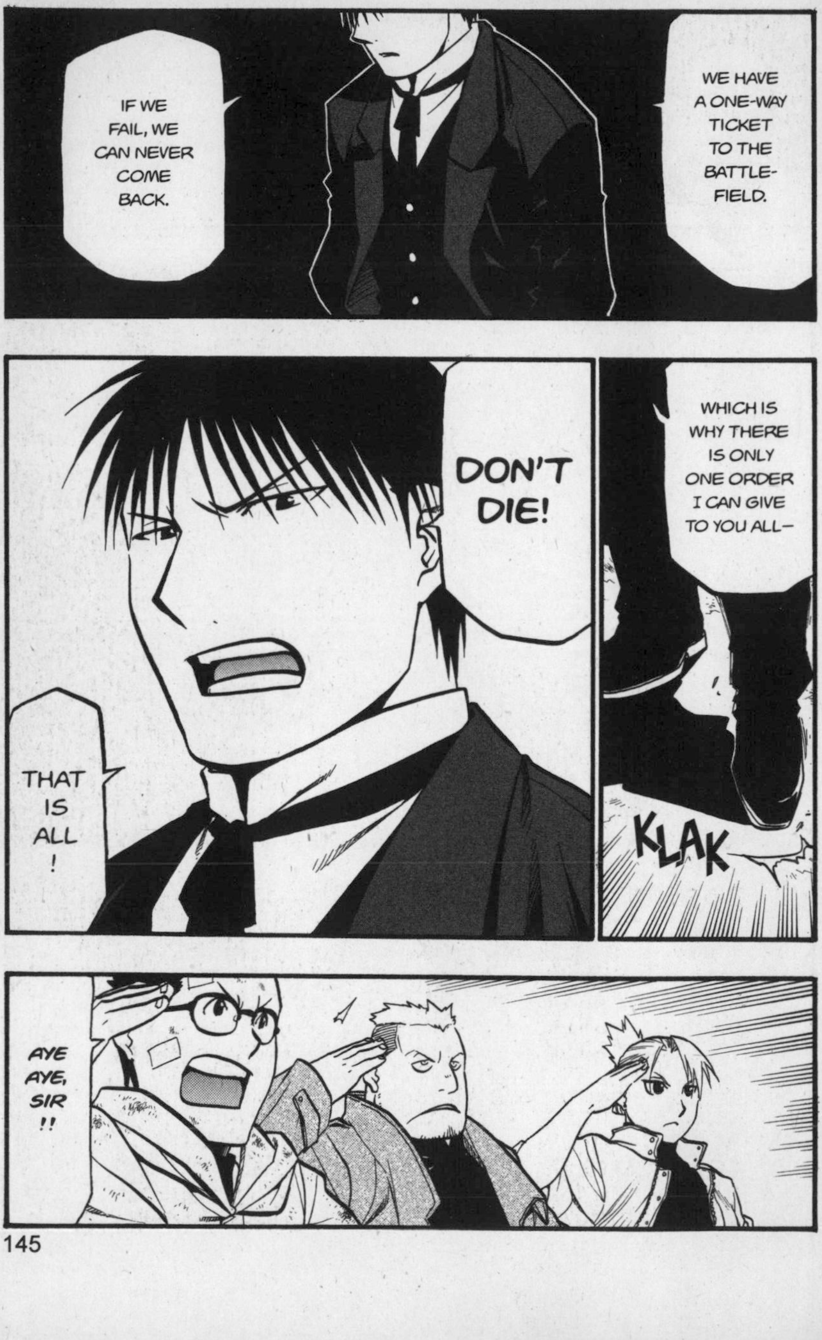
WE HAVE A ONE-WAY TICKET TO THE BATTLE-FIELD.
IF WE FAIL, WE CAN NEVER COME BACK.
WHICH IS WHY THERE IS ONLY ONE ORDER I CAN GIVE TO YOU ALL—
KLAK
DON'T DIE!
THAT IS ALL!
AYE AYE, SIR!!

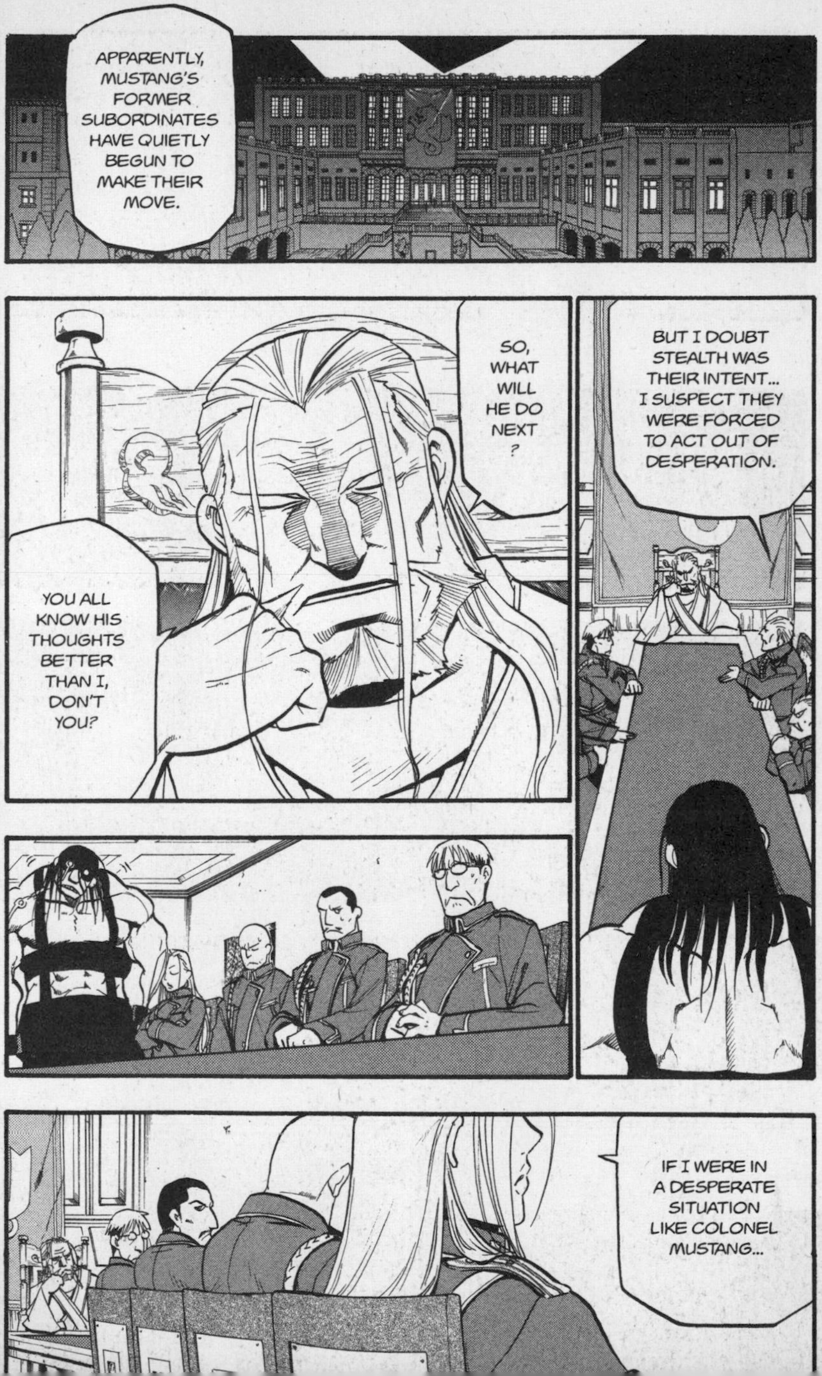
APPARENTLY, MUSTANG'S FORMER SUBORDINATES HAVE QUIETLY BEGUN TO MAKE THEIR MOVE.
BUT I DOUBT STEALTH WAS THEIR INTENT... I SUSPECT THEY WERE FORCED TO ACT OUT OF DESPERATION.
SO, WHAT WILL HE DO NEXT?
YOU ALL KNOW HIS THOUGHTS BETTER THAN I, DON'T YOU?
IF I WERE IN A DESPERATE SITUATION LIKE COLONEL MUSTANG...

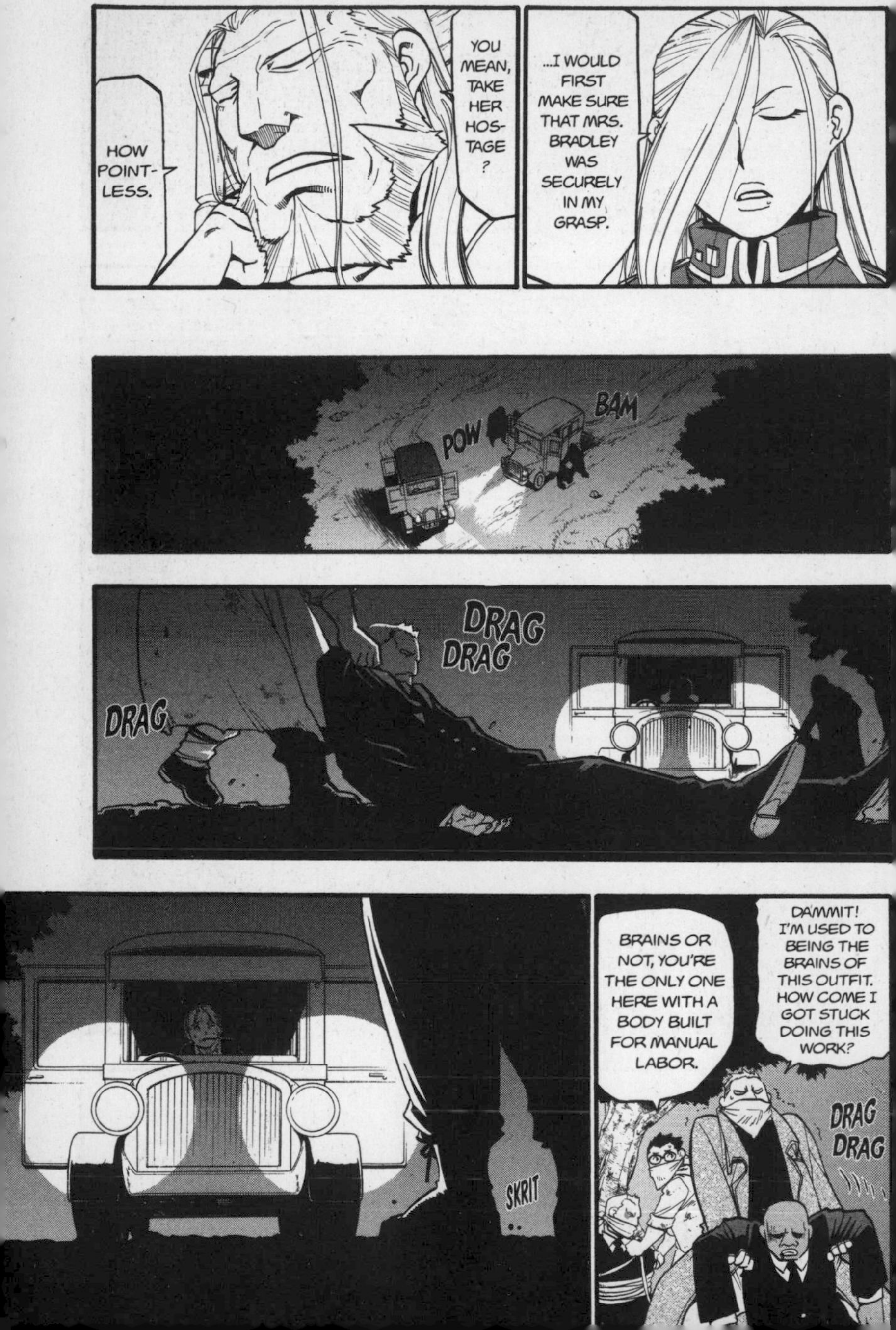
...I WOULD FIRST MAKE SURE THAT MRS. BRADLEY WAS SECURELY IN MY GRASP.
YOU MEAN, TAKE HER HOS-TAGE?
HOW POINT-LESS.
BAM
POW
DRAG DRAG
DRAG
DAMMIT! I'M USED TO BEING THE BRAINS OF THIS OUTFIT. HOW COME I GOT STUCK DOING THIS WORK?
BRAINS OR NOT, YOU'RE THE ONLY ONE HERE WITH A BODY BUILT FOR MANUAL LABOR.
DRAG DRAG
SKRIT

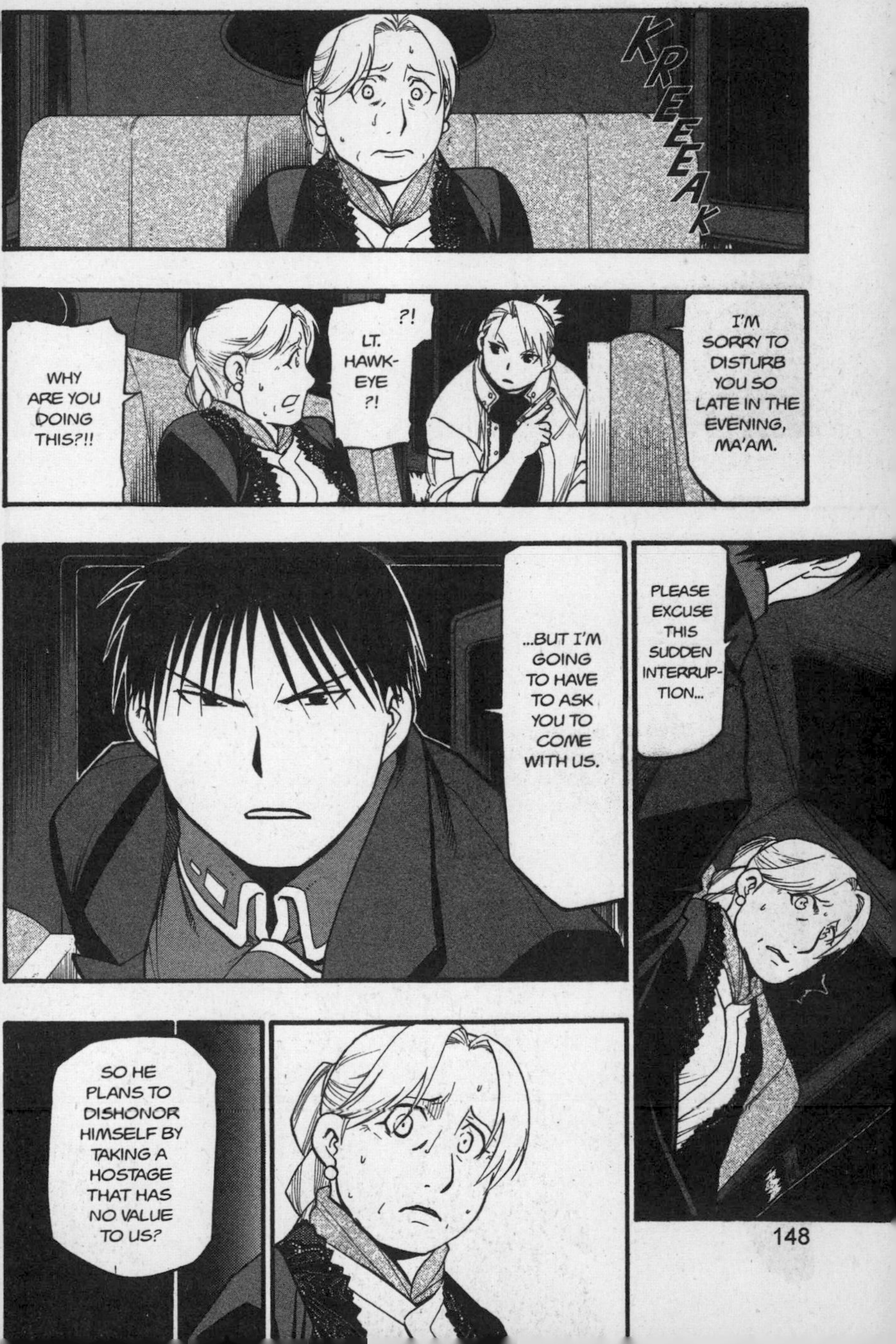
KREEEAK
I'M SORRY TO DISTURB YOU SO LATE IN THE EVENING, MA'AM.
?! LT. HAWK-EYE ?!
WHY ARE YOU DOING THIS?!!
PLEASE EXCUSE THIS SUDDEN INTERRUP-TION...
...BUT I'M GOING TO HAVE TO ASK YOU TO COME WITH US.
SO HE PLANS TO DISHONOR HIMSELF BY TAKING A HOSTAGE THAT HAS NO VALUE TO US?

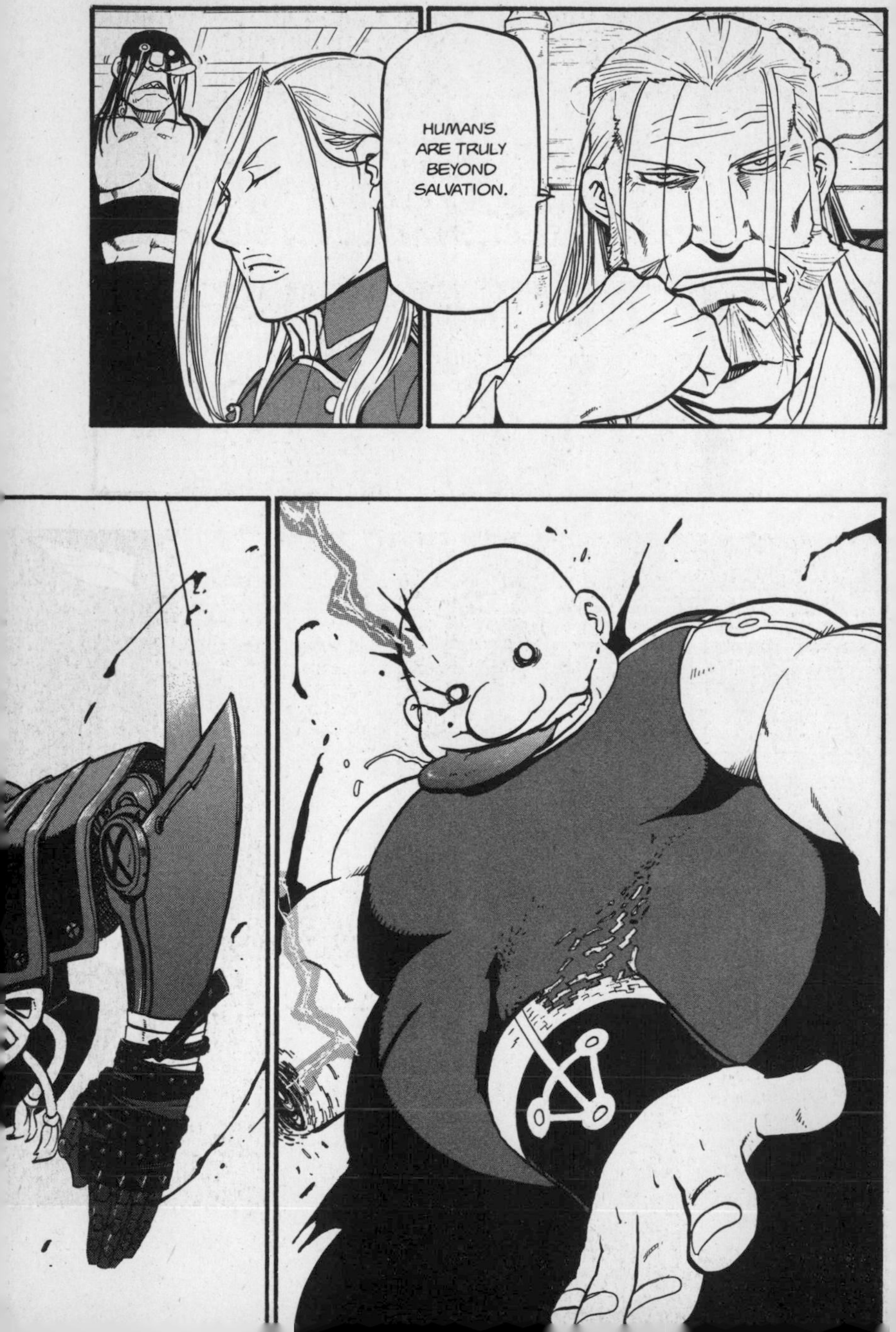
HUMAN'S ARE TRULY BEYOND SALVATION.

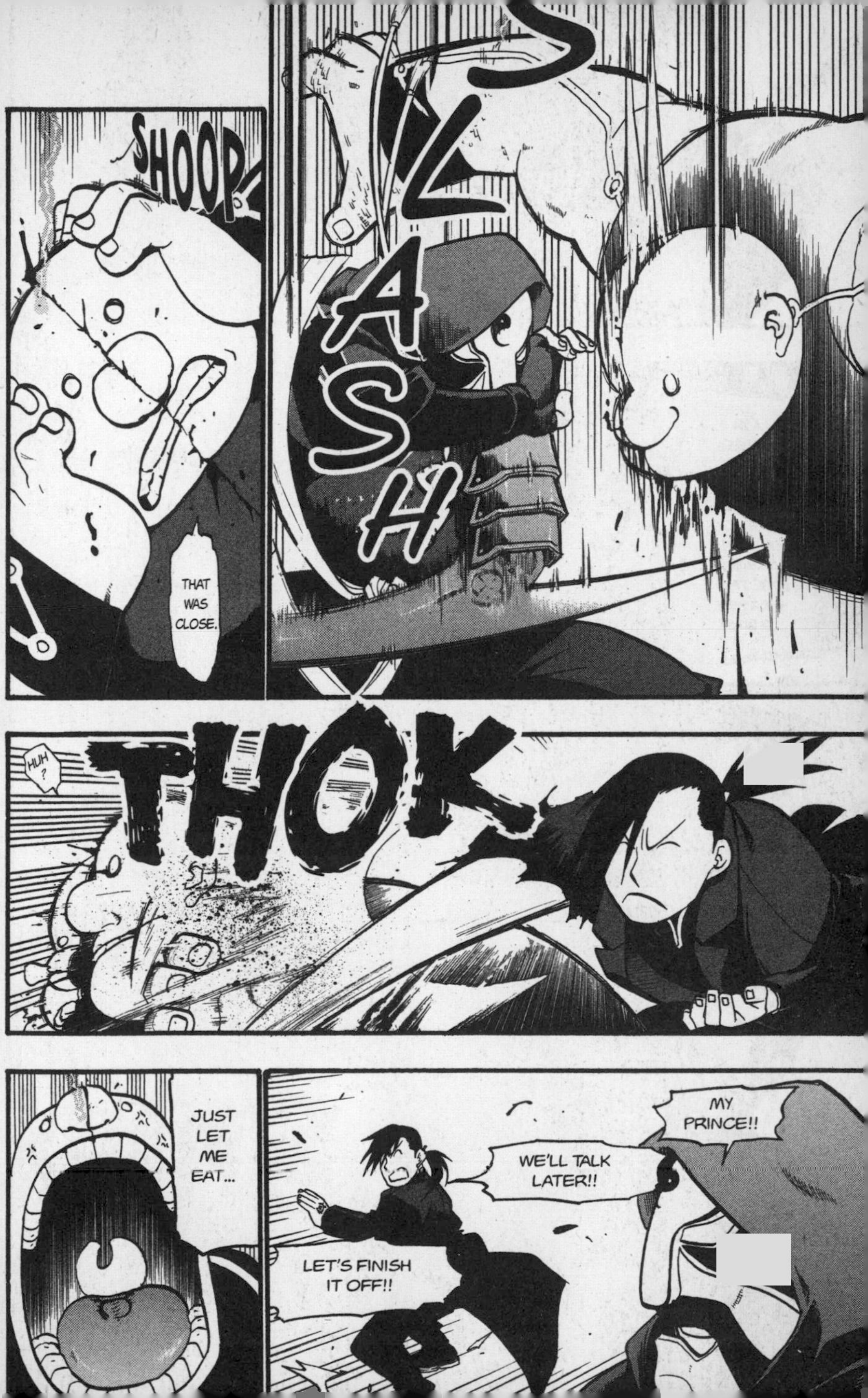
SLASH
SHOOP
THAT WAS CLOSE.
THOK
HUH?
MY PRINCE!!
WE'LL TALK LATER!!
LET'S FINISH IT OFF!!
JUST LET ME EAT...

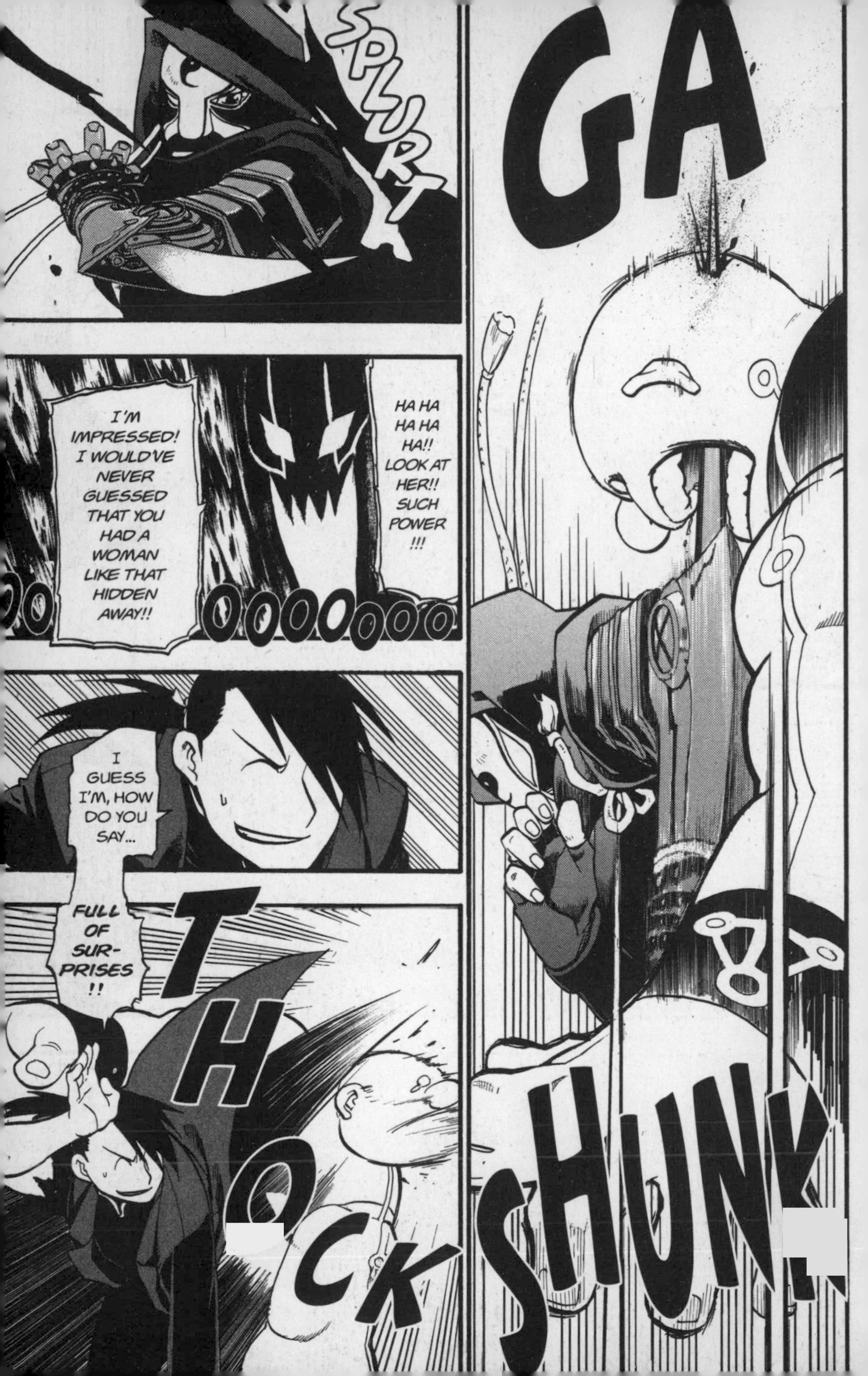
GA
SHUNK
SPLURT
HA HA HA HA HA!! LOOK AT HER!! SUCH POWER!!!
I'M IMPRESSED! I WOULD'VE NEVER GUESSED THAT YOU HAD A WOMAN LIKE THAT HIDDEN AWAY!!
OOOOOOO
I GUESS I'M, HOW DO YOU SAY...
FULL OF SUR-PRISES!!
THOCK

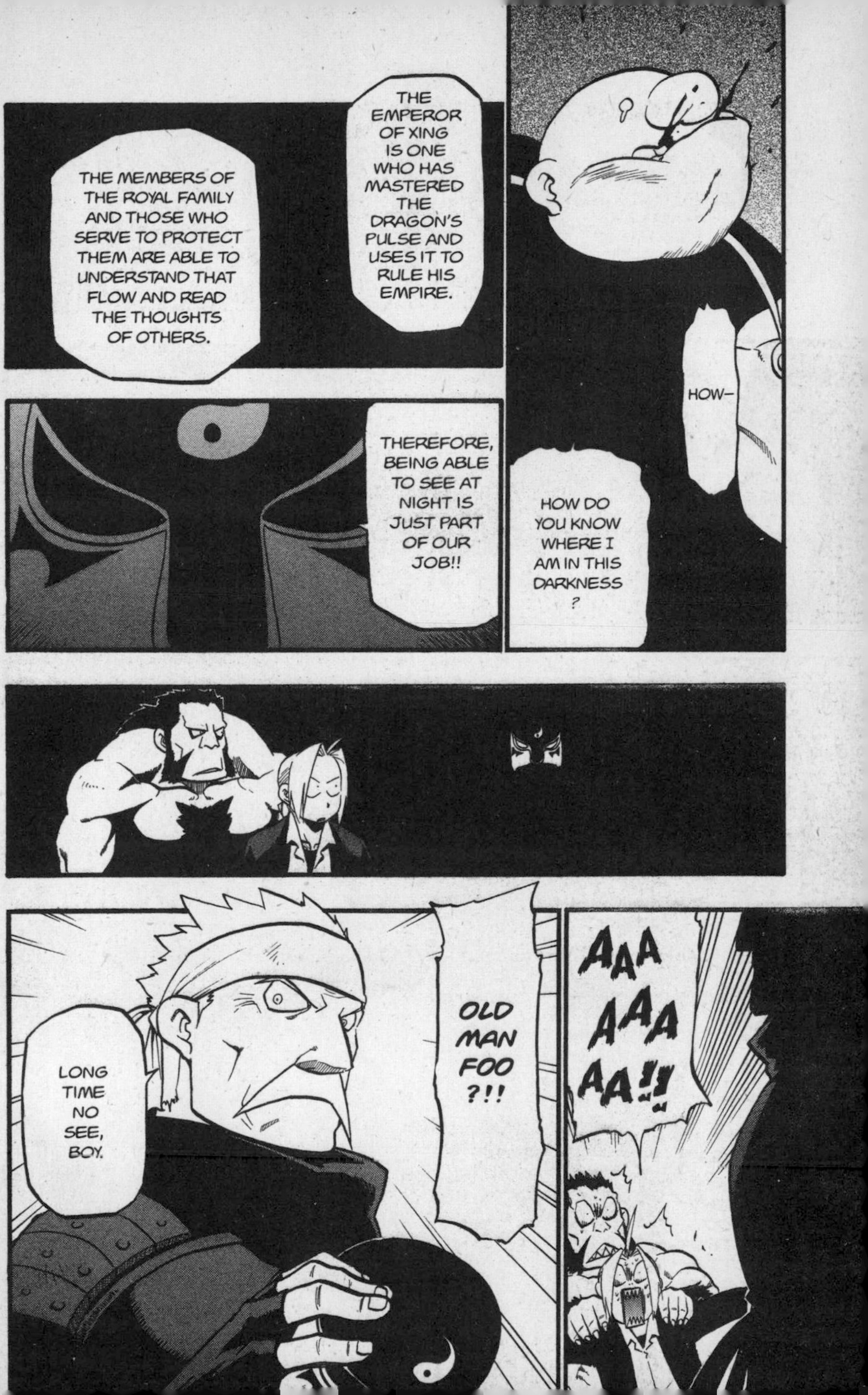
HOW—
HOW DO YOU KNOW WHERE I AM IN THIS DARKNESS?
THE EMPEROR OF XING IS ONE WHO HAS MASTERED THE DRAGON'S PULSE AND USES IT TO RULE HIS EMPIRE.
THE MEMBERS OF THE ROYAL FAMILY AND THOSE WHO SERVE TO PROTECT THEM ARE ABLE TO UNDERSTAND THAT FLOW AND READ THE THOUGHTS OF OTHERS.
THEREFORE, BEING ABLE TO SEE AT NIGHT IS JUST PART OF OUR JOB!!
AAAAAAAA!!
OLD MAN FOO?!!
LONG TIME NO SEE, BOY.

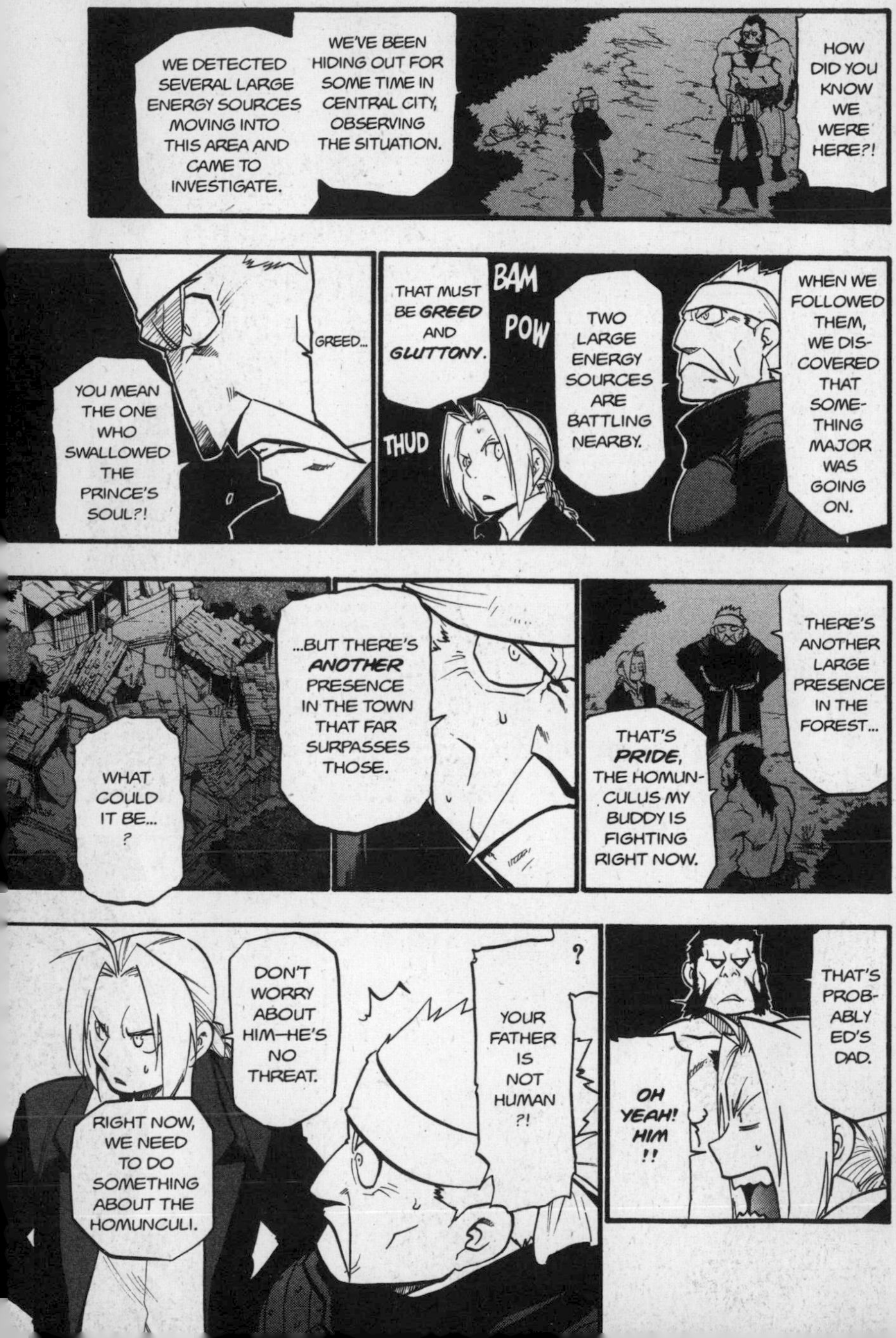
HOW DID YOU KNOW WE WERE HERE?!
WE'VE BEEN HIDING OUT FOR SOME TIME IN CENTRAL CITY, OBSERVING THE SITUATION.
WE DETECTED SEVERAL LARGE ENERGY SOURCES MOVING INTO THIS AREA AND CAME TO INVESTIGATE.
WHEN WE FOLLOWED THEM, WE DIS-COVERED THAT SOME-THING MAJOR WAS GOING ON.
TWO LARGE ENERGY SOURCES ARE BATTLING NEARBY.
BAM
POW
THAT MUST BE GREED AND GLUTTONY.
THUD
GREED...
YOU MEAN THE ONE WHO SWALLOWED THE PRINCE'S SOUL?!
THERE'S ANOTHER LARGE PRESENCE IN THE FOREST...
THAT'S PRIDE, THE HOMUN-CULUS MY BUDDY IS FIGHTING RIGHT NOW.
...BUT THERE'S ANOTHER PRESENCE IN THE TOWN THAT FAR SURPASSES THOSE.
WHAT COULD IT BE... ?
THAT'S PROB-ABLY ED'S DAD.
OH YEAH! HIM !!
?
YOUR FATHER IS NOT HUMAN ?!
DON'T WORRY ABOUT HIM—HE'S NO THREAT.
RIGHT NOW, WE NEED TO DO SOMETHING ABOUT THE HOMUNCULI.

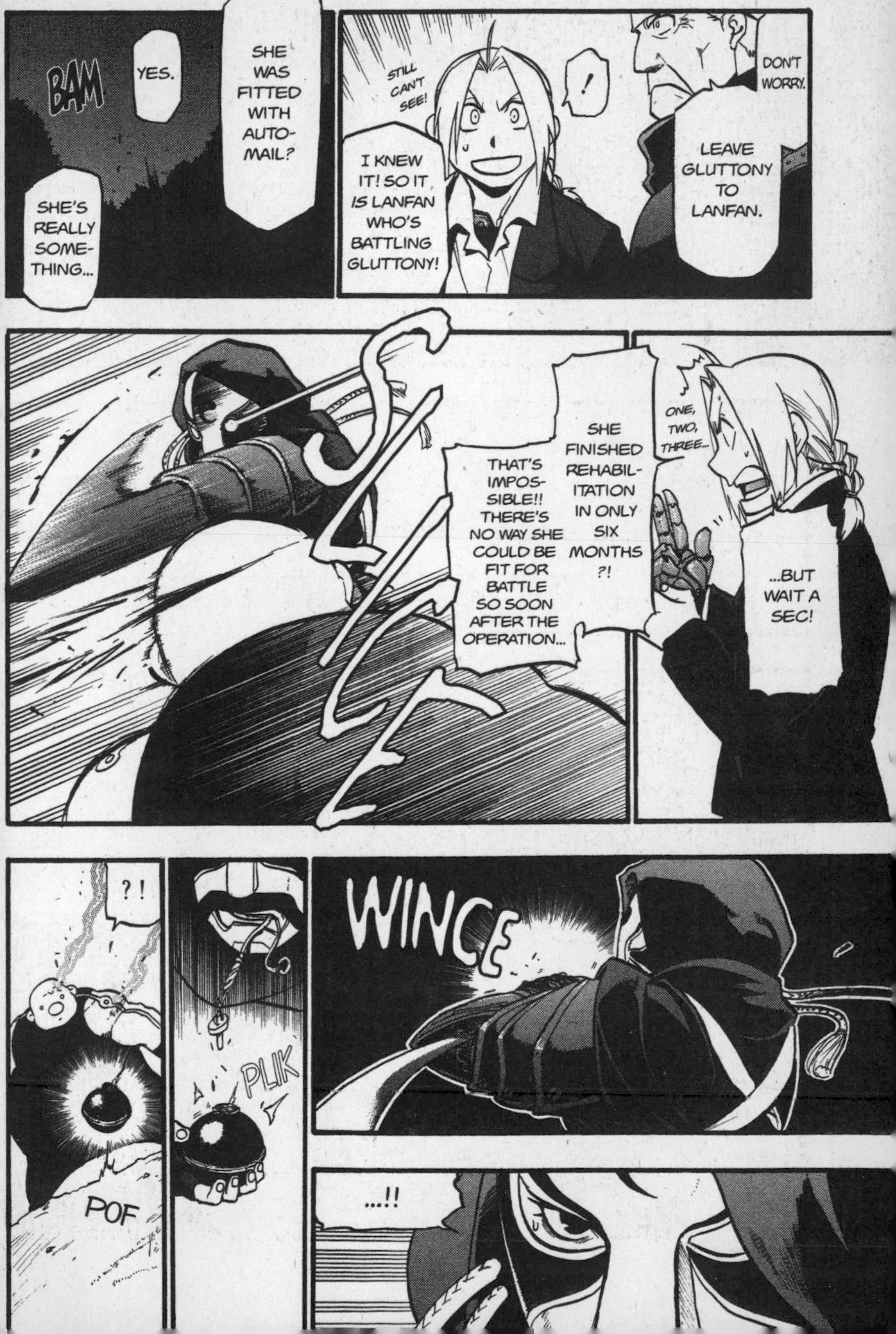
DON'T WORRY.
LEAVE GLUTTONY TO LANFAN.
!
STILL CAN'T SEE!
I KNEW IT! SO IT IS LANFAN WHO'S BATTLING GLUTTONY!
SHE WAS FITTED WITH AUTO-MAIL?
YES.
BAM
SHE'S REALLY SOME-THING...
ONE, TWO, THREE...
...BUT WAIT A SEC!
SHE FINISHED REHABIL-ITATION IN ONLY SIX MONTHS ?!
THAT'S IMPOS-SIBLE!! THERE'S NO WAY SHE COULD BE FIT FOR BATTLE SO SOON AFTER THE OPERATION...
WINCE
...!!
PLIK
?!
POF

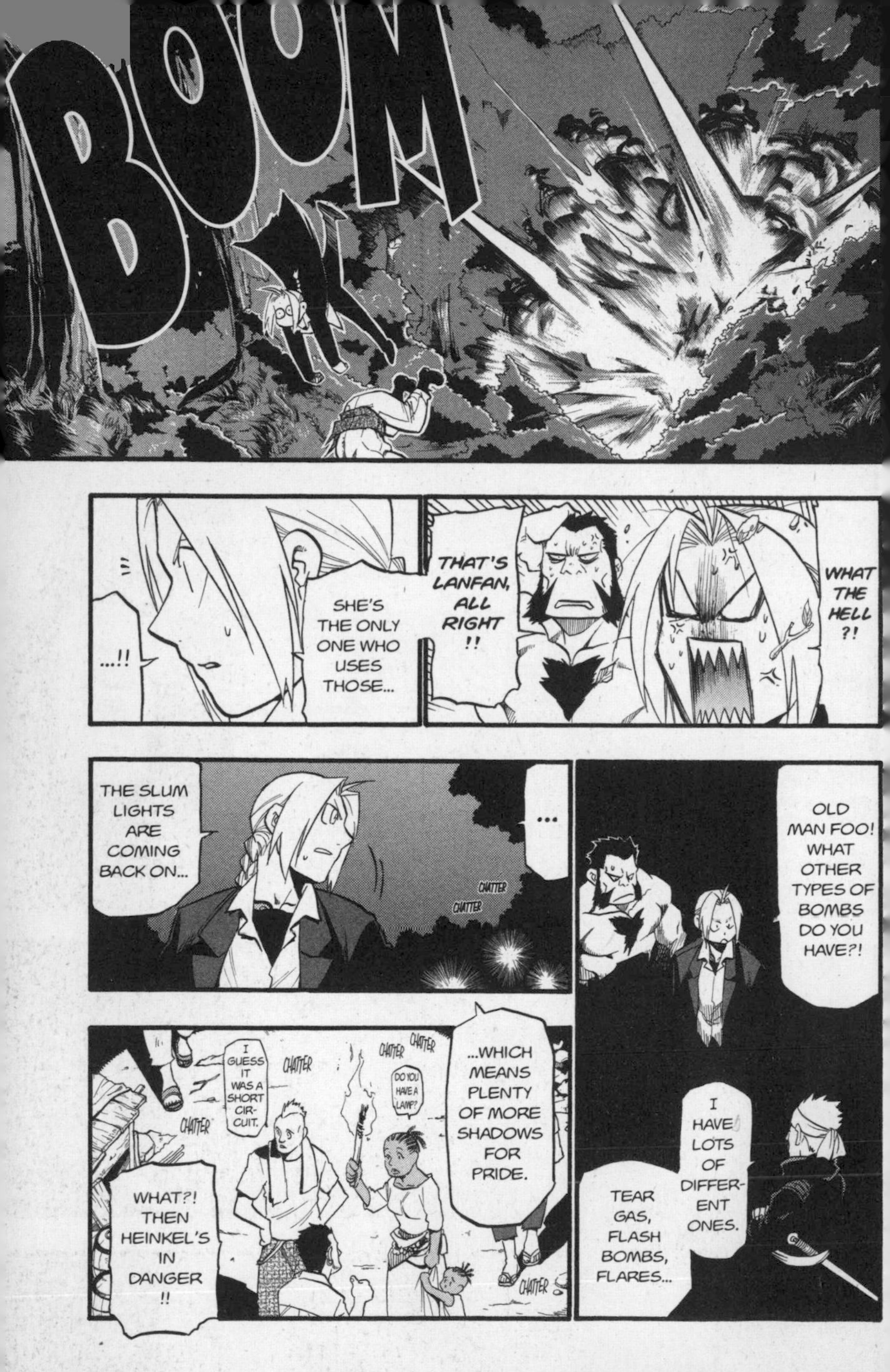
BOOM
WHAT THE HELL ?!
THAT'S LANFAN, ALL RIGHT !!
SHE'S THE ONLY ONE WHO USES THOSE...
...!!
OLD MAN FOO! WHAT OTHER TYPES OF BOMBS DO YOU HAVE?!
I HAVE LOTS OF DIFFER-ENT ONES.
TEAR GAS, FLASH BOMBS, FLARES...
...
THE SLUM LIGHTS ARE COMING BACK ON...
CHATTER
CHATTER
...WHICH MEANS PLENTY OF MORE SHADOWS FOR PRIDE.
CHATTER
CHATTER
DO YOU HAVE A LAMP?
CHATTER
I GUESS IT WAS A SHORT CIR-CUIT.
CHATTER
WHAT?! THEN HEINKEL'S IN DANGER !!
CHATTER

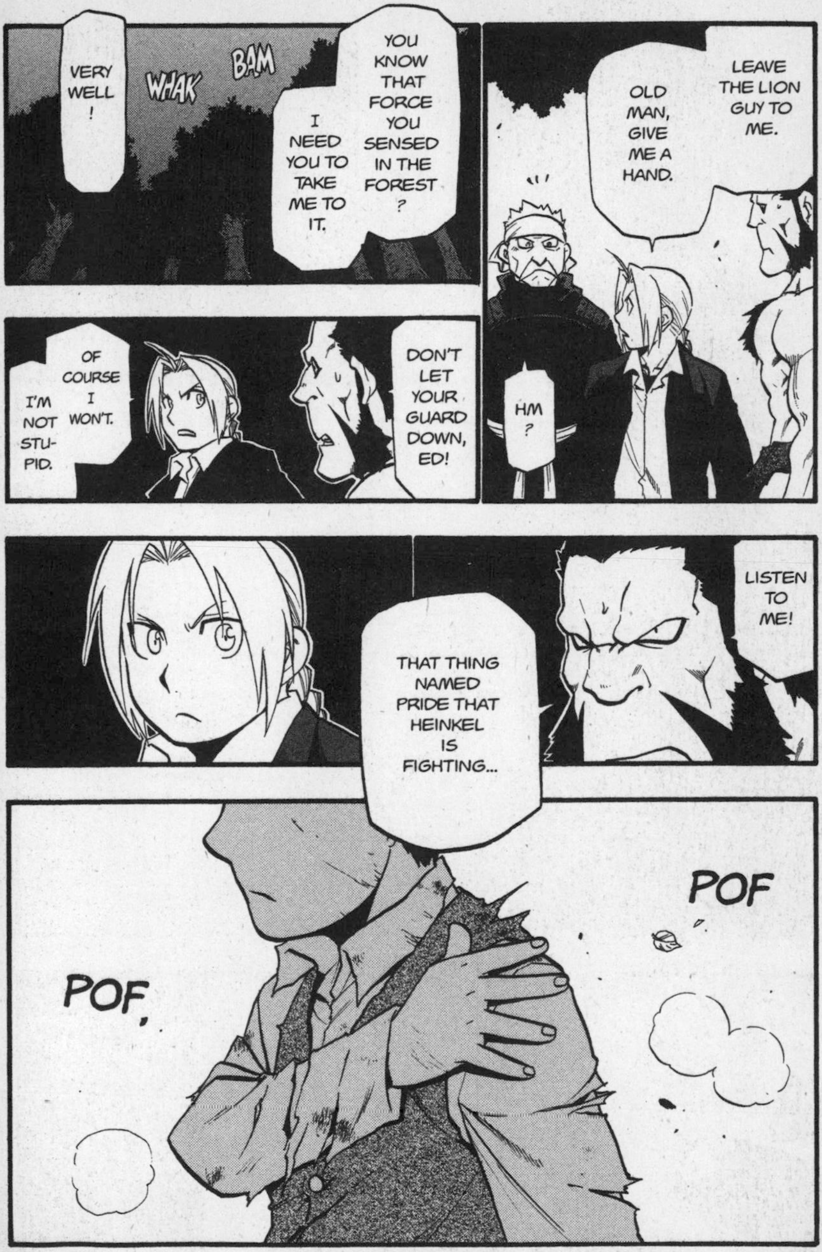
LEAVE THE LION GUY TO ME.
OLD MAN, GIVE ME A HAND.
HM?
YOU KNOW THAT FORCE YOU SENSED IN THE FOREST?
I NEED YOU TO TAKE ME TO IT.
BAM
WHAK
VERY WELL!
DON'T LET YOUR GUARD DOWN, ED!
OF COURSE I WON'T.
I'M NOT STU-PID.
LISTEN TO ME!
THAT THING NAMED PRIDE THAT HEINKEL IS FIGHTING...
POF
POF

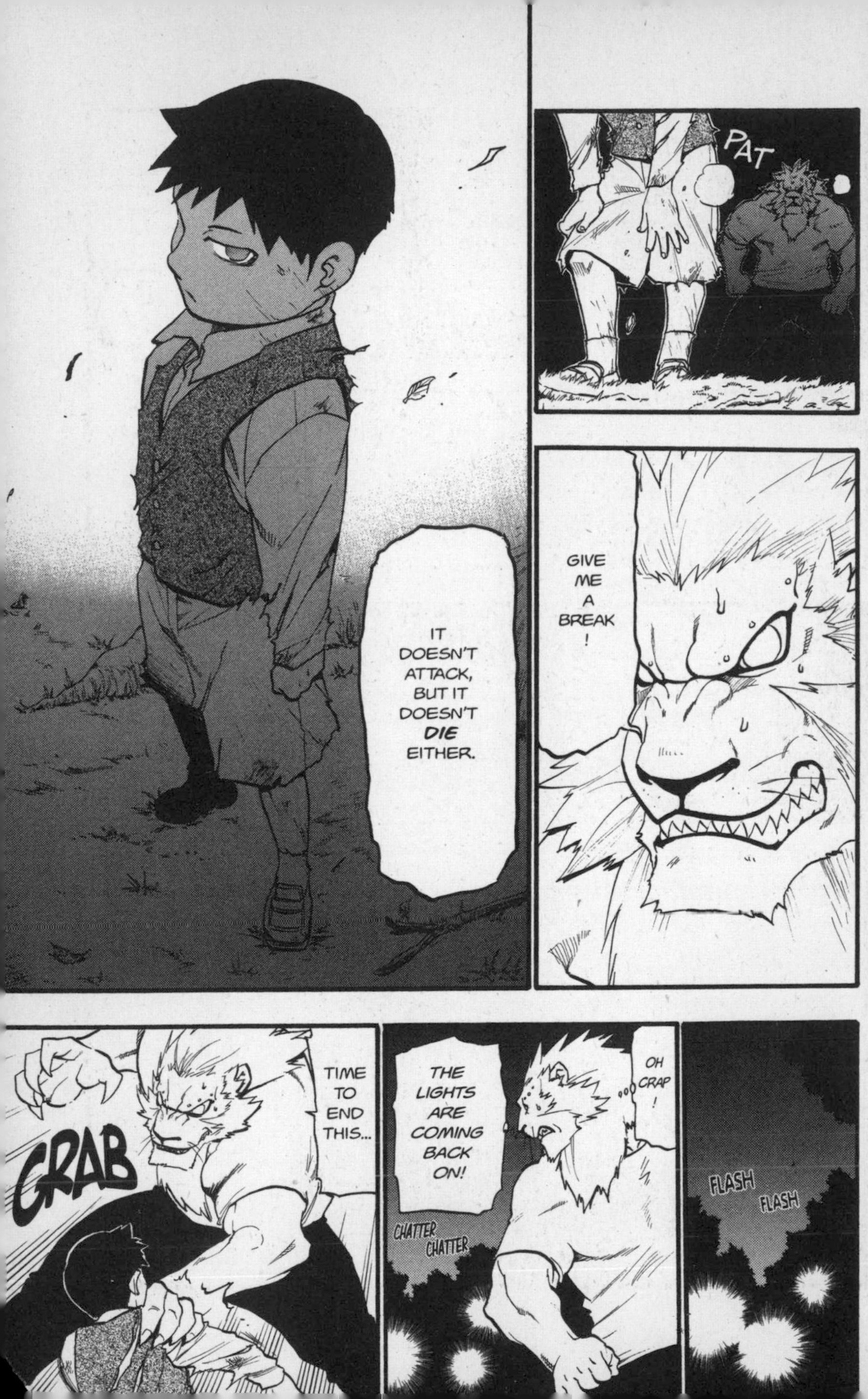
PAT
GIVE ME A BREAK!
IT DOESN'T ATTACK, BUT IT DOESN'T **DIE** EITHER.
FLASH
FLASH
OH CRAP!
THE LIGHTS ARE COMING BACK ON!
CHATTER
CHATTER
TIME TO END THIS...
GRAB

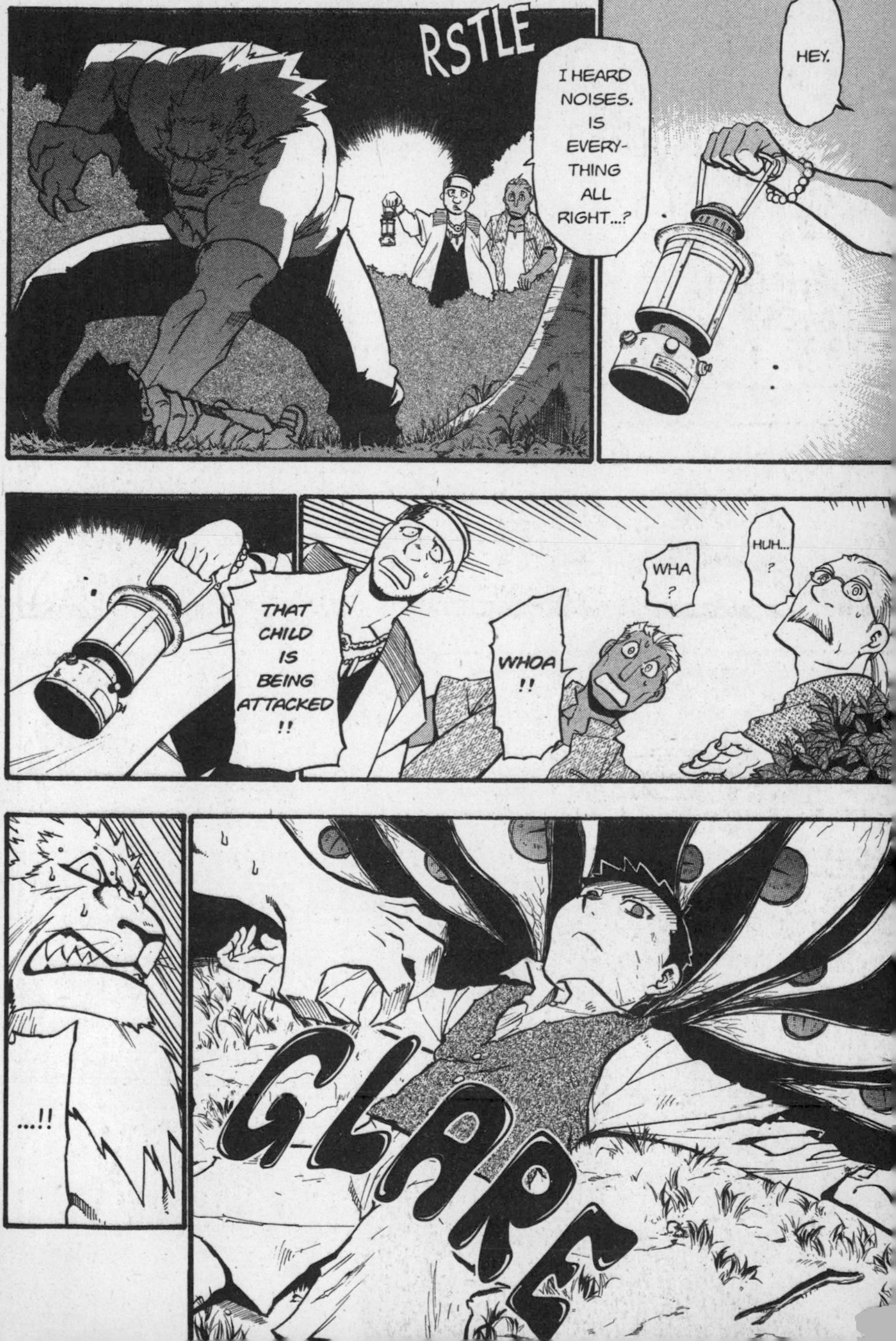
HEY.
RSTLE
I HEARD NOISES. IS EVERYTHING ALL RIGHT...?
HUH... ?
WHA ?
WHOA !!
THAT CHILD IS BEING ATTACKED !!
GLARE
...!!

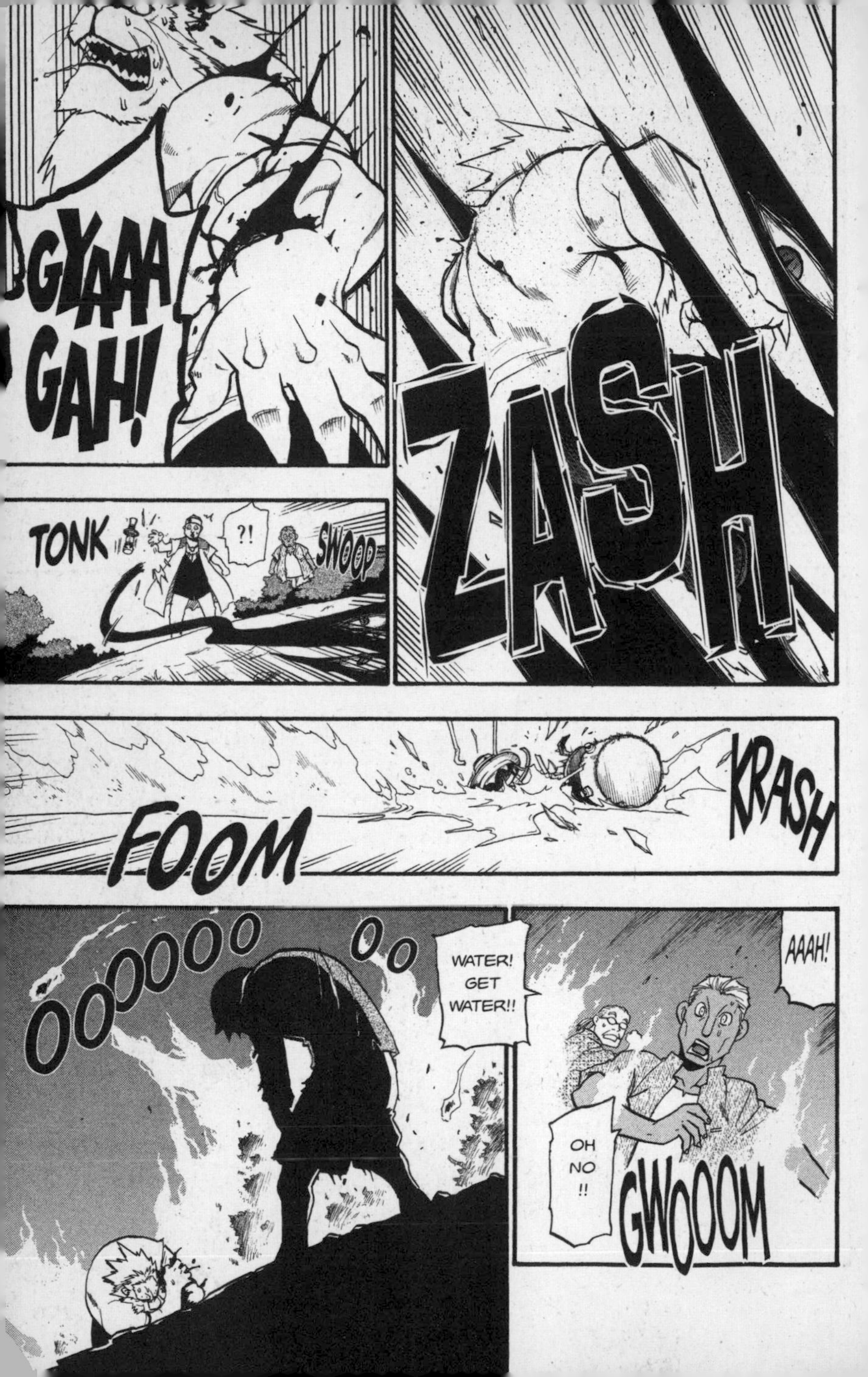

ZASH
GYAAA GAH!
SWOOP
?!
TONK
KRASH
FOOM
AAAH!
OH NO !!
GWOOOM
WATER! GET WATER!!
OOOOOOO
OO

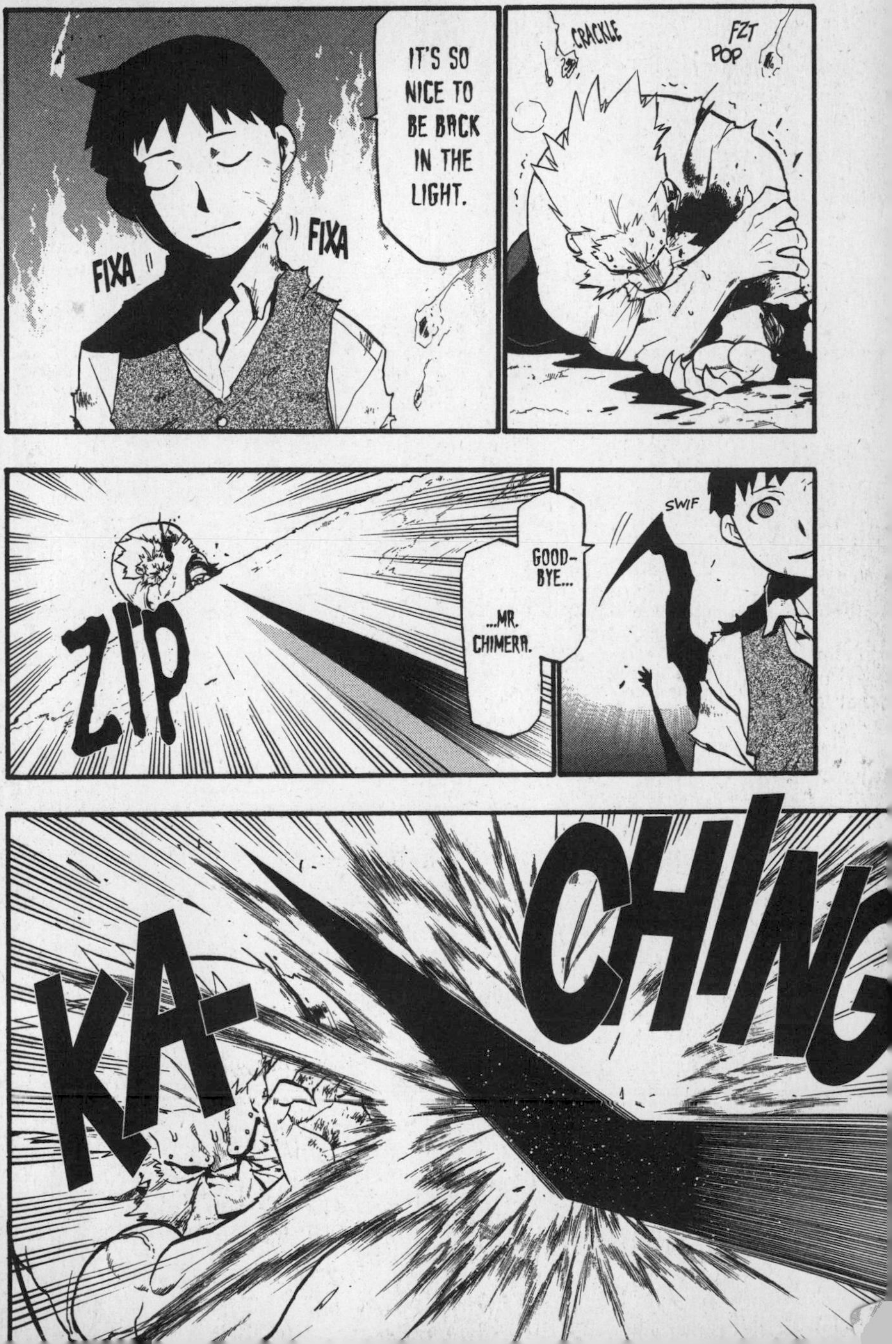
CRACKLE
FZT
POP
IT'S SO NICE TO BE BACK IN THE LIGHT.
FIXA
FIXA
SWIF
GOOD-BYE...
...MR. CHIMERA.
ZIP
KA-CHING

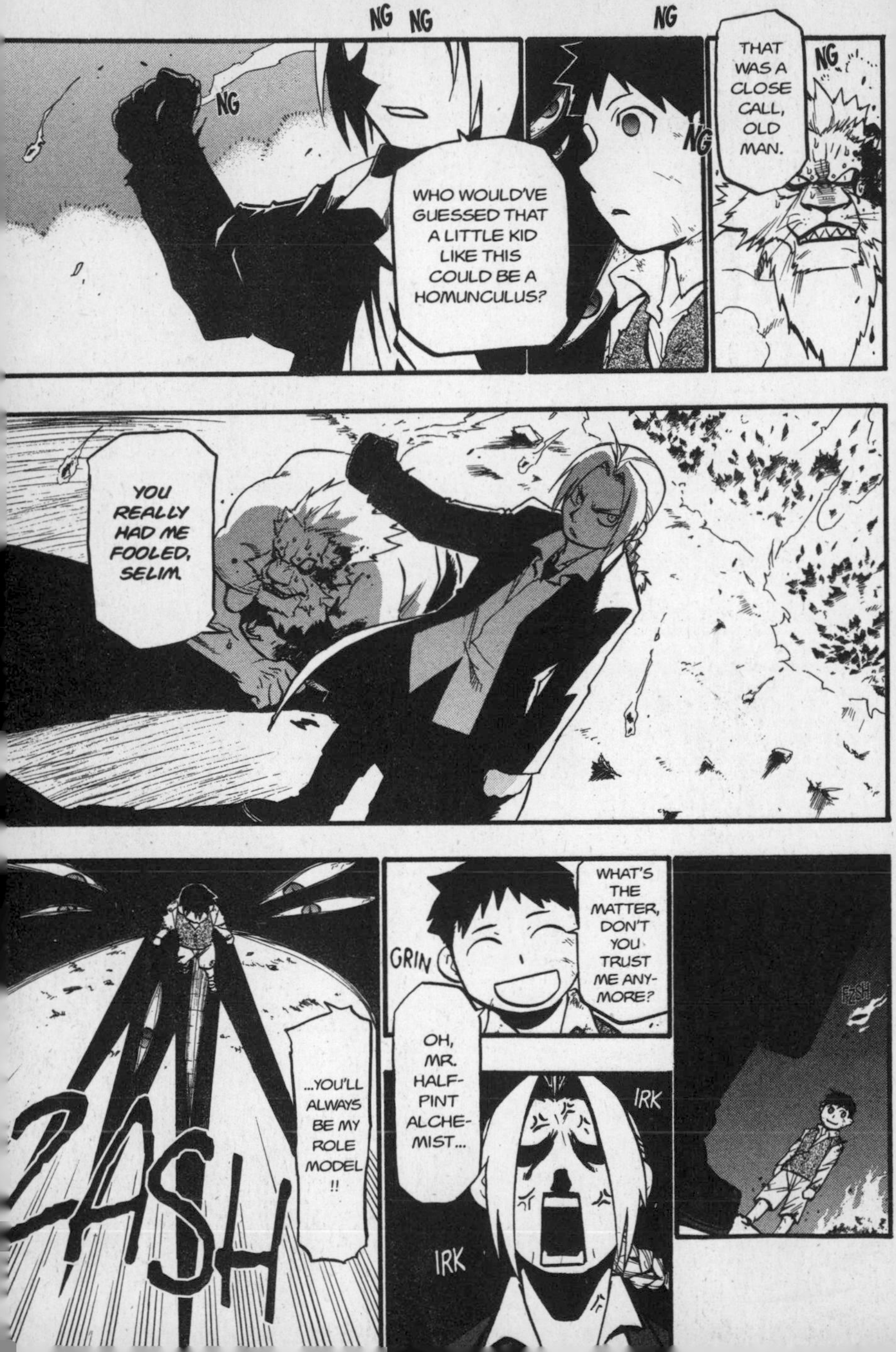
NG
THAT WAS A CLOSE CALL, OLD MAN.
NG
NG
WHO WOULD'VE GUESSED THAT A LITTLE KID LIKE THIS COULD BE A HOMUNCULUS?
NG NG
NG
YOU REALLY HAD ME FOOLED, SELIM.
FZSH
GRIN
WHAT'S THE MATTER, DON'T YOU TRUST ME ANY-MORE?
IRK
OH, MR. HALF-PINT ALCHE-MIST...
IRK
...YOU'LL ALWAYS BE MY ROLE MODEL!!
ZASH

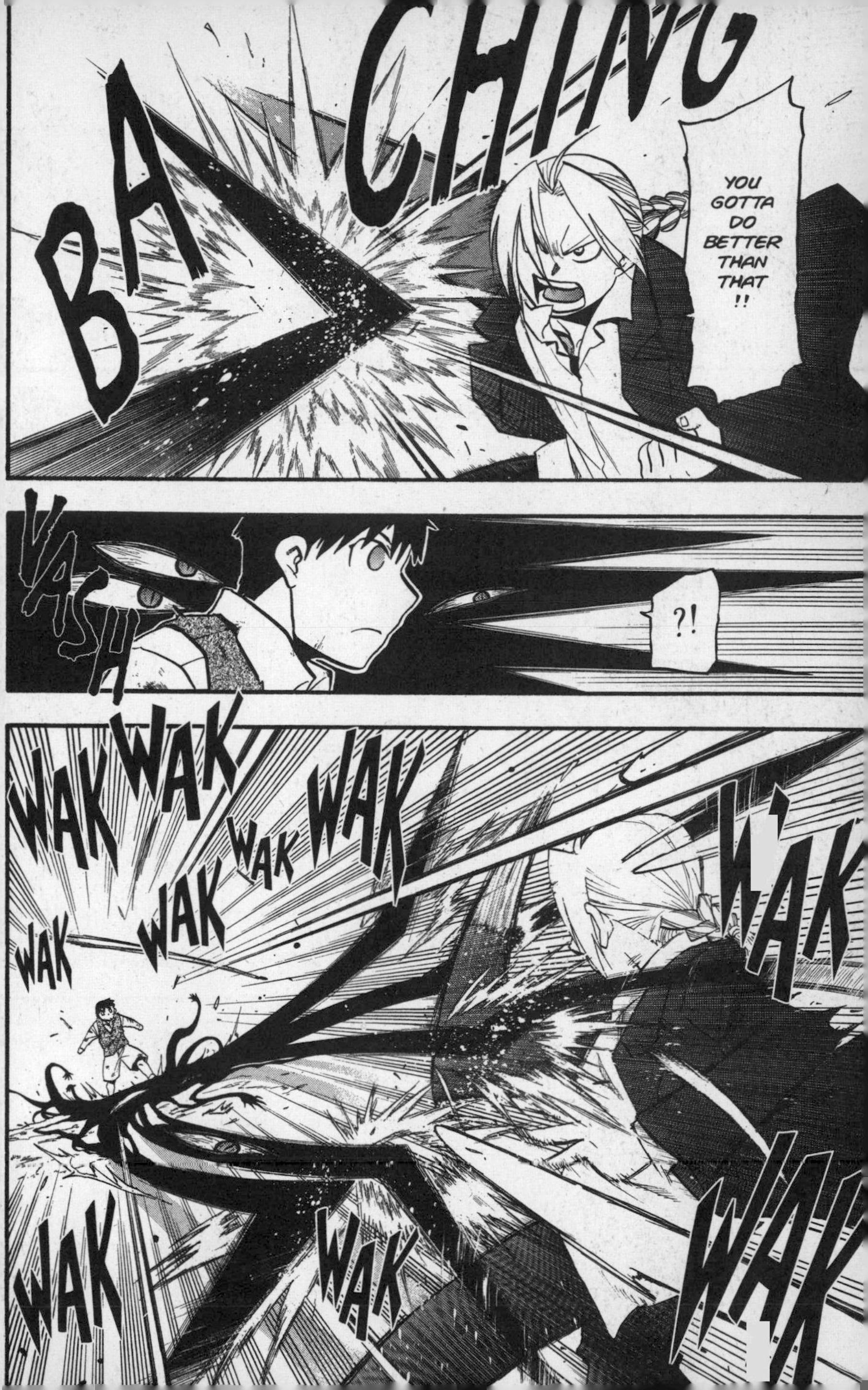
BA CHING
YOU GOTTA DO BETTER THAN THAT !!
?!
VASH
WAK
WAK WAK
WAK WAK
WAK
WAK WAK
WAK
WAK WAK

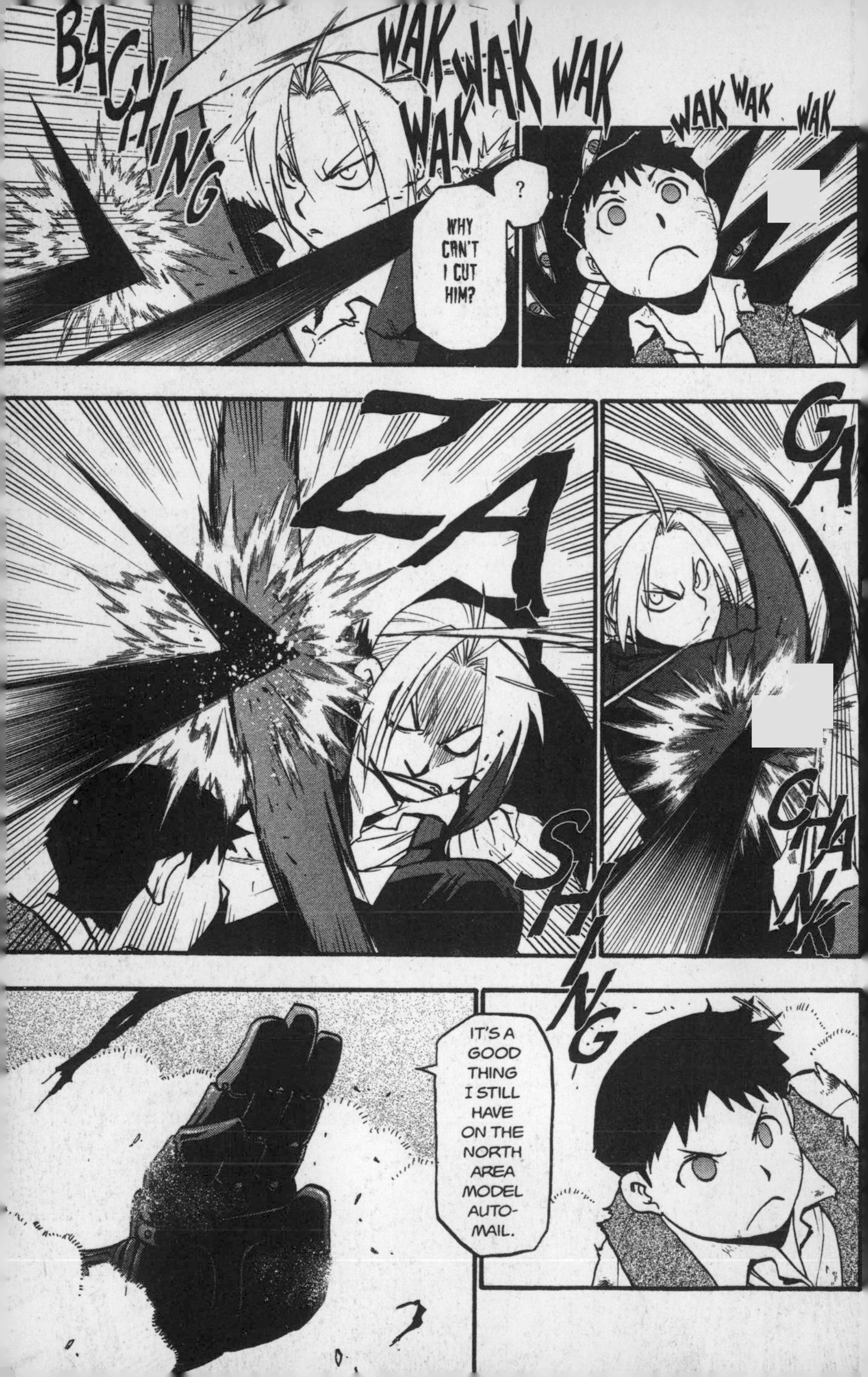

WAK WAK WAK
?
WHY CAN'T I CUT HIM?
WAK-WAK WAK WAK WAK
BACHING
GA CHANK
ZA
SHING
IT'S A GOOD THING I STILL HAVE ON THE NORTH AREA MODEL AUTO-MAIL.

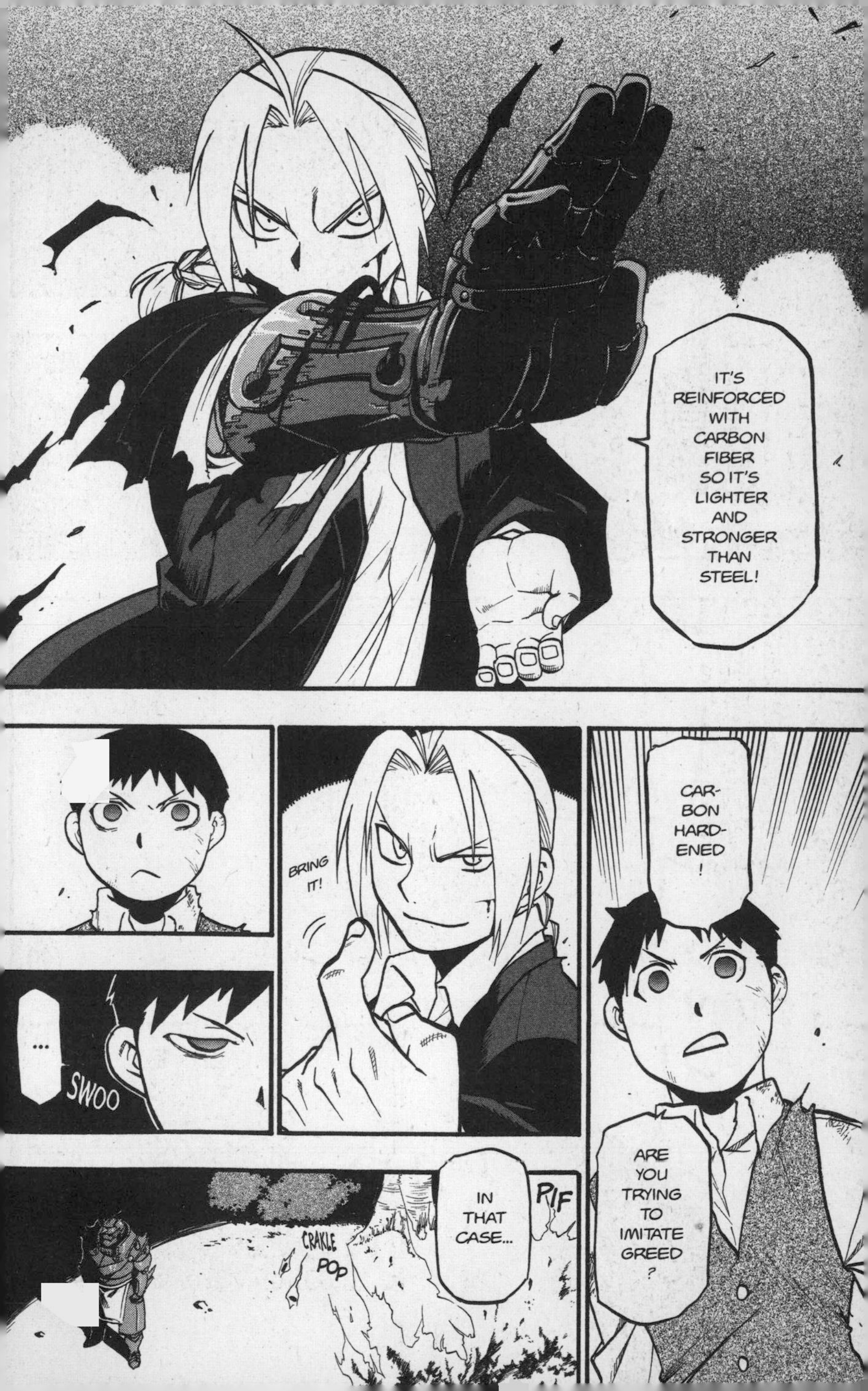
IT'S REINFORCED WITH CARBON FIBER SO IT'S LIGHTER AND STRONGER THAN STEEL!
CAR-BON HARD-ENED!
ARE YOU TRYING TO IMITATE GREED?
BRING IT!
...
SWOO
IN THAT CASE...
PIF
CRAKLE
POP

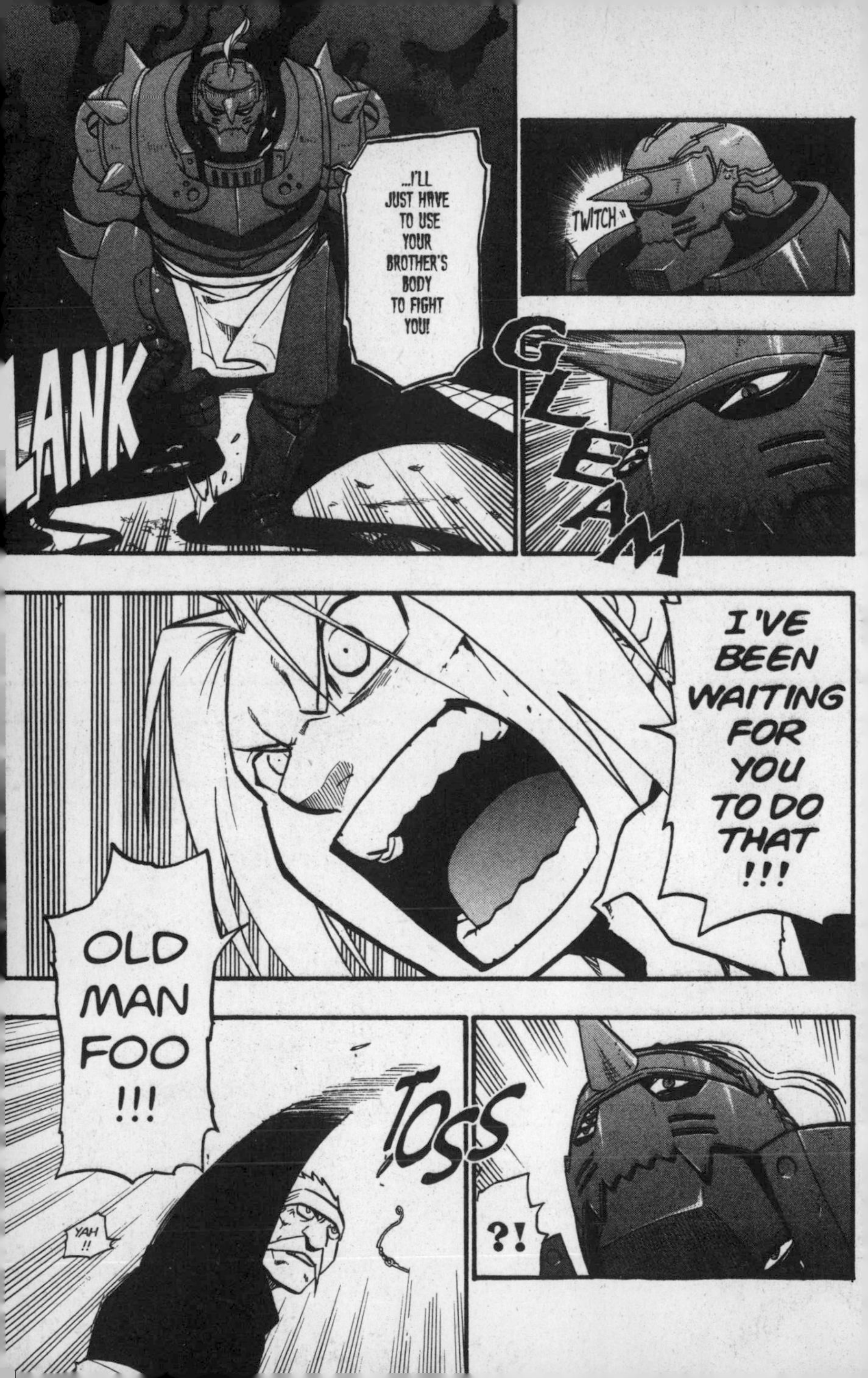
TWITCH
GLEAM
...I'LL JUST HAVE TO USE YOUR BROTHER'S BODY TO FIGHT YOU!
LANK
I'VE BEEN WAITING FOR YOU TO DO THAT!!!
OLD MAN FOO!!!
?!
TOSS
YAH!!

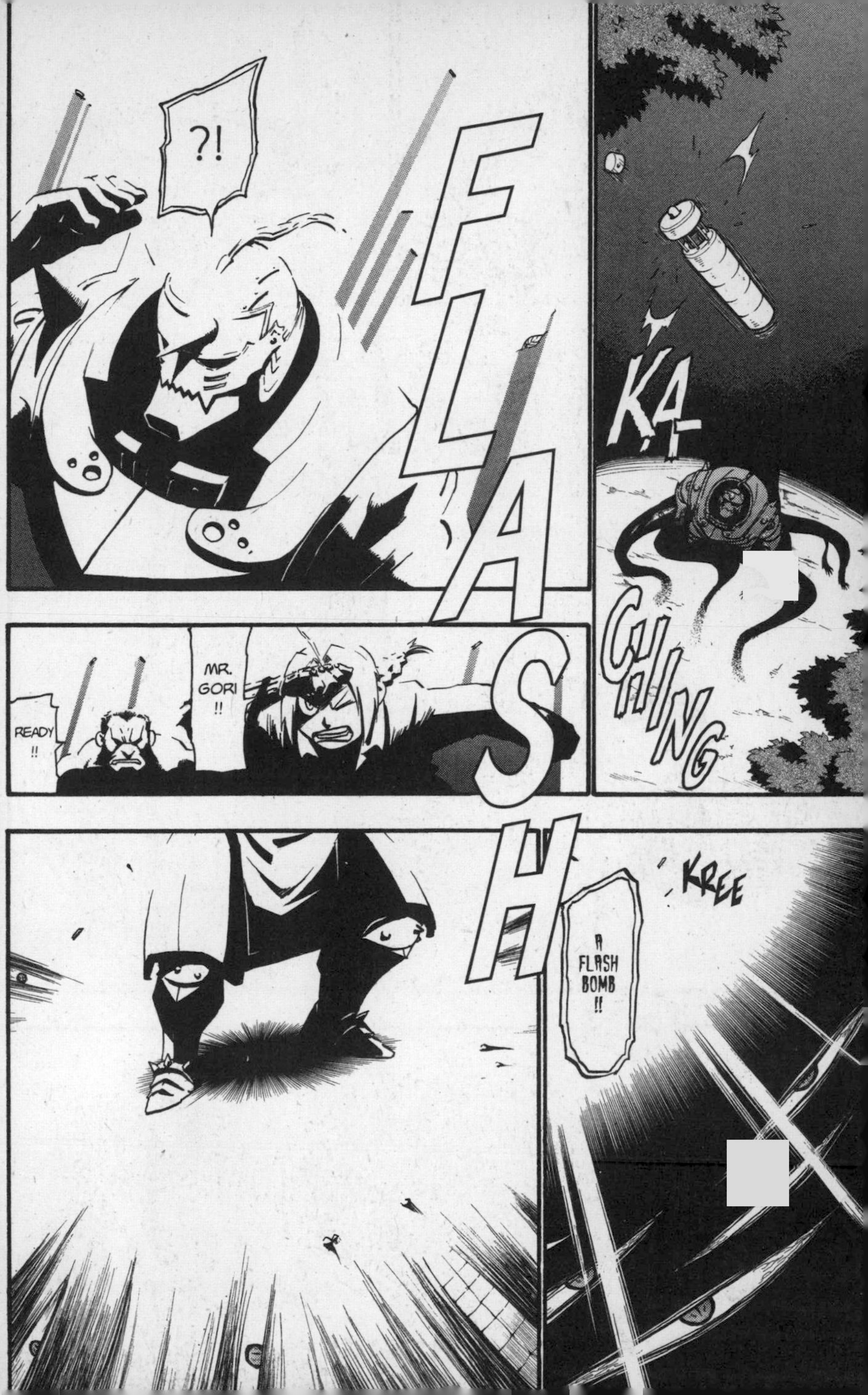
KA-CHING
?!
MR. GORI!!
READY!!
KREE
A FLASH BOMB!!
FLASH

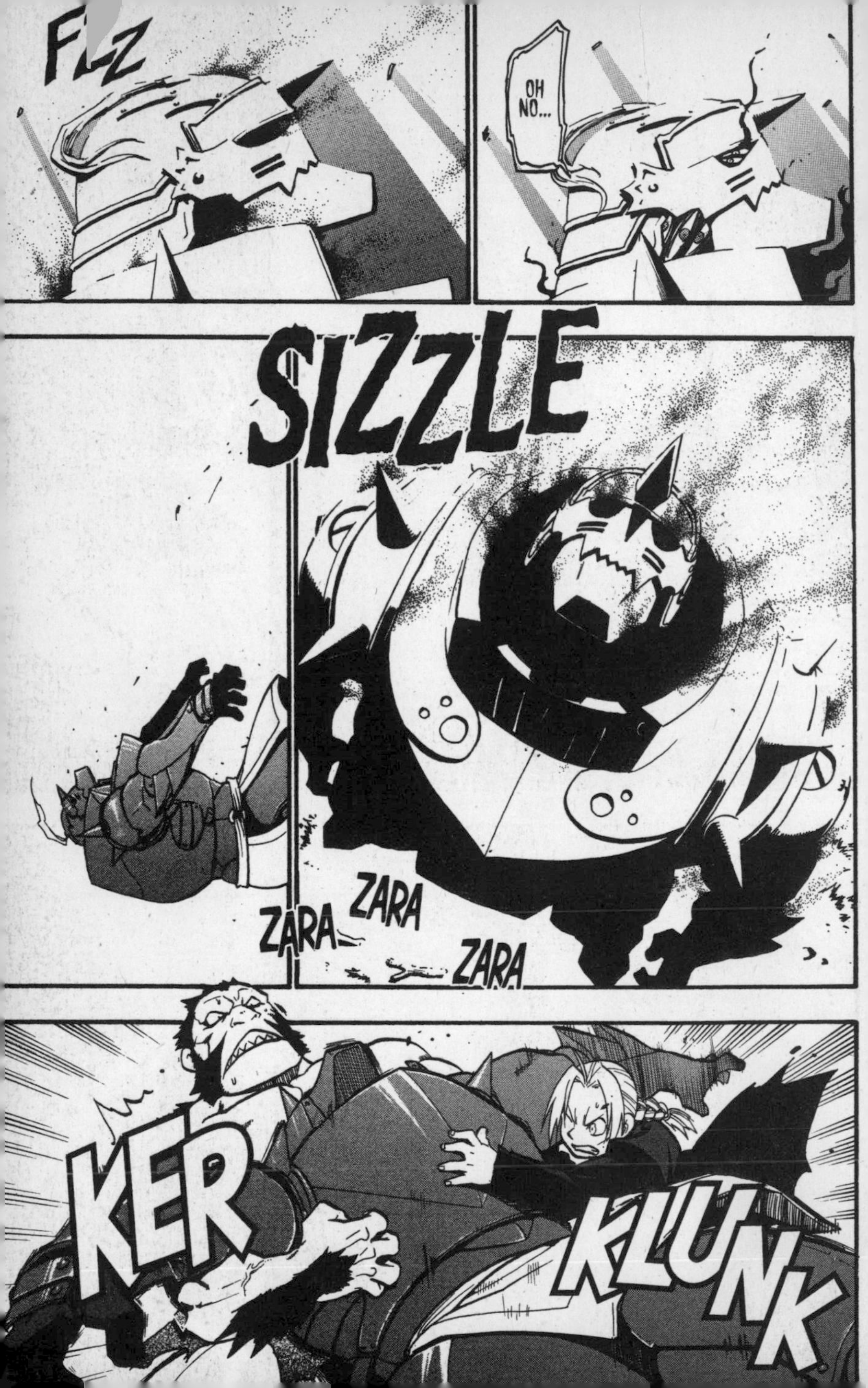
OH NO...
SIZZLE
ZARA
ZARA
ZARA
KER
KLUNK

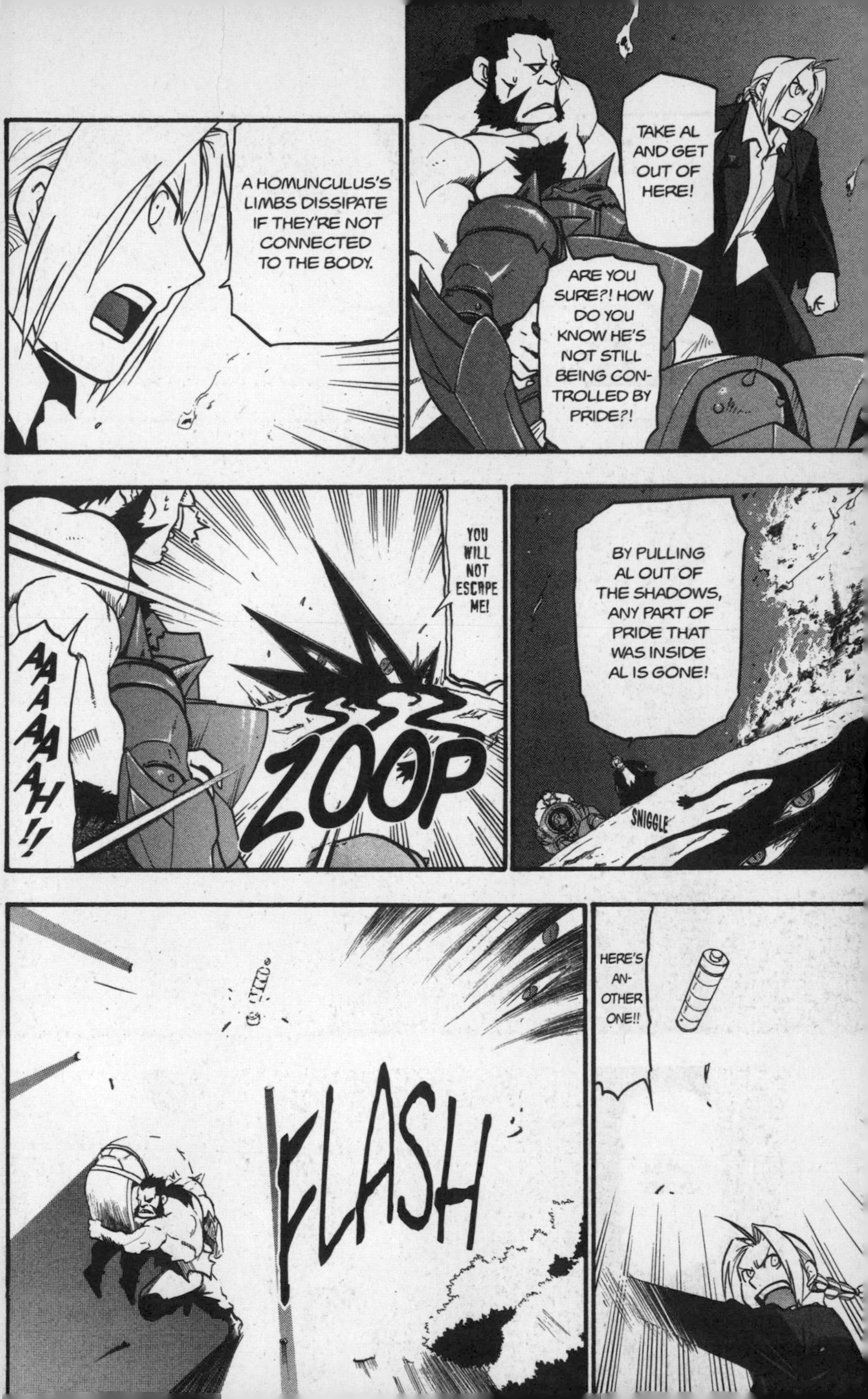
TAKE AL AND GET OUT OF HERE!
ARE YOU SURE?! HOW DO YOU KNOW HE'S NOT STILL BEING CONTROLLED BY PRIDE?!
A HOMUNCULUS'S LIMBS DISSIPATE IF THEY'RE NOT CONNECTED TO THE BODY.
BY PULLING AL OUT OF THE SHADOWS, ANY PART OF PRIDE THAT WAS INSIDE AL IS GONE!
SNIGGLE
YOU WILL NOT ESCAPE ME!
ZOOP
AAAAAAH!!
HERE'S AN-OTHER ONE!!
FLASH

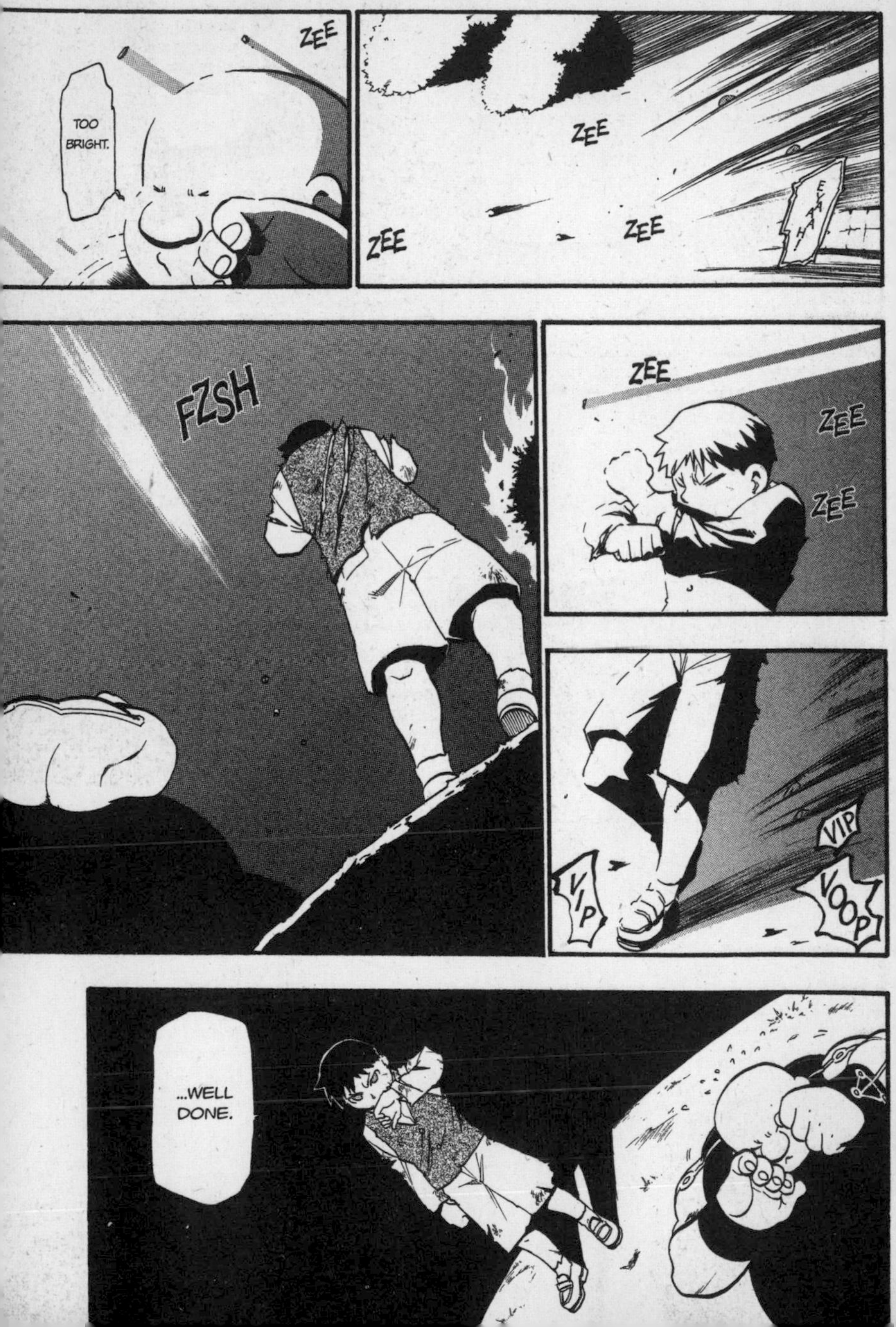
ZEE
EYAAH!
ZEE
ZEE
ZEE
TOO BRIGHT.
ZEE
ZEE
ZEE
VIP
VOOP
VIP
FZSH
...WELL DONE.

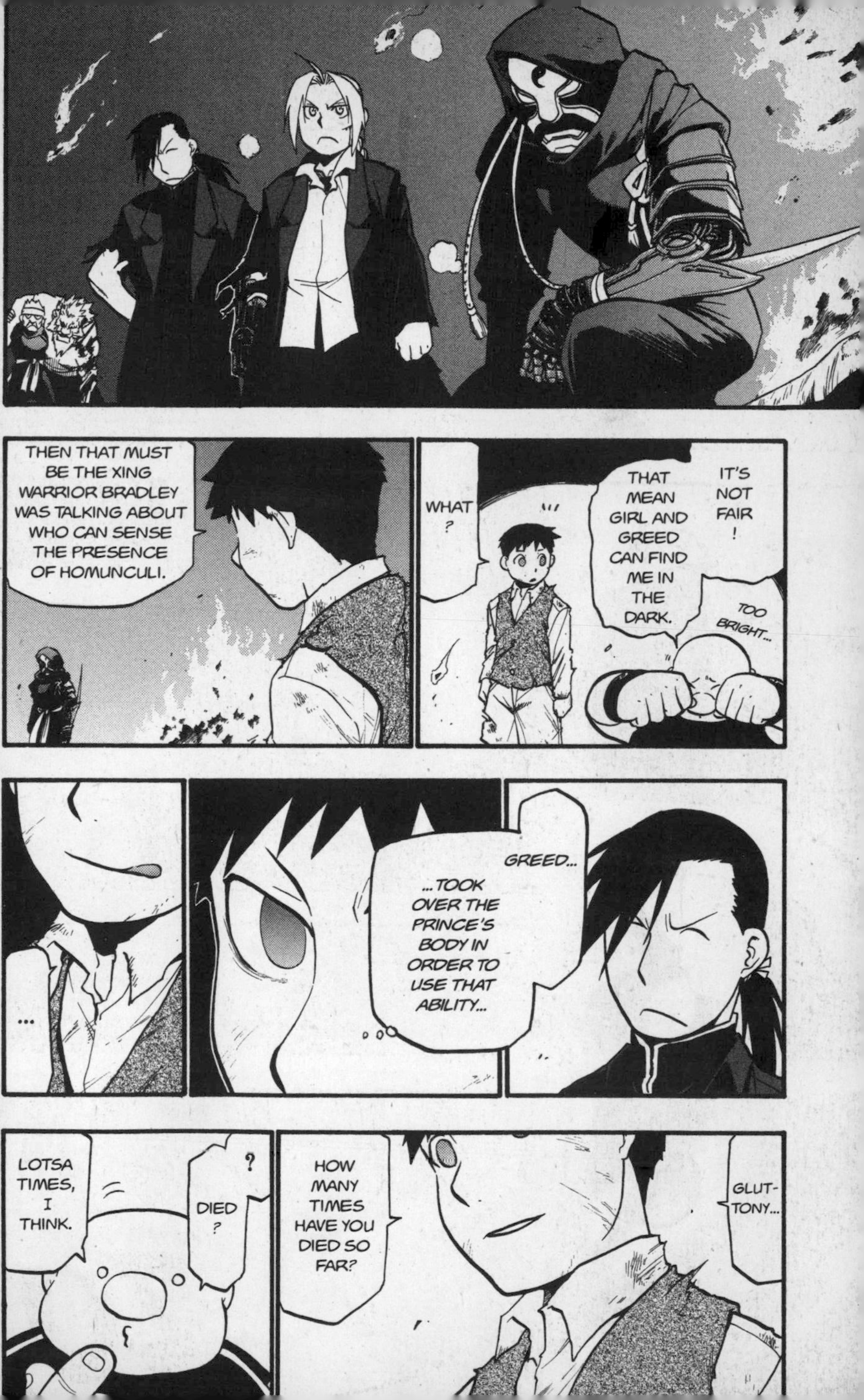
IT'S NOT FAIR!
THAT MEAN GIRL AND GREED CAN FIND ME IN THE DARK.
WHAT?
TOO BRIGHT...
THEN THAT MUST BE THE XING WARRIOR BRADLEY WAS TALKING ABOUT WHO CAN SENSE THE PRESENCE OF HOMUNCULI.
GREED...
...TOOK OVER THE PRINCE'S BODY IN ORDER TO USE THAT ABILITY...
...
GLUT-TONY...
HOW MANY TIMES HAVE YOU DIED SO FAR?
?
DIED?
LOTSA TIMES, I THINK.

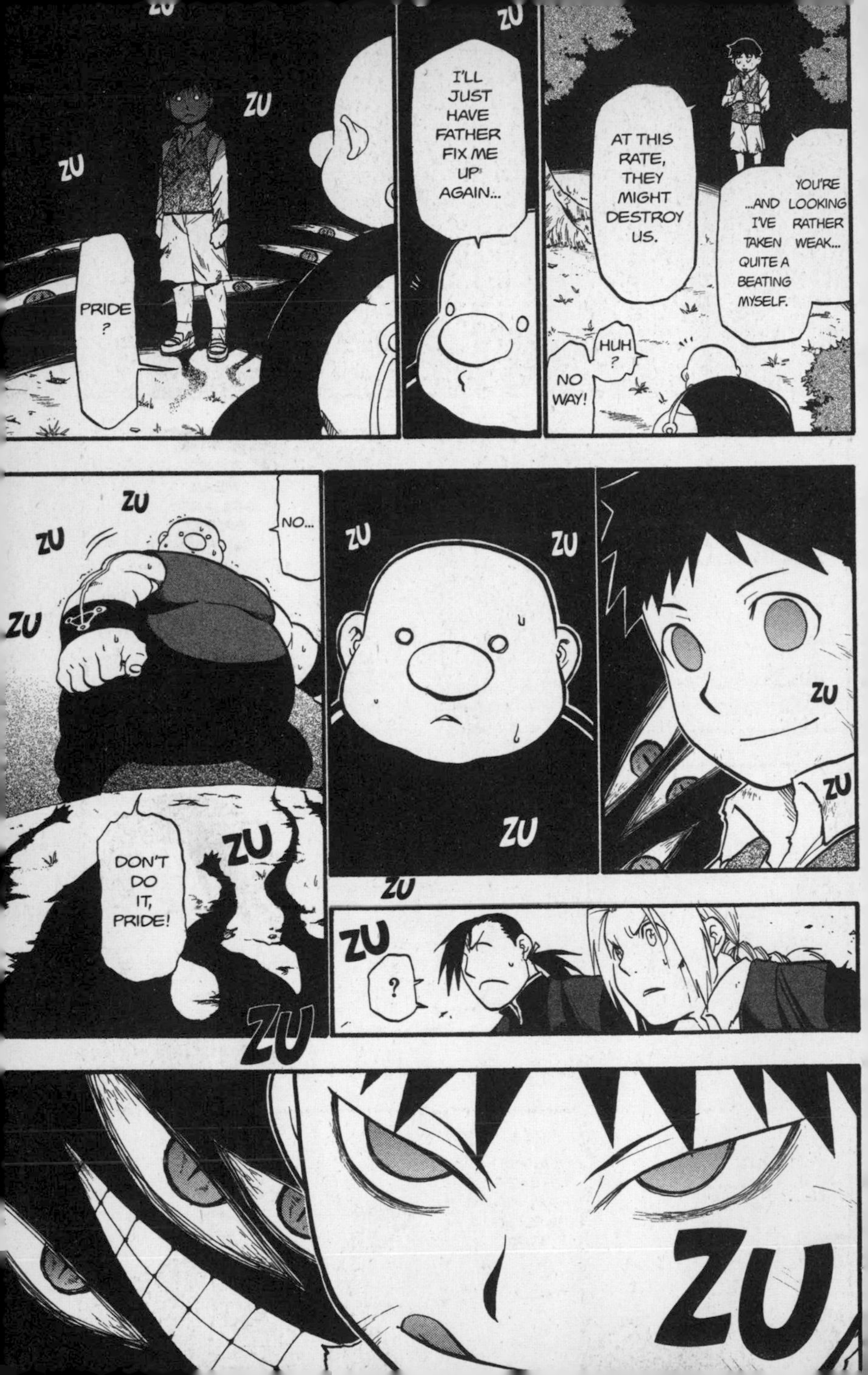
YOU'RE LOOKING RATHER WEAK...
...AND I'VE TAKEN QUITE A BEATING MYSELF.
AT THIS RATE, THEY MIGHT DESTROY US.
HUH?
NO WAY!
ZU
I'LL JUST HAVE FATHER FIX ME UP AGAIN...
ZU
ZU
ZU
PRIDE?
ZU
ZU
ZU
ZU
ZU
ZU
NO...
ZU
ZU
ZU
DON'T DO IT, PRIDE!
ZU
ZU
ZU
ZU
?
ZU

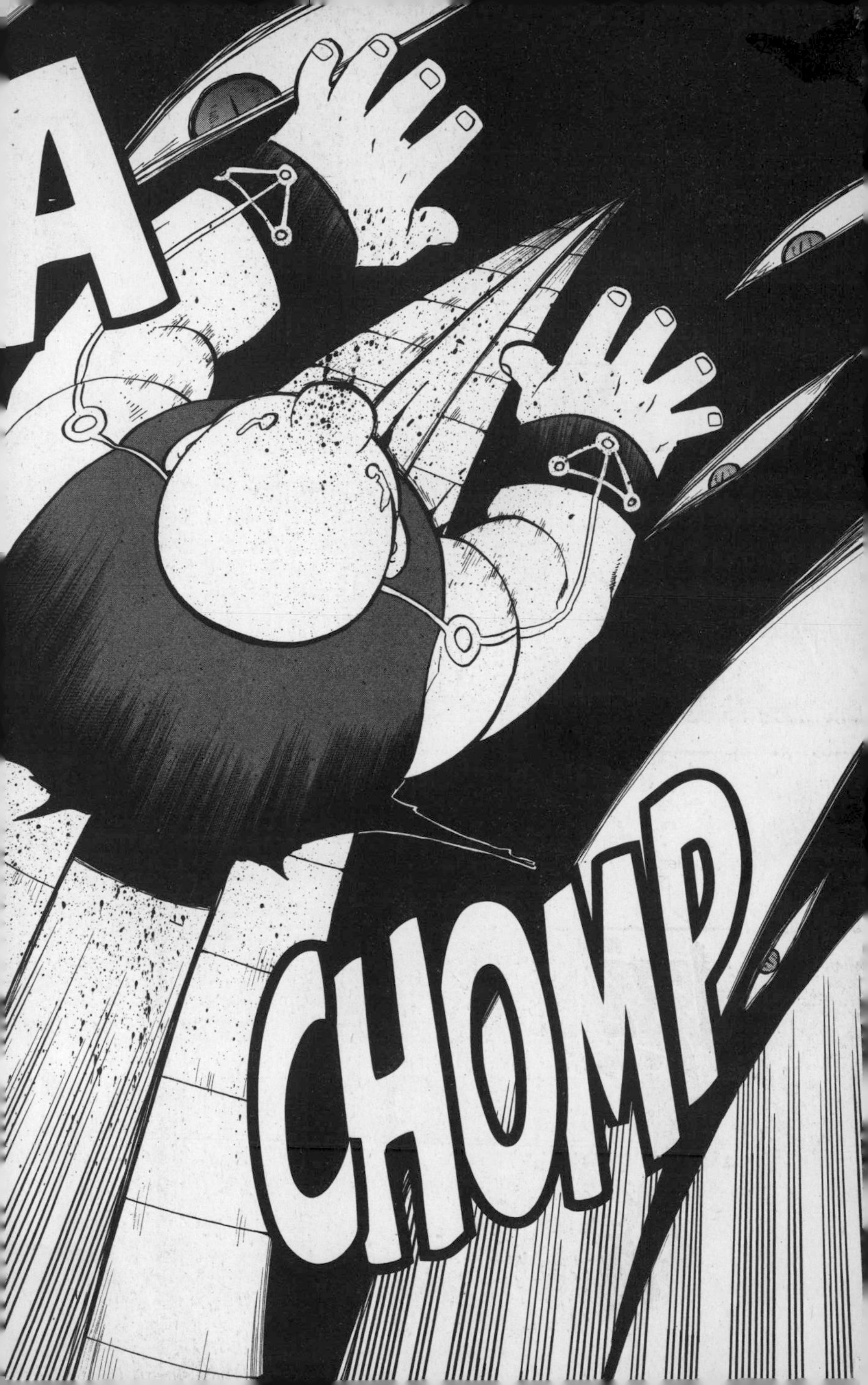
A
CHOMP

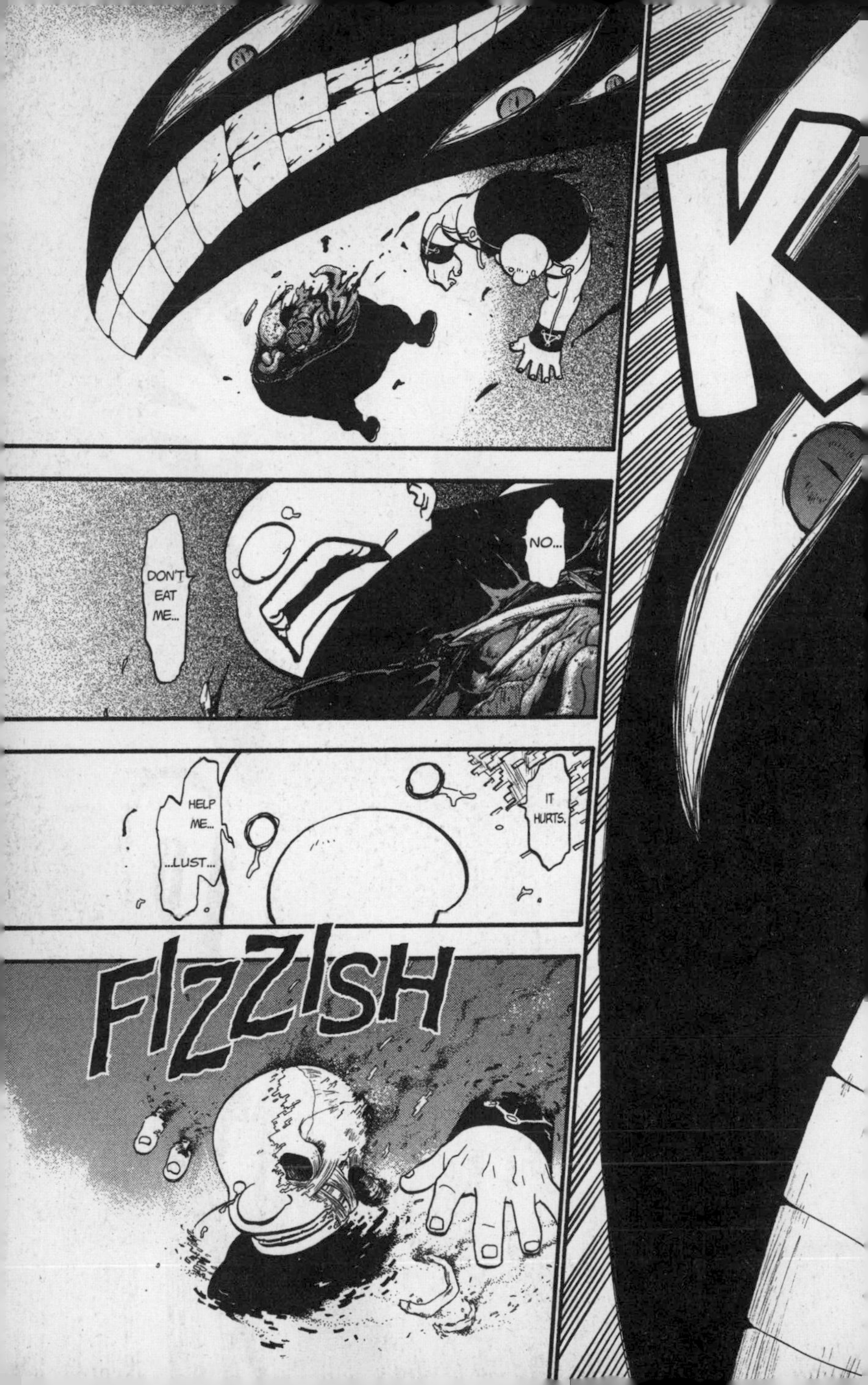
K
NO...
DON'T EAT ME...
IT HURTS.
HELP ME...
...LUST...
FIZZISH

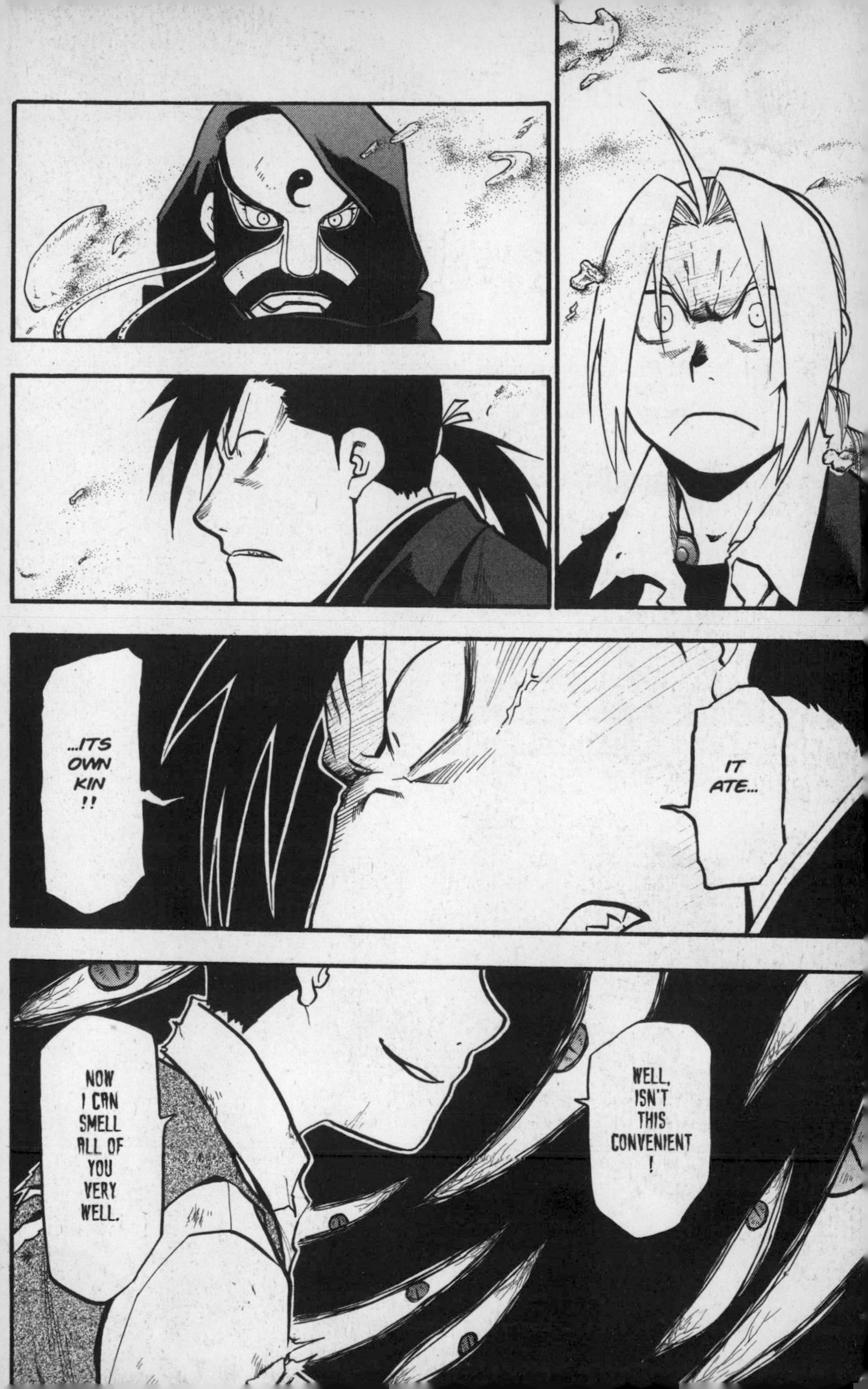
IT ATE...
...ITS OWN KIN!!
WELL, ISN'T THIS CONVENIENT!
NOW I CAN SMELL ALL OF YOU VERY WELL.

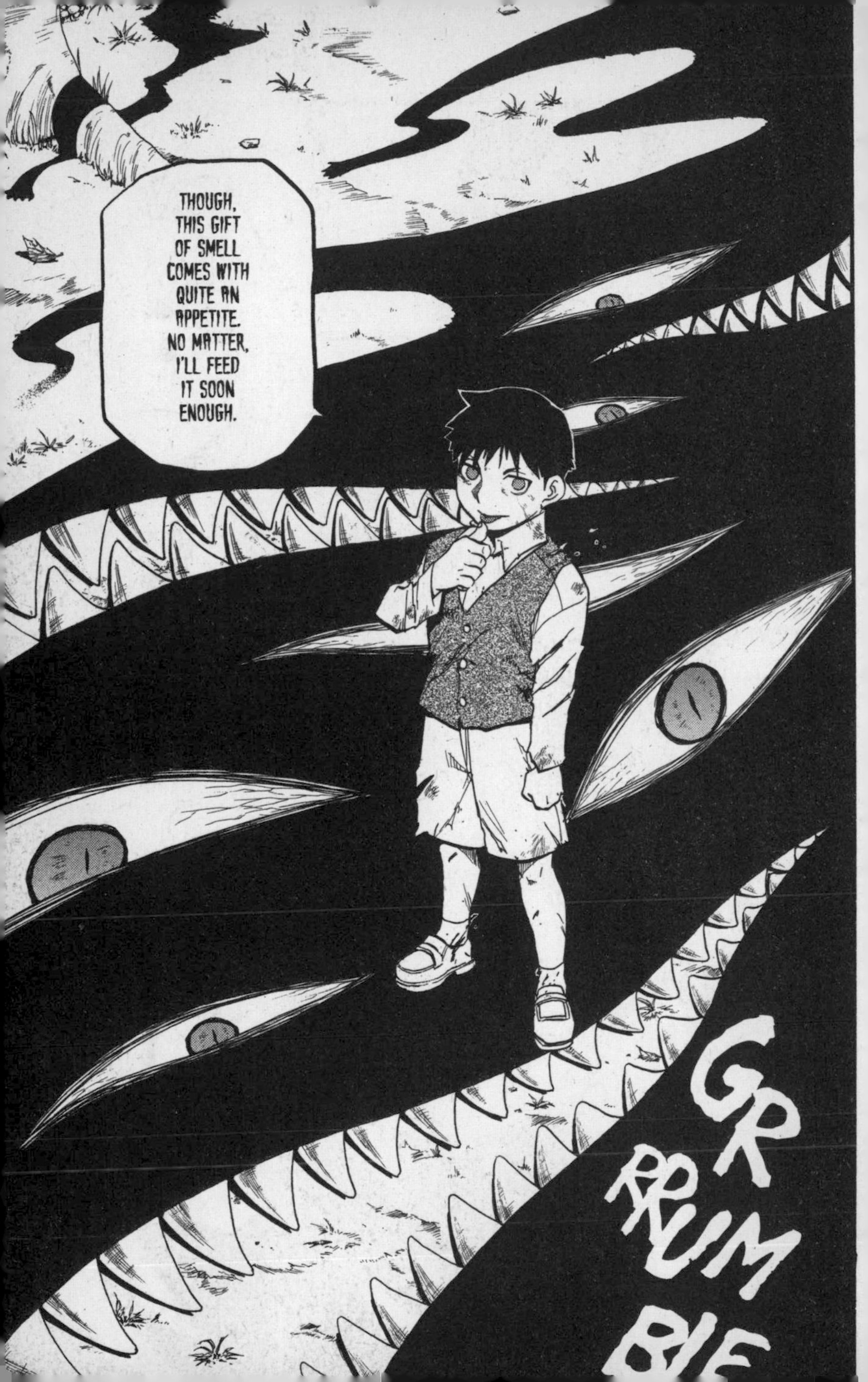
THOUGH, THIS GIFT OF SMELL COMES WITH QUITE AN APPETITE. NO MATTER, I'LL FEED IT SOON ENOUGH.
GRRRUMBLE

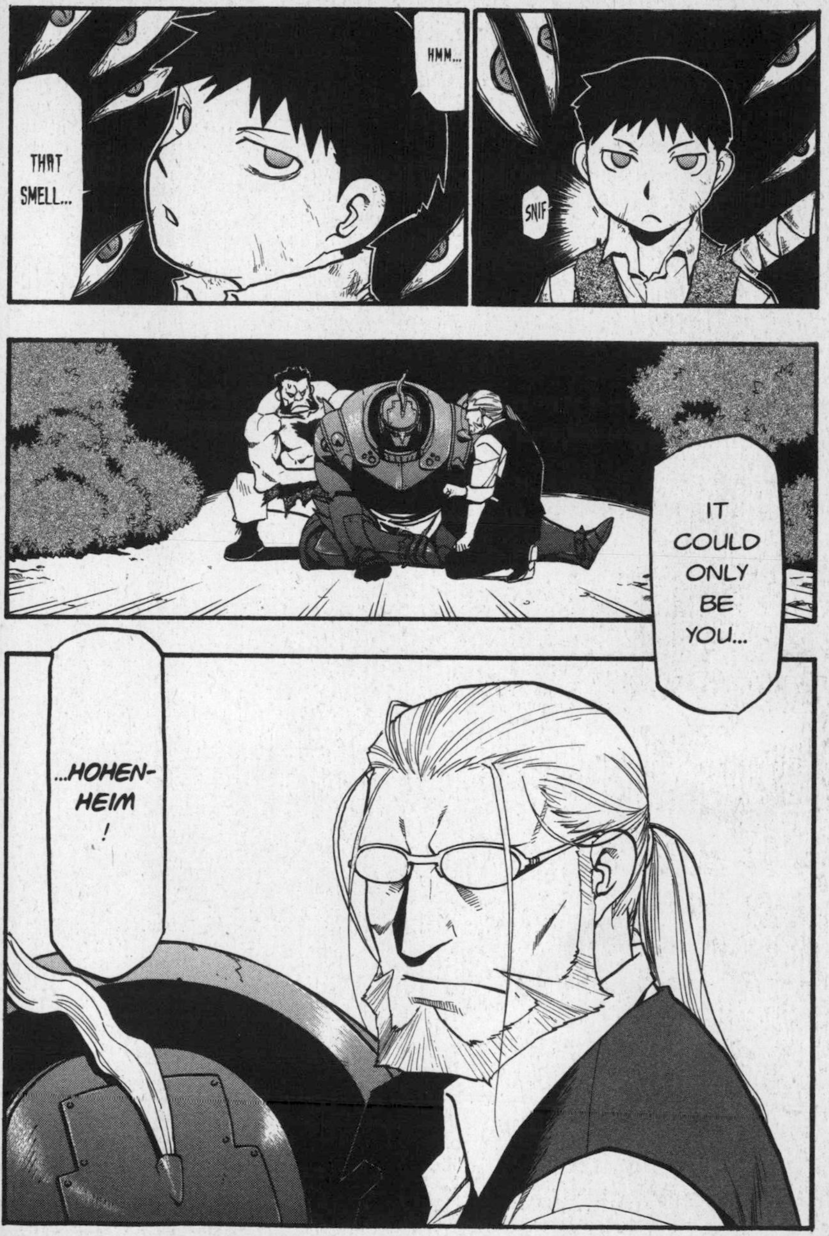
SNIF
HMM...
THAT SMELL...
IT COULD ONLY BE YOU...
...HOHENHEIM!

Fullmetal Alchemist 21 End

FULLMETAL
ALCHEMIST

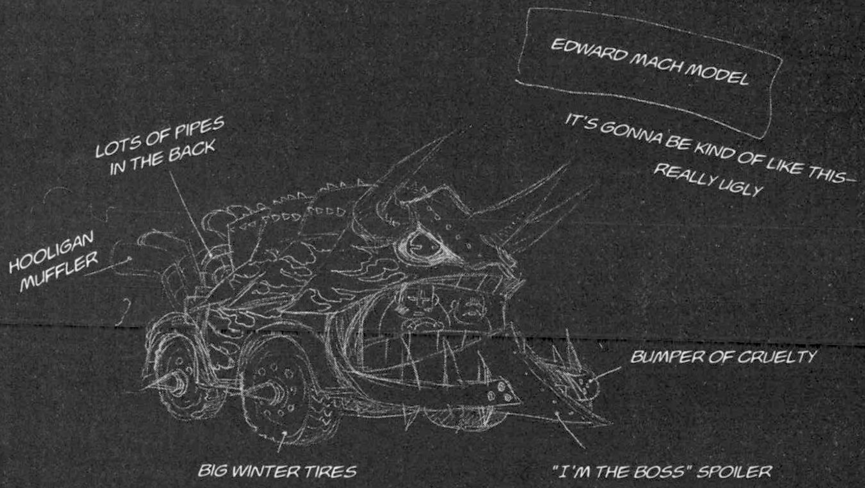
EDWARD MACH MODEL
IT'S GONNA BE KIND OF LIKE THIS-
REALLY UGLY
LOTS OF PIPES
IN THE BACK
HOOLIGAN
MUFFLER
BUMPER OF CRUELTY
BIG WINTER TIRES
"I'M THE BOSS" SPOILER

EXTRAS

THAT SMELL...
SNIF SNIF
IT COULD ONLY BE YOU, HO...
POOT
AAAAAAAH!!
IT STINKS!!
AAAAAAAH!!
SQUIRM SQUIRM
?

NICE ONE, MR GORI!!!

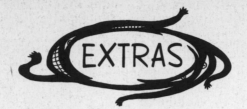

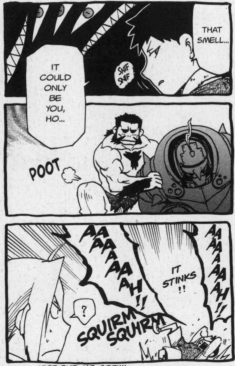

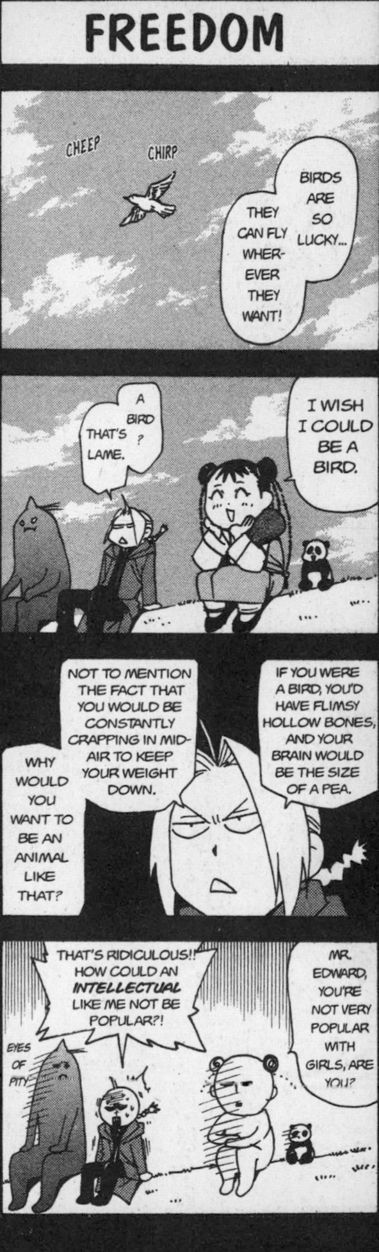
FREEDOM
BIRDS ARE SO LUCKY...
THEY CAN FLY WHEREVER THEY WANT!
CHIRP
CHEEP
I WISH I COULD BE A BIRD.
A BIRD?
THAT'S LAME.
IF YOU WERE A BIRD, YOU'D HAVE FLIMSY HOLLOW BONES, AND YOUR BRAIN WOULD BE THE SIZE OF A PEA.
NOT TO MENTION THE FACT THAT YOU WOULD BE CONSTANTLY CRAPPING IN MID-AIR TO KEEP YOUR WEIGHT DOWN.
WHY WOULD YOU WANT TO BE AN ANIMAL LIKE THAT?
MR. EDWARD, YOU'RE NOT VERY POPULAR WITH GIRLS, ARE YOU?
THAT'S RIDICULOUS!! HOW COULD AN *INTELLECTUAL* LIKE ME NOT BE POPULAR?!
EYES OF PITY
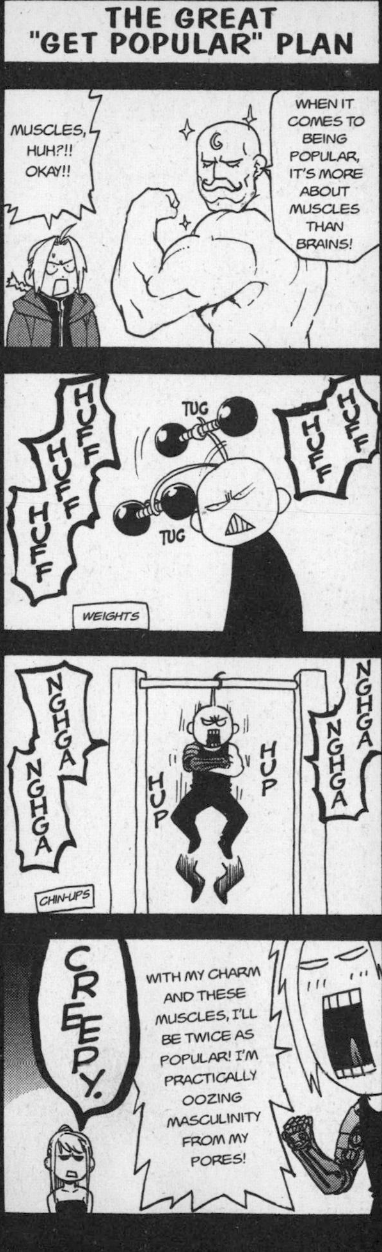
THE GREAT "GET POPULAR" PLAN
WHEN IT COMES TO BEING POPULAR, IT'S MORE ABOUT MUSCLES THAN BRAINS!
MUSCLES, HUH?!! OKAY!!
HUFF HUFF
TUG
TUG
HUFF HUFF HUFF
WEIGHTS
NGHGA NGHGA
HUP
HUP
NGHGA NGHGA
CHIN-UPS
WITH MY CHARM AND THESE MUSCLES, I'LL BE TWICE AS POPULAR! I'M PRACTICALLY OOZING MASCULINITY FROM MY PORES!
CREEPY.

HAWKEYE'S HOMECOMING

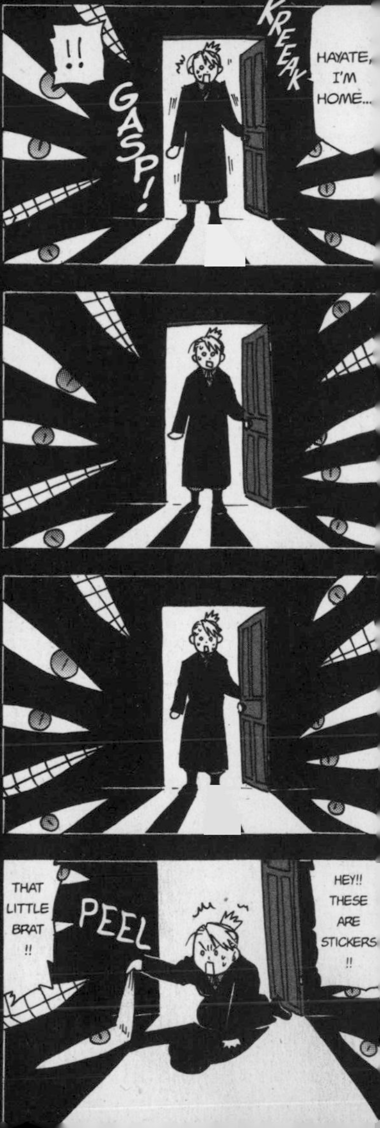
KREEAK
HAYATE, I'M HOME...
!!
GASP!
HEY!! THESE ARE STICKERS!!
PEEL
THAT LITTLE BRAT!!

MUGGER

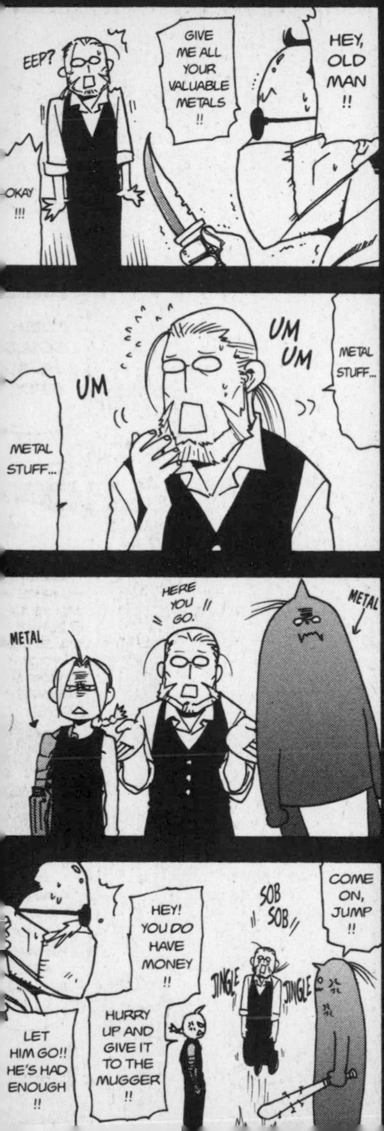
HEY, OLD MAN!!
GIVE ME ALL YOUR VALUABLE METALS!!
EEP?
OKAY!!!
METAL STUFF...
UM UM
UM
METAL STUFF...
METAL
HERE YOU GO.
METAL
COME ON, JUMP!!
SOB SOB
HEY! YOU DO HAVE MONEY!!
JINGLE
JINGLE
HURRY UP AND GIVE IT TO THE MUGGER!!
LET HIM GO!! HE'S HAD ENOUGH!!

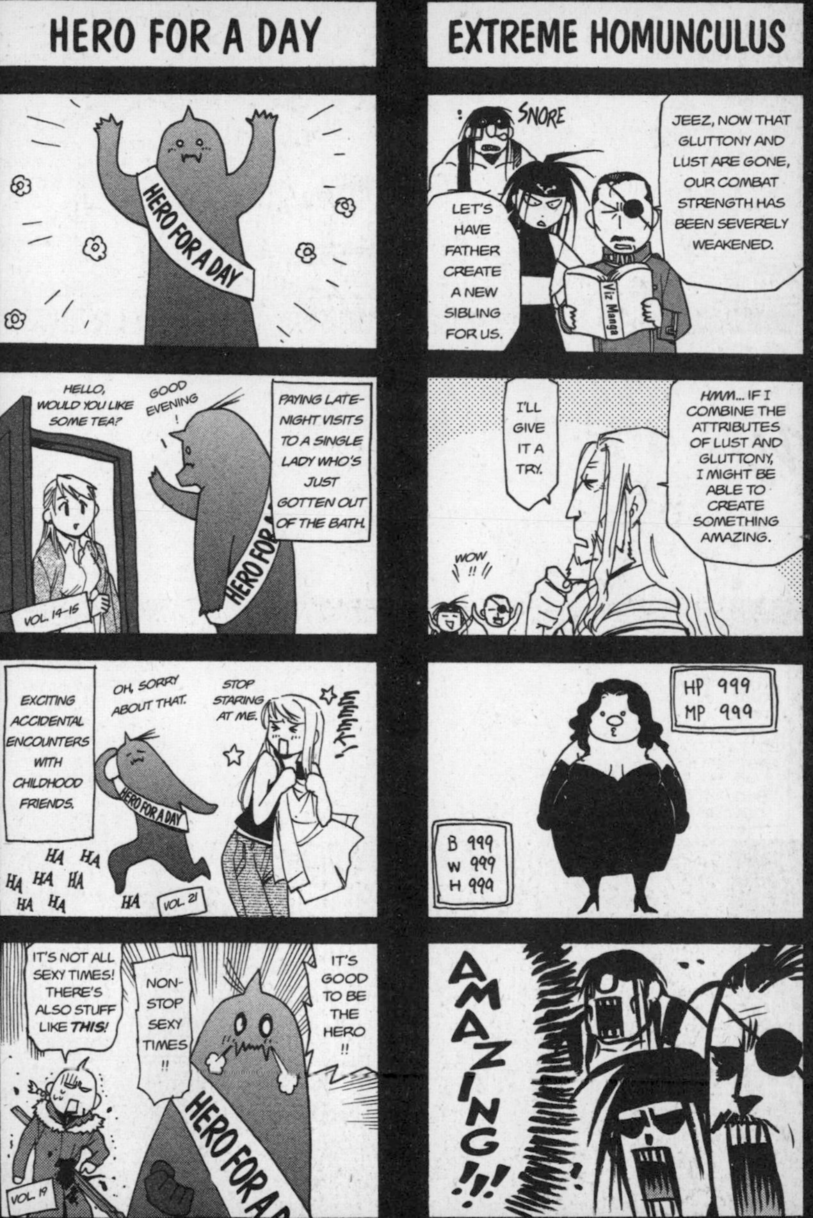
EXTREME HOMUNCULUS
JEEZ, NOW THAT GLUTTONY AND LUST ARE GONE, OUR COMBAT STRENGTH HAS BEEN SEVERELY WEAKENED.
SNORE
LET'S HAVE FATHER CREATE A NEW SIBLING FOR US.
Viz Manga
HMM... IF I COMBINE THE ATTRIBUTES OF LUST AND GLUTTONY, I MIGHT BE ABLE TO CREATE SOMETHING AMAZING.
I'LL GIVE IT A TRY.
WOW !!
HP 999
MP 999
B 999
W 999
H 999
AMAZING!!!
HERO FOR A DAY
HERO FOR A DAY
PAYING LATE-NIGHT VISITS TO A SINGLE LADY WHO'S JUST GOTTEN OUT OF THE BATH.
GOOD EVENING !
HELLO, WOULD YOU LIKE SOME TEA?
VOL. 14-15
STOP STARING AT ME.
OH, SORRY ABOUT THAT.
EXCITING ACCIDENTAL ENCOUNTERS WITH CHILDHOOD FRIENDS.
HERO FOR A DAY
HA HA HA HA HA HA HA HA
VOL. 21
IT'S GOOD TO BE THE HERO !!
NON-STOP SEXY TIMES !!
IT'S NOT ALL SEXY TIMES! THERE'S ALSO STUFF LIKE THIS!
VOL. 19

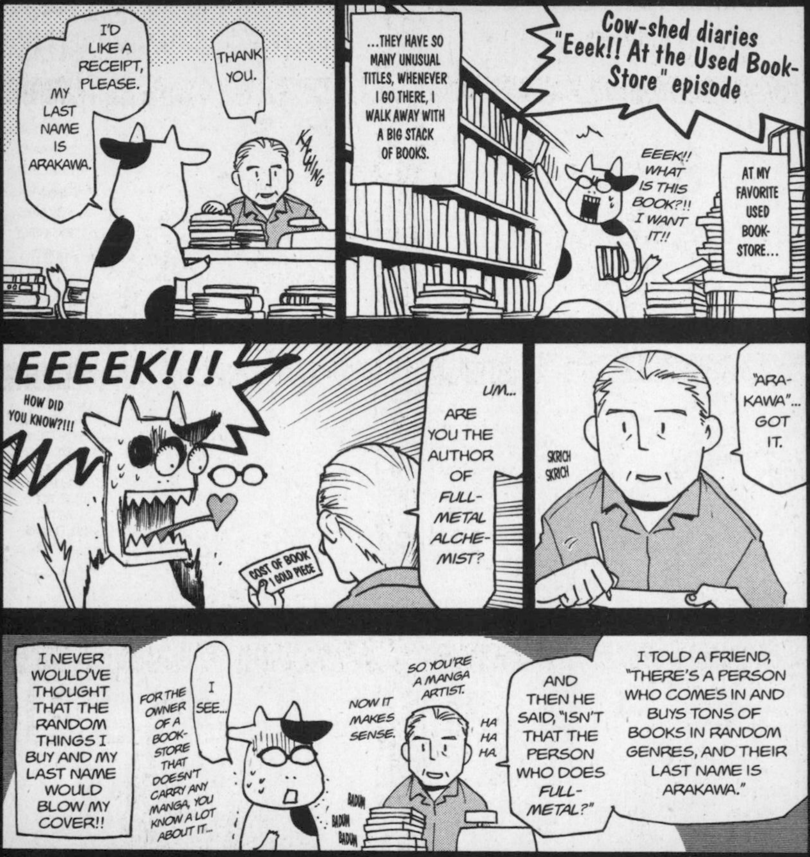
Cow-shed diaries "Eeek!! At the Used Book-Store" episode
AT MY FAVORITE USED BOOK-STORE...
EEEK!! WHAT IS THIS BOOK?!! I WANT IT!!
...THEY HAVE SO MANY UNUSUAL TITLES, WHENEVER I GO THERE, I WALK AWAY WITH A BIG STACK OF BOOKS.
THANK YOU.
KACHING
I'D LIKE A RECEIPT, PLEASE. MY LAST NAME IS ARAKAWA.
"ARA-KAWA"... GOT IT.
SKRICH SKRICH
UM... ARE YOU THE AUTHOR OF FULL-METAL ALCHE-MIST?
COST OF BOOK 1 GOLD PIECE
EEEEK!!!
HOW DID YOU KNOW?!!!
I TOLD A FRIEND, "THERE'S A PERSON WHO COMES IN AND BUYS TONS OF BOOKS IN RANDOM GENRES, AND THEIR LAST NAME IS ARAKAWA."
AND THEN HE SAID, "ISN'T THAT THE PERSON WHO DOES FULL-METAL?"
SO YOU'RE A MANGA ARTIST.
HA HA HA
NOW IT MAKES SENSE.
BADUM BADUM BADUM
I SEE...
FOR THE OWNER OF A BOOK-STORE THAT DOESN'T CARRY ANY MANGA, YOU KNOW A LOT ABOUT IT...
I NEVER WOULD'VE THOUGHT THAT THE RANDOM THINGS I BUY AND MY LAST NAME WOULD BLOW MY COVER!!

FULLMETAL ALCHEMIST 21
SPECIAL THANKS to:

Jun Tohko
Noriko Tsubota
Mitsuri Sakano
Masashi Mizutani
Haruhi Nakamura
Manatsu Sakura
Mr. Coupon
Kazufumi Kanek
Kei Takanamazu
Editor—Yuichi Shimomura

AND YOU!!

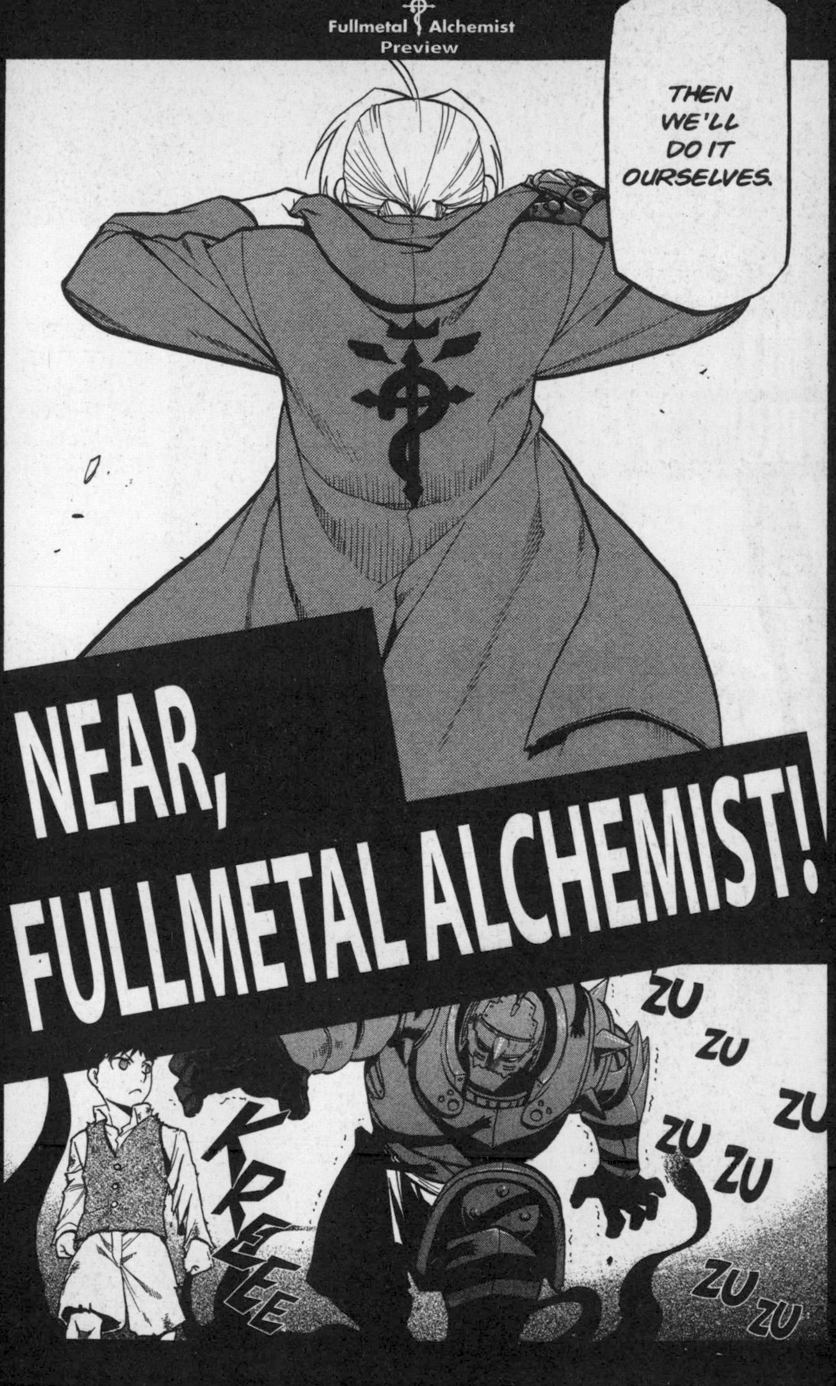
THEN WE'LL DO IT OURSELVES.
NEAR, FULLMETAL ALCHEMIST!
ZU ZU ZU ZU ZU ZU ZU ZU
KREEEE

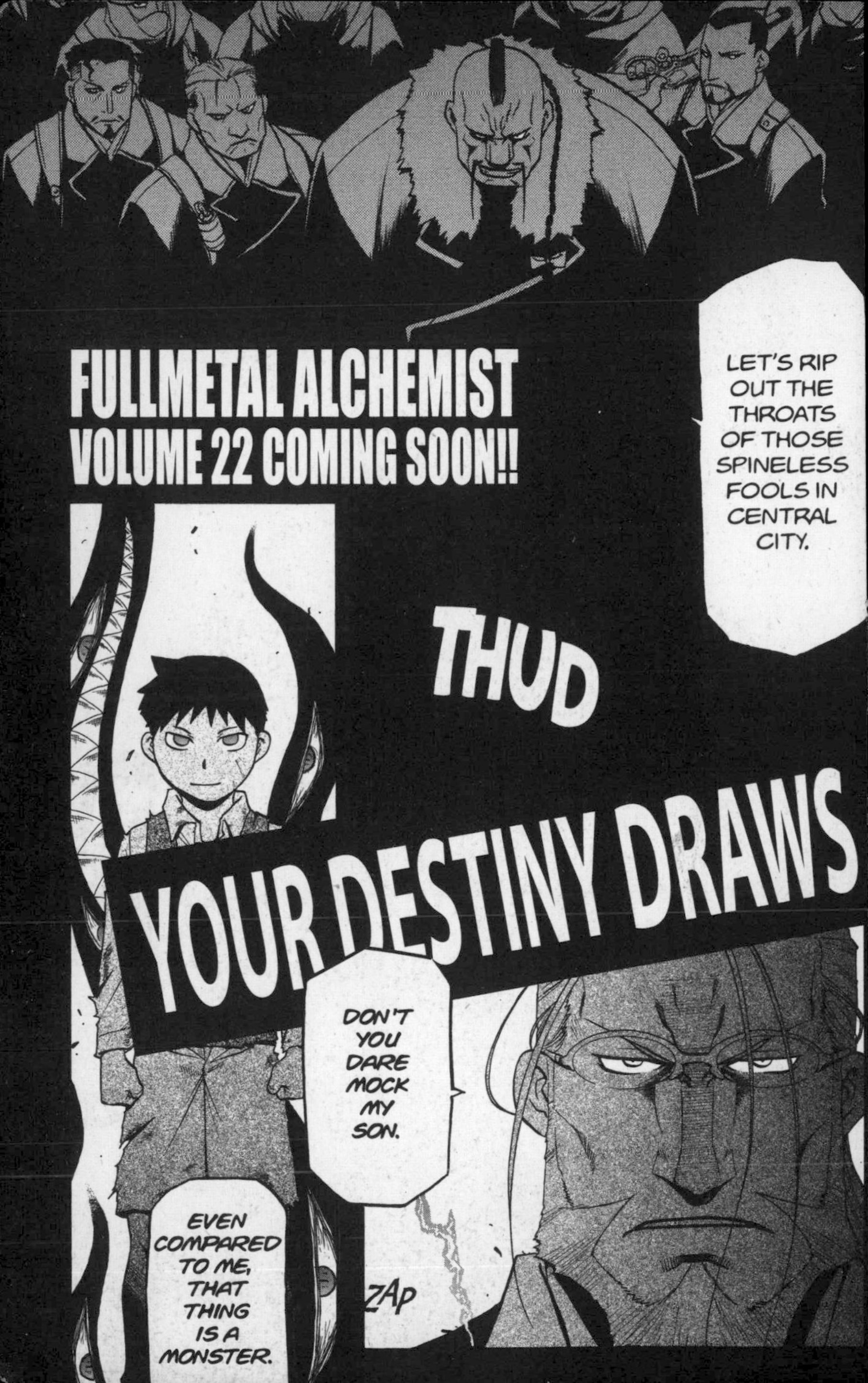
FULLMETAL ALCHEMIST
VOLUME 22 COMING SOON!!
LET'S RIP OUT THE THROATS OF THOSE SPINELESS FOOLS IN CENTRAL CITY.
THUD
YOUR DESTINY DRAWS
DON'T YOU DARE MOCK MY SON.
EVEN COMPARED TO ME, THAT THING IS A MONSTER.
ZAP

Fullmetal Alchemist 21

A DAY IN THE LIFE OF FATHER

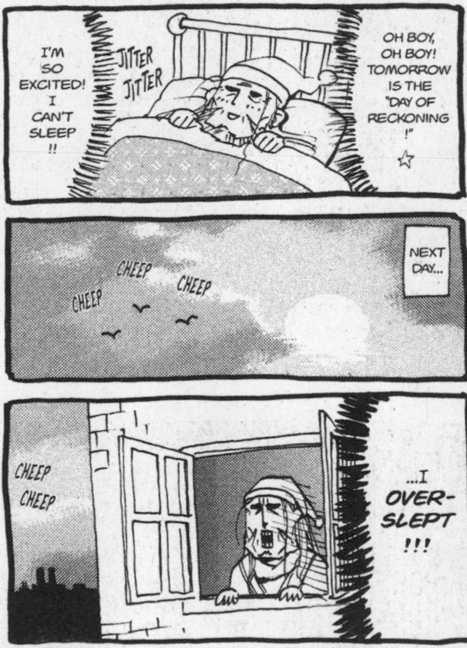
OH BOY, OH BOY! TOMORROW IS THE "DAY OF RECKONING!" ☆
JITTER JITTER
I'M SO EXCITED! I CAN'T SLEEP!!
NEXT DAY...
CHEEP
CHEEP
CHEEP
...I OVER-SLEPT!!!
CHEEP CHEEP

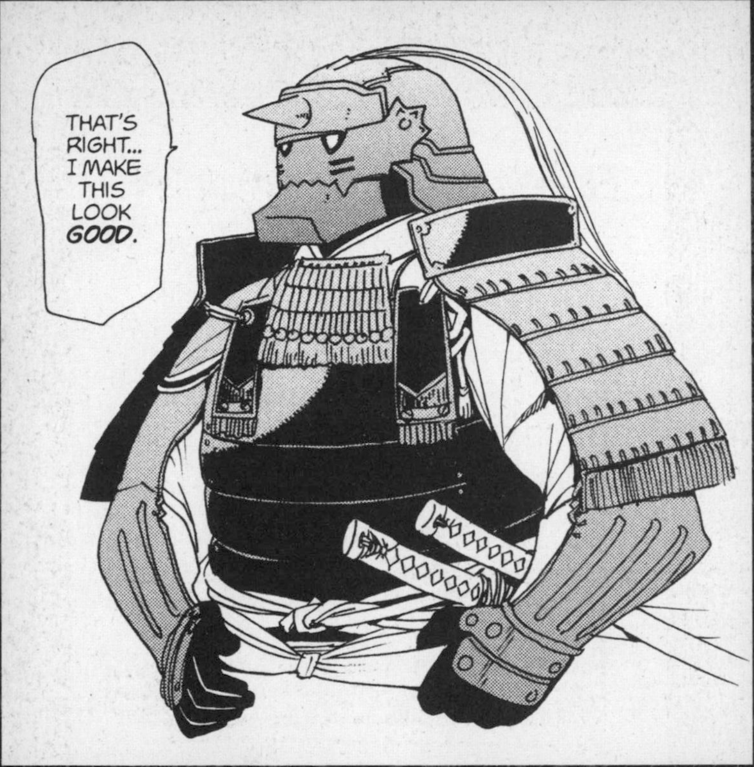
THAT'S RIGHT... I MAKE THIS LOOK GOOD.
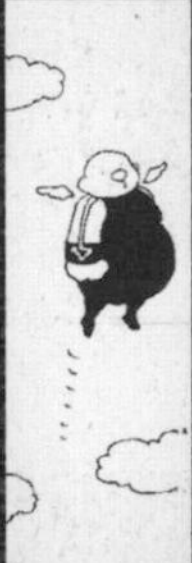

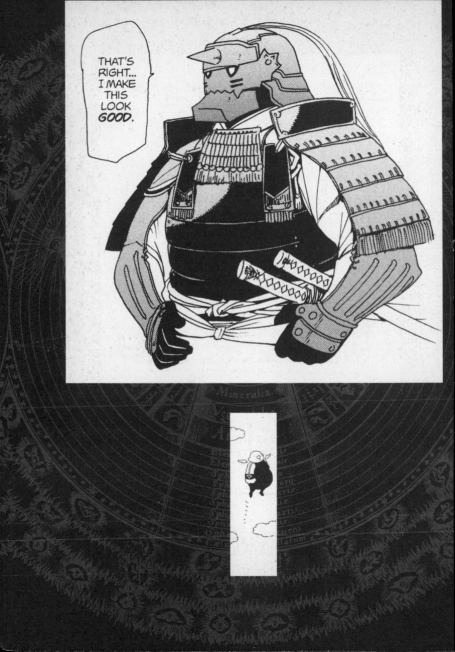

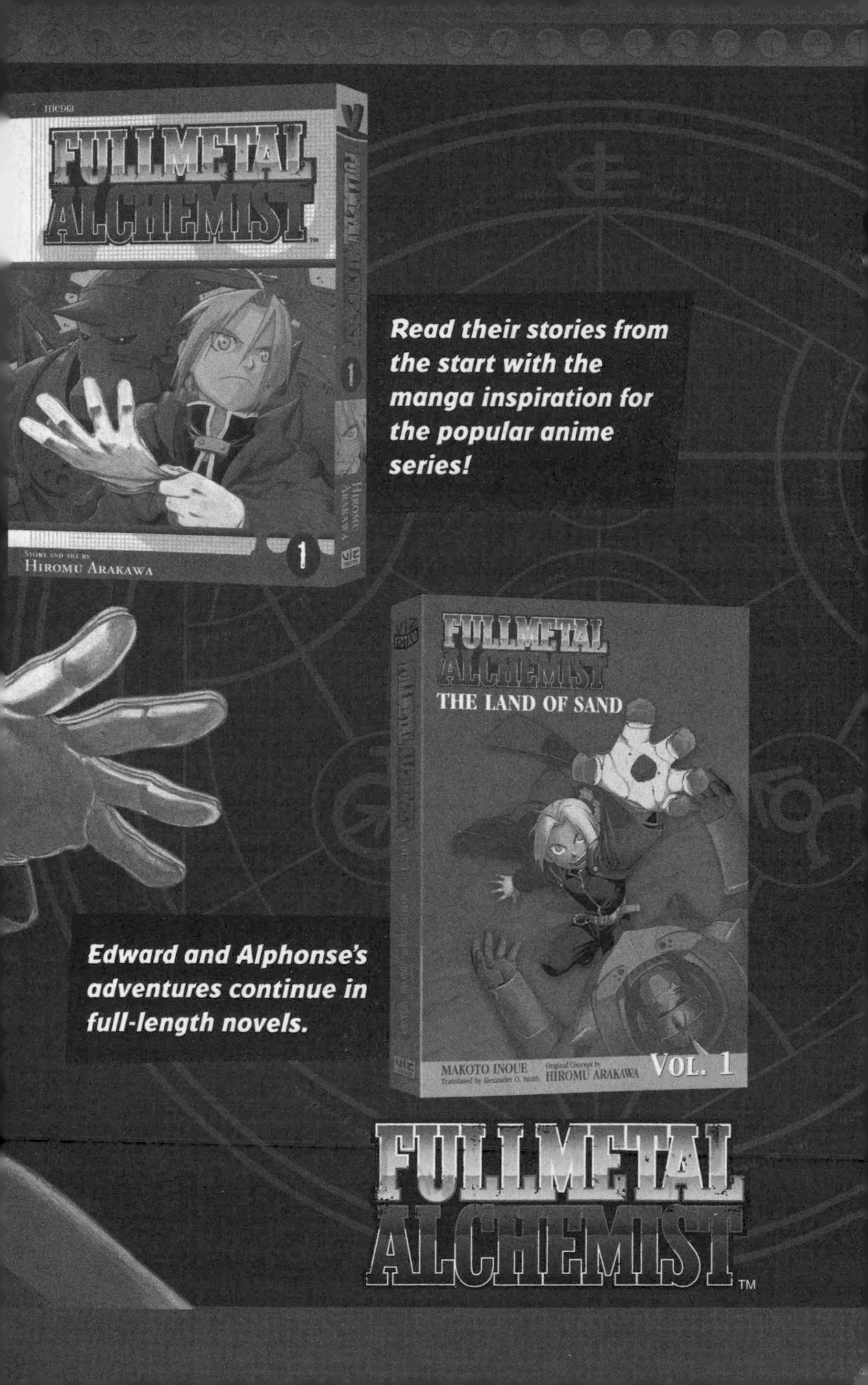
FULLMETAL ALCHEMIST
STORY AND ART BY
HIROMU ARAKAWA
Read their stories from the start with the manga inspiration for the popular anime series!
FULLMETAL ALCHEMIST
THE LAND OF SAND
MAKOTO INOUE
Translated by Alexander O. Smith
Original Concept by
HIROMU ARAKAWA
VOL. 1
Edward and Alphonse's adventures continue in full-length novels.
FULLMETAL ALCHEMIST™

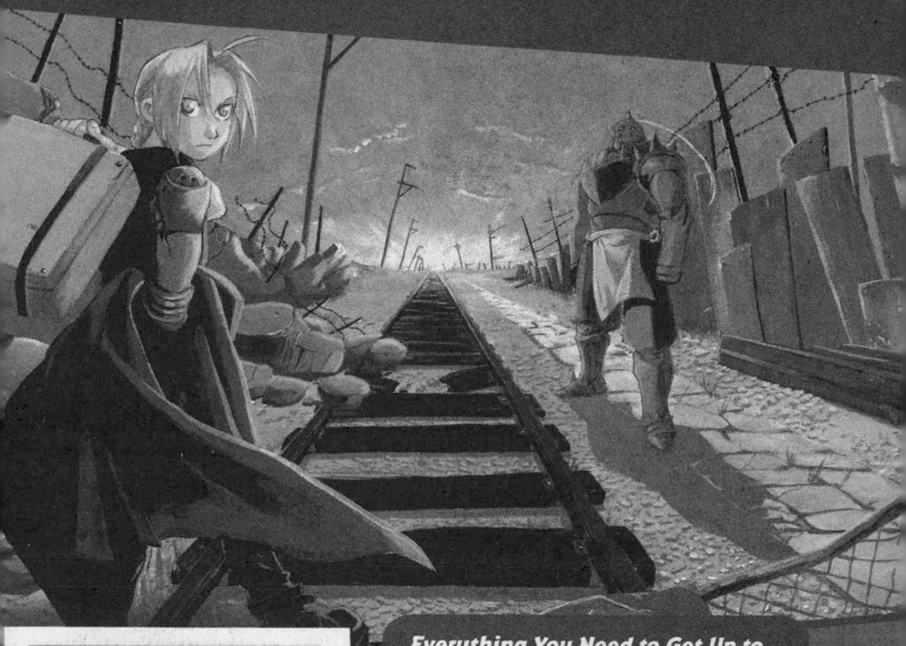

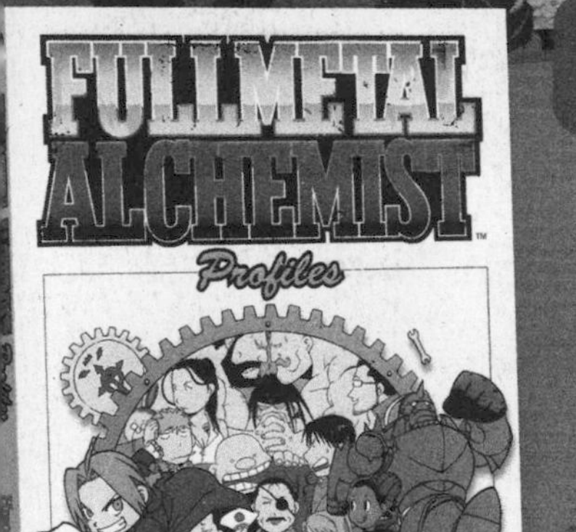
FULLMETAL ALCHEMIST
Profiles
HIROMU ARAKAWA
$14.99

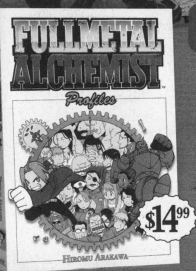

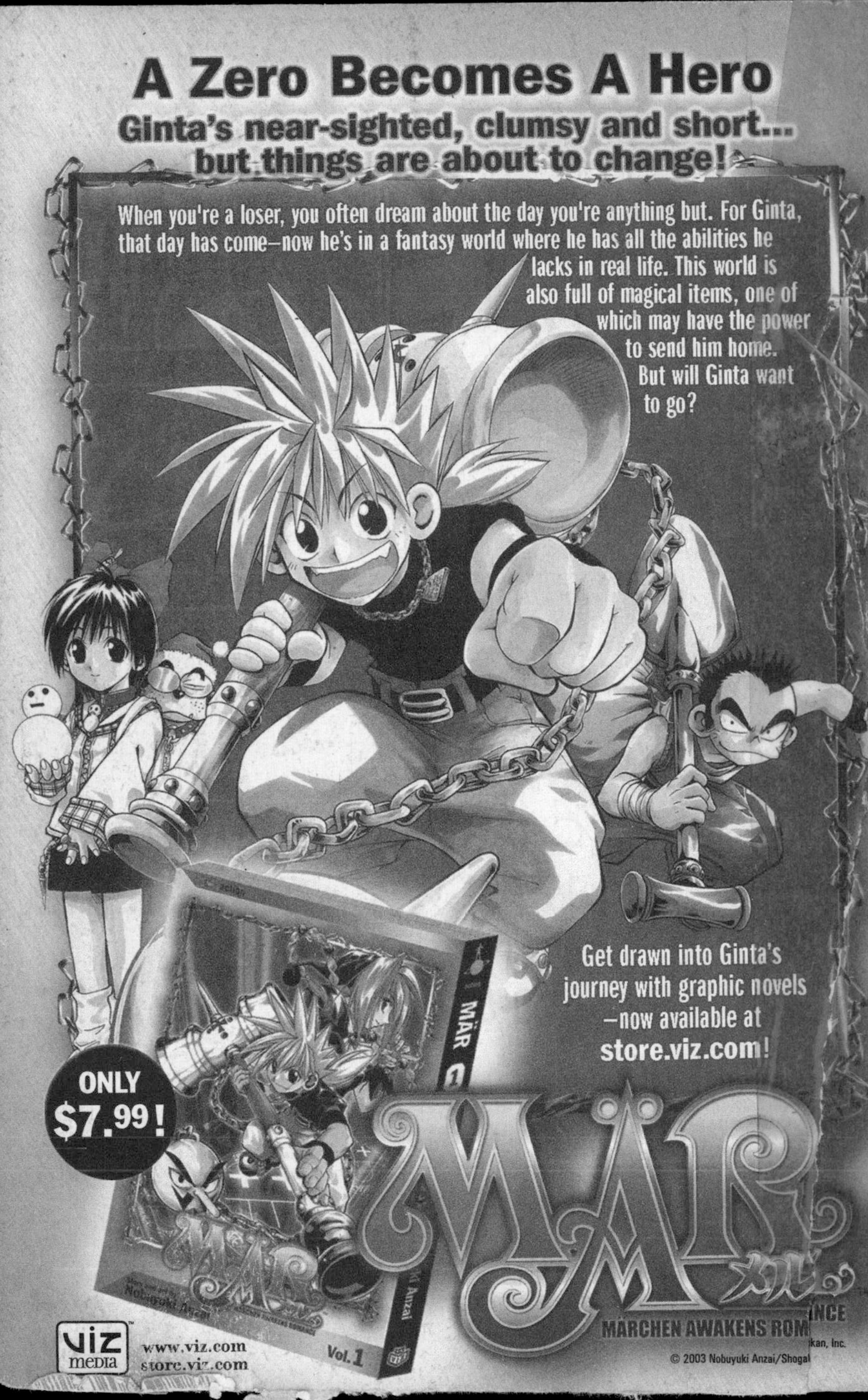
A Zero Becomes A Hero
Ginta's near-sighted, clumsy and short...
...but things are about to change!
When you're a loser, you often dream about the day you're anything but. For Ginta, that day has come—now he's in a fantasy world where he has all the abilities he lacks in real life. This world is also full of magical items, one of which may have the power to send him home. But will Ginta want to go?
Get drawn into Ginta's journey with graphic novels —now available at store.viz.com!
ONLY $7.99!
MÄR
Vol. 1
MÄR
MARCHEN AWAKENS ROM
INCE
viz media
www.viz.com
store.viz.com
© 2003 Nobuyuki Anzai/Shogal
kan, Inc.

LOVE ♥ MANGA?

what you think.

Our **MANGA SURVEY** is now available **ONLINE.**

Please visit: **VIZ.COM/MANGASURVEY**

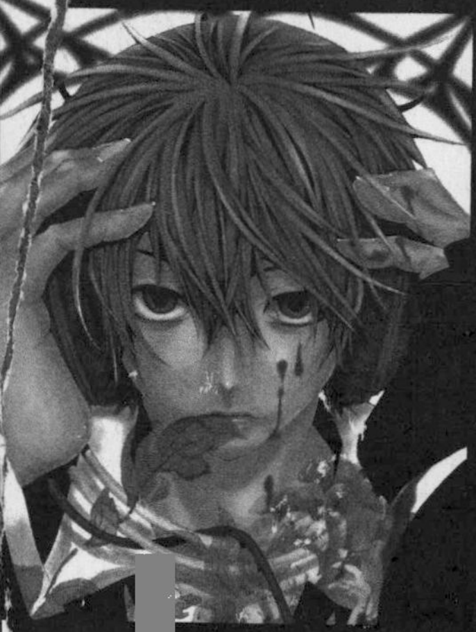

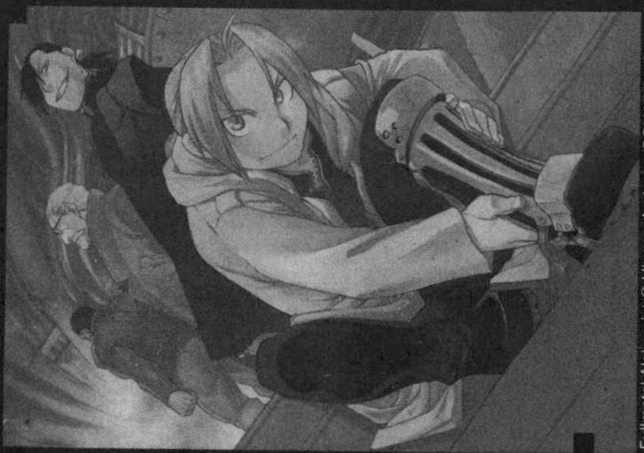

Fullmetal Alchemist © Hiromu Arakawa/SQUARE ENIX

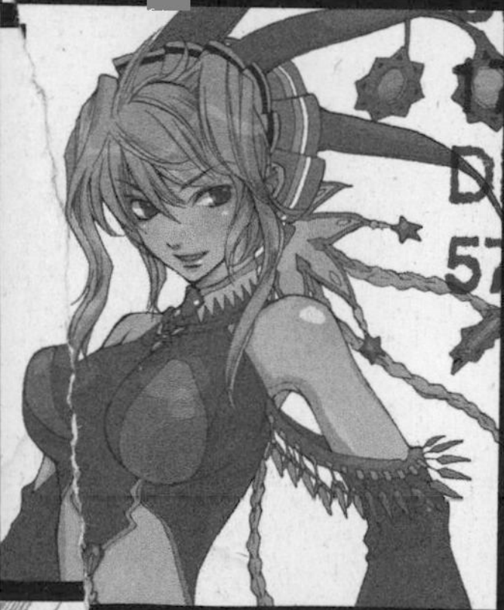

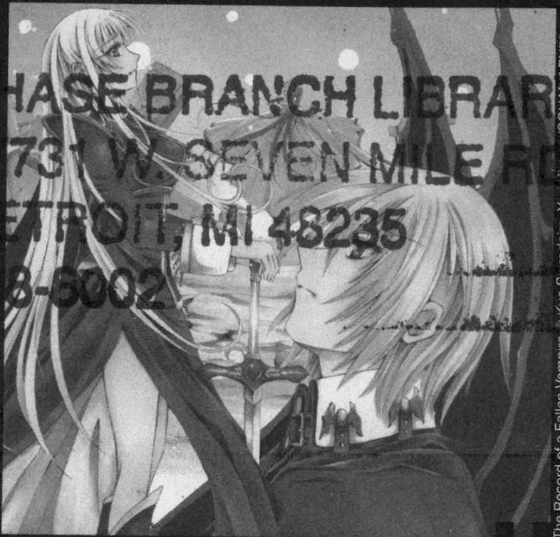

The Record of a Fallen Vampire © Kyo Shirodaira, Yuri Kimura/SQUARE ENIX

Help us make the **manga** you love **better!**